Thinking/Writing

Thinking/Writing

Fostering Critical Thinking Through Writing

Carol Booth Olson

University of California, Irvine
California Writing Project

HarperCollins*Publishers*

Executive Editor: Christopher Jennison
Development Editor: Anita Portugal
Project Coordination, Text and Cover Design: Caliber/Phoenix Color Corp.
Production Manager: Michael Weinstein
Compositor: Caliber/Phoenix Color Corp.
Printer and Binder: R.R. Donnelley & Sons Company
Cover Printer: The Lehigh Press, Inc.

THINKING/WRITING: FOSTERING CRITICAL THINKING THROUGH WRITING

Library of Congress Cataloging-in-Publication Data

Thinking/writing: fostering critical thinking through writing/
[edited by] Carol Booth Olson.
     p. cm.
    Includes bibliographical references (p.) and index.
    ISBN 0-673-46346-X
    1. English language—Composition and exercises—Study and teaching—California. 2. Critical thinking—Study and teaching—California. I. Olson, Carol Booth.
LB1576.T495   1991
808' .042'0710794—dc20

91-19785
CIP

92 93 94 9 8 7 6 5 4 3 2

This book is dedicated to Owen Thomas who taught us that our job is not to put language into kids' heads, but to help them express "the extraordinary wealth of linguistic knowledge" that each of them already possesses through writing.

We have to reinvent the wheel every once in a while, not because we need a lot of wheels, but because we need a lot of inventors.

Bruce Joyce

Contents

PART ONE
The Thinking/Writing Model   1

PART TWO
The Demonstration Lessons   29

PART THREE
Making Thinking/Writing Your Own   397

What About the Affective Domain?   399
Russ Frank

Thinking and Writing About Thinking/Writing   403
Todd Huck and Jerry Judd

Foreword

Reflections on the Thinking/Writing Project

My connection with the teachers who are the authors of this book began nearly ten years ago when I was invited by the National Writing Project site at the University of California, Irvine (UCI) to serve as a consultant to an advanced summer seminar on writing and critical thinking for thirty experienced teachers who had previously completed a UCI Writing Project Summer Institute in Composition. I found there an indefatigable group of teachers, thoroughly committed to each other and to their ambitious collaborative goal. Their aim was to forge a theoretical framework and a set of workable lessons for systematically using writing to promote more cognitively demanding and more refined thinking in students at all grades and in all subjects. To this end they embarked first on the task of familiarizing themselves with the current state of knowledge about writing as a cognitive process, about learning theory, and about intellectual development. By the time I arrived, they had been meeting for about a week and (guided by the organizational genius and intellectual resourcefulness of Project Director, Carol Booth Olson) had already collectively read, reviewed, and assimilated as large a body of professional literature as a graduate professor might assign in a semester. They had also begun to develop some exciting prototypes for classroom lessons and the outlines of a persuasive theory of instruction.

As I revisited these teachers over the years, watching the continuing growth of their expertise and of their manuscript, my admiration and affection for them also continued to grow, as did my sense of wonder at their continuing commitment to each other and to their collaborative project. I was particularly struck by the remarkable synergy that their collaboration seemed to produce. As a group they energized and continually drew out the best from all their members and from anybody else who came into their circle. In the middle of one of my own presentations to these teachers, I found myself articulating ideas that constituted a real advance for me in my own thinking about the teaching of literature. I hastily made some notes on a scrap of cardboard, outlining my new thinking. These notes became crucial to me in much of the research, writing, and instructional development work I have been engaged in over the past several years.

A Book for Our Time

Looking now at the finished manuscript which is the latest product of the synergy I experienced and witnessed on my visits to the thinking/writing project, I am struck most by how much this volume may be seen as emblematic not only of the processes that produced it, but of transformations that have taken place in the past decade in the teaching of writing and in the professional lives of writing teachers—transformations that the teachers of the thinking/writing project helped to pioneer and advance. I do not think I am claiming too much for this book, then, when I suggest that it is emblematic of the current moment in the field of language arts education and that its content, its rhetorical structure, and the conditions of its production all represent and enact what I take to be the most important developments of recent years in the teaching of writing and in the profession of teaching.

Thinking/Writing is first of all emblematic of the present moment in the history of teaching writing for its particular approach to the teaching of critical thinking through writing. It is unapologetically and emphatically a process-oriented book. Indeed, its fundamental premise is that the writing process itself is a model and enactment of the processes of critical thinking and an essential instrument for critical thinking in all disciplines. This approach to teaching writing and thinking reflects a body of research that has emerged over the past two decades in composition and allied fields, but has not found universal acceptance until recently in the larger community of teachers. The publication of *Thinking/Writing* at this moment testifies to the widespread need among teachers throughout the country for curricular materials, right now, that will help them implement a process-oriented approach to the teaching of writing and thinking in classrooms at every grade and in all academic subjects.

Thinking/Writing is also a representative book for our time in its fundamental rhetorical structure; that is, as a book in which classroom teachers present to other teachers model lessons that are research-based and classroom-tested. The key element here, marking this book as representative of an important transformation in our professional world, is that it is an instance of classroom teachers teaching other teachers—a concept for professional development programs that was largely dismissed by the educational community until it became the seminal principle of the National Writing Project professional development model in 1976—a principle that is only now gaining wide acceptance among district and school-site planners of staff development programs. The teachers who in this volume present lessons they have tested and perfected in their own classrooms presume to do so not because they hold advanced degrees or have been promoted to supervisory positions in their schools. Their principal qualification as authors derives from the commitment they made a decade or more ago to their own continuing professional growth through active membership in a community of professional colleagues. This meant that they committed themselves to learning from colleagues, to learning collaboratively with colleagues, and contributing their own expertise to colleagues.

The lessons presented in this volume are therefore much like the inservice workshops that these teacher/consultants/authors regularly conduct for teaching colleagues in schools and at conferences throughout the country. They demonstrate lessons that derive from actual classroom practices, that have been refined through discussions with colleagues and through an examination of current theory and research, and that are presented in the context of a theoretical framework which accounts for the efficacy; so that they meet the test of being both successful and principled practices.

Finally, as the collaborative effort of some 30 teacher-consultants from the National Writing Project site of the University of California, Irvine—all working under the inspired leadership of site director Carol Booth Olson—*Thinking/Writing* demonstrates the intellectual power and productivity that is possible within a community of teachers who continue to collaborate over the years for their own professional development and for the improvement of their teaching. Such collaborative communities, almost unheard of previously in American education, are at this moment becoming a regular feature of the academic landscape, variously organized as institutes, teacher-research groups, and special interest groups—most of them sponsored by National Writing Project sites.

In characterizing *Thinking/Writing* as a representative book for this moment in the history of American language arts instruction, I do not, of course, mean to suggest that it is a typical work or that its authors are typical teachers. The book and its authors are representative in the sense that they are exemplars for the profession of teaching, this book representing exemplary teaching practices and its authors representing model classroom practitioners working together in an exemplary community of colleagues. I feel blessed by the opportunity I had to become part of that community on my many visits to the UCI Writing Project over the past several years and I feel privileged now to be able to invite all readers of this volume to participate in that community by adapting the materials in this text to their own purposes as collaborators with the teachers who offer this book in the spirit of collegial generosity and professional fellowship.

Sheridan Blau, Director
South Coast Writing Project
University of California, Santa Barbara

Preface

What We Did Last Summer...Or...The Process of Collaborating on a Product

During the summer of 1982, thirty Teacher/Consultants who had been previously trained at the UC Irvine site of the California Writing Project returned to the campus for what would turn out to be the first of an ongoing series of Second Time Around Institutes. United by a common concern about the rather limited depth and range of critical thinking we were seeing in the writing of our students across grade levels, districts, and educational segments, we set out to explore ways to provide students with much needed practice in thinking and writing—practice that would enable them to tap the full range of their cognitive potential. With a lot of hard work, some healthy disagreement, and a certain amount of serendipity, we managed to forge a vision in that first summer of an instructional model designed to foster critical thinking through writing that combines basic principles of learning theory, composing process research, and the practical strategies of the National Writing Project. Further, we developed a core of rough drafts, many of which were refined to become the demonstration lessons which you will find in this book. The purpose of these demonstration lessons, simply stated, is to motivate teachers to think critically about critical thinking and to recognize the potential of using writing as a tool for promoting cognitive growth.

We were tremendously proud of the fact that we generated a product during that first Second Time Around project. However, it was the *process* of collaborating on that product that got us hooked, kept us coming back for the ensuing four summers to work on this concept and the curriculum materials which grew out of it, and which keeps us returning for projects which have spun-off the original Thinking/Writing effort even to this day, almost a decade later. It was the process and not the product which forged our "community" of learners, to use Donald Graves' term. It was and still is the intellectual stimulation of growing together as learners and the bonds of mutual respect and affection which gradually developed that inspired such an extraordinary commitment on the part of these extraordinary teachers.

A number of individuals facilitated our learning process by lending their support, encouragement and expertise to this project. Carl Hartman, former Associate Vice Chancellor of Academic Affairs at UCI, provided the impetus for our original Second Time Around program by requesting that the Writing Project focus its efforts on the translation of what we were learning in the Summer Institutes into some kind of curriculum materials, and by offering to provide seed-money to get this effort underway. Carolyn Lawson, Assistant Superintendent of Savannah School District, helped us to identify what we sensed was a missing stage in the writing process and to label it *precomposing*. While we did not have the pleasure of working with Linda Flower and John R. Hayes personally, their research on the role of planning in the composing process also contributed significantly to our emphasis on precomposing. Sheridan Blau, Director of the South Coast Writing Project at UC Santa Barbara, was a constant source of inspiration as we watched his own concept of humane literacy evolve over his several visits to our project. Aaron Fink, a consultant to The College Board, gave us a wonderful morale boost when he called our lesson the work of "scholar practitioners." Bill Strong, Director of the Utah Writing Project, offered support and encouragement by inviting us to present the Thinking/Writing model at his Summer Institute and identified a core of Utah teachers who participated in our first evaluation of the effectiveness of the Thinking/Writing lessons. Charles Cooper, Coordinator of the Third Writing Program at UC San Diego, helped us look more closely at our model and recognize the need for providing opportunities for student reflection. George Hillocks, Professor of English and Education at the University of Chicago, was instrumental in enabling us to re-see our lessons with an eye to whether or not they provided practice in the cognitive task called for in the writing prompt. And, finally, Owen Thomas, the former Co-Director of the UCI Writing Project, to whom this book is dedicated, taught us to believe in the remarkable linguistic abilities of our students and then modeled his own philosophy by believing in our ability to find our own voices as writers.

We were also fortunate to receive grant awards from several agencies to refine and enhance the Thinking/Writing concept and curriculum materials. The California Educational Initiatives Fund (Bank America/Chevron) provided the initial start-up funds in 1982-83 to further the work underwritten by the UCI in Summer '82. Subsequently, we received a three-year grant from the Fund for the Improvement of Postsecondary Education, 1983-1986, to build upon the work supported by the CEIF award. These funds were augmented by the California Writing Project Advisory Committee, who enabled us to allocate some of our stat support as matching funds. Most recently, the Office of the President, University of California contributed funding so that we could undertake a large scale research study of the Thinking/Writing model. The support of these agencies enabled those of us in the Thinking/Writing group to let ideas percolate and evolve over a number of years. The book you see today bears a resemblance to that original manuscript in 1982, but it is a product of much deeper reflection because of the revisions it underwent.

Sheridan Blau maintains that two kinds of thinking are entailed in composing and revising—commitment and detachment. *Commitment* involves finding enough value in what we have to say that we are likely to make the effort required to get our ideas straight, even for ourselves, and then having the faith (often in spite of feelings to the contrary) in our capacity to meet the challenge of articulating those ideas precisely for our readers. *Detachment* involves the intellectual skill of distancing ourselves from our writing in order to take the perspective of a reader. This perspective enables us to move from writer-based to reader-based revising—in other words, from getting things

straight for ourselves to getting things straight for a reader.[1] As Sheridan says, "The more writers want to have an impact on their readers, the more they need to understand how readers are likely to respond to their discourse."[2] Over the years, as the Thinking/Writing model and manuscript evolved, we experienced these twin processes of commitment and detachment over and over again. Working in small peer response groups, we served as an audience for each other's lessons, piloted them in our own classrooms to see what worked and what didn't, looked for missing rungs in the instructional ladder and collaborated on revisions. Interestingly, as our commitment to the total project grew, so did our detachment from our own individual work. In fact, ownership of the manuscript—the entire manuscript—became communal. Although the lessons and articles have individual by-lines, they are a product of a whole group process.

In a sense, then, the greatest debt we owe is to each other. In my own case, it has been the greatest privilege of my professional career to work with the colleagues listed below:

Susan Adams
English Teacher
Culver City High School
Culver City USD

Virginia Bergquist
Teacher
Meadowbrook Elementary School
Irvine USD

Brenda Borron
English Teacher
Saddleback High School
Santa Ana USD

Bill Burns
English Teacher
Sonora High School
Fullerton Joint Union HSD

Trudy Beck Burrus
Former English Teacher
El Toro High School;
Coordinator of Healthy Kids,
   Healthy CA
Sadleback Valley USD

Michael Carr
English Teacher
Valley Junior High School
Carlslbad USD

Evelyn Ching
English Teacher
Villa Park High School
Orange USD

Susanna Tracy Clemans
Instructor of English
Cerritos College

Catherine D'Aoust
Coordinator of Instructional
   Services, K-12
Saddleback Valley USD;
Co-Director, UCI Writing Project

Marie Filardo
Teacher
DePortola Elementary School
Saddleback Valley USD

Russ Frank
Former English and Journalism
    Teacher;
Assistant Vice Principal
Chaparral Intermediate School
Diamond Bar USD

Patti Gatlin
Teacher
S.A. Moffett Elementary School
Huntington Beach City SD

Sue Ellen Gold
English and History Teacher
Irvine High School
Irvine USD

Paulette Morgan Hill
English Teacher
El Monte High School
El Monte USD

Todd Huck
Former English Teacher
Thurston Intermediate School
Laguna Beach USD;
Instructor of English
Rancho Santiago College

Jerry Judd
English Teacher
Irvine High School
Irvine USD

Sheila Koff
Instructor of English
Orange Coast College

Erline Krebs
Lecturer, Department of Education
California State University,
Fullerton

Shari Lockman
Special Education Teacher
Saddleback High School
Santa Ana USD

Mindy Moffatt
English and History Teacher
Thurston Intermediate School
Laguna Beach USD

Mike O'Brien
Former English Teacher
Irvine High School Irvine USD
Instructor of English
Alan Hancock College

Laurie Opfell
Former English Teacher
Irvine High School
Irvine USD

Glenn Patchell
English Teacher
Irvine High School
Irvine USD

Elizabeth Reeves
Former Teacher
Los Alamitos Elementary School
Los Alamitos USD

Harold Schneider
Former Instructor of Composition
    and Film Studies, UCI;
Instructor of English
American River College

Peg Serences
Retired English Teacher
San Clemente High School
Capistrano Valley USD

Julie Simpson
English Teacher
Sunny Hills High School
Fullerton Joint Union HSD

Dale Sprowl
Former English Teacher
Irvine High School
Irvine USD

Sue Radar Willett
English Teacher
Capistrano Valley High School
Capistrano Valley USD

Susan Starbuck
English Teacher
Long Beach Polytechnic High
School

Special thanks to Catherine D'Aoust for her thoughtful reassessment of several sections of the manuscript.

Members of the UCI Writing Project staff also contributed to the production of the *Thinking/Writing* manuscript. Henia Alony and Greta Brooks painstakingly typed all the lessons before we had access to computers. Sheryl Palmer and Penelope West transferred the manuscript onto the Macintosh and created all of the computer graphics. When the Writing Project Office was burglarized, leaving nothing but the telephone hook up and one xeroxed copy of *Thinking/Writing*, Anna Manring patiently embarked upon a "cut and paste" to insert all of the revisions. And Chris Emerson-Orbaker kept the UCIWP inservice ship afloat while we all pursued the completion of this collaborative effort.

In the same way that we came to value the process of collaborating on a product as much or more than the product itself, we hope that it is the model which underlies our demonstration lessons rather that the individual lessons themselves that informs your thinking about thinking and writing. Our intention is that these lessons will serve as a vehicle for you, as teacher/readers, to discover your own process. Therefore, we invite you to collaborate with us— to make *Thinking/Writing* your own by rethinking, reshaping, and modifying the lesson prompts and activities to fit the interests and needs of your students. In short, we encourage you to use the lessons as a point of departure to arrive at your own destination.

Our hope for students is much the same. What we're really after is to provide students with enough guided practice—enough points of departure, if you will—to enable them to develop a range and repertoire of conceptual, problem-solving strategies that they can apply with confidence as *autonomous learners* to future thinking/writing challenges.

It is with these hopes in mind and in the spirit of collaboration that we offer you this book.

Carol Booth Olson

Notes

[1]Sheridan Blau, "Competence for Performance in Revision," in *Practical Ideas for Teaching Writing as a Process*, ed. Carol Booth Olson, (Sacramento: California State Department of Education, 1986), 140.
[2]Blau, 141.

PART ONE

The Thinking/Writing Model

A Rationale for Fostering Critical Thinking Through Writing
Carol Booth Olson

Basic Tenets of the UCI Writing Project
*Dale Sprowl, Glenn Patchell, and UCI Writing Project Teacher/
Consultants*

Thinking Levels
*Susan Adams, Michael Carr, Evelyn Ching, Catherine D'Aoust,
Patti Gatlin, and Peg Serences*

Taxonomy of Thinking Levels
*Susan Adams, Bill Burns, Evelyn Ching, Patti Gatlin,
Paulette Morgan Hill, Glenn Patchell, and Peg Serences*

Writing as a Process
Catherine D'Aoust

Thinking/Writing Charts
Bill Burns, Catherine D'Aoust, and Carol Booth Olson

The Domains of Writing
Trudy Beck Burrus and Elizabeth Reeves

The Goals of a Writing Program: Fluency, Form, Correctness
Virginia Bergquist, Brenda Borron, Bill Burns, Russ Frank,
Mindy Moffatt, Paulette Morgan Hill, Laurie Opfell, Glenn Patchell,
Peg Serences, and Dale Sprowl

A Rationale for Fostering Critical Thinking Through Writing

The heart of this book is a series of demonstration lessons, primary to college, that provides students with much needed practice in thinking and writing. But before you turn to those lessons, we would like to explain why we have taken an integrated approach to thinking and writing, acknowledge the influences that enabled us to shape our thoughts and develop premises, describe the results of our efforts, and share what we learned in the process. The purpose of our Thinking/Writing lessons, simply stated, is to motivate teachers to think critically about critical thinking and to recognize the potential of using writing as a tool for promoting cognitive growth. Combining basic principles of learning theory, composing process research and practical strategies of the National Writing Project, the Thinking/Writing lessons are intended to help teachers re-see, rethink, and redesign their own lessons with a greater awareness of their specific instructional goals.

Why Create a Thinking/Writing Project?

Established in 1978 as a site of the National Writing Project, the UCI Writing Project first addressed the issue of providing students with ongoing practice in sustained thinking and writing in a two-week curriculum conference in August 1982. Funded by the Office of Academic Affairs at the University of California, Irvine, with supplementary support from the California Writing Project, the conference brought together thirty Teacher/Consultants, K-College (who had been previously trained in the UCI Writing Project Summer Institute on the Teaching of Composition), to exchange ideas, experience, and expertise. Although we shared a perception that today's students are deficient in their thinking and writing ability when compared with students of a decade ago, we had very little data to verify our collective intuition nor any clear idea of what we might do to remedy the situation.

Two documents were especially significant in determining our focus. The first was *Reading, Thinking and Writing,* a recent report of a national reading and literature assessment of over 100,000 American school children. This document cited as its "major and overriding finding" that although students at each age level had little difficulty making judgments about what they read, most lacked the problem-solving and critical thinking skills to explain and defend their judgments in writing.[1] According to the authors of this report (Applebee, Brown, Cooper, and others), the results of this assessment do not point to any cognitive inability on the part of students to respond analytically. Rather, because of the current emphasis in testing and instruction on multiple choice and short answer responses, students are simply unused to undertaking critical thinking tasks. A separate research study, *Writing in the Secondary School* (Applebee, Auten, and Lehr), corroborates these findings. In an intensive one-year observation of two high schools, the researchers reported that 44 percent of the lesson time in six major subject areas involved writing activities of some kind; yet only 3 percent of that time was spent in writing tasks of a paragraph or longer.[2]

The second document that helped us establish our objectives was a draft of the *Statement on Competencies in English and Mathematics Expected of Entering Freshmen,* a joint publication of the Academic Senates of the California Community Colleges, the California State University, and the University of California, which was later distributed to every school in the state. This document stressed that before entering college it is crucial that students develop the ability "to understand, organize, synthesize, and communicate information, ideas, and opinions" and be able to demonstrate those thinking skills by "writing compositions, reports, term papers, and essay examinations."[3] When we contrasted the current emphasis on teaching to the proficiency test in the public schools with the expectations of California's college system, we had to ask ourselves: When, where, and how will students get the wide-ranging practice in thinking and writing that will enable them to tap the full range of their cognitive potential? In asking this question, we identified our ultimate concern: What contribution could we make to assist teachers in activating the thinking and writing skills of their students? This was the beginning of the Thinking/Writing Project.

Learning About Learning

Most people take as a given that depth and clarity of thinking enhance the quality of writing. What may not be so readily apparent is that writing is a learning tool for heightening and refining thinking. As writing teachers, we acknowledged that we intuitively foster critical thinking through our prewriting, writing, and postwriting activities. But before making our integrated thinking/writing approach a conscious one, we first had to learn more about how people think and learn.

From the learning theorists (Bloom, Bruner, Gagné, Guilford, Perry, Piaget, Taba, and others), we became reacquainted with the premise that there is a developmental sequence in the growth of thought and that this sequence progresses from the ability to operate at the most concrete level to the most abstract levels. Because one of the primary modes of learning is discovery, thinking cannot simply be taught like facts from a textbook. Maturity, experience, and practice all play a role in the development of a range of thinking abilities. However, as a facilitator and a guide, the teacher can create an environment that activates discovery and thereby fosters learning. Structured activities that gradually increase in complexity can become stepping-stones to higher levels of thinking. Taba acknowledged the crucial role of the teacher in this process when she concluded, ''how people think may depend largely on the kinds of 'thinking experience' they have had.''[4]

Once we established a theoretical framework from which to talk about thinking, we turned our attention to that most challenging of thinking experiences: writing. As we reviewed the studies of what people do when they compose (Bereiter, Britton, Emig, Flower and Hayes, Moffett, Perl, Scardamalia, and others), we gained a greater appreciation of the complexity of the act of transforming thought to print. As Flower and Hayes have pointed out, ''Writing is among the most complex of all human mental activities.''[5] Essentially, it is a form of problem solving because the writer must ''produce an organized set of ideas for a paper by selecting and arranging a manageable number of concepts and relations from a vast body of knowledge'' and ''fit what they know to the needs of another person, a reader, and to the constraints of formal prose.''[6] In short, we learned that researchers are currently looking to the field of cognitive psychology for new insights into the constraints that affect the composing process, such as the knowledge we have to construct and express meaning, the language we have to communicate what we know, the audience and purpose for writing, and the context in which writing occurs.[7]

Making the Abstract Concrete

At this point, we faced a challenging problem—how to apply what we had learned about thinking and writing by transforming abstract concepts into concrete demonstration lessons that would be meaningful to the classroom teacher. Since Bloom's taxonomy of educational objectives seemed to be compatible with the writing process and familiar to most classroom teachers, we decided to use his levels of thinking as a point of departure. (See Thinking Levels, pp. 14–16.) On looking closer, we experienced a shock of recognition: all of Bloom's categories in the cognitive domain—knowledge, comprehension, application, analysis, synthesis, evaluation—are integral to composing. In other words, the thinking process recapitulates the writing process and vice versa (see figure on next page).

To produce a composition, writers must tap memory to establish what they know, review the information they have generated and translate it into inner speech or print, organize main ideas into a logical sequence, discover specific support for those main ideas, re-see the whole to find a focus, construct a structural framework for communicating an intended message, transform this network of thought into a written paper, and evaluate the product. Thinking and writing are recursive processes; one often has to go back to go forward. It is inappropriate, therefore, to describe the act of composing in a linear fashion. One can argue (and we did!)

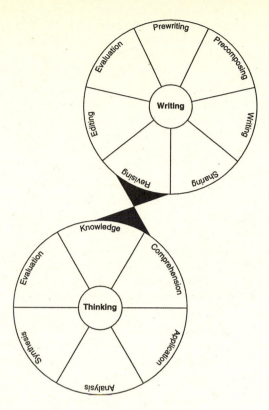

The Student's Process

whether evaluation should precede synthesis and whether one has to analyze in order to apply. We also acknowledged that certain stages in the writing process may simultaneously tap two or more thinking levels. The important point, we felt, was that composing involves all of the skills in the taxonomy regardless of the nature of the writing task. To understand this concept, it is helpful to think of two questions that the writer must constantly keep in mind while composing. The first—*What do I want to say?*—is a content-oriented concern that focuses on the written product. The second—*How will I get the ideas in my head into written form?*—is a procedural concern that relates more to the process of transforming thought into print than to the final product. Whether we ask a student to describe what it's like to peel an orange in rich sensory detail (a comprehension-level task) or to interpret and comment on the significance of the "Turtle Chapter" in *The Grapes of Wrath* (an analysis-level task), the process of writing requires tapping all of the levels of thinking. Given this premise, we concluded that providing students with ongoing practice in a range of thinking and writing activities would make the *what* in their papers more accessible and would also allow students to focus more attention on the *how* of composing.

In this way, we would reduce the constraints placed on student writers. By helping students become better thinkers, we would enable them to become better writers and vice versa.

The Demonstration Lessons

With a common philosophy about the interdependent nature of thinking and writing behind us and a common goal before us, we launched into the creation of our demonstration lessons. We first turned to Bloom's taxonomy of the cognitive domain as a way of identifying the thinking skills to be fostered in the content of our lessons. Many of us were uncomfortable with the idea of levels of thinking and the implication that these are hierarchical. Nevertheless, we recognized in Bloom's taxonomy a rough progression from *what,* to *how,* to *why,* to *so what* that made sense to us—as did the premise that concrete experiences can become a bridge to more abstract or formal operations. Ultimately, we concluded that all thinking is critical and that the goal of our lessons should not be to reach the top of any "hierarchy," but, as Moffett puts it, "to play the whole range."[8]

We also wrestled with our dislike of categorizing as we debated the specific abilities associated with each of Bloom's cognitive levels and began adapting and modifying his terms to reflect more closely the language that teachers use in phrasing writing assignments. The chart on page 7 is the latest version of what the subcommittee of Writing Project Teacher/Consultants called "the flowering of Bloom." While we see the categories and the "cue words" within them as fluid and sometimes overlapping, we have, nevertheless, found the chart to be helpful in identifying the key cognitive task within a writing prompt, whether it be to recall, describe, analyze, speculate, persuade, etc.

While our adaptation of Bloom's taxonomy served as a useful tool in examining what it is we ask students to do when they undertake a specific writing task, the stage process model of composition—prewriting, precomposing, writing, sharing, revising, editing, and evaluation—provided a way to format activities that would help students move from conception to completion.

Flower and Hayes have observed that the stage process model makes composing sound like it can be accomplished in a "tidy sequence of steps," like baking a cake or filling out a tax return, when, in actuality, " a writer caught in the act looks much more like a busy switchboard operator," juggling constraints and working on "cognitive overload."[9] While there is no one description of THE writing process, this model can serve as a teaching tool which provides students with a language with which to talk about writing and which builds in "think time" for ideas and expression to evolve.

What we wish to provide students with, through exposure to the Thinking/Writing model, is a progression of activities, somewhat like a ladder, that leads them to increasingly complex levels of thinking. Our goal is to give students enough guided practice to enable them to develop a range and repertoire of conceptual

Level	Cue Words	
Knowledge *Recall* Remembering previously learned material	Observe Repeat Label/Name Cluster List Record Match	Memorize Recall Recount Sort Outline/Format Stated Define
Comprehension *Translate* Grasping the meaning of material	Recognize Locate Identify Restate Paraphrase Tell Describe	Report Express Explain Review Cite Document/Support Summarize Précis/Abstract
Application *Generalize* Using the learned material in new and concrete situations	Select Use Manipulate Sequence Organize Imitate Frame	Show/Demonstrate How To Apply Dramatize Illustrate Test Out/Solve Imagine/Information Known
Analysis *Break Down/Discover* Breaking down material into its component parts so that it may be more easily understood	Examine Classify Distinguish/Differentiate Outline/No Format Given Map Relate To Characterize Compare/Contrast	Question Research Interpret Debate/Defend Refute Infer Conclude Analyze
Synthesis *Compose* Putting material together to form a new whole	Propose Plan Compose Formulate Design	Construct Emulate Imagine/Speculate Create Invent
Evaluation *Judge* Judging the value of material for a given purpose	Compare Pro/Cons Prioritize/Rank Judge Decide Rate Evaluate Predict	Criticize Argue Justify Convince Persuade Assess Value

strategies that they can apply as autonomous learners to future thinking/writing challenges.

The Process of Thinking and Writing About Thinking and Writing

As Bruce Joyce says, "We have to reinvent the wheel every once in a while, not because we need a lot of wheels, but because we need a lot of inventors."[10] As we thought and wrote about thinking and writing, it began to dawn on us that were concretely experiencing the levels of Bloom's taxonomy. This was a welcome and validating discovery.

The first phase of our endeavor generated what Sheridan Blau, Director of the South Coast Writing Project, would call "creative chaos." Ideas were voiced, pondered, debated, tabled, and reintroduced as we struggled to establish and define what we knew. We soon became aware of our differing learning styles. Some people had to hear an idea over and over again in order to grasp it, while others had to verbalize their thoughts—using the group as a sounding board. During these lofty and often circular discussions, our more visual learners pleaded with us to translate abstract concepts into diagrams on the board; strips of colored butcher paper with lists, charts, and favorite quotations began to adorn the walls of our room. Meanwhile, those of us who explore what we think by writing it down were furiously scribbling in our notebooks.

Through this process, knowledge gradually became comprehension. But we did not make what we understood our own until we began to apply the taxonomy to our writing assignments. Since old lessons would now take on a new thinking/ writing focus, it was necessary to analyze them carefully. Many of us were surprised to find great gaps in our writing assignments where students were expected, without direction, to make significant leaps in levels of thinking. No wonder we saw puzzled faces in the classroom when we explained some of these writing tasks. After we broke the lessons down, we reformulated them and put them back together. Writing was our synthesis.

What we developed was a series of five demonstration lessons (one each for primary, elementary, intermediate, high school, and college) at each thinking level: knowledge, comprehension, application, analysis, synthesis, and evaluation. Rather than by grade level, the lessons are grouped according to the category of the taxonomy on which they focus because we recognize that within any classroom some students will be ready for stretching experiences, while others need exercises that reinforce previous learning. Moreover, since students bring differing degrees of maturity and experience to any writing assignment, most of these lessons can be repeated (with modifications, if necessary) with younger or older students. We like to think of them as an "accumulating repertory" of ideas, to use James Moffett's term.[11] In addition to identifying the thinking and writing skills being fostered and offering specific ideas for each stage of the composing process, we also include extension activities that take the lesson into another domain of writing and/ or to the next step in the taxonomy and also provide across the curriculum ideas for writing assignments at the particular thinking level, when applicable. After pilot-testing these lessons during the 1982–83 school year, we returned to UCI the succeeding four summers with support from the Fund for the Improvement of Postsecondary Education and the California Writing Project to evaluate and refine our model, to revise what we had written, to create additional lessons, and to conduct training sessions to disseminate our work.

Reactions to Thinking/Writing

Since that intensive two-week curriculum conference in 1982 when we ''invented'' the Thinking/Writing Project, we have had many opportunities to present our model and demonstration lessons locally, state-wide and nationally. We have been gratified by positive responses such as the ones below from teachers at all levels of the curriculum:

The Thinking/Writing model has enabled me to fill in the gaps in my lessons. Too often, I have expected my students to know how to arrive at places they have never been.

More than anything, I learned how to stair-step up to the top of the process instead of just pushing the kids off the balcony and praying for a good landing.

Have you ever intuitively sensed that something was right—sort of felt it in your bones—and followed that feeling in a fumbling way until suddenly a 250-watt light bulb clicks on for you and you feel and say, ''That's what I thought''? The link between thinking and writing that I sensed is now very clear for me.

The theory behind Thinking/Writing gives me a good ''because'' to support curriculum choices. I don't need to rely on luck, habit, personal bias or whimsical caprice to explain why I teach the particular sequence I do.

I learned that I sometimes ask students to leap tall buildings in a single bound. They would be more likely to make it with a ladder.

Occasionally, we do hear teachers raise this concern: ''*Well, this may be relevant for those of you who have college-bound students; but I have the slow kids, and they just can't do this.*'' At this point, someone at the other end of the room usually counters with, ''*I totally disagree . . . This would be great for my Basic Comp class, but I know my Honors students won't go through all these thinking and writing steps. They'd get bored.''* We would urge those who react to the Thinking/Writing lessons in this book from either perspective to give the model a try before deciding whether or not or with whom it will work. It seems to us that the "slow" kids, those with the least practice, need the ladder of thinking/writing activities the most. As for the "bright" kids, if they don't need the structure, it's probably because they have internalized the necessary steps for solving that particular thinking/writing problem. For those students, you can move to more complex content or stay with the same content but provide activities which lead to a more sophisticated cognitive task.

We have also been asked whether this model provides too much "hand holding" for students—whether we, through our structured activities, are doing the thinking for the students in our lessons rather than prompting them to think for themselves. Since some of us used to be the kind of teachers who required papers to be handed in on the day before class discussion on the assigned topic so that students couldn't "steal" ideas from each other, we can relate to this concern. But since we've been developing these Thinking/Writing lessons, we have reassessed our role as teachers and changed our priorities. No single written product is as important to us as the process of getting to that product. What we're really after is to help students develop and internalize a set of conceptual strategies that can be applied to any writing task as well as to solving problems in everyday life.

We leave the final task of evaluating the value and usefulness of our efforts to you. If what we have shared in this book motivates you to think critically about critical thinking and to foster those skills in writing, then we have achieved our objective.

Notes

1 Arthur Applebee et al., *Reading, Thinking and Writing,* National Assessment of Educational Progress, Report No. 11-L-01, 1981, 31.

2 Arthur N. Applebee, Anne Auten, Fran Lehr, *Writing in the Secondary School,* National Council of Teachers of English, Research Report No. 21, 1981, 93. (Note: The percentage of time in English classes in writing tasks of a paragraph or more in length was higher than other disciplines—10 percent.)

3 Academic Senates of the California Community Colleges, The California State University, and the University of California. *Statement on Competencies in English and Mathematics Expected of Entering Freshmen,* 1982, 5.

4 Hilda Taba, *Thinking in Elementary School Children,* U.S. Department of Health, Education and Welfare, Cooperative Research Project No. 1571, 1964, 25.

5 Linda Flower and John R. Hayes, "Plans That Guide the Composing Process," in *Writing: The Nature, Development and Teaching of Written Communication,* eds. Carl H. Frederiksen and Joseph F. Dominic, Vol.2, (Hillsdale, NJ: Lawrence Erlbaum Associates, 1981), 39–40.

6 Flower and Hayes, 40.

7 Carl H. Frederiksen and Joseph F. Dominic, "Introduction: Perspective on the Activity of Writing," in *Writing: The Nature, Development and Teaching of Written Communication,* Vol. 2 (Hillsdale, NJ: Lawrence Erlbaum Associates, 1981): 19.

8 James Moffett, *Active Voice: A Writing Program Across the Curriculum* (Portsmouth, NH: Boynton Cook Publishers, Inc., 1981), 10. Note: James Moffett's writing sequences in *Active Voice* which involve a progression in overall types of writing, specific modes, audience, time, space and perception were influential and validating.

9   Linda Flower and John R. Hayes, ''The Dynamics of Composing,'' in *Cognitive Processes in Writing,* eds. Lee W. Gregg and Erwin R. Steinberg, (Hillsdale, NJ: Lawrence Erlbaum Associates, 1980), 33.

10   An analogy frequently cited by Bruce Joyce, coauthor of *Models of Teaching* (Englewood Cliffs, NJ: Prentice-Hall, 1972), at various conference presentations and professional addresses.

11   Moffett, 12.

Basic Tenets of the UCI Writing Project

- Writing is a tool for learning which fosters critical thinking.

- Writing as a learning tool should be used across the curriculum.

- An integration of the literacy skills (listening, speaking, reading, and writing) is essential to a writing program.

- Reading enhances writing skills.

- The teacher is a facilitator of the learning process who creates an environment conducive to learning and who demonstrates by encouragement and example what it means to ask challenging questions and to take intellectual risks.

- Assigning writing is not teaching writing. Practice in writing will not by itself lead to improved writing skills; only frequent writing experiences combined with instruction built on a sound theoretical framework can improve written expression.

- The composing process—prewriting, precomposing, writing, sharing, revising, editing, and evaluation—involves all levels of critical thinking and is a recursive process (students must go back to go forward.)

- The writer must juggle a variety of cognitive, linguistic, communicative, and contextual constraints in transforming thought into print.

- The more specific the writing assignment, the clearer the criteria for evaluation, the better the student will be able to respond effectively.

- Writing for a variety of audiences helps students develop voice, style, and purpose.

- Student should write for audiences other than the teacher-as-assessor. A proposed order of audiences is self, peers, trusted adult, teacher-as-collaborator, teacher-as-assessor, and unknown audiences.

- Peer sharing groups validate writing; group members function as supportive listeners, constructive critics, and editors.

- Writing in different domains should be emphasized at every level of learning. The domains discussed in this book are:
  - sensory/descriptive
  - imaginative/narrative
  - practical/informative
  - analytical/expository

- Each domain of writing has its purpose; no domain has more value than the others.

- The formal study of grammar in itself has no significant correlation to the improvement of writing skills.

- Teachers should stress fluency before correctness; students must be able to produce text before they can edit it.

- Teachers of writing should write; good teachers are themselves learners.

Thinking Levels

Most writing teachers would readily acknowledge that depth and clarity of thinking enhance the quality of writing and, at the same time, that the writing process is a tool that fosters thinking. Yet, in the classroom, we have not always integrated these interdependent processes. The demonstration lessons in this book represent our attempt consciously to integrate thinking and writing. The goal of this integration is to create thoughtful classrooms in which teachers model and foster thinking.

On the following pages, you will find a taxonomy of thinking levels which we have adapted from Benjamin Bloom's *Taxonomy of Educational Objectives: Cognitive Domain*. In modifying this taxonomy for writing teachers, we have reworded, eliminated, and/or added words under the categories of cognition to reflect more accurately the thinking/writing process. The cue words, listed next to the thinking levels, are commonly used as imperative verbs in the writing prompts and assist the teacher and student in assessing the cognitive task demanded by the writing prompt.

Bloom proposed six major categories of thinking levels: Knowledge; Comprehension; Application; Analysis; Synthesis; Evaluation.

The KNOWLEDGE level requires recall and remembering specifics, such as facts, terminology, events, and relationships. COMPREHENSION encompasses the ability to understand the meaning of the material or ideas contained in it. This level also involves the translation of knowledge from ideas and thought into print. APPLICATION includes the ability to apply what has been learned to new situations and to make appropriate generalizations or to derive principles. ANALYSIS is the breaking down of materials into their component parts. SYNTHESIS involves composing the parts of the material into something original—a creative act in which elements or parts are put together to form a new whole. EVALUATION refers to making judgments according to established criteria. EVALUATION includes rating, ranking and persuading.

In our integration of thinking and writing, we have reconceptualized Bloom's taxonomy in light of our own classroom experiences and thirty years of research. We perceive all thinking, whether it be at the knowledge level or evaluation level, to be *critical*. Generative writing requires that writers tap into all levels of the taxonomy—to recall, to express, to organize, to examine, to create, and to evaluate. However, these acts of cognition do not necessarily occur one at a time or progress in a certain order. At any stage in the process of transforming thought into print, the writer may, simultaneously, tap two or more thinking levels. Envision the graphic of the double wheels representing the thinking and writing process on pages 20–21, which is shown one-dimensionally as a kind of figure eight, as two roulette wheels superimposed upon one another, and you will have a sense of the complexity of the thinking/writing connection.

We also contend that all thinking levels pose their own difficulty; knowledge is not always a simpler behavior than comprehension. It is erroneous to describe one thinking level as more difficult than another without reference to the thinking experiences, background and behaviors which a student brings to the cognitive task as well as the content being explored. The taxonomy is not simply linear but is, instead, multidimensional. (See Table 1.) However, we do know from our own classroom experiences and research that the cognitive tasks of synthesis and evaluation which can require a high degree of content mastery are greatly facilitated by content experiences at the knowledge, comprehension and application levels.

TABLE 1: Taxonomy of Thinking Levels

Level	Cue Words	Sample Directions	Lesson
Knowledge *Recall* Remembering previously learned material	Observe Repeat Label/Name Cluster List Record Match Memorize Recall Recount Sort Outline (Format Stated) Define	• Recall and vividly describe a memory from your childhood. • Recall names and relationships of characters in the drama. • Cluster the characteristics of the Hemingway Code. • Define denotation and connotation.	• Watermarks • Character as Onion • After the Storm • Is He Your Daddy?
Comprehension *Translate* Grasping the meaning of material	Recognize Locate Identify Restate Paraphrase Tell Describe Report Express Explain Review Cite Document/Support Summarize Precis/Abstract	• Explain how words and actions affect our perception of the play's characters. • Identify the use of hands in playing jacks. • Paraphrase sections of the song as well as describe real events, people, battles, feelings, happenings, etc. • Restate the story of Christ in your own words, incorporating all parts contributed by the class.	• Character as Onion • News About Hands • Songs of an Era • After the Storm
Application *Generalize* Using the learned material in new and concrete situations	Select Use Manipulate Sequence Organize Imitate Frame How To Apply Dramatize Illustrate Test Out/Solve Imagine/Information Known Show/Demonstrate	• Imitate the story of "Alexander and the Terrible. Horrible. No Good. Very Bad Day" by writing a narrative about an abominable day in your life. • Explore how important or unimportant you feel birth order is in determining personality traits, based on your careful selection of data. • Using "barbaric" as defined in "The Lady or the Tiger?" apply the definition to a modern sport.	• The Horrible Day • Birth Order Essay • Should I or Shouldn't I?

TABLE 1: Taxonomy of Thinking Levels (cont.)

Level	Cue Words	Sample Directions	Lesson
		• Select you favorite sentence. • Find passages which illustrate scenes from *Old Man and the Sea* that demonstrate the Hemingway Code.	• Who Are You? • After the Storm

Analysis
Break Down/Discover
Breaking down material into its component parts so that it may be more easily understood
	Examine
	Classify
	Distinguish/
	  Differentiate
	Outline/No Format
	  Given
	Map/Relate To
	Characterize
	Question
	Infer
	
	Compare/Contrast
	  (Similarities/
	  Differences)
	Research
	Interpret
	Debate/Defend
	Refute
	Conclude/Draw
	  Conclusions
	Analyze
		• After looking at songs from two historical eras, compare and contrast the similarities and differences between the two eras.
		• Analyze which letter would be more likely to persuade a reader.
		• Examine Thanksgiving from the point of view of a child, a parent and a turkey.
		• If this were the only toy a person had, what would it tell you about the person?
			• Songs of an Era
			
			• Laws of Probability
			
			• It's All in the Way You See It
			
			• Pac Man

Synthesis *Compose* Putting material together to form a new whole	Propose Plan Compose Formulate Design Invent Construct Emulate Imagine/Speculate Create	• Imagine you have discovered an entirely new animal no one knows exists and write an encyclopedia entry. • Speculate about the happiness of a person based on only a photo. • Speculate about Kurtz. • Compose an ending for the Langston Hughes' short story "Thank You Ma'am following the lines "The door was open . . ."	• Darwin Redone • Who Are You? • A Letter from the Heart of Darkness • "Thank You Ma'am"

TABLE 1: Taxonomy of Thinking Levels (cont.)

Level	Cue Words		Sample Directions	Lesson
Evaluation *Judge* Judging the value of material for a given purpose	Compare Pro/Cons Prioritize/Rank Judge Decide Rate Evaluate Predict	Criticize Argue Justify Convince Persuade Assess Value	• Persuade a specific audience by predicting possible reactions and justifying your arguments. • Assess the behavior of a character, justifying his actions in terms of his values. • Pretending that you are a judge of a cookie "taste-off," write your choice of the best cookie and explain why. • Assess the overall learning experience in writing a personalized research paper.	• Persuasive Letters • Justifying a Decision • How Does Your Cookie Crumble? • Personalizing the Research Paper

Adapted from Bloom's Taxonomy of the Cognitive Domain [See *Taxonomy of Educational Objectives—Handbook 1: Cognitive Domain*. ed. Benjamin Bloom (New York: David McKay, Company, Inc., 1956)]

Writing as a Process

Writing, when viewed as a process, has strong pedagogical implications. It means abandoning the traditional classroom practice of simply assigning and grading papers for a more interactive role with students. It means that teachers interact with students and facilitate the development and discovery of their individual writing processes. Teachers who adopt the concept of writing as a process create enabling environments in which they assist students in their efforts to the finished product. Too often, teachers have overlooked the significant role they play in the students' discovery of their writing processes.

This change in the teacher's role does not simplify the teaching of writing. Teaching writing will always be a challenging task because writing itself is so difficult. Research helps us to understand rationally why this is so. P.C. Wason hypothesizes that the difficulty stems from a writer's attempts, simultaneously, to accomplish two incompatible objectives: "to say something, and to say it in an acceptable way."[1] This creates an incredible double bind for the writer who must generate and edit at the same time—a near impossibility.

Linda Flower and John R. Hayes contend that the conscious attempts on the part of the writer to gain control over all the demands (constraints) facing him or her will result in cognitive strain. They describe effective writers as those who juggle constraints throughout their writing process.[2] The difficulty arises for those writers who are unskilled or unpracticed in juggling constraints.

We writing teachers have known for a long time that writing is difficult. (What we did not know was the close connection between thinking and writing.) "Writing," according to Flower and Hayes, "is among the most complex of all human mental activities."[3] The cognitive scientists, who are investigating writing as a problem-solving activity, describe writing as a human production activity which requires decision making and planning skills. We know that writing is a vehicle for thought; it plays an important facilitative role in the development of thinking. In fact, the act of writing itself often leads to a discovery on the conscious level of what was previously only available to the writer unconsciously—a discovery only made possible through the transformation of thought into symbolic form. The nature of writing means that writing teachers teach for thinking. They create contexts where thinking is an integral and natural activity.

Within this context, we writing teachers have sought to discover the process students go through to produce written discourse. Research has revealed that students engage in a multitude of processes rather than a singular one. In other words, there is no straight line from conception to completion; each writer develops writing skills and manages the constraints of writing uniquely. Writing is *NOT* a linear process with a series of discrete, teachable stages. It is, instead, an interactive and recursive process that varies with each individual and each writing task.

In order to facilitate each student's discovery of his or her own unique writing process and to foster the development of a range of thinking skills, the teacher can provide a sequence of activities that enhance student attainment. This progression of activities structured by the teacher is like a cognitive ladder—the rungs are spaced at reachable distances for the student writer but far enough for intellectual challenge. The structure we chose within our lessons to create this ladder is the stage process model of prewriting, precomposing, writing, sharing, revising, editing, and evaluation.

Although the stage process model is not a description of the student writing process, it is a viable pedagogical tool to promote each student's thinking and writing development. It provides a common writing vocabulary and activities through which students discover their own writing process. The activities also associated with this model can increase a student's awareness of his or her own spontaneous, inner subprocesses as a writer. The stage process model, therefore, is a discovery tool. What follows is a description of the stages which provide the format for the demonstration lessons.

Prewriting

Prewriting is a generative activity to initiate thinking and fluency. It aims to stimulate a free flow of ideas through activities which require a writer to process new experiences or retrieve past experiences. In our lessons, we have structured prewriting activities both to generate ideas and provide practice for the thinking skills inherent in the writing prompt.

Precomposing

Flower and Hayes point out that writers must not only think about what they are going to say, but also how they are going to say it. The writer plans both for the process as well as the product.[4] Precomposing is the stage in which writers make initial plans about how they will approach the blank page. Precomposing activities usually follow the introduction of the writing prompt. In its most formal structure, precomposing can take an outline form. In our lessons, however, we tend to be less formal and have students make lists, organize through the use of charts and diagrams, and brainstorm as planning activities. Writers will find that these plans are essential for getting started but often change as they discover through writing itself what they want to say and how they want to say it.

Writing

Writing is drafting to give ideas shape and form in the symbols of written language. As mentioned earlier, it is a juggling of constraints requiring high level critical thinking skills. The writer is a decision maker constantly determining which demands need attention. The teacher assists this transformation in a number of ways in our lessons.

Sharing

In sharing, writing that is essentially one way communication becomes two-way communication. Through sharing activities, a writer receives feedback from other writers concerning how his or her words affect the reader. The writer who thinks and talks about the writing of others is preparing to review his or her own writing. In other words, this practice of being an audience for someone else's writing provides a distancing necessary to re-see one's own work. In structuring sharing activities, the teacher must consider who is to be the audience, what kinds of feedback would be most beneficial, and what kinds of feedback the potential responders are capable of providing. Sharing activities are sometimes unsuccessful because students have not been adequately prepared concerning how to respond to someone else's paper and/or the writer does not know how to receive feedback. In our lessons, sharing activities include read-around groups, peer response groups, and conferencing with the teacher.

Revising

In a certain sense, revision begins even before a writer puts pen to paper as thoughts are formulated, verbalized internally, and organized. Once the writer has generated a draft and received feedback, the revision stage allows time to reflect upon what has been written—to rethink, re-see, and reshape words and ideas. Using the skills gained in sharing and responding, the student must now become his or her own audience and assess the quality of the written work to enhance communication. In other words, revision is an act of creative criticism; for out of this careful scrutiny must come a reshaping of thought through the addition, substitution, deletion, and rearrangement of words. Revision can also be described as a juggling of constraints. Demands that a writer could not consciously attend to while drafting can be considered during revision. Revision activities in our demonstration lessons most commonly take the form of a series of questions which motivate the writer to read his or her paper critically. These questions may be the same ones used in the sharing groups or may stem from the evaluation criteria.

Editing

Young writers often have a difficult time differentiating between revising and editing. Revision is actually the reshaping of thought, while editing is the polishing of that thought. Editing is a particular subcategory of constraints in the composing process involving conforming to the conventions of written English, including accurate use of grammar, punctuation, and spelling. The goal is for the paper to stand alone without needing interpretation or explanation by the writer because of distractions caused by errors.

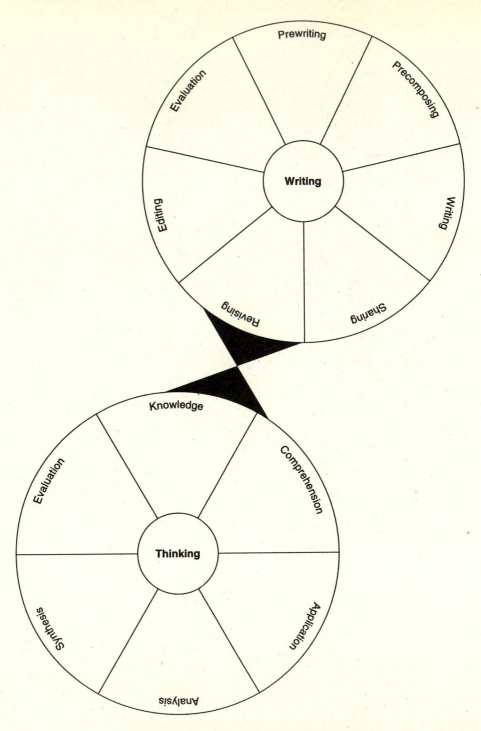

Thinking/Writing Chart: The Student's Process

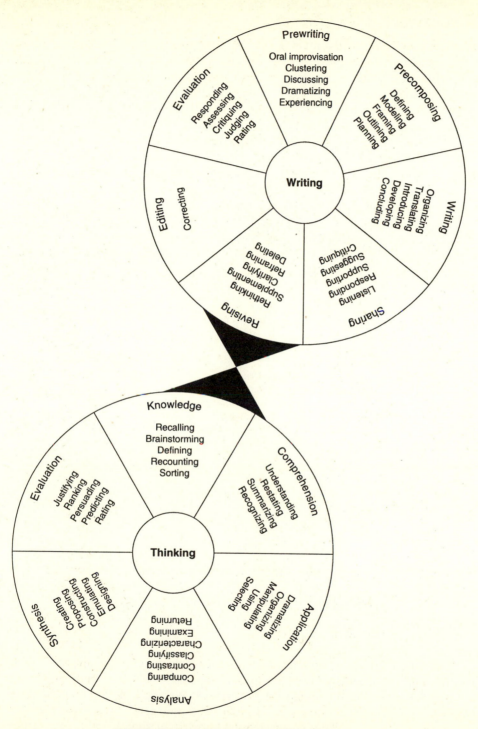

Thinking/Writing Chart: The Teacher's Process

Evaluation

Evaluation is a special form of sharing in the writing process. It is final feedback given to a writer when a paper is completed. Hopefully, this evaluation will give confirmation to the assessments made by the writer throughout the writing process. This feedback in our lessons is provided either by the teacher, other students, or the writer himself or herself. The criteria for evaluation is communicated early in our lessons—most often with the writing prompt. In some lessons, the teacher introduces the prompt and generates the criteria for evaluation from the students who will actually be writing to that topic. Later, as the students become more actively involved in writing, the evaluation criteria may be reassessed. Our lessons utilize a variety of evaluation techniques. Holistic scoring with rubrics, primary trait scoring, and analytic scoring are just a few of those included. In some lessons, formal evaluation of the final product is not suggested. All student writing does not need to be formally evaluated, in the sense of being given a grade. Ongoing student assessment during the writing process may, in fact, be sufficient evaluation for that product.

Notes

1 P.C. Wason, "Specific Thoughts on the Writing Process," in *Cognitive Processes in Writing*, eds. Lee W. Gregg and Erwin R. Steinberg, (Hillsdale, N.J.: Lawrence Erlbaum Associates, 1980), 132.
2 Linda S. Flower and John R. Hayes, "The Dynamics of Composing: Making Plans and Juggling Constraints," in *Cognitive Processes in Writing*, 31.
3 Linda S. Flower and John R. Hayes, "Plans that Guide the Composing Process, in *Writing: The Nature, Development and Teaching of Written Communication*, H. Frederiksen and Joseph F. Dominic, Vol.2, (Hillsdale, N.J.: Lawrence Erlbaum Associates, 1981), 39.
4 Linda S. Flower and John R. Hayes, "Plans That Guide the Composing Process," in *Writing: The Nature, Development and Teaching of Written Communication*, 39–57.

The Domains of Writing

Each of the Thinking/Writing lessons specifies a domain (or domains) of writing into which the final written product of that lesson falls. As Nancy McHugh pointed out in her chapter "Teaching the Domains of Writing" in *Practical Ideas for Teaching Writing as a Process*, "Dividing the 'universe of discourse' into domains is not new."[1] Educators have used a variety of approaches to characterize written discourse. James Britton's division of writing into three "function categories" —transactional, expressive and poetic[2]—and James Moffett's discourse schema based on the progression of speaker-subject relationships—recording (drama), reporting (narrative), generalizing (exposition), inferring (logical argumentation)—are two such approaches.[3] For the lessons in this book, we have chosen to use the "broad concept of domains" adopted by the Los Angeles Unified School District composition program. This model establishes four categories—sensory/descriptive, imaginative/narrative, practical/informative, and analytical/expository—for defining the purposes of writing. Each of the domains is described below.

Sensory/descriptive writing is based on concrete details. The writer gathers information through all five senses and uses those details to present a word-picture of a person, place, or object. His goal is to provide vivid, concrete details which will allow the listener or reader to recapture the author's perceptions. It is within this domain that the student learns to focus and to sharpen his powers of observation and to choose precise words to convey the sensory description. In the "On the Nose" lesson, for example, students practice identifying and describing smells. The activities promote close attention to details and to words that appeal to the reader's senses. The skills developed in this domain provide a foundation for writing in the remaining three domains.

Imaginative/narrative writing tells a story. It requires the student to focus on events, actual or imaginary, and to arrange the parts in a time/order frame. Here, the student learns ordering; beginning and ending; transition and balance; suspense and climax. The action of an event, placed in proper sequence, is embedded with "observed" sensory details, thus enriching the story. Look at the "Watermarks" lesson. In it, students recall events that have made lasting impressions on their lives. Not only do they examine their "watermark" experience, but they also identify events which lead up to it, and they select important details which will bring the situation to life for the reader.

Practical/informative writing provides clear information without much interpretation or analysis. Working in this domain, students learn accuracy, clarity, attention to facts, appropriateness of tone, and conventional forms. "Handy News" demonstrates the cumulative nature of the domains because, in the process of reporting about how a person uses his hands on the job at school, the writer may both rely on his sensory perceptions of the hands and employ narration to tell about the job being performed.

Imaginative/narrative and practical/informative writing incorporate several interrelated and overlapping skills. Regardless of the order in which these domains are taught, the skills in one will enhance and build on those of the other. For example, the ordering task of narrative enables the writer to produce a more successful practical/informative composition. Likewise, providing clear information in an appropriate tone enhances the narrative process. Both require the use of sequencing skills and description; both may focus on a breadth of topics from real to imagined, from concrete to abstract.

Writing in the **analytical/expository** domain explains, persuades, and influ-

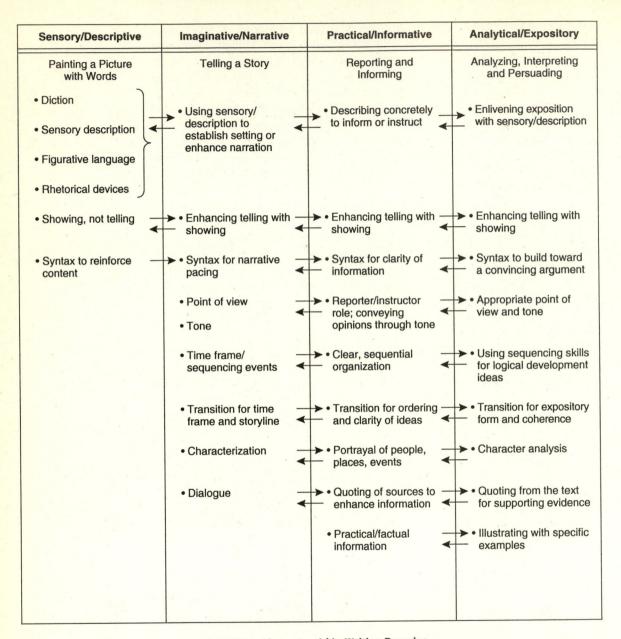

Sensory/Descriptive	Imaginative/Narrative	Practical/Informative	Analytical/Expository
Painting a Picture with Words	Telling a Story	Reporting and Informing	Analyzing, Interpreting and Persuading
• Diction • Sensory description • Figurative language • Rhetorical devices	• Using sensory/ description to establish setting or enhance narration	• Describing concretely to inform or instruct	• Enlivening exposition with sensory/description
• Showing, not telling	• Enhancing telling with showing	• Enhancing telling with showing	• Enhancing telling with showing
• Syntax to reinforce content	• Syntax for narrative pacing	• Syntax for clarity of information	• Syntax to build toward a convincing argument
	• Point of view • Tone	• Reporter/instructor role; conveying opinions through tone	• Appropriate point of view and tone
	• Time frame/ sequencing events	• Clear, sequential organization	• Using sequencing skills for logical development ideas
	• Transition for time frame and storyline	• Transition for ordering and clarity of ideas	• Transition for expository form and coherence
	• Characterization	• Portrayal of people, places, events	• Character analysis
	• Dialogue	• Quoting of sources to enhance information	• Quoting from the text for supporting evidence
		• Practical/factual information	• Illustrating with specific examples

FIGURE 1: Elements within Writing Domains

ences. It emphasizes analysis, organization, and development. The author examines closely, sees relationships, and builds a logical argument in order to successfully complete his writing task. "Theme Explanation Using *Lord of the Flies*" does precisely that. Students are asked to examine various characters, objects and events in the novel for symbolic significance. They explore ways in which these parts of the book interrelate, and they attempt to make new connections by moving beyond simple plot to the *how's* and *why's* of the story. The purpose of the essay is to explain how the specific parts of the novel are used to reflect a theme statement.

It would be a serious mistake to view these four domains as completely separate realms of writing. Research and practice show that these categories are interdependent and that they combine elements in varying proportions. Narration frequently utilizes description; exposition often incorporates aspects of all writing domains. A practical/informative letter of complaint, for example, might lean heavily on description and narration to make its point. A successful analytical/expository editorial may employ precise description, narrative ordering, and informative presentation of facts in order to convince the reader.

Finally, it is clear that the levels of complexity in the domains of writing vary according to the thinking and writing skills being practiced, as well as to the sophistication of the subject matter. Cartoon captions, dialogues, autobiographies, and allegories represent the wide range of difficulty possible within the imaginative/narrative domain. Analytical/expository writing can be a single paragraph definition or a multi-page research paper. The developmental lessons in this book have been designed to sample and span this complex network and to provide models which demonstrate the major domains of discourse.

Notes

1 Nancy McHugh, "Teaching the Domains of Writing" in *Practical Ideas for Teaching Writing as a Process*, ed. Carol Booth Olson (Sacramento: California State Department of Education, 1987), 81.

2 James Britton ed., *The Development of Writing Abilities* (11–18) (London: Macmillan Education LTD, Schools Council Publications, 1975), 88–91.

3 James Moffett, *Active Voice* (Portsmouth, NH: Boynton Cook Publishers, 1981), 13.

The Goals of a Writing Program: Fluency, Form, Correctness

The graphic below (Figure 2) represents the three goals of a writing program: fluency, form, and correctness. Notice that these goals are depicted in a triangle. No one facet of this triangle is more important than another. However, fluency is at the base of the triangle. Once students feel comfortable with expressing what they have to say, they are much better able to attend to concerns of form and correctness. Therefore, in the early stages of the writing process, fluency should be encouraged, whereas correctness should be emphasized in the later stages. The chart on the next page defines fluency, form, and correctness and lists writing skills and strategies one might focus on to promote each of these goals.

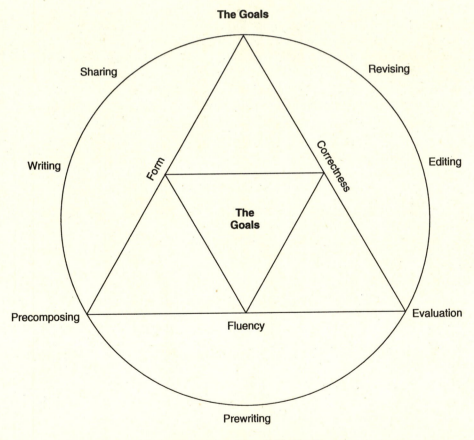

FIGURE 2: Writing Skills Chart

Fluency	Form	Correctness
The ability to comfortably and easily express ideas in writing. It includes the ability to overcome writer's block and to suspend judgment on the initial writing. Prewriting strategies promote fluency.	The ability to respond to a writing task, work through and choose an appropriate shape or format for the piece, execute a plan (the precomposing step) which fulfills that format and select the domain and style of writing based upon the audience.	The ability to use the conventions of written English in order to communicate effectively.

Prewriting Strategies

- Recalling prior knowledge
- Tapping prior experience
- Clustering
- Brainstorming
- Freewriting
- Guided imagery
- Showing films, slides, pictures
- Using models for writing
- Stylistic imitation
- Reading silently or aloud
- Discussing a topic or issue
- Singing/listening to music
- Drawing
- Taking field trips or walks
- Role playing
- Pantomiming
- Listening to guest speakers
- Conducting interviews
- Peer group activities

Audiences

- Self
- Peers
- Trusted adult
- Teachers as collaborator
- Teacher as assessor
- Unknown audiences

Precomposing Strategies

- Focused freewriting
- Oral composition/ improvisation
- Writing down inner speech
- Informal outlining
- Formal outlining
- Organizing a cluster
- Mapping
- Charting
- Framing
- Writing an abstract
- Formulating a writing plan

Domains

- Sensory/descriptive
- Imaginative/narrative
- Practical/informative
- Analytical/expository

Style

- Diction
- Figurative language
- Rhythm
- Sentence pacing
- Sentence variety
- Rhetorical devices
- Point of view
- Tone
- Personal voice

Standards of Written English

- Spelling
- Capitalization
- Punctuation
- Grammar/usage
- Penmanship/neatness

Formats

- Poem
- Song
- Paragraph
- Journal or diary
- Short story
- Vignette
- Myth or fable
- Play
- Monologue
- Dialogue
- Script
- Biography
- Autobiography
- Letter
- Application
- Ad
- Captions
- Resume
- Notes
- Directions
- Essay
- Editorial
- Review
- Research paper
- Footnote
- Bibliography entry

PART TWO

The Demonstration Lessons

The heart of this book is a series of thirty demonstration lessons—one each for primary, elementary, intermediate, high school, and high school/college at each thinking level: knowledge, comprehension, application, analysis, synthesis, evaluation. Rather than by grade level, the lessons are grouped according to the category of the taxonomy on which they focus because we recognize that within any classroom some students will be ready for stretching experiences while others need exercises that reinforce previous learning. Moreover, since students bring differing degrees of maturity and experience to any writing task, most of these lessons can be replicated (with modifications, when necessary) with younger and older students.

Integrating learning theory, composing process research, and the practical strategies of the National Writing Project, the lessons stress the importance of thinking about what you write and writing about what you think. Each lesson identifies the specific thinking and writing skills to be fostered; offers concrete ideas for implementing each stage of the writing process—prewriting, precomposing, writing, sharing, revising, editing, and evaluation; provides suggestions for extension activities which take the lesson to another level of the taxonomy, offer examples of related writing prompts in other domains, or explore the implications of the lesson for a different content area. Topics for the lessons range from open-ended to more closed-ended, although almost all are built upon a strong personal experience base.

We have chosen the term *demonstration* with some care because its dictionary definition, ''a description or explanation, as of a process, illustrated by examples,''[1] conveys our intent to share a *model* for providing students with much needed practice in thinking and writing rather than a rigid formula for generating particular written products. Granted, you will find that some of the authors of these lessons use a step-by-step or Day 1/Day 2 approach to constructing the ladder of thinking/writing activities that will facilitate a student's progress from conception to completion. But we invite you to look at these lessons as a point of departure and, if you wish to replicate them, to add, modify or remove the rungs in those ladders to suit your own instructional needs and student population. As Madeline Hunter points out, *"There are no absolutes in teaching! . . .* There is no substitute for a teacher's considered judgment . . . about *these* students in *this* learning situation at *this* moment in time.''[2]

Before you turn to these lessons, we also encourage you to look ahead to the chapter "Operation Robot or How We Made Thinking/Writing Our Own" which describes a unit of activities developed by Patti Gatlin and Erline Krebs that draws from Thinking/Writing concepts but which branches out from and experiments with the model—reflecting the creative and comprehensive plan Patti and Erline envisioned for a specific group of young writers. It is in the spirit of that chapter that we offer you these demonstration lessons. To quote Patti and Erline:

> We have found that making Thinking/Writing our own was like designing our own robot. We had to give it our own shape and design useful appendages. It had to be comfortable to be with and easy to maneuver wherever we needed to go. It didn't require excessive maintenance, and there were plenty of accessible emergency parts. Piece by piece, it became our own creation. Please accept our invitation to make Thinking/Writing *YOUR* own!

The following charts outline the format of the demonstration lessons, define the activities or goals of each stage in the lesson, and provide directions to the teacher regarding how to design and implement a demonstration lesson.

Notes

1 *The Random House Dictionary of the English Language.* New York: Random House, 1983: 531.
2 Madeline Hunter. "Madeline Hunter in the English Classroom." *English Journal* 78, September 1989, 17–18.

Demonstration Lesson Chart

Writing Domain

Title

Lesson	
Objectives	

The Process

Prewriting

Prompt

Precomposing

Writing

Sharing

Revising

Editing

Evaluation

Structured

Demonstration Lesson Chart

Title

Lesson	A brief description of the final writing assignment.
Objectives	THINKING: Specific skills from Bloom's taxonomy.
	WRITING: Specific writing skills utilized in the writing.

The Process

Prewriting	Activities and experiences that capture students' attention and promote students' confidence in themselves as writers, that generate ideas—setting the stage for the prompt, that give practice in higher level thinking skills.
Prompt	A specific writing task.
Precomposing	Activities and experiences that promote the development of a plan for writing to a particular prompt and provide practice in the skills taught in the lesson.
Writing	The first draft—aims for fluency, for rapid, rough completion, for discovery of content rather than refinement of thought.
Sharing	Writing being read by another that allows for input to be refined by the writer.
Revising	Rethinking, re-seeing, reformulating the content and clarity of the first draft, incorporating the sharing.
Editing	Proofreading the surface of the writing to ensure that it conforms to standards of correctness.
Evaluation	Judging the writing to determine if it satisfies the writer and reader as well as fulfills the requirements of the prompt.

—**Defined**—

Demonstration Lesson Chart

Writing Domain

Taxonomy Level
Grade Level

Title

Lesson	Briefly describe the final writing assignment.
Objectives	THINKING: Choose and specify thinking levels students will attain.
	WRITING: Delineate specific writing skills taught or utilized.

The Process   Writing the lesson plan

Prewriting

Specify activities that lead into the writing. Provide for the visual, auditory, kinesthetic, or experiential needs of the students and the writing and thinking skills being called for.

Prompt

Write specific directions for the writing task. Tell what is required in terms of fluency, form, and correctness. Explain what is expected in the content of the final piece of writing. The more specific the prompt, the clearer the criteria for evaluation, the better able the student is to respond effectively.

Precomposing

Structure activities to help students generate ideas that are specific to the prompt and lead to a writing plan. Activities can be varied including providing models.

Writing

Stressing fluency, provide specific guidelines to assist students in composing a first draft.

Sharing

Decide how best to allow students to read and comment on each other's writing. Possibly provide a list of questions to direct students in their responses. Decide what the role of the teacher will be in the sharing process.

Revising

Give students an opportunity for individual reassessment of their work based on insight from sharing.

Editing

Specify and reinforce the correctness requirements of the prompt.

Evaluation

Decide what method to use to judge the writing. Specify and reinforce the requirements of the prompt. The evaluation criteria must be specific and addressed from the time the prompt is given to enable the student to know what is expected.

—— **Processed** ——

1 Knowledge

Color Poems

Lesson

Having listened to poems on color from the book *Wishes, Lies, and Dreams* by Kenneth Koch, students will write a poem about a color.

Objectives

Thinking Skills
Students will function at the *KNOWLEDGE* level of the taxonomy by *RECALLING* and *RECORDING* objects that are of a particular color.

Writing Skills
Students will be expected to recall their color items and list them in the prescribed poetic form.

The Process

Prewriting

1. To help students focus in on the format of color poems, read selected samples from ''Colors'' in Kenneth Koch's book *Wishes, Lies, and Dreams* (New York: Chelsea House, 1970).

   Red
   Red is the sun setting at night
   Red is the color of love
   Red is the color of a cherry
   Red is the color of an apple
   Red is the color of a nice person
   Red is the color of sweetness
   Red is the sun rising

   Marion Mackles (206)

*Note: This lesson will need to be adapted for K-1 students. For example, during prewriting, the teacher might have the students draw color words which the teacher can transcribe (with picture and word) onto a composite cluster on the board. Students can then make their own picture cluster. Instead of writing a color poem, the students can dictate to the teacher and then copy in their own handwriting or trace the teacher's writing.

Pink is my color. I like pink because it is bright. When I think of it, it makes me think of a pink sky, an Easter Bunny, a dress, a baby in a crib and it makes me think of myself.

Lorraine Fedison (205)

2. After hearing the poems, select a color and have the class cluster objects that they associate with that color. Write their responses on the chalkboard and remind them to list responses that are familiar to their classmates. A sample cluster might look like this:

Sample Cluster:

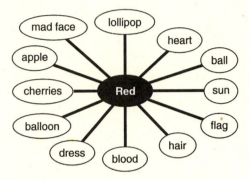

3. Select some of the objects and write them on the board in the poetic format.

K–1	**2–3**
Red is a hard lollipop	Red is a falling sun
An apple	Red is a cut on my finger
A flag in our room	Red is a heart beating loudly
A hot sun	Red is a round bouncing ball
A mad face . . .	Red is a balloon far overhead . . .

When completed, read and explain to the students that they have created a poem.

Prompt:

Now that you have heard poems about color, have named things of the same color, and have written one poem as a group, choose a color and then write a color poem. List at least five interesting things that you can recall that remind you of the color you have chosen. Your list should include items that are of interest to your classmates, and are clear and easy to understand. Remember that the poem can be written in phrases or sentences and should follow the poetic format demonstrated on the board.

Precomposing

To assist students in planning their writing, ask that they:

- Use the clustering technique to generate ideas for their poems.

- Use the poetic format demonstrated on the board, and include at least five clear and interesting examples.

    (*color*) is _____ _____ _____ _____ _____

Writing

Students will now write a poem about one color. This is a first draft writing that stresses fluency.

Sharing

Before students read their rough drafts in small groups, the teacher can read a sample poem and model the types of feedback students can give one another.

Example Poem:	**Sample Response:**
Blue	I like the way you put blue with rainy days and then rainbows.
Blue is like a person Blue is like cookies Blue is like a mountain Blue is like a rainy day Blue is like a rainbow	I don't understand why blue is like a cookie. Would you explain this connection?

Revising

Students can expand on the parts of the poem people liked, revise parts of the poem that were not clear, or they can resequence the poem. Students can refer to the primary trait scoring guide below for specific requirements.

Editing

Students will meet with sharing groups or have individual conferences with the teacher to edit their work for capitals and spelling. Students can refer to the secondary trait scoring guide for correctness requirements.

Evaluation

Students and/or the teacher may score papers according to primary and secondary traits.

Primary Trait Scoring Guide

3 Writer used one color in his/her poem and had at least five clear and interesting examples. Used correct poetic format.

2 Writer used one color in his/her poem and included some clear and interesting examples. Used correct poetic format.

1 Writer may have used more than one color in his/her paper or may not have used clear and interesting examples. Problems in the use of poetic format.

Secondary Trait Scoring Guide

3 Paper demonstrated correct use of capitals and spelling.

2 Paper had some errors in the use of capitals and spelling.

1 Paper had many errors in the use of capitals and spelling.

Note: If students are given the option of following the sentence format modeled on the top of page 37, you may want to add correct use of commas and periods to the scoring guide.

Extension Activities

Application

Prompt: Write your color poem on the color paper it describes. You may also want to illustrate your poem to add a visual effect so that we can see it better.

_____

Analysis

Prompt: Write another poem in which you compare and contrast two colors on alternating lines.
For example:

Green is . . .
Red is . . .

_____

Writing Domain: Imaginative/Narrative   Thinking Level: Knowledge
                                                         Grade Level: Elementary

Book Wheels
A Book Reporting Activity Involving
Reading, Writing, Speaking, Listening, and Art*

Lesson

As part of an oral book report presentation called a ''book talk,'' students will
create a visual aid, a ''book wheel,'' containing a written list of incidents from an
episode in the book they have read.

Objectives

Thinking Skills
Students will:

- *DEFINE* ''episode'' (Knowledge);

- *IDENTIFY* three episodes in the book they have read (Comprehension);

- *SELECT* an episode from their book which they think will appeal to peer group
  members (Application);

- *LIST* and *RECOUNT* the incidents in the episode they have selected (Knowledge).

Writing Skills
Students will:

- List in order and in complete sentences three incidents in an episode from the
  book they have read;

- Write a parallel list based on the first list which uses key words and phrases
  rather than whole sentences;

- Revise each episode list for proper sequencing, clarity, and required content;

- Edit for correct spelling, capitalization, and end punctuation.

*This lesson is based upon one designed by a colleague, Tina Knowlton.

The Process

Introduction

Since the writing, reading, speaking, listening, and art work related to this assignment culminate in the construction and use of a visual aid called a "book wheel," it is a good idea right here at the beginning to get a clear understanding of what a book wheel is and how it works.

You might first want to look over the diagram of the book wheel and the sample book wheels which follow the *EVALUATION* section of this lesson. (See page 51.)

As you can see, the book wheel is a visual aid which students make and then use to help recount the events of an episode from a book that they have read. This recounting of events is done informally in small groups and is called a "book talk."

The right-hand side of the backing paper for the book wheel contains basic information about the book and an abbreviated list of the incidents in the episode that the student is going to recount. The student may use this list as a set of notes when he gives his book talk. (A corresponding unabbreviated list of incidents in the episode will be written on the back of the backing paper. See *PRECOMPOS-ING*, Step 3, page 44.)

On the left-hand side of the backing paper, a circular pattern is drawn. Inside this circle, the student glues or draws small pictures and words which will help to illustrate, in order, the incidents in the episode. The circular pattern is then overlaid with a "window wheel," a matching circular piece of paper from which a wedge has been cut. The window wheel is attached to the backing paper with a brad fastener which allows it to rotate. The student may then rotate the window wheel, revealing through its pie-shaped cut-out one or two pictures at a time. As the book talk progresses, the student continues to rotate the wheel to reveal pictures and words which correspond to the incidents in the episode that the student is recounting.

Prewriting

1. Three to five weeks prior to the due date of this assignment, have students begin reading the book of their choice. Fiction works best for this assignment. However, nonfiction books which contain facts about a person's life, a historical incident, the steps in a process, what parts make up a whole, etc., can be easily adapted for this assignment. You may wish to inform students at this time that an oral book report called a "book talk" which requires the use of a visual aid will be due at the end of the specified reading and report preparation time.

2. A week before the "book talk" is due:

    •   Remind students that a "book talk" which involves the use of a visual aid is due in a week. Tell them that they are going to spend most of the next five days in class preparing for their "book talk" and making their "book wheel."

- Begin a discussion of the term "episode" by asking volunteers to explain what happened in the latest episodes of their favorite TV shows. (You needn't define the term at this point.) After several examples have been shared, ask the students to deduce and then define what an episode is. Be attentive to what is accurate in their answers and repeat it. To corroborate student definitions, a student may look up the term in the dictionary and report back to the class. Finally, you may wish to restate for the whole class what an episode is. (An episode is a developed situation in a work of fiction that is part of the continuous narrative, the larger whole, but which may be identified and discussed separately because it has its own distinct beginning, middle, and end.)
- Ask for a volunteer to recount briefly an episode from the book he has just finished reading. When he is done, ask him (or the class in general) to state why his example is an episode.
- Explain that, although an episode may be written as a single chapter, it may also be longer or shorter than a chapter. The following "Example Episodes" may be used as models:

Shorter than a chapter: The chapter "Flies and Spiders" from *The Hobbit* (Ballantine) contains an episode in which Bilbo encounters the spiders of Mirkwood, first killing one and then rescuing his friends, the dwarves, from the rest, and finally all battle the spiders until they retreat.

A chapter: Chapter 11 in *To Kill A Mockingbird* (Popular Library edition) is an episode. In it, Mrs. Dubose insults Jem and Scout's father, and Jem, in anger, knocks the tops off of her camellias. As punishment Jem is forced to read to her after school every day for a month. Shortly thereafter, Mrs. Dubose dies, and Jem learns from his father that she had been trying to kick a morphine addiction during the month of the afternoon readings. Finally, Jem's father, Atticus, gives Jem a gift sent to him by Mrs. Dubose just before she died: a perfect, snow-white camellia.

Longer than a chapter: Chapters 12 and 13 in *The Count of Monte Cristo* (Bantam Books edition) comprise an episode in which Edmond Dantes makes his escape from the Chateau d'If by hiding in the burial sack of his dead friend, Abbe Faria, which is flung into the sea by the guards. Dantes cuts his way out of the sack, rides out a storm at sea, and is rescued by a small smuggling vessel.

3. During class discussion, take a quick check of the students' comprehension of the term "episode." Ask volunteers to provide examples of episodes from books, films and television shows. Be sure to have students identify the beginning and ending of each example episode that they provide. As a summary activity, you may wish to have students write their own definitions of the term "episode."

4. At this point, introduce the ''book wheel'' itself. Explain that the book wheel is a visual aid that the students will make to help them share with their peer groups a colorful episode from the books they have read. This sharing is called a ''book talk.''

Now would be a good time to model a book wheel that you have constructed. Show the students the different parts (front list, back list, circle patterns with pictures, window wheel.) Talk them through the episode depicted in your book wheel.

If you haven't made a book wheel, draw a large mock-up of the book wheel on the board, or pass out to the class the student directions for making a book wheel. Once again, go over the parts of the book wheel.

Tell students that the first step in building a book wheel is selecting a colorful, interesting episode from the book they each have read and then writing a ''front'' and a ''back'' list of events from that episode.

Prompt:

1. In six to twelve sentences list the main incidents in the episode from the book which you have chosen to share with your peer group. Sentences in your list must:

    - be numbered
    - be in proper narrative sequence (the order in which they appear in the book)
    - mention the setting of the episode
    - mention the names of main characters in the episode
    - relate an episode which has a clear beginning, middle, and end.

2. The list must be copied neatly on the back of the book wheel card.

3. For the front of the book wheel (see ''book wheel'' format, following page), write a second list. This list must cover, point by point, the same incidents mentioned on the first list but with this important difference: because space on the front of the book wheel is limited, each incident on this second list may be represented by a key word, a phrase, or a shortened sentence based on the sentence already written on the first list. Copy this shortened list on the right-hand side of the front of the book wheel card.

4. You will use your lists as notes when you give your ''book talk'' to your peer group.

Precomposing

1. Tell students that the audience for their book talk is their peer response group and that their purpose in selecting and later presenting an episode is to encourage them to read the book. They should, therefore, select an episode which they think will appeal to their peers. (Should you find a student who wishes to dissuade his peers from reading his book, have him select his episode accordingly.)

2. Based on their understanding of the term "episode," students will:

   - identify three separate episodes in their novel
   - restate in writing, in one to four sentences, the basic action of each of the three episodes they have identified
   - select the one episode from their novel which they think will most appeal to members of their peer group

3. Model a backlist (sentences) and a frontlist (words and phrases) of incidents from an episode. Following are example lists from *Tom Sawyer:*

Example Lists

Backlist	Frontlist
1. On a beautiful Saturday morning, Tom is depressed because he must whitewash the fence as a punishment.	1. Saturday—Tom depressed—whitewash
2. Tom begins working, but he is soon discouraged by the long stretch of fence left to paint.	2. Tom begins—discouraged
3. Jim, the slave boy, passes by, and Tom tries to bribe him with a marble to paint the fence.	3. Jim arrives—Tom bribes
4. Aunt Polly gives Jim a swift kick and sends Tom back to work.	4. Aunt Polly's kick
5. Soon, Ben Rogers arrives pretending to be a steamboat.	5. Ben "Steamboat" Rogers
6. Tom purposely ignores Ben and pretends to concentrate on painting and then suddenly "realizes" Ben is there.	6. Tom ignores, concentrates, and "realizes."

7. Ben tries to get Tom to give up painting and go swimming.

7. Ben wants to swim.

8. Tom tells Ben that painting is an important job that a person doesn't get a chance to do everyday.

8. Tom says painting is important.

9. Ben asks Tom for a turn painting, and when he bribes Tom with an apple, Tom lets him paint.

9. Ben asks, begs, bribes—Tom lets him paint.

10. Other boys come and fall for Tom's persuasion, and soon he has collected several "treasures" from them in return for letting them paint.

10. Other boys give "treasures" to paint.

11. The fence is soon finished, and Tom decides that work is doing whatever you have to do, and play is doing whatever you don't have to do.

11. Fence finished—Tom on work and play.

12. Tom goes in to report to Aunt Polly.

12. Tom reports to Aunt Polly.

Writing

Based on their understanding of the elements of an episode and of the modeling you have presented, the student will write a backlist and a frontlist for their episode according to the requirements stated in the prompt.

Hint: Once students have selected an episode they wish to use, you may wish to have them begin to collect and draw pictures and words that will illustrate that episode on their book wheel. Introducing this part of the process (#1 on ''Directions for Making the Book Wheel'') at this point will give them more time for picture gathering. It may also help them better tie the pictures and words they collect to the incidents in the written list on which they are now working.

Sharing

Students exchange completed back and front episode lists with a classmate who is preferably not a member of the peer response group that will hear the final book talk. The partner will read, analyze, and compare both lists against a list of eval-

Note: See the sample Book Wheel following the *EVALUATION* section of this session for a graphic representation of incidents 1, 9 and 12 of *Tom Sawyer.*)

uation questions written on the board (see below). If the peer partner answers "no" to any of the questions, he must write the author a brief note on his lists pointing out the areas which need attention.

- Sample backlist evaluation questions:

  - Is the list made up of six to twelve numbered sentences?
  - Are the sentences clearly written? (Do they make sense?)
  - Are the items in the list arranged in the proper order as far as you can tell?
  - Is the setting of the episode mentioned?
  - Are the names of the major characters in the episode mentioned?
  - Does the episode have a clear beginning, middle, and end?

- Sample frontlist evaluation questions:

  - Do the items match up point for point with the numbered sentences on the "back" list?
  - Are key words and phrases from the "back" list used in the "front" list?

Revising

Based upon the feedback they have received from their peer partner, students will add, delete, substitute, and rearrange details in their papers for improvements in content, clarity, and sequencing.

Editing

On the board, write a list of editing criteria for the final draft of the students' front and back lists which they will copy onto the book wheel card. Discuss these criteria with your students and have them copy them for further reference. Criteria may include correct spelling, capitalization, end punctuation, sentence completeness, overall neatness, and other elements of grammar, mechanics, and usage that the teacher deems appropriate.

A limited read-around group (see Glossary) may be used in which each student can have his or her paper checked by other students for established editing criteria. It is probably preferable if read-around responders are not members of the peer group which will finally hear the book talk.

The students then edit their own papers based on input from peer responders and their own careful proofreading. When both back and front lists have been edited, they may be copied onto the book wheel according to the following format.

Annotated Directions for Making the Book Wheel

After students have written their front and back lists and have begun collecting pictures to illustrate chosen episodes, they are ready to begin constructing their book wheels.

Listed below are the directions the students should follow in constructing a book wheel. Comments in brackets which follow the directions are intended for the teacher and suggest points of discussion, explanation, or clarification about the directions. A clean, unannotated set of student "Directions for Making a Book Wheel" is included at the end of the lesson. It is also advisable to give the students a copy of the qualities of an excellent book wheel at this time (#4 on the Holistic Scoring Guide).

1. Begin collecting small magazine pictures and words that illustrate incidents in the episode you are presenting for your book talk. You may wish to draw or paint pictures or print words to illustrate some incidents in your episode.

   (It is helpful at this point to show students the size of the book wheel circle [7-½" in diameter] and the size of the pictures which must fit within it. If you have constructed a book wheel to use as a model, show the students the pictures you have used. It is also worthwhile to give them a quick lesson in how to see "into" a magazine picture. Most magazine pictures are too large to fit within the diameter of the circle, so students need to practice seeing smaller components or details within larger pictures which they can cut out and use. Warn them that they may not be able to find every picture or word they need to explain their episode, in which case hand-drawn pictures and printed words can be used in place of magazine pictures.)

2. The diagram on page 48 is a "blueprint" or pattern for the book wheel. Follow this pattern in constructing your book wheel. (Background paper should be heavy stock, white, and 8-½" by 11".)

3. Using the circle pattern supplied by the teacher, and placing your paper horizontally rather than vertically, trace a circle on the left side of your sheet of paper, leaving room on the right for captions. (7-½" circle pattern to be supplied by teacher.)

4. Using the window wheel pattern supplied by the teacher, trace and cut out a window wheel from the construction paper. (The window wheel pattern is a circle of exactly the same diameter as the circle pattern except that it has a wedge cut out of it. The wedge allows the student to reveal, one or two at a time, the pictures and words placed on the circle pattern underneath. When making the window wheel pattern, do not cut the wedge all the way to the center of the circle. Leave a bit of space for the brad fastener which attaches the window wheel to the circle pattern. See Figure 3.)

5. The window wheel and/or the background circle upon which you will glue your pictures and words must be in a color(s) reflecting the mood or tone of your episode. (You may wish to stop and have the students discuss how certain colors evoke certain moods and vice versa. You might also give some examples of how color is used on the covers of paperback books to suggest or reflect the mood of the story. For instance, books of suspense, fright, or

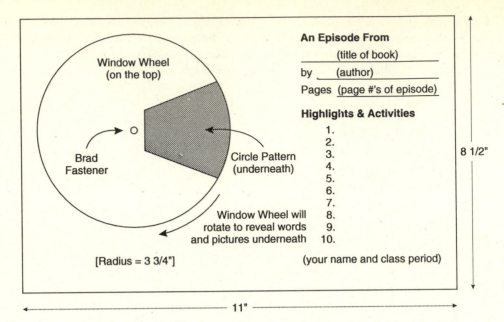

FIGURE 3: Making a Book Wheel

adventure might be done with dark colors such as black or red, while books about young romance might be done with bright colors or pastels.)

6. Glue your pictures, words, and drawings within the circle you have drawn on the left side of your paper. Remember to keep them in the order of the incidents in the episode which they illustrate so that your window wheel will reveal them one or two at a time in the proper sequence as you rotate it around the circle.

7. You may decorate your window wheel in any way you like as long as it relates in some way to your episode. You can achieve different and original effects if you decorate your wheel using materials with different colors and textures, such as foil, cloth, lace, leaves, etc.

8. Attach the window wheel over the pictures in the circle with the brad fastener supplied by your teacher.

9. Copy your list of six to twelve numbered sentences about your episode on the back of the book wheel paper. You may find it helpful to draw some faint lines with a ruler on the back of the paper. This will help keep your copied sentences neat. Finally, copy your front list on your book wheel.

10. (At this point you may once again wish to model how a completed book wheel is used to give a book talk. Be sure the students can see the connection be-

tween the words and pictures you have used in your model book wheel and the incidents in the episode you are describing. Let them know that the "book talk" is not a formal speech assignment. The emphasis should be on good storytelling. They may use the front and back lists on their book wheels as notes while they are telling their story, but under no circumstances are they to read them.)

Evaluation

Book wheels and book talks will be evaluated by student peer groups. Book wheels will also be evaluated by the teacher.

Peer Evaluation. Students will meet in peer response groups of four or five, and each member of the group will present his book talk using his book wheel. Other members of the group will listen to the book talk and respond by filling out an evaluation sheet which uses sliding scale measurements. The sliding scale is used to rate specific features of the book wheel and the book talk. The scale does not use letters or numbers, but rather a set of qualitative terms arranged at opposite ends of a row of plusses. Student evaluators select a plus mark near that end of the scale which they think most closely represents the quality of the student's effort for that feature. (See the *STUDENT EVALUATION SHEET.*) The teacher should discuss and demonstrate the use of the evaluation sheet before any evaluation of book talks takes place. At the end of the sharing session, the teacher will collect the evaluation sheets and the book wheels. Student evaluation responses will be returned to each student along with the teacher's holistic score and the book wheel. How peer evaluations and holistic teacher scores relate to any "grade" given to the book wheel is up to the discretion of the teacher.

Student Evaluation Sheet for Book Wheels and Book Talks.

Student's Name: ——————— ——————— **Title of Book:** ——————— ——————— ———————	**Format followed**	+ + + + + + + + Several errors Excellent job
	Color, pictures, & word usage	+ + + + + + + + Needs work Excellent job
	Originality	+ + + + + + + + Average Very unique
	Oral presentation	+ + + + + + + + Seemed unsure Very well told
	Give one reason why you would or wouldn't read this book: ————————————————	

Four-Point Holistic Scoring Guide

4 A 4 book wheel demonstrates overall excellence and has most of these qualities:

- Follows format
- Uses several pictures and words
- Uses color to express the mood of the episode
- Clearly shows originality
- Has parallel numbered front and back written lists
- Lists are sequenced properly
- Lists mention setting of the episode
- Lists mention main characters
- Uses complete sentences and is nearly error-free
- Is neat
- (*Optional*) Has received above average marks on oral presentation from half of the peer response group members

3 A 3 book wheel is generally well done and has most of these qualities:

- Has minor errors in the format
- Uses some pictures and words
- Uses color to express the mood of the episode
- Shows some originality
- Has parallel numbered front and back written lists
- Lists are generally sequenced properly
- Lists mention setting of the episode
- Lists mention main characters
- May have an incomplete sentence and some editing errors
- Is fairly neat in appearance
- (*Optional*) Has received one above average mark on oral presentation from peer response group members

2 A 2 book wheel, which is only fair, has most of these qualities:

- Has a major error in the format
- Uses some pictures and words
- Has not clearly used color to express the mood of the episode
- Shows little originality
- Has differences in the numbering and ordering of front and back written lists
- Lists are not sequenced properly
- Lists mention setting or main characters but not both
- Has incomplete sentences and several editing errors
- Lacks neatness in overall appearance
- (*Optional*) Has not received an above average mark on oral presentation from peer response group members

1 A 1 book wheel does not meet most of the requirements for the assignment and is poorly done. It has most of these qualities:

- Has several major errors in the format
- Has made limited use of pictures and words
- Has not used color to express the mood of the episode
- Has several differences in the numbering and ordering of front and back written lists
- Lists are not sequenced properly
- Lists fail to mention setting or main characters
- Has several incomplete sentences and many editing errors
- Lacks neatness in overall appearance
- (*Optional*) Has received below average marks on oral presentation from peer response group members

Directions for Making a Book Wheel

The book wheel you will make will be a visual aid which you will use when giving your book talk to other students. Both your book wheel and your book talk must focus on a single episode from your book.

1. Begin collecting small magazine pictures and words that illustrate incidents in the episode you are presenting for your "book talk." You may wish to draw or paint pictures or print words to illustrate some incidents in your episode.

2. The diagram below is a blueprint or pattern for the book wheel. Follow this pattern in constructing your book wheel.

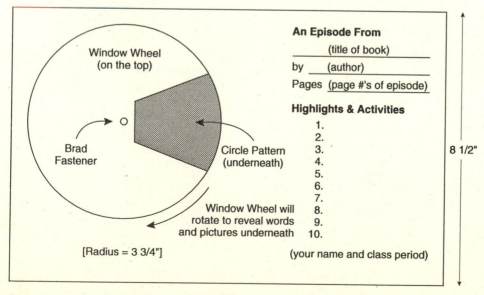

Window Wheel (on the top)

Brad Fastener

Circle Pattern (underneath)

Window Wheel will rotate to reveal words and pictures underneath

[Radius = 3 3/4"]

An Episode From
_____
(title of book)

by _____
(author)

Pages (page #'s of episode)

Highlights & Activities
1.
2.
3.
4.
5.
6.
7.
8.
9.
10.

(your name and class period)

8 1/2"

11"

3. Using the circle pattern supplied by the teacher, and placing your paper horizontally rather than vertically, trace a circle on the left side of your sheet of paper, leaving room on the right for captions.

4. Using the window wheel pattern supplied by the teacher, trace and cut out a window wheel from construction paper.

5. The window wheel and/or the background circle upon which you will glue your pictures and words must be in a color(s) reflecting the mood or tone of your episode.

6. Glue your pictures, words, and drawings within the circle you have drawn on the left side of your paper. Remember to keep them in the order of the incidents in the episode which they illustrate so that your window wheel will reveal them one or two at a time in the proper sequence as you rotate it around the circle. (See Figure 4: a, b and c for examples from an episode from *Tom Sawyer*.)

7. You may decorate your window wheel in any way you like as long as it relates in some way to your episode. You can achieve different and original effects if you decorate your wheel using materials with different colors and textures, such as foil, cloth, lace, leaves, etc.

8. Attach the window wheel over the pictures in the circle with the brad fastener supplied by your teacher.

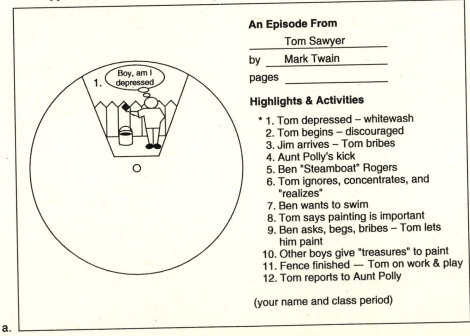

An Episode From

Tom Sawyer

by   Mark Twain

pages _____

Highlights & Activities

* 1. Tom depressed – whitewash
2. Tom begins – discouraged
3. Jim arrives – Tom bribes
4. Aunt Polly's kick
5. Ben "Steamboat" Rogers
6. Tom ignores, concentrates, and "realizes"
7. Ben wants to swim
8. Tom says painting is important
9. Ben asks, begs, bribes – Tom lets him paint
10. Other boys give "treasures" to paint
11. Fence finished — Tom on work & play
12. Tom reports to Aunt Polly

(your name and class period)

a.

FIGURE 4: Sample Book Wheels

9. Copy your list of six to twelve numbered sentences about your episode on the back of the book wheel paper. You may find it helpful to draw some faint lines with a ruler on the back of the paper. This will help keep your copied sentences neat. Finally, copy your front list on your book wheel.

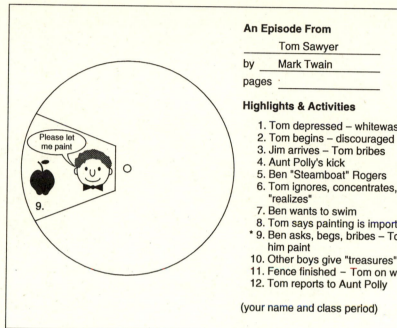

An Episode From

Tom Sawyer

by   Mark Twain

pages _____

Highlights & Activities

1. Tom depressed – whitewash
2. Tom begins – discouraged
3. Jim arrives – Tom bribes
4. Aunt Polly's kick
5. Ben "Steamboat" Rogers
6. Tom ignores, concentrates, and "realizes"
7. Ben wants to swim
8. Tom says painting is important
* 9. Ben asks, begs, bribes – Tom lets him paint
10. Other boys give "treasures" to paint
11. Fence finished – Tom on work & play
12. Tom reports to Aunt Polly

(your name and class period)

b.

An Episode From

Tom Sawyer

by   Mark Twain

pages _____

Highlights & Activities

1. Tom depressed – whitewash
2. Tom begins – discouraged
3. Jim arrives – Tom bribes
4. Aunt Polly's kick
5. Ben "Steamboat" Rogers
6. Tom ignores, concentrates, and "realizes"
7. Ben wants to swim
8. Tom says painting is important
9. Ben asks, begs, bribes – Tom lets him paint
10. Other boys give "treasures" to paint
11. Fence finished – Tom on work & play
* 12. Tom reports to Aunt Polly

(your name and class period)

c.

Extension Activities

Comprehension:

Prompt: Create a mock book cover for the book you have read. Include cover art, format components, (title, author, etc., on front and back covers), and a written summary of the plot action up to a tantalizing, dramatic moment. Include the names of the major characters and establish the setting, just like the blurb on a real book jacket.

_____

Application

Prompt: Create a book wheel with sections of the circle specified for words and pictures illustrating each of the following major elements of fiction:

- character
- setting
- plot
- point of view
- theme
- tone

(In writing on the back of the book wheel, students will demonstrate and apply their comprehension of literary terms by using examples from their novel to illustrate those literary terms.)

_____

Analysis

Prompt: Create a character analysis wheel based on the book wheel format. Analyze a literary character in terms of his/her appearance, thought, and action by illustrating each of those aspects with words and pictures. On the back of the book wheel or on a separate companion page, draw conclusions and make inferences about the character's personality based on evidence and examples from the story. Relate the evidence and the examples to the three aspects of character mentioned above.

_____

Writing Domain: Sensory/Descriptive

Thinking Level: Knowledge
Grade Level: Intermediate

Bobby B. Bored Teaches Writing
Introducing Showing Writing With Role-Playing

Objectives

Thinking Skills
Students will work at the knowledge level of Bloom's taxonomy to *OBSERVE, CLUSTER, LIST,* and *RECOUNT* a role-play between the teacher and several students.

Writing Skills
Students will sharpen their visual and auditory perception skills by showing, in as much vivid detail as possible, a subject who role-plays a bored student. The lesson emphasizes the use of:

* relevant visual and auditory details to create a vivid picture;
* an abundance of factual information based upon observation;
* apt word choice (precise nouns, descriptive adjectives and active verbs);
* figurative language (one or more similes or metaphors);
* sequencing skills (attention-getting beginning, logically connected middle, and interesting conclusion);
* correct sentence structure, spelling, and punctuation.

The Process

This lesson can be used to begin a study of descriptive writing and to introduce the concept of Rebekah Caplan's "showing, not telling."* It is aimed at sharpening visual and auditory sensitivity and at enhancing skills of conveying this vision to an audience.

The following audiovisual equipment will be needed for this lesson: video camera, VHS monitor and playback, slide projector, and screen.

Prewriting

1. Role-play
   Select three students (or ask for volunteers) to participate with you in a role-play and meet with them in advance to sketch out each person's role. During this role-play, the teacher will play the role of Bobby (or Bobbi) B. Bored, a

---

*Please see the Glossary for detailed information about showing, not telling.

terminally bored, chronically distractable eighth grader. The teacher should play this role in class as most teachers probably can exhibit a wider variety of bored behaviors for a longer period of time than most students and because some students can get out of hand when acting. By playing the role of the bored student, the teacher also maintains control over the direction of the role-play.

One volunteer is to act as the teacher. Find an article from a high school or college text and ask the volunteer to read it in the flattest monotone that he/she can possibly muster. (I use a well written, college level essay entitled "Photosynthesis" by Eric Marcusson in the *St. Martin's Guide to Writing* by Charles Cooper and Rise Axelrod.) The volunteer must continue reading at all times and not be distracted by the class's reactions to your role-playing. The other two volunteers are to dutifully take notes, listen to the "lecture" and ignore you as much as possible. The students should pretend they do not want to be bothered by your antics. (*Note*: You might even consider dressing in the latest school attire for your part.)

The four role-players should be positioned at the front of the class so that everyone can see clearly. At the back of the class, a videotape camera should be set up and a cameraman should record the role-play for later reference.

Before beginning the role-play, tell the class to observe what is about to take place as closely as possible because they will be asked to recount it afterwards. During the role-play, the volunteer teacher should read the article for approximately three to four minutes. While he or she is reading, you should let loose of the old (and hopefully few) painful memories of bored student behavior that have gathered dust in your long term memory. I suggest: tapping fingers, yawning loudly, sighing, rubbing watery eyes, squinting, frowning, dozing, gazing across the room, propping your head in your hands and pushing your face into wrinkled rolls, staring at the floor, tapping your fingers, pencil, pen, bouncing or rocking your chair, doodling, glancing at the clock, passing notes (actually signs which your observers can read), checking out the boy/girl in the next seat who's taking notes, winking at the boy or girl, writing them a note asking what their name is, other flirtatious behavior, making paper airplanes, etc. As the essay is concluding, I suggest that you doze off to sleep.

2. Writing
   After the role-play is over, ask students to take five minutes to recount, as precisely as possible, what they just observed.

   When they have finished, ask for volunteers to read their accounts. Typically, their descriptions will be short and rather matter of fact as in the examples below:

   The teacher pretended to be a bored student.

   While the person playing the teacher read from a book, two students took notes and the other one goofed off.

The student (really the teacher) seemed bored. He was yawning and doo-dling on the desk. He tried to pass notes to the other two students, but they ignored him.

Explain that these examples all *tell* that the teacher role-playing the student was bored but they don't *show* us. They don't create a vivid picture that the reader can visualize. (*Note*: If some students do write rich showing descriptions, ask the class to discuss how their writing differs from most of the examples.)

3. Showing, not telling

To illustrate the difference between telling and showing, give students an example—such as the one below—of a telling sentence and a showing paragraph:

Telling Sentence

The roller coaster was the scariest ride at the fair.

Showing paragraph

As I stood in line, I gazed up at the gigantic steel tracks that looped around three times. The thunderous roar of the roller coaster sounded like a thunder cloud that had sunk into my ears and suddenly exploded. The wild screams of terror shot through me like a bolt of lightning and made my fingers tingle with fear. Soon I heard the roar of the roller coaster cease. As the line started to move forward, I heard the clicking of the turnstile move closer and closer. Finally, I got onto the loading deck and with a shaking hand gave the attendant my ticket.

It seemed like I barely got seated when I felt a jolt which signified the beginning of the ride. While the roller coaster edged up the large track, I kept pulling my seatbelt tighter and tighter until it felt like I was cutting off all circulation from the waist down. At the crest of the hill, I caught a glimpse of the quiet town which lay before me and gave me a feeling of peace and serenity. Suddenly my eyes felt like they were pushed all the way back into my head, and the town had become a blur. All I could see was a mass of steel curving this way and that as the roller coaster turned upside down. I was squeezing the safety bar so tight that my fingers seemed to be embedded in the metal. I could see the landing deck, and I let out a deep breath that had been held inside ever since the first drop. As the roller coaster came to a halt, I felt weak and emotionally drained. When I stepped off onto the deck, I teetered a bit to the left, but caught my balance quickly when I saw my friends waiting for me at the exit gate. I tried to look "normal," while trying to convince them in a weak voice that, "Oh, it was nothing."

> Quoted in Rebekah Caplan's chapter "Showing, Not Telling: A Training Program for Student Writers" in *Practical Ideas for Teaching Writing as a Process,* ed. Carol Booth Olson, (Sacramento: California State Department of Education, 1987), 56.

After reading the example aloud, ask students to make a list of the words and phrases that show the reader that the roller coaster (or whatever subject you give them) was the *scariest* ride at the fair.

4. Videotape Replay #1: Clustering Showing Details

Since many students need to be exposed to more than one example of showing writing to comprehend the distinction between showing and telling and translate that understanding into their writing, involve them in generating a list of showing details and developing a telling sentence which those details illustrate. Replay the videotape of Bobby B. Bored for the class. Then, lead the class in clustering the behaviors they observed. One at a time, cluster on the board details which students provide. When starting, leave the center circle empty as in Figure 5: a on page 59.

Most likely, students will come up with the telling sentence "Bobby was bored." If it is mentioned ask, "How did you know that?" and continue clustering details. At this time, students may mention other "telling" phrases. When this happens, highlight the "telling" phrase in red to flag it as a "telling" phrase. Then elicit from students words or phrases which explain this "telling" word or phrase. For example, if students mention "he flirted" ask "how did you know?" "What made you think so?" "What things did he do to show you he flirted?" Students will offer more specific showing details such as "he winked" or "he smiled in a sexy way" or "he wrote a note." (See Figure 5: b on page 59.) You may want to develop the last response more fully by asking, "What did the note say?" and add their responses to the cluster. Finally, when the cluster is completed, elicit from the class that all these details together show or reveal that Bobby was bored. Write this in the center circle at the end of the discussion, highlighting the difference between "showing" and "telling." (See Figure 5: c on page 59.)

Prompt:

Using factual information based upon your observation of the role-play of Bobby (or Bobbi) B. Bored, write a description which shows the behavior of the bored student. Your writing should be so vivid that an eighth grader from another class can visualize exactly what happened as if a videotape with clear sights and sounds were playing in his/her head. Use precise nouns, descriptive adjectives, active verbs, and at least one simile or metaphor to vividly show what you observed. Your writing should have an interesting beginning, middle, and end which are logically connected and flow smoothly. It should also use correct sentence structure, spelling and punctuation. (Note: In your paper, assume that the teacher actually *was* the bored student rather than just role-playing.)

Precomposing

1. Visual Perception Exercise*
   • Find a series of three or four slides to present to your class. A slide with a simple foreground and background, a large simple center of interest prefer-

*Adapted from ideas presented in Sue Rader Willet's article, "Using Visual Stimuli to Motivate Writers and to Foster Descriptive Writing Skills," in *Practical Ideas for Teaching Writing as a Process*, ed. Carol Booth Olson (Sacramento: California State Department of Education, 1987), 92.

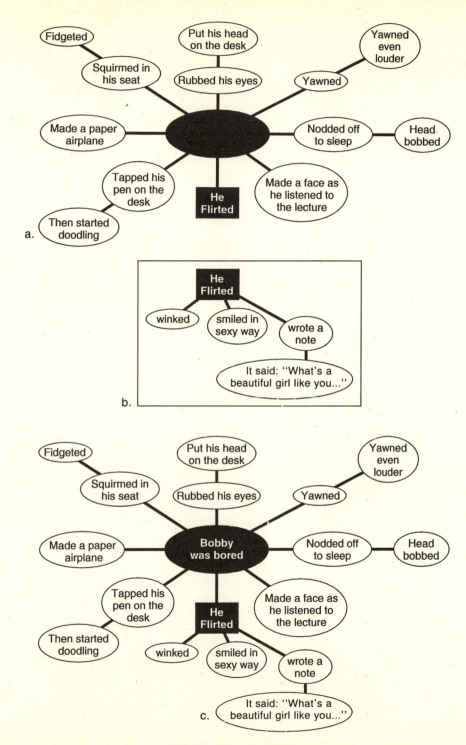

FIGURE 5: Sample Cluster

ably of people interacting with each other or their environment works best. Seat students so that their backs are facing the screen and they cannot see the projection. Project the slide and describe the image to the class so clearly that the students can picture in their heads what is on the screen. Depending on the nature of the slide, the teacher may want to describe first the foreground or background and then focus on the center of interest. You may give a brief, overall sense of the photo first before getting into details, or move from top to bottom or vice versa. Mention the relative size of the center of interest, the angle of view, the time of day or kind of lighting, dominant colors, and the feeling the slide evokes.

- After the description, allow time for students to ask questions which clarify their visions. Then ask students to turn around and view the slide.
- Ask students to respond to the following as a whole class:

  - How close was your visualization to the actual slide?
  - How were your own visions different or the same? Why?
  - What kind of information would have given a more complete picture in your mind?

- Ask for two or three volunteers to describe the next slide after they have spent a few minutes of quiet time studying the slide. Repeat steps A and B.
- As students describe the slide, record on scratch paper some of what you consider to be vague, nonspecific words in their oral description. When their discussion is over, and students have observed the slide, ask the class to identify words or phrases in the description that they could not picture and record them for the entire class. See if these words/phrases match your list. If not, elicit from the class the words you wrote. Ask the class to substitute more specific, descriptive words and phrases which would have created a more vivid vision.

Vague Image	More Specific Revision
• Big dog	• Great Dane
• Huge tree	• Gnarled trunk of a giant redwood tree
• Flowers	• Field of orange poppies with purple stains at the center

Elicit from the students during the discussion the difficulty of communicating the image with words and how specific, precise nouns and vivid adjectives paint clearer pictures for the listener.

2. Videotape Replay #2: Listing Visual Details
   - Show the videotape a second time. Ask students to pay particular attention to the visual details. As they take notes about what they see, remind them

to be as specific as possible. Remind them to pay attention not only to visual details related to Bobby but to the details related to his fellow students and the teacher.

- After they have taken notes, make a class list of details on the board.

Example

Bobby

- wearing a shirt, blue jeans, and tennis shoes
- wrote a word on the desk
- made a paper plane

- Select details from the class list which could be more vividly described and revise them as in the Visual Perception Exercise.

Example

Vague Image	More Specific Revision
• Wearing a shirt, blue jeans and tennis shoes	• Wearing a purple Izod shirt with an ink stain in the pocket, faded blue jeans and Nike tennis shoes
• Wrote a word on the desk	• Etched the word "BORING" on the lower right hand corner of the desk
• Made a paper airplane	• Folded blue and yellow lined notebook paper into a bird-like airplane

- Now, ask students to rephrase these showing revisions into complete sentences.

Example

Bobby is wearing a purple Izod shirt with a blot of ink in the pocket where his pen has leaked, faded blue jeans, and Nike tennis shoes.

After carefully etching the word "BORING" on the lower right hand corner of his desk, he folded a piece of yellow and blue lined notebook paper into a bird-like airplane and sailed it across the room.

3. Videotape Replay #3: Auditory Perception Exercise
   Replay the tape again, asking students to pay particular attention to the sounds they hear. Have them record what they see Bobby (or other role-players) doing in one column and to think of a simile or metaphor to describe what the sound that action reminds them of in a second column:

Action	What the sound reminds me of . . .
• Bobby yawns	• It's like the roar of a tired lion
• He taps his pen on the desk	• Sounds like pennies on a tin roof
• Teacher reads his lecture	• He drones on like a record stuck on the same groove

5. Focusing on Attention-Getting Details

Ask students to return to their cluster and select an interesting, attention-getting detail with which they may start their description. They should pay particular attention to choosing a detail which will enable them to show Bobby's bored behavior. Once they have selected their detail, ask them to freewrite for five or ten minutes and see where their writing leads them.

Example

Detail—Yawning/then yawning louder

Bobby shuffled into class and slumped into his seat. Before he was even settled, he stretched his arms out, tilted his head back and let out a weary yawn which sounded like the roar of a tired lion. As the teacher began to drone on about photosynthesis, Bobby yawned again but louder this time. Both students sitting next to him stopped taking notes, looked up and frowned at him.

Ask students to meet in peer groups and share their freewrites. Each group should choose one example to read aloud to the class. Discuss which beginnings seem most interesting and why.

6. Formulating a Writing Plan

Students are now ready to formulate a plan for writing. On a piece of paper, have them make headings for introduction, main body and conclusion.

Introduction—Under introduction, students can list the detail they have already developed in their freewrite or choose a different detail to open their description that will capture their reader's attention.

Main Body—Under the main body, students should list at least four more details they plan to use and to sequence these in a logical order.

Conclusion—For their conclusion, students should sketch out an idea for an ending which will not only be interesting but give their piece a sense of closure.*

*Note: Writing plans can be used for one-on-one conferences between the teacher and his/her students.

Writing

Using their clusters, descriptive sentences, freewrites, and writing plans, students should compose their sensory/descriptive papers.

Sharing

Ask students to select a partner and exchange their papers. (Note: It would be helpful if partners could exchange a xeroxed or carbon copy.)

Then replay the videotape of the role-play. Give the following directions:

1. Read over your partner's description.

2. Watch the tape carefully.

3. As the tape is playing, write quick notes in the margins at places where you would like to convey something to the writer about his/her piece.

   After viewing the videotape:

- Star * the words, phrases or sentences which you think are your partner's best showing writing.

- Put a bracket [ ] around any similes or metaphors you find. Do they make sense? Do they seem natural or forced? Are they interesting? Comment in the margins.

- Reread you partner's draft, putting parentheses ( ) around telling words, phrases, sentences, or paragraphs you think your partner should add more showing description to.

- Put an X by details which you think are vague or insignificant.

- Mark spots in the draft where you feel your partner may have left important gaps with a question mark *?*.

- At the bottom of your partner's paper, please make an overall comment about the organization of their paper. Does it have an attention-getting opening, logically connected middle, and interesting ending? Discuss what you like and make suggestions for improvement.

Revising

1. Generating Ideas for Revision
   Students should use the feedback they received from their partner and from

comparing their own draft to a final replay of the videotape to make notes for revising their descriptions.

2. Critique of a Student Model

   Ask for a volunteer who is willing to share his or her paper or use the following example and project it on an overhead. As a class, critique the student model, highlighting its strengths and making suggestions to improve its weaknesses. Record their comments and suggestions as in the example below:

We can sort of picture this but it's not very attention-getting.

Did the lecture make Bobby yawn or was he just tired?

(Bobby came into class and sat down.) Before he was even settled, he stretched his arms out, tilted his head back and let out a weary yawn which sounded [like the roar of a tired lion.] As the teacher began to (lecture) about photosynthesis, Bobby yawned again but louder this time. Both students sitting next to him stopped taking notes and (looked at him.)

* *Great showing. We like the simile: it shows loudness.*

What kind of look did they give him?

We can see his shirt. * Very vivid.

Bobby was determined to make a pest of himself so he reached into the ink-stained pocket of his purple izod shirt and pulled out his pen. He wrote a note on some paper and passed it to one of the two students. (She tried to ignore him.)

We can't picture what she did.

What did the lecture sound like?

What do airplanes sound like?

Bobby could (hear the teacher lecturing) and decided he needed to make some noise to get his classmates' attention. So, he quickly folded a paper airplane and (made airplane sounds) as he sailed it across the room. When that didn't work, he settled back in his chair and started to doze off— [his head bobbing up and down like a yo-yo.] *

? Not sure of what "when that didn't work" means.

Great simile. We like it! Good way to end.

Overall, this seems well organized. It's interesting and easy to follow. It had a distinct beginning, middle and end.

Optional: If you wish to, you can then assign small groups to revise certain parts or work as a class to generate a group revision as in the following example:

> Bobby shuffled into class and slumped into his seat. Before he was even settled, he stretched his arms out, tilted his head back and let out a weary yawn which sounded like the roar of a tired lion. As the teacher began to drone on about photosynthesis, Bobby yawned again but louder this time. Both students sitting next to him stopped taking notes and frowned at him disdainfully.
>
> Bobby was determined to make a pest of himself so he reached into the ink-stained pocket of his purple Izod shirt and pulled out his pen. After opening his three-ring notebook with an intentionally loud *CLICK,* he scribbled a note which said "What is a beautiful girl like you doing in a place like this?" on a piece of notebook paper, folded it in half and passed it to the studious-looking girl with the horn-rimmed glasses that was sitting next to him. She tried to ignore him by leaving his note unopened and by staring straight ahead at the teacher. But Bobby opened it for her and pushed it in on top of her notes. She blushed but continued to stare straight ahead while scribbling even more furiously in her notebook. Tired of passing notes, Bobby began to work on a paper airplane. He could hear the teacher's monotonous voice still droning on—like a record player stuck on the same groove—and he decided that a little sound effects of his own were in order. So, as his plane sailed down the aisle, he recreated every sound he could think of from old World War II movies: the RAT-TAT-TAT of machine gun fire, the *BOOM* of exploding jet engines, and the winding scream of a plane going down, down, down and *CRASHING* into the sea.
>
> When even World War II failed to get his classmates to so much as look up from their notes, Bobby settled back in his seat to devise a new tactic. But the teacher's voice was so hypnotic that Bobby soon began to doze off—his head bobbing up and down like a yo-yo.

After completing their critique of the student model, each student should review his or her paper one more time and add to his or her notes for revision.

3. Individual Revision
   After making notes for revision based on feedback from their peers, comparing their description to the videotape, and reviewing their original draft one final time in light of the students model they just critiqued, students should individually revise their papers.

4. Revising Checklist
   Upon completing their second drafts, students should review the requirements of the prompt to ensure that their papers meet the criteria that it outlines. The following checklist of questions may be helpful:

Revising Checklist

☐ Did I show the behavior of a bored student using factual information based on my observation?

☐ Is my writing so vivid that someone else can visualize what I am describing?

☐ Did I describe clear sights and sounds?

☐ Did I use precise nouns, descriptive adjectives, active verbs, and at least one simile or metaphor?

☐ Does my writing have an interesting beginning, middle and end which are logically connected and flow smoothly?

Editing

Students bring in their final drafts written in pencil or erasable ink on the due date.

Put dictionaries on each student's table or desk. Then, ask students to pass their papers around the team of four in read-around fashion.* Each teammate reads one other teammate's paper for a minute or two, searching for words which may be misspelled, sentences that may be run-ons or fragments or errors in punctuation. If a student spots an error, he/she should lightly checkmark the line in which the error occurs in the left margin.

Pass the papers around once again so everyone has another teammate's paper and repeat the process. If another student spots the same error, he/she should again lightly mark the paper next to the previous checkmark. If a student does not see an error, then no marks should be made. After four passes of the papers, each student should have his/her own paper and can examine the paper for possible errors in spelling, punctuation or sentence structure. Students are then free to use dictionaries and each other as resources in correcting and cleanly editing their papers. This process should take 10–15 minutes, depending on the average length of the papers to be submitted.

Evaluation

A 9–10 Paper:

- Uses factual information based upon observation to show Bobby's bored be-havior.

- Uses many relevant visual and auditory details to create a vivid picture.

- Uses many precise nouns, descriptive adjectives and active verbs.

*See the Glossary for information about read-around groups.

- Contains at least one original simile or metaphor.

- Has an interesting beginning, middle, and end which are logically connected and flow smoothly.

- Is spelled correctly, punctuated properly and has no run-ons or fragments.

A 7–8 Paper:
   Has many of the qualities of a 9–10 paper but doesn't create quite as vivid an image for the reader. It may not have quite as interesting a beginning, middle or ending or the language may not be as descriptive and original as a 9–10. It should not have any major errors in spelling, punctuation or sentence structure.

A 5–6 Paper:

- Uses less factual information than a 7–8 paper to show Bobby's bored behavior.

- Uses fewer relevant visual and auditory details; the picture created is not as vivid as a 7–8 paper because telling language creeps into the description.

- Does not use as many precise nouns, descriptive adjectives and active verbs.

- Does not contain a simile or metaphor or uses an unoriginal simile or metaphor.

- Has some sense of beginning, middle and end but at least one section is weak.

- Has some problems in spelling, punctuation and sentence structure.

A 3–4 Paper:

- Does not use factual information to show Bobby's bored behavior.

- Creates a vague picture with a few visual or auditory details; tells more than shows.

- Uses imprecise and/or overly-general word choice.

- Does not contain a simile or metaphor.

- Does not contain a definite beginning, middle and end.

- Has many problems in spelling, punctuation and sentence structure.

   A 2–1 paper does not respond to the criteria in the writing prompt and contains all of the weaknesses of the 4–3 paper.

Extension Activities

Application   Have students rewrite their description of Bobby B. Bored for the following contexts and audiences:

- Imagine you are one of the students in class who is taking notes and trying to ignore Bobby. Write an entry for your journal which describes this kid's behavior in class.
- Imagine you are Bobby. Describe what you did in class today and why.
- Imagine you are the teacher who is trying to ignore Bobby B. Bored so that you can finish your lecture. Write a description of Bobby's behavior from your point of view.

Comprehension   Have students choose a place in the community to go to where they can observe and record everything that happens for 15–20 minutes. After recording all the visual and auditory details, the students should decide on a statement which describes this place or, in other words, create a telling sentence for a descriptive piece about this place.

Examples

- Rudi's Pizza is a fun place to be on Friday night.
- The playground was jammed with kids on Sunday afternoon.
- The mall is a great place to meet boys.

These observations can become the foundation for the writing of a descriptive/narrative report called a "Saturation Report"— which relies heavily on showing, not telling.

Comprehension   Observe a friend doing an activity which he/she likes and is good at. Write a description and a telling sentence which shows him/ her doing this activity:

Examples

- Jeremy is a great skateboarder.
- Shirley drives her Mom crazy because she's on the phone so much.
- Lorinda is an expert typist.
- Robert is a slick basketball player.

When reading the pieces back to class, do not reveal the telling sentence. Ask students to guess what the telling sentence was.

Synthesis   With your response group, design a role-play involving four people which conveys a specific theme. Videotape it or perform it in front of the class as the class takes notes and writes a descriptive piece showing what took place.

Writing Domain: Imaginative/Narrative   Thinking Level: Knowledge
                                                                         Grade Level: High School

Is He Your Daddy, Pop, Or Old Man?

A Lesson on Connotation and Denotation

Lesson

Students use several writing exercises and class discussions to learn the difference between connotation and denotation, a crucial distinction for students studying language. Students will also demonstrate in writing how words come to have connotative meaning.

Objectives

Thinking Skills
Students will *RECORD* the meaning of connotation and denotation, *LIST* both connotative and denotative meaning of given words, then *LABEL* words according to their connotations. Finally, they will *RECOUNT* in a paragraph how a word came to have its connotative meaning for them.

Writing Skills
Students will write a narrative which will recall in a paragraph an incident which helps to explain why a word has a particular connotation for them.

The Process

Because the understanding of connotation and denotation looms so large in many subjects, this functions best as a groundwork lesson. For instance, it can be an introduction to further vocabulary study, the study of diction in a given piece of literature, the study of diction used in student writing, or the importance of connotative meanings in areas as diverse as political speeches and psychological terminology.

The lesson itself involves several steps, taking about three class periods; however, some of the steps can be eliminated to fit a tighter schedule. You will need a classroom set of dictionaries. Since most students have already internalized the narrative form at an early age, this mode does not usually have to be taught.

Prewriting

Dictate to the student the meanings of the terms *connotation* ("something suggested by a word or thing") and *denotation* ("a direct, specific meaning"), as they record them on paper.

- Write these three words on the board and ask for volunteers to briefly tell what each word means:
  - restaurant
  - café
  - coffee shop

- Ask them to do a cluster for each word, listing all of their associations for each. An example might be:

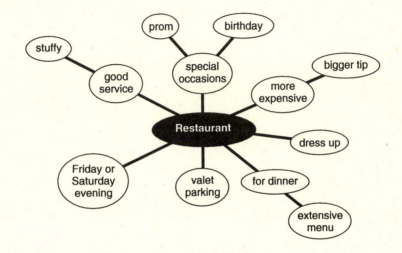

- When they are done clustering, ask students to volunteer some of their associations and record them on the board. Then, with their help, write an extended connotative definition of each. For example, *restaurant* implies a more prestigious public eating place. The food may be fancier and also more expensive than in a fast food place. One would tend to dress up to go to a restaurant. The word café, on the other hand, implies a more humble public eating place. The food may tend to be simpler (e.g, ''home cooked'') and less expensive than in a restaurant. *Coffee shop* is again associated with informality. It may have a less extensive menu than a restaurant or café, but the prices will, like a café's, tend to be modest. Unlike a restaurant or café, one might drop in at just about any time to have a bite at a coffee shop.

- Now, ask the students to use dictionaries to list the denotative meanings of the three words:

  - restaurant: ''public eating place''
  - café: ''restaurant''
  - coffee shop: ''a small restaurant especially for light refreshments''

- Next, ask students to give synonyms for the word "father." Write the synonyms on the board. (Likely responses are: "dad," "pop," "daddy," "old man," "pa," "papa.")

Ask them to make a chart that would look like this:

Word	Associations	Connotation	Denotation

Then instruct them to fill out the chart by writing down *father* and its synonyms, any of their associations with those words, what the connotation is, and finally, the denotative meaning, in the example below:

Word	Associations	Connotation	Denotation
• daddy	• childhood • protector • love • playing catch	• an endearing form of "father" • informal	• "father"
• father	• head of family • strength • deep voice	• figure of authority • formal	• "one who has fathered a child"

- When they are done, ask students to help you fill out the blank chart you have written on the board. As you fill it out, don't neglect to discuss some of the implications of the chart. Some possible points to work toward in the discussion are:
  - People react emotionally based on their past experiences. For instance, even *daddy* might carry a negative connotation for a child who has just been punished by his/her father.
  - One may often predict how others may react to a particular word *if* one is aware of its connotative meaning.
  - Being aware of connotations makes one a more perceptive reader and a more powerful writer.

- An interesting activity at this point would be to discuss the connotation of *papa* (if it hasn't already been discussed) and *waltz*. Then pass out copies of Theodore Roethke's "My Papa's Waltz" and read it with the class:

My Papa's Waltz

The whiskey on your breath
Could make a small boy dizzy;
But I hung on like death:
Such waltzing was not easy.

We romped until the pans
Slid from the kitchen shelf;
My mother's countenance
Could not unfrown itself.

The hand that held my wrist
Was battered on one knuckle;
At every step you missed
My right ear scraped a buckle.

You beat time on my head
With a palm caked hard by dirt,
Then waltzed me off to bed
Still clinging to your shirt.

From Theodore Roethke, *Collected Poems*
(New York, Doubleday Publishing Co., 1966)

- A good question for discussion would be: "How does Roethke play off of the connotations of the words *papa* and *waltz*?"

    (The papa in the poem seems to love his son, but, because he has been drinking, he is also hurting the child. The waltz in the poem is a drunken parody of an elegant waltz one might do in a ballroom.)

- For the final part of the prewriting stage, give students a list of these words:

adolescent	teenager	kid
shack	house	mansion
belly	stomach	tummy
puny	small	petite
clothes	apparel	duds

- Ask the students to get into small groups and have them add their own sets of words to the lists. After fifteen minutes of this activity, the group should write out the denotative meanings for the words on their lists. Ask the groups to share with the rest of the class some of their more interesting combinations.

- When they are done, ask students to choose one word that was either on their group's list or one that was shared by another group. Ask them to cluster for their associations with the word they have chosen. Finally, ask them to fastwrite an explanation of why they chose that word, what connotation it has, and how it came to have that connotation. For instance:

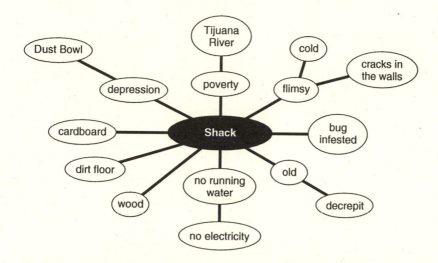

I chose the word *shack* because of an experience I had some time ago when I walked across the Mexican border into Tijuana. As I walked over a bridge that spans the Tijuana River, I saw hundreds of wood and cardboard shacks, homes for the people who lived there. This sight shocked me. For me the main connotation of *shack* is poverty. This is because people who live in shacks usually have no other choice because they are poor. Similar to photographs I have seen of families living in the Dust Bowl during the 1930's, the impression I got of the inhabitants of the Tijuana River was that they were poor. Their homes looked flimsy, as if the cold wind at night would blow right through the cracks. I imagined that their floors were simply the dirt that the homes were built over. They obviously had no running water or electricity. As I got to the other side of the bridge, I felt sadder, and luckier.

Prompt:

Choose a word that has a special connotation for you. At the top of the page, write a title which includes the word you chose. Skipping about an inch, write the denotative meaning of that word. Then skip one line and, in a well-developed paragraph, explain why you chose the word, describe what connotation it has for you, and recount how it came to have that connotation. Your audience will be your classmates, so make it interesting by using descriptive details.

Precomposing

- Ask the students to devise a topic sentence that expresses the main idea found in their fastwriting. Then they should arrange the important details in chronological order. They could do this by numbering their sentences in order of occurrence.

- Show them a sample that you have written. As you are discussing your sample, point out how you have accomplished all three parts of the assignment, and how you tried to use descriptive details.

- Ask them to use their clusters as sources for their own details.

Example:

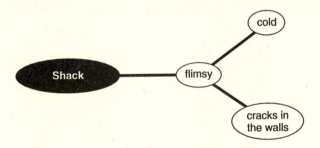

Their homes looked flimsy, as if the cold wind would blow right through the cracks.

Writing

Ask students to write a rough draft of a paragraph.

Sharing

In their response groups, students will read their paragraphs aloud and then record the oral responses from the group. When all the papers have been read aloud, they will be passed around for silent rereading and written comments. The oral and written comments will be based upon the traits of the following guides, which will have been distributed to the students.

Primary Trait Scoring Guide

5 A 5 paragraph clearly explains why the student chose the word, what connotation it has for the student, and how it came to have that connotation. Sufficient descriptive details are used so that the reader can easily understand how the word has that connotation. The piece is obviously written for an audience of the writer's peers and would be interesting to them.

4 A 4 paragraph follows all three parts of the assignment. However, it will be thinner in details than a 5 paragraph and, thus, less interesting. It may be inappropriate to its audience.

3 A 3 paragraph will not fulfill all three parts of the assignment. Or, it fails to show logically the connections between how the word came to have the connotation and the connotation itself.

Secondary Trait Scoring Guide

3 A 3 paragraph follows all the directions for format and has few mechanical errors.

2 A 2 paragraph follows the format exactly, but there are several bothersome mechanical errors.

1 A 1 paragraph may have serious problems with format, mechanical errors, or both.

Revising

After the group sharing, the student will take into account the oral and written comments on his rough draft and write a revision. (If possible, it might also be a good idea to read a few top-notch rough drafts aloud as models.)

Evaluation

The teacher will evaluate the final draft according to the scoring guide. To receive full credit, the student will have had to submit all of the clusters, the charts, earlier drafts, and so on.

Extension Activities

Analysis

Prompt: Collect several magazine advertisements aimed at the adolescent. From these advertisements, derive a list of ten words whose connotative meanings are used to sway the adolescent reader. Then, record both connotative and denotative meanings for the words. Finally, using the list for examples, write a paper *ANALYZING* how advertisers use connotative meanings to sell products.

Analysis   • Dictate the opening of Chapter 2 in Fitzgerald's *The Great Gatsby* (New York: Scribners, 1953):

About halfway between West Egg and New York the motor road hastily joins the railroad and runs beside it for a quarter of a mile, so as to shrink away from a certain desolate area of land. This is a valley of ashes—a fantastic farm where ashes grow like wheat into ridges and hills and grotesque gardens; where ashes take the forms of houses and chimneys and rising smoke and, finally, with a transcendent effort, of men who move dimly and already crumbling through the powdery air. Occasionally a line of gray cars crawls along an invisible track, gives out a ghastly creak, and comes to rest, and immediately the ash-gray men swarm up with leaden spades and stir up an impenetrable cloud, which screens their obscure operations from your sight.

Prompt: Identify words that have obvious connotations in this passage by Fitzgerald. Discuss the impact of these words on the reader, and analyze and describe the tone Fitzgerald is trying to establish in this passage.

A Rose-Colored Life By Any Other Name. . .

A Lesson Recalling What We Imagined/Expected and Recounting What Actually Happened

Lesson

Students will write a narrative describing a real event that fell short of their expectations.*

Objectives

Thinking Skills
Students will use critical thinking skills at the·*KNOWLEDGE* level to *RECALL* and *RECOUNT* an event in their lives that turned out differently than they expected.

Writing Skills
The lesson taps the sensory/descriptive and imaginative/narrative domains. It:

- reinforces sensory/descriptive skills, such as the use of precise, vivid language as the student recalls concrete details from imagined and actual experiences;

- stresses imaginative/narrative elements, such as chronological sequencing of events with a beginning, a middle, and an end; the use of connecting transitions, and parallel construction for coherence and clarity;

- encourages the student's awareness of his/her audience who should be able to paraphrase what the writer intended.

The Process

Although this introductory lesson can lead to numerous extension activities, at the *KNOWLEDGE* level it is intended to remain strictly as a reminiscence and as a warm-up to writing. Here is an opportunity for the students at the beginning of the semester to meet each other and to be introduced to sensory/descriptive and imaginative/narrative writing.

*Note: This lesson is adapted from John Langan's original suggestion in ''My Senior Prom,'' *English Skills* (New York: McGraw-Hill Book Company, 1977), 108.

Prewriting

Explain to the class that very often when we anticipate something that is about to take place—whether it is a first date with someone, a new job, or a special vacation—we often create our own scenario of the experience beforehand and color it with our own expectations. In other words, we often look at life through "rose-colored glasses."

In order to permit students time to "rediscover" their recalled events, begin naturally by discussing a concrete anecdote of your own. Describe a fantasy or expectation you once had for an actual event. Then detail how it really turned out.

For example, I begin by describing my hopes for my marriage. Then I give concrete examples, as suggested below, of what really happened the first week of my marriage:

Expectations	What Actually Happened
1. I thought that my husband, Tom, would earn the money—at least the major share.	1. What an eye-opener when during the first week of marriage, he signed up for a full-time Master's program while I took a typing test for full-time work.
2. I expected to continue my usual habit of showering the night before in order to sleep in until the last minute, dashing out the door with no breakfast.	2. However, Tom liked to shower in the morning, and he looked forward to a leisurely breakfast with his morning paper; he assumed I would keep him company.
3. Since I don't like to cook, I assumed that we would continue visiting restaurants, like we did when we were courting.	3. But after much discussion, we concluded that there'd be tremendous savings if I cooked. Therefore, instead of sleeping in, I was up and dressing while he showered. Then, by the time he had shaved and dressed, I had breakfast ready for us both.

To engage your students' interest and get them thinking, initiate a discussion using such questions as these:

- Did anyone else ever have an experience that fell way short of your expectations, for example, a date, a party, or a new job?
- Have you ever gone on a date and had the reality (what actually happened) fall short of your expectations? (Or did the opposite happen and your low expectations turn into pleasant surprises?)
  - What are some concrete examples of what you expected and what actually happened?

- What sights, sounds, smells, tastes, or touch words can you use to help someone else picture what you imagined and what actually happened?
- Have you ever attended a party where your rosy hopes for an especially exciting time fizzled with flat, dreary, or boring experiences?
  - What are some lively, vivid examples of what you hoped for and of what really happened?
  - How can you make the details more vivid for your readers so they can experience your event through the sights, sounds, smells, tastes, and/or feeling senses that you had?

Brainstorming Groups

After discussing as a whole group the questions listed above, have the students form small groups of four or five and take five to ten minutes to share other situations where their actual happenings fell way short of their hopes. Ask one member of each group to record the group's situations. The instructor then lists these on the board, including a few concrete details, where possible:

Expected (Hoped For) Event	What Actually Happened
a. On a birthday Smiling faces of 30 friends yelling "Surprise!" would greet me with a yellow, rose-covered cake.	a. On a birthday No one was home, and only a day-old hard cinnamon roll remained.
b. On a Date He would arrive in a fire-engine red Camaro dressed in a suit for the prom.	b. On a Date He arrived in a rusty Chevy pick-up, wearing an Izod shirt and tennis shoes.
c. At a Bar A Richard Gere look-alike would give me the eye while the band plays some of the latest Cars music.	c. At a Bar The most obnoxious person in the bar got fresh while a tired Lawrence Welk band droned on.
d. On a New Job I would have a gentle, patient, helping boss, direct me to office files so organized that I could easily figure them out.	d. On a New Job My boss was angry at having to train his fifth secretary—me. No filing had been done in five months.
e. Having a Friend Visit I hoped she'd be neat, cheerful, quiet, and stay only a few days.	e. Having a Friend Visit She smoked throughout the house all day, drank beer because she was depressed, and left beer cans—even in the bathroom. To top it off, she stayed a full week.

Prompt:

Recall and recount an event in which what you hoped for, imagined, or expected was very different from what actually happened. Be sure you have a beginning, a middle, and an end. Develop your narrative with a point-by-point description of what happened. Or develop it with one-side-at-a-time form (i.e., by first providing a complete account of what was imagined/expected and then by recounting what actually happened.). Use clear connecting and sequencing transitions. Include vivid, concrete details and appropriate sensory descriptions. Your narrative should be clear and complete enough that your reader can paraphrase your detailed hopes and can contrast them with the actual happening.

Precomposing

The following group of activities will help students zero in on their selected event and plan their compositions.

Phase One

Using the contrast between an ideal and a real date as an example, draw two clusters on the board. Ask students to contribute their ideas about what they hoped for in a date versus the actual date they had. Record their suggestions around the central cluster. (See Figure 6 on page 81.)

Because students need much assistance with specificity and precise word choice, the second cluster on page 82 includes more *nonspecific* descriptors. Contrasting the original pair of clusters with this second, more general pair, will help students appreciate the more vivid language due to proper nouns, strong verbs, and vivid modifiers that help readers to experience their writing.

Phase Two

To help students understand and implement time sequencing and parallel structure for coherence, guide them through Model A pointing out the connecting and time-ordering transitions.

Model A (Point-by-Point Development):

My date with Harvey Sprinklestein was nothing like I had hoped it would be. *FROM THE START*, I thought he would arrive early, relaxed, with a large, fragrant gardenia corsage. What a shock when, *INSTEAD* he came dashing to my door an hour late, arriving with a single, odorless sunflower, just ripped from my garden. I had also imagined him escorting me to his shiny new black BMW, looking debonair in a handsome tuxedo. *BUT INSTEAD,* he charged ahead of me to his rusty 1965 Impala, looking harried and embarrassed in his Izod shirt and shorts.

IN ORDER to keep my hopes up, I fantasized about our $100-a-plate dinner at

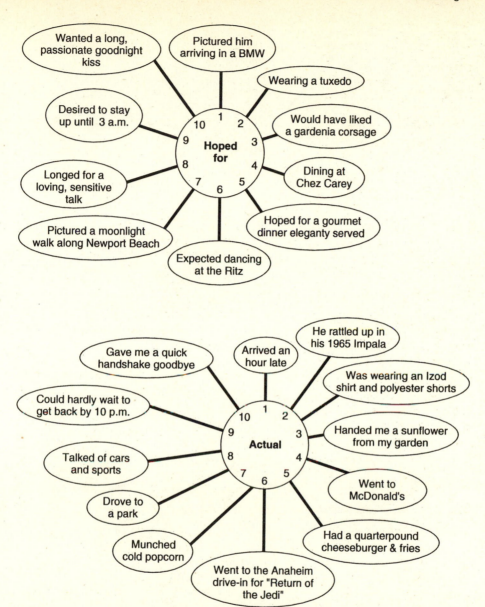

FIGURE 6: Sample Cluster for "The Date"

Chez Carey, *BEGINNING* with escargot, *FOLLOWED* with pheasant smothered in lindenberry wine sauce, and as a *FINAL TOUCH*, cherries flambé for dessert. My heart dropped in my chiffon dress *WHEN* he skidded into McDonald's for a quarterpound cheeseburger and fries.

Note: You need not number the spokes during this spontaneous clustering, but doing so would facilitate later sequencing and parallel structure using the point-by-point or one-side-at-a-time form.

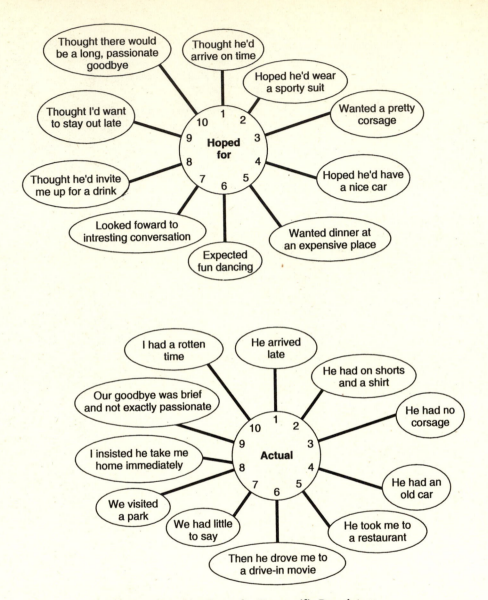

FIGURE 7: Sample Cluster for Nonspecific Descriptors

EVEN THOUGH this evening got off to such a poor start, I ignored reality, clinging to the hope that it would turn around. Maybe to work off our greasy calories, Harvey would suggest we dance until dawn—preferably at the Ritz. Well, he did a turnaround, all right, *BUT* it was into the Anaheim Drive-In for "Return of the Jedi," where we sat all evening munching on greasy popcorn and drinking

Pepsis. *IF ONLY* after the boring movie we could have a long walk, strolling along the sands of Newport Beach—watching the sky until the sun rose. What a disappointment *WHEN* Harvey left the drive-in and turned inland, instead of toward the beach, for the darkest park in town where couples go to neck.

BY NOW I'd given up hopes for an interesting, informed conversation. It was difficult to keep from nodding off to sleep as he rambled on about cars and sports. No longer did I yearn to remain with him past 3 a.m. *INSTEAD*, I professed a severe headache across my left eye and secretly yearned to be delivered to my front door by 10 p.m. *IN CONTRAST* to the long, passionate kiss I had fantasized *EARLIER*, with me modestly insisting that Harvey not come in, I gave him, instead, the briefest handshake goodnight—and bid good riddance to my romantic dreams—at least for that evening.

Have the students list all transitions in Model A as suggested on the chart below:

Transition List-Connectives*

Addition Signals	**Change-of-Direction Signals**	**Illustration Signals**
first	but	for example
in the first place	however	for instance
first of all	in contrast	specifically
one	yet	as an illustration
for one thing	even though	
secondly	otherwise	**Conclusion Signals**
third	still	
the third person	on the contrary	therefore
last of all	on the other hand	then
finally	a final reason	consequently
a final reason		thus
also		as a result
too	**Emphasis Signals**	to conclude
in addition		in summary
moreover	most importantly	last of all
likewise	the most important reason	finally
furthermore	the best (worst) thing	a final touch
next	the chief factor	
another	principally	
again	most of all	
and	a major concern	

*Note: Adapted from John Langan's *English Skills* (New York: McGraw-Hill, Inc., 1977), pp. 26–32.

For awareness of parallel structure, have the students underline from Model A all the actual events in one color and all the hoped for events in another color.

Then ask the students to read Model B and:

- list transition words
- underline in two distinct colors hoped for versus actual events
- make a list of these hoped for versus actual events

Model B (One-Side-At-A-Time Development):

My date with Harvey Sprinklestein was nothing like I had expected it to be. From the start I thought he would arrive early with a large fragrant gardenia corsage. After placing it gently on my wrist, I imagined him escorting me to his shiny black 1986 BMW, looking debonair in a handsome tuxedo. Our evening would begin at Chez Carey with a $100-a-plate dinner, consisting of escargot, pheasant with lindenberry wine sauce, and cherries flambé for dessert. After dinner, to work off these calories, I hoped we would dance until dawn at the Ritz and then watch the sun rise while strolling along the sands of Newport Beach. Because I expected he would have me captivated with his informed and interesting conversation, I knew I would yearn to stay up with him past 3 a.m. Finally, to cap the evening, I imagined a long, passionate kiss at my front door while I modestly insisted that he not come in.

To say that I was disappointed with my actual date with Harvey would be putting it mildly. He came dashing to my door an hour late, arriving with a single odorless sunflower just ripped from my garden. After placing the mud-covered plant on my shiny walnut table, he charged ahead of me to his rusty 1965 Impala, looking harried and embarrassed in his Izod shirt and shorts. I felt a little silly, too, in my chiffon summer dress, especially when we skidded into McDonald's for a quarterpound cheeseburger and fries. I never did get a chance to work off my dinner calories as we sat all evening munching on greasy popcorn, and drinking Pepsis, watching ''Return of the Jedi'' in the Anaheim Drive-In. Hopes of a romantic beach walk were also squashed as Harvey headed for the darkest park in town where couples go to neck. It was difficult to keep from nodding off to sleep as he rambled on about cars and sports. Harvey never got beyond the preliminaries as I professed a severe headache across my left eye and secretly yearned to be delivered to my front door by 10 p.m. With the briefest handshake, I bid good riddance to Harvey—and farewell to my romantic dreams—at least for that evening.

By the end of Phase Two, the students are ready to select their own topic and to write a narrative. At this point, pass out a blank chart for students to list incidents in their lives that they imagined/expected would turn out one way but which actually turned out quite differently.

Incident as I Imagined/Expected	What Actually Happened
1.	1.
2.	2.
3.	3.
4.	4.
5.	5.

Have students break into pairs, discuss their charts, and choose the most interesting incident for writing a lively narrative.

Once students have a topic, have them sequence events within their incident on the Time Frame of Events next.

Time Frame of Events	
Hoped for events	**Actual events**
First, _____ _____ _____	But instead, _____ _____ _____
Next, _____ _____ _____	However, _____ _____ _____
Then, _____ _____ _____	But, _____ _____ _____
After this, _____ _____ _____	Yet, _____ _____ _____
Then, _____ _____ _____	But, instead, _____ _____ _____
Finally, _____ _____ _____	In contrast to _____ _____ _____

Writing

Either at home or in class, students write their narratives using point-by-point or one-side-at-a-time development.

Sharing

Each student will then bring four copies of his/her rough draft narrative to be read aloud and responded to by a peer group, using Peter Elbow's "pointing method."* (Once a student-writer reads his/her paper to the group, he/she should not speak until all in the group have made positive comments and have then either offered suggestions for improvement or have raised questions as to where they are confused.) The following questions may also prove helpful for the responders:

Student Responses on Substance:

- Did the student-writer successfully convey to you what his/her expectations were and what really happened?
- If not, how might he/she improve it so you can better experience the event? Tell the writer, "For *me*, it would work better if you would . . . ? (Add, delete, change, whatever.)
- Were the examples precise and vivid enough for you, the listener, to adequately put into your own words the difference between what the writer expected and what actually happened?

Student Responses on Form:

- Did the student-writer use parallel construction with either point-by-point or one-side-at-a-time development? Was it easy to follow?
- Is there a narrative form with a beginning, a middle, and an end?
- Is there adequate use of transitions for coherence? Does the paper seem logically arranged?

Once all listeners have responded positively and have suggested improvements or raised questions, then the student-writer can respond.

Revising

Once all group members have shared their papers, each group should pick a favorite to be shared with the entire class. Each group is then responsible for presenting to the class specific examples of why their favorite paper worked. The rest of the class can then add additional positive comments or suggestions for improvement. (All opinions are valid if—and only if—the commenters can point to exact words or phrases that caused them to find papers effective or ineffective.)

---

*For further reference, see Peter Elbow's *Writing Without Teachers* (New York: Oxford University Press, 1973).

Based on the students' explanations of why their favorite papers succeeded, the instructor can write a 6-point rubric on the board. Since this is an early assignment, first stress the use of concrete details, and, second, sequencing (with a beginning, a middle, and an end) and parallel structure (point-by-point or one-side-at-a-time). A sample rubric is included in the *EVALUATION* section of this lesson.

The students may now either rewrite their first drafts or begin anew if they have found a more exciting experience from listening to others' attempts.

Editing

Encourage students to proof and edit their own work. Permit them one last rewrite.

Evaluation

Using the 6-point rubric developed by the students, the instructor can score their papers and discuss why some received 6's and some received lower scores. Or better yet, give your students this responsibility. Permit them to "practice" the evaluation process by having them defend why they scored a paper a certain way. (Early on, you might use student models from another class and share comments using transparencies.)

Sample Rubric

6 Substance:
- With numerous lively sensory details, the student-writer recounts and conveys his/her expectations of a hoped for experience and what really happened.
- Concrete examples are sufficient so that readers can paraphrase the difference between what was imagined/expected and what actually happened.
- The language is sufficiently lively to hold the reader's interest.

Form:
- Construction is parallel with either point-by-point or one-side-at-a-time structure.
- Within the narrative form, events are sequenced, tightly organized, and contain a clear beginning, a middle, and an end.
- There is adequate use of transitions for logical coherence.

5–4 The student-writer meets the requirements of the prompt, but the paper is a thinner version, possibly lacking in a couple of these areas:

Substance:
- With a few lively sensory details the student is still able to recount and convey his/her expectations of a hoped for experience and what really happened.

- Concrete details are sufficient enough for the readers to somewhat paraphrase the difference between the imagined/expected and the actual event.

Form:

- Construction is fairly parallel with a semblance of either point-by-point or one-side-at-a-time structure.
- The narrative form has some sequencing of events with a loose organization, containing a vague beginning, a middle, and an end.
- There are some transitions for coherence.

3–2 The student-writer just barely meets the requirements of the prompt. There are major flaws in some of these areas:

Substance:

- With vague and often dull details, the student-writer may recount or convey his/her expectations of a hoped for experience and what actually happened.
- Lack of concrete details may make it difficult for the readers to paraphrase the difference between the imagined/expected and the actual event.

Form:

- There is little parallel structure with either point-by-point or one-side-at-a-time development.
- The form has little narrative sequencing and lacks a clear beginning, a middle, and an end.
- There may be too few transitions for adequate coherence.

Extension Activities

These are variations on the theme of expectations versus reality. The *Los Angeles Times* newspaper article (Model C), reprinted on the following pages, is the springboard.

Knowledge

Prompt: Read the *Los Angeles Times* article on the woman who divorced her husband, hoping for greener pastures with a new mate. Make a list of what the writer said about how this decision to leave her husband affected her life.

_____

Comprehension

Prompt: Paraphrase (put in your own words) what the writer said about older married women who are unhappy with their husbands and with their lives. What does she suggest they do with their ''great expectations''?

Synthesis

Prompt: Imagine yourself as the husband of the woman who desires greener pastures. Write an editorial reply from his view, addressing the *Los Angeles Times* article.

Analysis

Prompt: Examine a situation you are now in, or were in, that was disappointing. List the advantages and disadvantages of that situation, concluding with why a change might or might not be better. Then, write a letter defending why you are leaving, why you left, or why you chose to stay. The letter can be addressed to the person directly involved in the situation or to a friend who knows about your predicament.

Evaluation

Prompt: After reading the *Los Angeles Times* article, discuss whether you empathize with the woman who "traded a great life-style with a less-than-perfect husband for a stressful and lonely existence" or whether you feel she got what she deserved. Use evidence from the article to support your opinion.

Model: From the *Los Angeles Times*, August 15, 1983

Don't Let "Greener" Grass Fool You Into a Divorce
By Lois Marie

A friend and I had lunch a few weeks ago. She is an attractive woman in her mid-40's, very bright, and has a good job as a manager of a busy medical office.

She looked at me over a glass of Chablis and said, "I really made a mess of my life. When I asked my husband for a divorce, I got rid of an insensitive, mediocre man, but in the process I lost a wonderful life style. Before my divorce, I had security and freedom to do what I wanted with my life. I worked part-time, played tennis, enjoyed my children, and had no financial worries.

"Now, I work full-time and can barely keep my head above water. I feel bad about having to leave my children alone so much. The guilt I feel keeps me from using the little free time I do have for things that I enjoy, like tennis.

"I feel lonely. I haven't met any men of real interest to me. I just didn't realize how difficult this new life would be. If I could go back to everything as it was, I would. But my husband remarried as soon as our divorce was final. I traded a great life style, with a less-than-perfect husband, for a stressful and lonely existence.

"I do like my job; it definitely has its rewards, but the money is not adequate for my needs. I hope that someday I'll meet 'Mr. Right,' but so far it doesn't look too encouraging. Every time I meet a possible 'Mr. Right,' 'Mrs. Right' is on his arm."

It's rare to find a woman who will admit she made a mistake in leaving her husband. But I find many lonely and stressed women who are not finding a better life after divorce. We all have read the statistics on the growing problem of poverty among women. It's not a happy picture. It's frightening to hear about the numbers of men who do not even help support their children. Men have lost their feelings of responsibility. The growing, almost aggressively insistent demands of women to be responsible for their own lives have tended to free men from their traditional feelings of caring and concern for women.

I'm not suggesting that every woman should stay with her man, no matter how he treats her. Obviously, there are situations that are intolerable to human dignity. I'm just saying that I fear many women are acting hastily, without enough reason and without giving enough serious thought to the consequences. Life is not a fairy tale, and not all our stories have happy endings.

My findings are that all too many women are leaving their husbands simply because they are not giving the emotional support that today's women think they deserve. It just may be that women are demanding something of their men that most men are not biologically or culturally equipped to provide.

Too Much Leisure

Maybe our problem, society's problem, is that we have too much leisure time, and amateur psychology has become a popular pasttime. Books and magazine articles tell us what we should expect from a relationship. Both men and women are bombarded daily with unrealistic expectations for life, love and marriage.

It just may be that today's couple is expecting too much from a marriage. We need to treat our mates as vulnerable human beings, capable of making terrible mistakes on our way through life. We need to remember to be kind, loving and most of all to forgive and to adjust.

If we're not getting 100% of what we need from our mates, maybe we should evaluate the 60% or 75% that we do get and try to fill in the empty spaces of our lives with work or friends. It's probably a rare couple, indeed, that can satisfy all of each other's needs.

By saying this, I'm not suggesting infidelity as a way to fill out one's life. It's a very dangerous way to go unless you don't mind inflicting crippling hurt on those you love. Many find that the "highs" you get from an affair are not really worth the devastation that often follows. But, as we all are human, it does happen. As hard as it is to do, if the marriage is basically worth saving, we should try to forgive and go on with our lives, stronger, hopefully, for the experience.

Unhappy, Lonely People

I think it's time we all look around us at the many unhappy, lonely people out there. As in most areas of life, men have the advantage over women. They are in the minority and much in demand. Most men who want to remarry can and do. Women, especially older women or those with children, do not fare so well. For several demographic and cultural reasons, there just are not enough eligible men to go around. The statistics, and the reality, are lopsided. Face it, if you are a married woman and become single, your chances of remarriage to a better man are very slim.

Sometimes being alone is preferable to being stuck in a bad marriage. Just make sure your marriage is really all that bad before you throw away a life style and a love you may never be able to replace.

Great expectations often precede great disappointments.

2 Comprehension

Writing Domain: Practical/Informative   **Thinking Level: Comprehension**
                                                   Grade Level: Primary

Handy News

Lesson

Having visited an employee at the school site, students will write a news story reporting about and describing how one person's hands help them do his or her job.

Objectives

Thinking Skills
Students will function at the *COMPREHENSION* level of the taxonomy by *RE-PORTING* about and *DESCRIBING* how one person's hands help him/her perform a specific job at school.

Writing Skills
Students will be expected to write an accurate news story which is descriptive and informative. The news story will be about one person doing a job at the school.

The Process

This lesson could be incorporated into a unit on the community or into one on career awareness.

Prewriting

In the weeks prior to the written assignment, it is helpful if students have participated in some of the following learning experiences:

1. Doing fingerplays such as "Open Shut Them";

2. Tracing their own hands and labeling the parts of their hands;

3. Listening to someone read *My Hands* by Aliki, a Let's Read-and-Find-Out Science book (New York: Thomas Y. Crowell, Co., 1962);

4. Making handprints with tempera paint and composing a sentence telling something they use their hands for at school;

5. Clustering the activities they participate in at school which require the use of their hands;

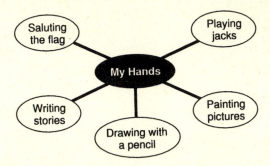

6. Reading (echo, choral and/or dramatic) the following poem written by Mary O'Neill:

Fingers are always
Bringing me news
Toes never know
Because of shoes.
They tell me what
Is hot or cold,
And what is too heavy
For me to hold.
They lift my crayons,
Smooth my hair,
And tuck me into
My underwear.

Prompt:

Today you are a newspaper reporter. Select one person who works at our school who you would like to write a news story about. You will then interview this person and make a list of all of the ways the person uses his or her hands to do a job at school. Since your news story will be placed in the classroom's *Handy News* book, it should be interesting and informative so your classmates and other people will want to read it.

Precomposing

1. Brainstorm a list of people who work at the school. Examples:

cook	principal	attendance clerk
cashier	custodian	assistant principal
teacher	parent	volunteer nurse
secretary	aide	resource teacher
counselor		

2. Ask children to select one person they would like to write about.

3. Show the children a model of a complete book page. The Primary and Secondary Trait Scoring Guides may be discussed.

4. After appointments with school staff have been arranged, allow children—in groups or alone—to visit the person they want to write about during class time, recess, or at lunch. Older children may be asked to take notes. Younger children may go with an adult or cross-age tutor who can help make a list.

5. During their visit, children should trace the outline of the hands of the person on a piece of construction paper so they may be cut out and pasted on the book page.

6. After returning to class, allow children to draw a picture of the person doing his/her job at the school, cut out the hands, and paste them on the book page.

7. It is helpful if children are given time to do an oral improvisation of what they want to say in the news story. This can be done in a small group or dictated into a tape recorder.

Writing

Students may dictate or write the first draft of their news story as in the following example:

Vic

Vic's hands are big. He cleans with his hands. He sweeps with his broom. He erases chalkboards. He closes windows. He fixes things. He waves at me. I like Vic because he is nice. Do you know what Vic's job is?

—Composed by a first grader

Sharing

News stories may be read to peer response groups, peer partners, or an assisting adult. The following set of questions will be helpful in structuring feedback:

To be asked of response partner(s):

- Which part did you like best?

- Do all the sentences tell about how someone uses his or her hands while doing a specific job at out school?

- Does the news story match the picture on the book page? Does it show the person doing his or her job?

- Was the story easy to understand? Do you have any questions to ask about the job the person does?

- Can you think of anything else that should be included in the news story?

- Referring to the scoring guide, do you think the news story, as it is written now, should get a:

Revising

If older students start every sentence with the same word, the teacher may wish to encourage students to be sure that No Two Sentences Begin With the Same Word (NTSBWSW). Students may add, delete, or rearrange information, based on the sharing feedback.

Editing

Students who are writing independently may edit their news stories with a peer partner. Students should refer to the Secondary Trait Scoring Guide before their story is handed in to the teacher for evaluation.

Evaluation

In the early grades, the teacher may only wish to evaluate the stories informally. However, a formal evaluation instrument is included for you to use if your children are ready for it.

Vic

Vic's hands are big. He cleans with his hands. He sweeps with his broom. He erases chalkboards. He closes windows. He fixes things. He waves at me. I like Vic because he is nice. Do you know what Vic's job is?

Primary Trait Scoring Guide

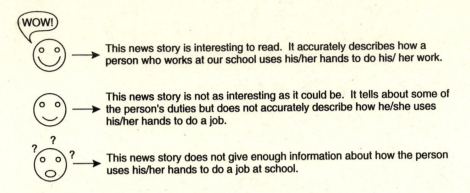

This news story is interesting to read. It accurately describes how a person who works at our school uses his/her hands to do his/ her work.

This news story is not as interesting as it could be. It tells about some of the person's duties but does not accurately describe how he/she uses his/her hands to do a job.

This news story does not give enough information about how the person uses his/her hands to do a job at school.

Secondary Trait Scoring Guide

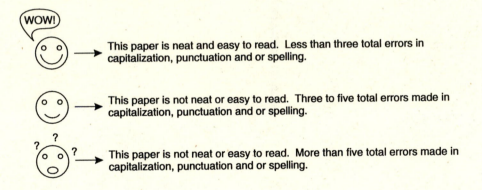

This paper is neat and easy to read. Less than three total errors in capitalization, punctuation and or spelling.

This paper is not neat or easy to read. Three to five total errors made in capitalization, punctuation and or spelling.

This paper is not neat or easy to read. More than five total errors made in capitalization, punctuation and or spelling.

Extension Activities

Comprehension _____

Prompt: Interview parents or adults you know and then write a news story for a book entitled *Handy News at Home*.

Writing Domain: Sensory/Descriptive   **Thinking Level: Comprehension**
          Grade Level: Elementary

On the Nose

A Sensory/Description of a Favorite Place

Lesson

Students will write a paragraph describing a favorite place by focusing on the sense of smell.

Objectives

Thinking Skills
Students will function at the *COMPREHENSION* level of Bloom's taxonomy by *IDENTIFYING* a place and then *DESCRIBING* it.

Writing Skills
Students will practice and reinforce skills in the sensory/descriptive domain of writing by writing a paragraph using precise, vivid language and rich, sensory details.

The Process

This seven-day lesson may be used as an introduction to or as part of a unit on the use of sensory description.

Prewriting

Teacher Preparation (The night before Day One)

1. Raid your spice rack and round up all the different ''smells'' you can find. Some good scents to use are:

mint	rosemary
dill	cinnamon
nutmeg	celery salt
ginger	whole allspice
coffee	sweet basil
lemon peel	fine herbs
orange peel	smoke flavored garlic salt
cloves	onion powder
bay leaves	vanilla bean

2. Wrap the jars or little cans in heavy, brown wrapping paper so that the labels are covered but the tops are easily opened. Although it works best if all the containers are the same size (eliminates visual clues), a mixture of jars and cans may also be used.

3. Next, with a thick, black marking pen, number each package and record the name of the spice on a sheet of paper (eg., 1 = cloves; 2 = orange peel; 3 = vanilla bean, etc.). You will need to use this sheet later as an answer key.

4. Bag the wrapped and numbered spices and take them to school with you the next morning.

Day One—Senses Surveyed

1. Introduce the use of sensory description by having students volunteer to describe how something smells. Their descriptions will probably be vague, colorless, and limited to only one or two words. List the descriptions on the board. For example:

   - *nice* perfume
   - *delicious* apple pie
   - *smelly* sweatshirt
     etc.

2. Explain to the students that our six senses (taste, touch, smell, sight, sound, and movement) are the ways that our brain receives information about the world around us and that if, as writers, we want to bring the reader into the worlds that we create on the page, then we must use vivid, precise words that appeal to our reader's senses.

3. Then, having them keep that point in mind, ask students to make their previous descriptions more vivid. Give them some of your own examples:

   - a *fresh, flowery* perfume
   - a *hot, mouth-watering* apple pie
   - a *soiled, sweat-streaked* sweatshirt
     etc.

Have them come up with more examples of their own. Write their new descriptions on the board next to their first ones. For example:

Descriptions

Without Sensory Details	With Sensory Details
1. *nice* perfume	1. *fragrant, gardenia-scented* perfume
2. *delicious* apple pie	2. *newly baked, appetizing* apple pie
3. *smelly* sweatshirt	3. *Nauseating, stenchy* sweatshirt

4. Ask the students to compare the two sets of descriptions and decide which set they like best and why it appeals more to them. Invariably, they prefer the second set of descriptions because they find them more alive and interesting.

5. Tell them that during today's activity, they will think up some precise, vivid words to describe how something smells. Tell them that they will also be playing a kind of "guessing game."

6. To begin the activity, pass out the "sniff sheets" and give every other student a wrapped spice jar/can.

7. Note: When giving the following directions, it helps to model the process with a willing student.

Have the students open the lid of each bottle, sniff the contents, screw the lid back on (this makes the scent come out in a rush every time a new student opens it), and pass the jar/can to the student directly behind them.

8. Then, while the second set of students are smelling the contents of the containers, have the first set of students write down (next to the number that corresponds to the number on the spice container that was just sniffed) two words that describe how that spice smelled to them. For example:

Sense Surveyed: **Smell**   Name: Jose Guerrero
                                    Period: 5

Sniff Sheet

Directions: After you have smelled each secret spice or hidden herb, write
             down two or more words that describe its scent

1. sweet, tasty, tantalizing   10. bitter, distinct
2. repugnant, strong   11. fruity, overpowering, sickening
3. sharp, crisp, zesty   12. sugary, strong, exotic

Note: See Figure 8 on page 103 for a complete sniff sheet.

9. After that, on the lower half of their worksheets, have the students try to
   identify what it was that they smelled. (All possible answers should be included on the worksheet in order to ensure that some correct guesses will be
   made.)

10. It takes about 2–3 minutes to sniff and about the same amount of time to write
    the answers down; so after the first few minutes, everyone should have some-
    thing to do at all times.

Have students continue to pass the containers around until the activity is finished.
Total working time runs from 30 to 40 minutes, depending on how many scents
are used. (One spice for every two students works out well.)

11. Finally, as each spice is unwrapped and its identity is revealed, have the students share some of the words used to describe it. For example, ask:

- What are some words that you used to describe scent #1? (Take three or
  more examples.)
- Who wants to make a guess as to what #1 is? (Take three or more answers.)

Calling on the person who has that numbered container on his/her desk, ask:

- Would you unwrap that package and reveal the answer for us? (Students
  really enjoy unwrapping the "packages" and often remark that it reminds
  them of Christmas.)

Sense Surveyed: **Smell**

Name: _____

Period: _____

Sniff Sheet

Directions: After you have smelled each secret spice or hidden herb, write
down two or more words that describe its scent

1. _____   10. _____
2. _____   11. _____
3. _____   12. _____
4. _____   13. _____
5. _____   14. _____
6. _____   15. _____
7. _____   16. _____
8. _____   17. _____
9. _____   18. _____

Directions: Now try to guess the name of the secret spice or hidden herb that
you have just described.

mint	cloves	sweet basil
dill	bay leaves	orange peel
nutmeg	rosemary	fine herbs
ginger	cinnamon	vanilla bean
coffee	celery salt	onion powder
lemon peel	whole allspice	smoke-flavored garlic salt

1. _____   10. _____
2. _____   11. _____
3. _____   12. _____
4. _____   13. _____
5. _____   14. _____
6. _____   15. _____
7. _____   16. _____
8. _____   17. _____
9. _____   18. _____

Number of correct guesses: _____

FIGURE 8: Complete Sniff Sheet

12. Keep on describing, identifying and unwrapping spices until all of the students have shared their descriptive words and corrected the bottom part of their worksheets. (A prize can be awarded to the one with the highest number of correct guesses.)

Day Two—Getting the Scent

1. Line up the unwrapped spice jar/cans in a row at the front of the room. (They fit easily into a chalk tray.) This will become a "reference rack" as students work on today's lesson.

2. Review yesterday's introduction to the use of sensory description, stressing the fact that the use of precise language and rich, sensory details helps draw the reader into the world of the story.

3. As you return their sniff sheets, read aloud some examples of the vivid words that the students wrote in response to yesterday's activity.

4. In groups of 3–4, have the students review and discuss the words on their worksheets in terms of each word's ability to describe the smells precisely and vividly. Students may, of course, use the "reference rack" to double-check the validity of their descriptions. Tell them to combine all of their words into one alphabetized group list. The group activity will take from 25 to 30 minutes.

5. At this point in the lesson, help the students generate words/phrases and give the students some practice in sentence combining by having them combine their descriptive words into phrases and the phrases into sentences. Introduce and stress the use of comparisons using "like" and "as." This activity can be done informally with frames developed by means of a whole group discussion or by the teacher. Students may work individually or in small groups. Here are some sample frames:

The, _____ , _____ perfume smelled like

_____ and reminded me of _____ and

_____ .

The _____ , _____ smell of the apple pie

made my mouth water and made me feel as if _____ .

When I opened the locker, the _____ , _____

sweatshirt smelled like _____ and told me that I'd better wash

it.

6. Collect the group word lists as the students leave the room. In preparation for tomorrow's activity, combine all of the lists into one long list which will become a sort of student thesaurus that students can use as a reference tool when they write their paragraphs.

Day Three—The Thesaurus Page

1. Pass out and read aloud the thesaurus page. Remind the students that a thesaurus can be referred to whenever they get "stuck" for a word to use in their descriptions. Urge them to use their thesaurus page on the upcoming assignment.

Sample Thesaurus Page

Words That Can Describe
How Something Smells

acrid	herbal	sharp
airy	licorice-like	smokey
appetizing	lifeless	snappy
bitter	light	spicy
blah	mellow	stale
burly	mild	stenchy
barky (barkish)	minty	sterilized
clean	mouth-watering	strong
crisp	nauseating	sugary
delicate	odorous	sweet
distinct	outdoorsy	tangy
dry	overpowering	tantalizing
dull	peppery	tart
dusty	perky	tasty
exotic	pleasant	tea-like
faint	powdery	weak
fiery	powerful	wholesome
flowery	pungent	wild
fresh	rancid	woodsy
fruity	repugnant	wretched
grassy	salty	yeasty
hearty	sickening	zany
	sickeningly sweet	zesty

FIGURE 9: Sample Thesaurus Page

Prompt:

Our sense of smell can vividly bring back a memory or create an impression. Think of a place that you associate with certain smells. Using your memories and sensory impressions of those smells, along with details that appeal to your other senses, write a paragraph identifying and describing that place. Make your writing so precise and vivid that your readers will smell that place and feel that they are there just as clearly as you are there when you remember that special place.

Make sure that your paragraph:

- includes four or more details that appeal to the sense of smell;
- includes four or more details that appeal to the other senses;
- has a strong topic sentence that draws the reader into the paragraph by appealing to the sense of smell;
- flows smoothly and tells how that place makes you feel;
- demonstrates a mastery of spelling and punctuation.

2. Read aloud and discuss the prompt. (You may want to write it on the board or xerox a copy for each student.)

3. As a means of discussing and modeling the prompt, read aloud the following student models, highlighting the way that the writers (students from a previous class) used their sense of smell, along with words that appeal to other senses, to bring back a memory or create an impression. Also, point out the ways that the writers referred to the sense of smell in their topic sentences as a way to draw the reader into the paragraph and how they ended the paragraphs by telling how the place made them feel:

The Smell of the Woods in Summer

The tangy smell of the pines rode with the forest breeze as I walked into the depths of the darkened forest. The summer sun burst down upon the land, but its rays couldn't penetrate the cool, sweet woods. The pungent odors of moss and lichen filled my nostrils. The air was thick with the spicy odors of the trees and plants. I felt surrounded with no room to breathe because of the potent smell of the vegetation around me, but I continued to walk on. Suddenly, the forest opened up to a bright, golden meadow that was dotted with flowers. The air was so wild and free that I wanted to run barefoot and pick flowers. The wind rippled through the golden blades of grass and the fragrance of the flowers touched my mind. I thought of faintly scented perfumes and sweet smelling soaps. The air was electric and every beautiful fragrance in the world filled it.

The Smells of the Seaside

The air was filled with many different but very familiar smells that I have known for a long time. The abundant smell of decaying fish and other marine life came to my attention first. After I got used to it, I identified the bitter smell of sea salt which was being released as the furious waves crashed upon the shore, sending their shimmery spray into the atmosphere. Some juicy, red steaks were also cooking somewhere along the crowded beach. I didn't know where, but the smell was driving me, and everyone else, up the wall. Because of this, I had to trudge across the hot sand to the snack bar to get some food to settle my churning stomach. After a couple of hours on the beach, I came to know the freshness of the on-shore winds, the woodsy smell coming from the debris that had washed ashore, and, most of all, I sensed the freedom that is mine while I sit here on the beach as the sun sets in the West.

4. Then, to bring the discussion closer to the students' own experiential level, ask and discuss the following questions while encouraging the students to start their descriptions with images that appeal to their sense of smell, to then expand those images to include as much sensory description as possible, and to tell why the place is important to them:

- Look closely at the beige top of your school desk. Can you remember the smell and feel of cleanser and rough paper towels the last time that you scrubbed that desk? Who can describe it for me?
- Picture yourself watching a movie at your favorite theater. What is the first smell you think of? Describe the situation for us.
- Do you remember your last Thanksgiving dinner? What was it like?
- Close your eyes and remember the smell of cookies baking. What does it smell like? Where, in your memory, does it take you? Describe it for us.

Precomposing

5. Now, begin to direct the students' focus inward upon their personal experiences by dimming the lights and using the following questions to guide the students' imagery.* Say to them:

- Close your eyes and relax. You may put your head on your desk or sit with your back straight and your eyes closed. The important thing is that you are as comfortable and relaxed as you can be.
- Imagine that all the tension in your body is running down from your head and right out through your toes. Picture it evaporating into the air and floating away as lightly as a fluffy white cloud. Your whole body is relaxed and you feel calm and peaceful.
- Breathe slowly and deeply, enjoying this calm and peaceful feeling.
- Turn your attention to the smells that make you think of school. Smell and imagine:
  - a row of lunches lined up at the back of the room;
  - the smell of a hot meal as you stand in the lunchline;
  - the smell of a pencil being sharpened;
  - the smell of wet coats drying near the furnace on a rainy day;
  - the smell of grass being cut on a warm spring day.

*See definition for Guided Imagery in Glossary.

- All those special smells bring back vivid memories for us. Now think of a
  smell that is special to you.
    - What is that smell like?
    - Where are you when you smell it? Are you at home? Away? Are you
      inside? Outside?
    - Is this place familiar to you? Unfamiliar?
    - What do you see as you look around this place?
    - Are you moving or are you still?
    - What are you touching? What is touching you? What do you feel?
    - What kind of sounds surround you?
    - What do you taste?
    - How does this place make you feel?

6. Slowly, turn up the lights and have the students draw a picture (on art paper)
   of the place that they visualized, incorporating as many details as they can into
   the drawing. This will help them visualize and, later, generate language. Many
   students will choose to finish their pictures at home.

Day Four—Following the Scent

1. Have the students share and discuss their drawings in small groups or as a
   whole class.

2. After that, have them cluster the place that they visualized, concentrating on
   words that describe by appealing to the senses, especially the sense of smell.
   Here is a sample cluster for the student model, ''The Smell of the Woods in
   Summer'':

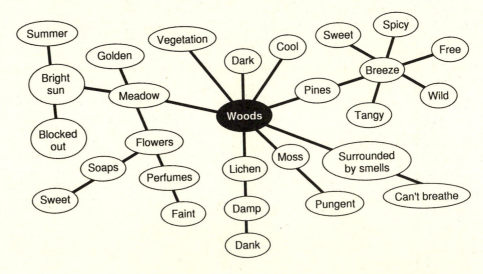

3. Then, to help them move from the chaos of a cluster to the continuity of a
   composition, have students classify and elaborate upon the details in their cluster by filling out a Memory Chart.

Example:

Memory Chart				
Details of Place	**Smells Recalled**	**Other Details Remembered**	**Memory They Trigger**	**How It Makes Me Feel**
pine trees	sweet, tangy, spicey	walking in the woods	cool, dark, needles crunching	peaceful, searching for myself
lichen, moss	pungent, damp, dank	surrounded by smells of the forest	can't breathe	boxed in
meadow	fresh	coming out of woods into meadow	bright sun, golden grass, flowers	free, relieved
flowers in meadow	sweet perfume like soap, faint	running barefoot	flowers waving in the breeze	wild, happy

4. Then, tell the students to look at their charts and determine their most vivid smell, the one that seems to trigger the memory of the place in their picture.

5. Have them use the description of that smell to formulate their topic sentences. The following frame may be used to help them get started:

As I walked into the _____, I was greeted by the
_____, _____ smell of _____ .
It reminded me of _____, and suddenly I am _____
again and back in _____ . I can see _____ .
I smell _____ again and, at that moment, it smells like _____

Writing

6. At this point in the lesson, students are ready to write the first draft of their paragraphs.

Day Five—Sharing and Revising for Content

Sharing

1. Break the students up into groups of three. Before they begin to share their paragraphs, have them answer and discuss the following questions (which can be written on the board):

• How did you put yourself into your special place? For instance, did you walk into and through it (as in the model, ''The Smell of the Woods in the

Summer''), or were you sitting still in your place (as in the model, ''The Smells of the Seaside'')?

- How did you focus on the details of your place? For instance, did you move around it or did you move outside and then back inside? What, if any, problems did you have describing your place and how did you solve them?
- How did you manage to include your feelings about the place in your paragraph? Did you have any trouble or triumphs when weaving your feelings into your description?

2. Conduct a read-around* to give students a chance to read others' first drafts and determine which paragraphs they like best. This activity will take from 20 to 25 minutes.

3. Read aloud the class favorites and discuss the reasons why the class picked them, stressing the use of precise language and vivid, sensory description. Here is a sample favorite:

What Love Smells Like

As I walked into the school cafeteria, I was greeted by the sweet, spicy smell of baking sugar cookies. It reminded me of my grandmother, and, suddenly, I am six years old again and back in her cozy kitchen on a lazy, summer afternoon. The hot, pungent smell of the green apples rotting on the ground underneath the gnarled old tree outside the kitchen door comes to my mind and I can hear the flies buzzing around the fallen fruit in the warm, prickly grass. Inside, though, it is cool, and a faint, musty smelling draft comes up from the open door that leads from the kitchen down the creaking stairs into the damp, moldy basement. Colorful little salt shakers that are shaped like a chubby boy and girl perch on the white stove. My grandmother lets me play with them on the cold linoleum floor while I wait impatiently for the cookies to cool. Lying flat on my stomach, I can smell the clean, pure Johnson's wax that is on the floor. I dreamily trace the shiny lines that the sun makes on the floor as it streams through the open window over the sink. Suddenly, my grandmother's soft chuckle calls me out of my daydream as she motions me toward a glass of milk and a plate that has three fresh cookies on it—all waiting for me on the kitchen table. The sunken brown eyes in her tanned, wrinkled face laugh quietly at my surprise and pleasure. I leap up, the salt shakers clatter across the floor, and I rush to hug my grandmother. My arms don't yet reach around her sturdy body. As I press close, I smell sugar cookies, and, at that moment, they smell like love.

Here are some things that students liked about this paragraph:

- The love between the child and the grandmother.
- The things that the people did (the child hugging the grandmother, the grand-

*See Glossary for definition of read-arounds.

mother "laughing quietly at my surprise and pleasure" and her "soft chuckle").

- The sensory details in the story (the "sweet, spicy smell" of the cookies, the "prickly grass," the "creaking stairs," etc.).
- The way the title told about the feelings in the last sentence of the paragraph.

4. Pass out colored pencils, and, working in their groups, have the students:

- circle in red and number all of the sensory details that appeal to the sense of smell
- circle the sensory details that appeal to the sense of sight in blue
- put a green ? in the margin next to the parts that they can't visualize
- underline the hear, touch, taste, and movement words in purple
- identify the sentences that show how the writer feels about the place by circling them in pink

Then, have students:

- identify one thing they liked best about the paragraph, and
- make one suggestion for improving the piece.

Revising

Give the students time to embellish and refine their paragraphs according to the new images and ideas that they have gained through the sharing process.

Day Six—Sharing and Revising for Form

Sharing

1. Pass out and discuss the scoring guide, concentrating on reviewing paragraph structure and the mechanics for which you hold your class responsible.

2. In their groups of three, have students share and discuss their second drafts in terms of the criteria presented on the scoring guide. (See *EVALUATION* section). Circulate to answer questions and to offer further guidance on using the scoring guide.

Revising

Give students time to make further revisions based on the suggestions that were made by their peer response groups.

Day Seven—Editing and Evaluation

Editing

1. Have students meet in their peer response groups and look over each others' papers for paragraph form and correct spelling and punctuation.

2. Conduct a second read-around in order to give the class a chance to evaluate the improvement in their work and, again, to determine the paragraphs that they like best. (Prizes can be awarded to the winning authors.)

Evaluation

Collect the papers and evaluate them according to the following 8-point scoring guide. (Points may be converted to a letter or a percentage grade that fits your grading system):

Primary Trait Scoring Guide

Descriptive Language

5 A 5 paper:
- uses memories and sense impressions to identify and vividly describe a place
- includes four or more details that appeal to the sense of smell
- includes four or more details that appeal to the other senses
- uses precise and descriptive language that engages the reader so that he/she can feel that he/she is in that place with the writer
- conveys how that place makes the writer feel
- flows smoothly and is easy for the reader to follow

4 A 4 paper:
- uses memories and sense impressions to describe a place but not as vividly as a 5 paper
- includes four or more details that appeal to the sense of smell
- may include less than four details that appeal to the other senses
- uses some precise and descriptive language but not so effectively that the reader can actually feel like he/she is in that place
- conveys how that place makes the writer feel but less specifically than the 5 paper
- generally flows smoothly and is easy for the reader to follow

3 A 3 paper:
- identifies and describes a place but the connection between that place and the writer's memories are not very clear
- includes less than four, but at least two, references to the sense of smell
- includes less than four, but at least two, references to the other senses
- the language is not precise or descriptive enough to help the reader feel like he/she is actually in that place
- conveys only indirectly how that place makes the writer feel
- does not completely flow smoothly and may not be easy to follow

2 A 2 paper:
- does not clearly identify or describe a place
- does not include more than two details that appeal to the sense of smell

- does not include details that appeal to the other senses
- uses overly general language
- does not convey how the place makes the writer feel
- does not flow smoothly and is hard to follow

1 A 1 paper fails to respond to the prompt.

Secondary Trait Scoring Guide

Form and Correctness

3 A 3 paper:
- is written in paragraph form
- contains a strong topic sentence that draws the reader into the paragraph
- has few, if any, errors in spelling and punctuation

2 A 2 paper:
- is written in paragraph form
- contains a topic sentence that partially draws the reader into the paragraph
- has errors in spelling and punctuation but none that interfere with the meaning of the paragraph

1 A 1 paper:
- is not written in paragraph form
- lacks a topic sentence
- has serious problems with spelling and punctuation

Extension Activities

Knowledge   In their learning logs, have students record and sort out the kinds of smells that they encounter during a typical school day.

Application   Working with a partner, have students read each other's paragraphs (from the *ON THE NOSE* prompt) and try to illustrate the place their partner's paragraph describes.

Analysis   Spray different kinds of perfume on cotton balls. Have students differentiate between the various types of scents and classify them into different groups (e.g., florals, musks, spicy scents, fruity scents). Have them write a paragraph that describes how they classified one of their groups and compares and contrasts that group with one of the other groups that they classified.

Songs of an Era

Expressing an Understanding of History

Lesson

After studying a historical era, students will explain how specific song lyrics reflect the social and cultural conditions of that era.

Objectives

Thinking Skills
Students will think on the *COMPREHENSION* level as they *EXPLAIN* how song lyrics from a historical era refer and allude to society. Students will *PARAPHRASE* sections of the song as well as *DESCRIBE* real events, people, battles, feelings, happenings, etc., that may be reflected in the song.

Writing Skills
Students will write an analytical/expository essay with a clear introduction, main body and conclusion explaining how song lyrics reflect the social and cultural conditions of a historical era. To support their interpretation of what and how the song reflects society's conditions, students will identify key words and phrases in the song that make references and allusions to the historical era.

The Process

Although this lesson focuses on the 1960s and the Vietnam War Era, it can easily be adapted to cover any historical period. Simply select a song which represents that era (or have students select one) and use the procedure that follows as a model.

Through the analysis of song lyrics and the writing of an analytical/expository essay, students will be able to demonstrate their understanding of how the people of a specific time felt about their society, what they thought, what they believed in, what they were for or against, etc.

This lesson takes about one week, not including the time necessary to study the historical period. If possible, team up with the social studies teacher to provide some of the necessary historical background.

The following sources are a partial list of those that might be used for background material on the Vietnam War:

Amter, Joseph A. *Vietnam Verdict: A Citizen's History.* New York: Continuum, 1984.
Baker, Mark. *Nam: The Vietnam War in the Words of the Men and Women Who Fought There.* New York: Morrow, 1981.
Isaacs, Arnold R. *Without Honor: Defeat in Vietnam and Cambodia.* Baltimore: Johns Hopkins University, 1983.

Prewriting

Pass out the lyrics to "For What It's Worth" by Buffalo Springfield reprinted on page 116.* Students must have a copy of the song, a pencil, and be ready to jot down ideas while they are listening to it on the record player. (If you are doing Civil War songs or material you don't have a recording for, pass out a copy of the lyrics and read them aloud as students follow along with their copies.) Before you play or read the song, tell students to do the following: [You might want to put these ideas from Peter Elbow's *Writing Without Teachers* (New York: Oxford University Press, 1973) on the board or on a handout.]

Underline words or phrases that:

- mean the most to you
- are important
- were repeated for a reason
- rang true

- carried special conviction
- strike you as particularly empty or weak
- rang false, hollow, or plastic
- didn't do anything for you

At the end of the song, see which words or phrases stick in your mind. Then go back and write down things you associate with any of these words or phrases. Allow time for students to work independently on this.

If necessary, replay the song and also read it aloud as many times as students feel they need to hear it in order to get down onto paper all the associations they can recall from previously learned material.

A sample response to this prewriting exercise might look like the one on page 117:

For What It's Worth

a demonstration

police
military

National Guard

Viet Cong

They're not "asking," they're "telling"

wants people to look

There's something happening here

What it is ain't exactly clear

There's a man with a gun over there

Telling me I've got to beware

I think it's time we stopped children

What's that sound?

Everybody look what's going down

against the war

It's not clear what's happening

scared

*Note: This song is available on several Buffalo Springfield anthologies and Stephen Stills' best hits albums. Specifically, it is available on "Buffalo Springfield," Atco Records: A Division of Atlantic Recording Corp., 75 Rockefeller Plaza, New York, NY 10010, © 1973.

battle lines
protest lines
boundary lines
political lines

through songs

saying they want peace

There's battle lines being drawn

Nobody's right if everybody's wrong

Young people speaking their mind

folk music

speeches

Getting so much resistance from behind

don't want to fight in Vietnam

It's time we stopped

Hey, what's that sound?

Everybody look what's going down

ballads

What a field day for the heat — *police*

protest

A thousand people in the street

a demonstration

political songs
feel united as a group

Singing songs and carrying signs

people united

crisis

Mostly say hooray for our side

bring attention

anti-war signs
peace signs

It's time we stopped

Hey, what's that sound?

Everybody look what's going down

paranoid because of what's unclear

Paranoia strikes deep

knowing who to beware of

of death

Into your life it will creep

beware

not sure what the other side is saying

It starts when you're always afraid

insecure

Step out a line

of the future

Police

The man come and take you away

Military

You better stop

police arrest

take into captivity

Viet Cong

Hey, what's that sound?

Everybody look what's going down

take time to stop and look at what's happening

You better stop

listen

Hey, what's that sound?

Everybody look what's going down

people are so involved that they won't stop to see what is really going on

You better stop

first time "now" is used, immediacy of the problem

Now what's that sound?

Everybody look what's going down

For What It's Worth

There's something happening here
What it is ain't exactly clear
There's a man with a gun over there
Telling me I've got to beware
I think it's time we stopped children
What's that sound
Everybody look what's going down

There's battle lines being drawn
Nobody's right if everybody's wrong
Young people speaking their mind
Getting so much resistance from behind
It's time we stopped
Hey, what's that sound
Everybody look what's going down

What a field day for the heat
A thousand people in the street
Singing songs and carrying signs
Mostly say Hooray for our side
It's time we stopped
Hey, what's that sound
Everybody look what's going down

Paranoia strikes deep
Into your life it will creep
It starts when you're always afraid
Step out a line
The man come and take you away
You better stop
Hey, what's that sound
Everybody look what's going down

You better stop
Hey, what's that sound
Everybody look what's going down
You better stop
Now what's that sound
Everybody look what's going down

Prompt:

Song lyrics are often an expression of the social and cultural conditions of the historical era in which they are written. After closely examining the song "For What It's Worth" [by Buffalo Springfield,] explain how this song is a reflection of the spirit of the 1960s. In your essay, paraphrase the main message of the song and explain how the song reflects the social and cultural conditions of the time. Support what you have to say with references to key words or phrases in the song and by describing specific events, people, issues, etc., of the Vietnam Era that the song may have been written about. Your essay should have a clear introduction, main body, and conclusion and provide logical connections and transitions between the key words in the song you mention and the real life events you think they refer to.

Precomposing

To help students organize their responses to "For What It's Worth," put five clusters on the board or an overhead transparency:

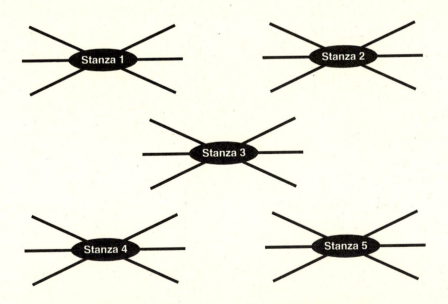

Students should make five clusters on their paper and, along with the instructor, they will record the ideas and associations of individual students on a group cluster. This will encourage the sharing of ideas and associations and will help students who are having difficulty relating to the song. Ask for associations someone had for the first stanza. Cluster their ideas off of stanza 1. Be sure to ask the student what word in the song sparked this association.

A sample cluster might look like this:

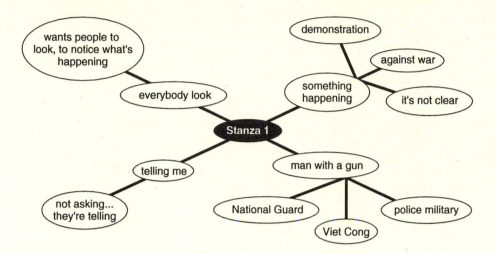

At this point, it will be helpful for most classes to go back to the prompt and define what the phrase "social and cultural conditions" means. Begin with definitions of social and cultural.

Social—of or relating to human society, the interaction of the individual and the group, or the welfare of human beings as members of a society.

Cultural—(from the noun *culture*)—the integrated pattern of human behavior that includes thought, speech, action, and artifacts and depends upon man's capacity for learning and transmitting knowledge to succeeding generations. The customs, beliefs, social forms, and material traits of a racial, religious or social group.

Have students answer the following set of questions for each stanza. Students will have five sets of answers (one for each stanza).

- What are the main points or feelings you got from the stanza?
- Summarize the stanza in a single sentence.
- Choose one word from the stanza that best summarizes it.
- Choose one word that isn't from the stanza that best summarizes it.

Writing

During the writing stage, students should refer back to the song with the key words from the song that they underlined and their original associations. They should also refer to the secondary clusters and the summary statements for each stanza completed during *PRECOMPOSING*. (Note: For some ability levels, it would be a good idea to have students write individual paragraphs centered around each stanza of the song instead of trying to write the entire essay in one sitting. Then, they can go back after five paragraphs are completed and work on an introduction, main body, conclusion and transitions.)

Optional: Have students begin the essay in class. After the first paragraph is written, do a read-around* so students can see how others started their essays.

Sharing

Before students split up into groups, read (or reproduce on the overhead, if possible) the following model of a student's first draft:

In the Streets During the '60's

The song "For What It's Worth," by Buffalo Springfield wanted people to stop, look and listen to what was going on in society during the 1960s. Something that might have been going on during this time would be the protests against the Vietnam War. The lines, "man with a gun over there telling me I've got to beware" could be talking about a scene at a college campus anti-war protest. The young people wanted to stop fighting in Vietnam, but the police tried to stop their demonstrations. It was probably pretty scary not knowing what was happening on either side.

The second stanza tells about lines being drawn. It could be boundary lines that the police had made to keep demonstrators where they wanted them. But the young people kept on talking, making speeches and "speaking their minds." They were probably talking about stopping the fighting. The "getting so much resistance" line might just mean that young people were getting hassled for carrying on their demonstrations.

The third stanza describes what an actual demonstration might have been like. "The heat" would refer to the police. There were times when hundreds of National Guardsmen would be lined up to stop a protest march.

The "paranoia" in the fourth stanza is important. The word really sets the mood of how it would feel in a war or demonstration. I'd probably be afraid. People weren't sure about what they were really doing. The idea of freedom of speech can be seen in the repetition of "what's that sound" in every stanza. It seems like everybody was talking and speaking, but nobody would listen to what anybody else was saying.

This song was probably written to help people realize that they weren't listening to each other and to now stop and listen to each other.

---

*See the Glossary for a definition of the read-around.

Ask the following questions:
Has the writer:

- Begun with a good opening?
- Explained how key words and phrases in the song refer to the 1960s Vietnam War Era?
- Described the social and cultural conditions of the 1960s Vietnam War Era?
- Written a well-organized paper that is easy for the reader to follow?
- Provided logical connections between key words in the song and what they might be referring to?
- Provided the reader with a good ending?

Then ask:

- What do you like best about this essay?
- What specific suggestions would you give the writer to improve the paper?

(Note: If you have this draft on an overhead, it would be helpful to write the students' suggestions for improving the paper directly on to the overhead.)

Students should split up into Peer Response groups of 3–5 students. If writers' groups have been used previously, students should go the their established writers' groups. If possible, students should make copies of their writing for their groups. Taking turns, the writer will read his writing to the group and listen to the group members respond.

Revising

At this stage, the writer is actually re-seeing and rethinking his first draft. Often, the comments from the peer response or writers' groups will be all the writer needs to revise the first draft. The discussion of how to improve the student model will also be useful for the writer to consider while revising his essay. The "Evaluation Checklist" (Figure 10 on page 122) can also be a valuable tool for the writer.

Editing

Although editing occurs continuously throughout the writing process and is automatic for many writers, a final correctness check should be used. The mechanical aspects of writing such as complete sentences, correct spelling, correct punctuation, capitalization, and form should be emphasized here. In particular, emphasize how to quote from the song lyrics accurately.

Evaluation

Content

5 A 5 essay expresses a good understanding of the 1960s Vietnam War Era:

- It explains how the song is a reflection of the social and cultural conditions of the times.

Have I . . .	First Draft		Second Draft		Change
	Yes	No	Yes	No	?
• expressed the main ideas, issues, or feelings of the song lyrics?					
• identified key words or phrases from the song to express the intended meaning?					
• described the social and cultural conditions that key words/phrases refer to?					
• described specific events, people, battles, feelings, happenings, etc., of the Vietnam War Era?					
• spelled everything correctly?					
• affected the reader the way I had intended?					
• incorporated any of the ideas the response group talked about during the sharing process?					
• **Additional Criteria**					
Comments:					

FIGURE 10: Evaluation Checklist

- It paraphrases the main message of the song.
- It supports main points with key words and phrases.
- It connects key words and phrases to the real life events that these lyrics might be alluding to.

4–3 A 4–3 essay expresses a fairly good to adequate understanding of the 1960s Vietnam War Era:

- It explains to some extent how the song is a reflection of the social and cultural conditions of the times.

- It paraphrases the main message of the song but may be overly general.
- It supports main points with a few key words and phrases.
- It does not always clearly connect key words and phrases to the real life events that these lyrics might be alluding to.

2–1 A 2–1 essay reflects little understanding of the Vietnam War Era:

- It does not explain how the song is a reflection of the social and cultural conditions of the times.
- It fails to accurately paraphrase the main message of the song.
- It cites few, if any, key words or phrases to support main points.
- It does not connect key words and phrases to real life events.

Form

3 A 3 paper:

- Has a clear beginning, middle and end.
- Has logical connections and transitions between key words and phrases and the real life events the song lyrics refer to.

2 A 2 paper:

- Has some semblance of a beginning, middle and end but at least one section is weak.
- Often fails to provide logical connections and transitions between key words and phrases and the real life events the song lyrics refer to.

1 A 1 paper:

- Lacks a clear beginning, middle and end.
- Has no logical connections or transitions between key words and phrases and the real life events the song lyrics refer to.

Correctness

2 A 2 paper:

- Uses, for the most part, corrects spelling, punctuation, and capitalization.
- Quotes key words and phrases from the song accurately and correctly.

1 A 1 paper:

- Has problems in correct spelling, punctuation, and capitalization that interfere with the reader's understanding of the essay.
- Fails to quote key words and phrases from the song accurately or correctly.

Extension Activities

Analysis

Prompt: After looking at songs from two different historical eras, compare and contrast the similarities and differences between the two eras. Be sure to quote key words and phrases from the songs to support your analysis.

Synthesis

Prompt: Using ''For What It's Worth'' as a model, write an original song of your own which reflects the cultural and social conditions of the present time.

Writing Domain: Imaginative/Narrative   **Thinking Level: Comprehension**
Grade Level: High School

Watermarks

Lesson

In a two to three page essay, students will narrate a significant or memorable event in their lives and explain its importance to them today.

Objectives

Thinking Skills
Students will practice *COMPREHENSION* skills of *IDENTIFYING, DESCRIBING,* and *EXPLAINING.*

Writing Skills
Students will practice narrative essay form and use of transitions.

The Process

Prewriting

This lesson may be used to stimulate writing in a composition class or to introduce a short story unit. Three to five class periods are required.

Session 1

Ask students for a definition of the word "watermark." Provide the following definitions:

- A mark on a wall, building, or measuring stick indicating the height to which water has risen. The mark could be the result of a regular recurring motion of water as in tides, or it could be made by a catastrophic event like a flood.
- A permanent marking produced in the making of good quality paper that is visible when the paper is held up to the light.

In relation to the assignment, a watermark is an event that has left a lasting impression on us.

Discuss how many events—both positive and negative—have made lasting impressions on our lives. Though these events sometimes coincide with the events that are "supposed" to be important for us like our sixteenth birthday, our first car, or New Year's Eve, other incidents—overlooked by the outside world—may actually be more meaningful.

Cluster on the board: What are some other kinds of events that might leave lasting impressions on us? (See the following example. Leave the completed cluster on the board or on a transparency for the next parts of the process.)

In addition, if a particular work of literature has been completed by students, do a cluster on that particular character's watermarks.

At this point, provide students with an opportunity to recall their personal watermarks, either by individually clustering these or by using a symbolic form. To use a symbolic form, give each student a large piece of blank paper and the following directions:

Think about all of your watermarks from childhood to the present. Using your own personal symbols—such as a broken heart to stand for a sad event, a trophy to represent an award, or any other thing that communicates to you—make a "picture" of the watermarks in your life. This picture could be like a monopoly game board, a road map, a chart, a diagram, or a timeline—whatever form you would like. The picture will help you to remember and to see how parts of your life fit together. The drawing will not be graded, and no one has to understand it but you.

This activity will take the rest of the period. While students are making their clusters or drawings, the teacher should walk around the room admiring the clusters or pictures and helping students who have trouble remembering. Students may share with each other or with the teacher throughout the process, but privacy should be respected. Some students will enjoy this so much that they will want to finish the paper at home. Encourage them to do this.

Session 2

Open the next class period with a review of the previous day's whole class cluster and a discussion of the kinds of impressions these events might make on us. The teacher may share one or more personal anecdotes from her life and explain what they mean to her today. Then the class should make a general cluster of how the events in our lives might affect us or what lasting impressions events might make on us.

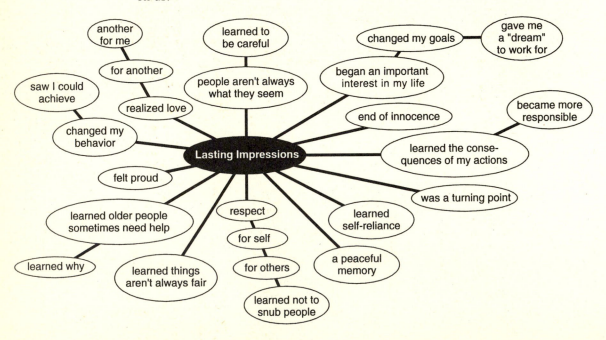

Prompt:

Choose one of the important watermarks in your life that you would like to share with the class and the teacher. In a two to three-page essay, first catch your reader's attention ("hook") and identify the watermark. Then describe the event that caused it, selecting important details to show the situation. Connect these with transitions. End your paper by explaining how this event is important to you today.

Precomposing

1. Review or introduce showing, not telling by clustering a telling sentence: *The girl was obviously nervous as she sat in the waiting room.** Have students contribute any things they might observe the girl doing or saying or any other aspects of her appearance that might make them draw the conclusion that the girl was nervous. An example might look like this:

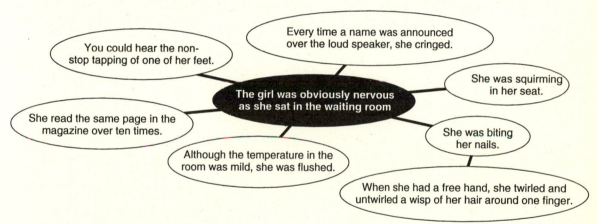

Explain that "showing" through these kinds of details, rather than "telling," will help make their watermark situation more alive for other readers.

2. Pass each student copies of the models that follow and give students practice in recognizing showing, not telling. After reading the first model aloud and providing time for students to respond to the text affectively, have students go back to the text and underline the details that show the telling sentence *The girl was very excited to show off her paper.* Have students share their underlined sections. Next, ask the students to find details that show *the girl was probably _____ years old.* (Students fill in the blank.) Finally, have them underline and share details that show *The girl was overcome with sadness.*

*See the Glossary for a further description of showing, not telling.

Model 1

"I Got An A!"

As I stepped onto the hulking yellow school bus, I tucked the paper into the pocket of my light blue sweat jacket. I patted the pocket, knowing that my first "A" spelling test was safe. I walked down the crowded aisle and found a seat next to my best friend, Vicky.

As we sat talking about everything and nothing, a wad of paper hit me on the side of my head. I picked it up and threw it back at the boy who had originally thrown it. Turning the corner nearing my bus stop, the last three blocks of our journey seemed endless and chaotic: Jeff Hannigan, a big fifth grader, got a citation for throwing the paper; the little red-headed kid wet his pants again (as always!); and as usual, the bus driver hit the curb, sending us all into hysterics.

In spite of it all, I looked out the window at the big, puffy, white clouds against the vivid blue sky. Even the clouds looked happy today, I thought, excited that I was almost home.

Breaks squeaked as the bus came to a halt. Kids scrambled off in every direction, dropping sweaters and jackets, throwing rocks, and kicking lunchpails. After picking up my stuff, I stepped off the bus, crossed the street, and headed for home. Cutting across someone's yard, the toe of my tiny Nike tennis shoe found a rock. "Maybe I could kick it home," I thought. The thermos rattled inside my empty metal Peanuts lunchbox as gravel crunched under my feet. I stopped to wipe my feet on the grass for a few rocks tried to catch a ride home by sticking to the tread on the bottoms of my shoes.

After a whole five minutes of brisk walking, I reached my street and turned right. Stuffing my fist into my pocket, I pulled out my test paper. I had finally gotten a "A"! Grandpa always told me to try and to think that I *can* do something, and then in the end, I *will*. He used to make me write my spelling words five times each. Then he'd take the papers away from me and make me spell them aloud. Sometimes he'd even have me spell them backwards so that I'd know every single letter. I guess he was right because it worked.

I quickened my pace as my house drew nearer. Finally, I could stand it no longer, and I started running. I turned up the driveway and barked at Mistie, who was barking back at me. I stopped at the gate and stuck my fingers through the diamond-shaped holes in the chain link fence that separated me from my grey and black poodle.

I walked up to the porch and flung open the door. Pulling off my jacket and dumping my lunchpail into a chair while trying to catch my breath, I yelled a quick hello to my mother. I raced past, and in a flurry of flying lips, gave her a quick smooch. I ran through the house to the den, clutching up my precious test paper and yelling, "Grandpa, I got an 'A'!"

Stopping at the top of the three brick steps that lead into our cozy den, I realized that Grandpa wasn't there. I walked over to the couch and sat on its arm. A hardening lump rose in my throat, and my eyes burned with wetness. I blinked hard, but it didn't help.

A fat tear escaped and rolled down my plump cheek, another one followed from the other eye. One tear jumped to his doom and splashed onto my chest. Another went a different direction and landed in the corner of my mouth. I licked it with the tip of my tongue and tasted its warm saltiness. I sniffed.

Then the tears flowed free and easy, and I slid off the arm onto a cushion of our couch. I cried and cried at the realization that Grandpa was gone and would never be back, sobbing myself to sleep.

I woke up some time later and looked about me. I was snug in bed. Realizing that Daddy must've carried me here while I was sleeping, I got up and went into the bathroom. Looking at my watch, I saw the big hand was on the twelve and the little hand was on the eight. "Gosh, it's late!" I thought, trying to convince myself that I could tell time.

I looked in the mirror at my red, swollen, tear-streaked face, puzzled. Then I remembered the paper. I walked through the cold, dark house, ever-so-cautiously. Shivering at the very thought of monsters and boogeymen watching me, I reached the den and, flipping on a dim light, I picked up the paper.

As I fought more tears, I stared glumly at the paper. I felt proud. Yet a certain deep sadness crept throughout my body. Another tear fought to get out, but I kept him back this time. I looked back at the pink bubble gum scratch-and-sniff sticker next to the big red "A."

"This is for you, Grandpa," I said softly as I smoothed the wrinkles out of my first "A" spelling test. I knew then his important gift of helping me develop a confidence in myself that continues to make me think positively and to succeed. Even to this day I have that paper locked in a special box. I have also the beloved memories of my grandfather locked in a special place in my heart.

—Patricia McCurley

Read the second model aloud. This time, ask students to create and share telling sentences that are supported by the details in the model. (For example, *The girls were bored, Smoking the cigarette was an unpleasant experience,* or *The punishment was painful.*) Have the students point out the details which show or illustrate the telling sentences they create.

Model 2

Lasting Impressions

Cancer, bad lungs, cloudy teeth, high heart attack risk—all of these are results of cigarette smoking. Can you imagine the effect it could have on a nine year old? Neither could I at that time, but I learned then that cigarettes were not for me.

After a week of ninety-degree August heat, Mary, my friend across the street, and I were tired of popping tar bubbles and running through the sprinklers. There just wasn't anything left to do. Getting a coke from the chronically roaring refrigerator in her kitchen, we wandered aimlessly into her den. Suddenly, Mary brightened. ''Hey, look what's on the coffee table,'' she invited. I spied the cellophane soft pack of Kools as she walked over to the table and picked them up. Knowing we had found a forbidden adventure, we snuck out back to the side of the house where we knew no one could see us from the street.

Then and there is when it all happened—the first wretched burn of the cigarette, very harsh and raspy in the lungs. As we each took a putrid puff, smug in our daring, I looked up and saw her coming toward us from the back gate. It was Kim, my younger sister, and in spite of our precautions, there I was, caught with a mouthful of smoke.

Choking, gasping, and frightened—I was in trouble. ''Kim, please don't tell. I'll do anything you want. I'll take you to the store. You can even ride my red bike. Please, please, please,'' I pleaded, ''don't tell.''

I can remember clearly the words she said as she skipped toward home. ''I'm not going to tell. I'm just going to the bathroom.''

Was my fear over? Not at all. At that precise moment I could hear my mother's anguished call, ''Versie, come here!''

Before going home I put toothpaste in my mouth, ate cheese, and even drank some milk. But a dead yellow taste lingered and I knew the scent was still there.

''What were you doing in the side yard?'' my mother calmly asked.

''Nothing,'' I whined like a little baby.

''Let me smell your breath,'' she commanded.

Very easily, I exhaled.

''You were smoking. Weren't you?''

''Yes,'' I answered meekly.

''You are getting a whipping!'' she sentenced.

''Please, Momma, no, I won't do it again. I swear I won't,'' I begged.

I can still see a slow motion mental picture of all the types of flips and turns I made as she beat me. I had never been able to do gymnastics before, but you can believe I did that afternoon. After the beating, I had a whole pack of cigarettes to smoke, one right after another. I took a puff; I wiped a tear. This was repeated until I finished. I never wanted to smell a cigarette again.

This has been a great learning experience for me. I don't feel that it is necessary to smoke. It doesn't give me any kind of pleasure. In addition, whenever I'm eating, I can't stand to smell cigarette smoke or ashes. Furthermore, if someone smokes around me, I feel dizzy. I often frown and usually move away. For in those clouds of smoke is a lasting impression.

—Versie Whitmore

3. Explain the concept of a ''hook'' to students—a bit of dialogue, a question, an unusual statement, an exciting moment from the story . . . that will spark the reader's curiosity. Ask students to identify the ''hooks'' in the two models and discuss what questions the ''hooks'' raise. (For example, why is the ''A'' spelling test so special? How did a nine year old tangle with cigarettes and what happened to her?)

4. At this point, review or introduce the idea of transition use. Returning to the models, have students circle which words, phrases, etc., alert readers to changes of time, place, and subject. Review some specific words to show time order. For example:

first	next	at once
last	after	before
when	later	finally
as soon as	afterward	meanwhile
since	then	following

Have students share their circled words, etc., in pairs.

In addition, discuss other ways of making transitions such as repeating key words or phrases. Explain that transitions are sometimes implied rather than stated. The important thing is that a reader understands how ideas follow one another.

5. Ask students to take out the cluster or "picture" of watermarks in their lives which they created previously. Have them select one that is especially meaningful to them. Then, have students individually cluster or brainstorm as many details as they can to "show" their selected watermark. They might also tell their story to a response partner before actually writing. The partner could ask questions such as "What did you see?" . . . "How did it feel?" . . . "What else was it like?" etc., to help the writer clarify and show the event.

6. Next, have students organize their papers by putting numbers beside the details in their cluster to indicate what they will write about first, second, etc.

You may want to provide less able students with a frame. A frame visually shows students how to organize a paper. It is meant to be just a suggestion of how the paper might be arranged, like the frame of a building to which is added the walls, colors, and other trimmings that make the house unique—in this case, their own words. They will need more sentences, more paragraphs, and different transitions than the frame includes.

Introduction

HOOK (Give a bit of dialogue, a question, an unusual statement, an exciting

moment from the story that will make the reader want to read on.):

_____

_____

GENERAL STATEMENT (Tell the who, what, where, when, and why of the in-

cident. If you choose to reveal this later for suspense, make sure you include it by the end and make a marginal note for the teacher about why you are not using one here.): _____

_____

_____

Body Paragraphs (Middle)

SHOWING, NOT TELLING DETAILS (Make the story as clear and vivid to your reader as possible, using transitions to connect the parts.) First of all, _____

_____ Next, _____. At the same time,

_____. Meanwhile _____

_____

_____ .

Later, (etc.) _____

_____ .

Finally, _____

_____

Conclusion

SUMMARY (Sum up your experience and what it means to you today. What do you have or know now that you wouldn't have had or known in the same way if this moment had never happened?) When I think of this experience today, I realize that

_____

_____ .

Writing

Students write the first draft.

Sharing

Students share in peer groups. One way this might be done is to have responders fill out sharing sheets after each writer reads his/her paper aloud. Sharing sheets focus the students' discussion and give the writer and the teacher a concrete version of what went on in the group, particularly if the students are new to the sharing process.

Sharing Sheet

1. Your paper does/does not "hook" me to read it because...

2. I like the following "showing" details in your paper...

3. I would like to read more "showing" about...

4. I can/cannot tell what came first, second, etc., because...

5. The parts I have trouble understanding are...

6. After reading this paper, what your watermark means to me is...

7. What I think this watermark means to you today is...

The written responses to these sentence completion queries will be the basis for revision.

Revising

Students revise according to new insights and perceptions gained in the sharing phase.

Editing

Have students concentrate on correctness and use of transitional words if the sequence of events and ideas is not clear. Have one or more other students in the class read each paper for errors and initial it.

Evaluation

Either peer or teacher evaluation may be used with this six-point rubric:

6 A 6-response is an excellent paper which completely and effectively addresses all aspects of the assignment. It will have all or most of the following:

- excellent organization and content
  - important watermark identified
  - vivid, imaginative description of the event which shows and doesn't just tell
  - a hook which catches reader's attention
  - an explanation of the event and its significance

- mature vocabulary
- varied sentence structure
- mastery of mechanics, spelling, and usage

5 A 5-response applies to a paper which is a thinner version of a 6. It includes all aspects of the assignment but with less depth or expression. It will have the following:

- good organization and content
  - watermark identified
  - vivid, imaginative description of the event which shows and doesn't just tell
  - a hook which may be less effective than a 6 paper
  - transition between ideas but not as smooth as a 6 paper
  - an explanation of the event and its significance
- less mature vocabulary
- less sentence variety
- a few errors in mechanics, spelling, and usage but none that interfere with the message

4 A 4-response includes all aspects of the assignment but may be weak in development of organization or content. It will be adequate but less mature and will have the following:

- basic organization, but less effective development in one or more of the following:
  - watermark not as clearly identified
  - description adequate but possibly unimaginative, containing less detail and more telling than showing
  - some transition but sequence of events is less clear
  - some explanation of the event but less emphasis on its significance
- adequate vocabulary
- less varied sentences
- some errors in mechanics, spelling, and usage but none that interfere with the message

3 A 3-response is a lower half paper whose writer has ignored part of the assignment, treating the subject superficially. Errors interfere with content. A 3-paper will have the following:

- addresses topic but is not fully organized
  - watermark not clearly identified
  - little description or flat description
  - few transitions, unclear sequence
  - inadequate explanation of event and its significance

- elementary vocabulary
- little sentence variety
- several errors in mechanics, spelling, and usage which interfere with the message

2 A 2-response is assigned to poorly written papers with inadequate content. Error dominates paper. A 2-paper will have the following:

- little organization
  - little or no description
  - no transitions
  - no explanation
- low vocabulary
- inadequate sentences
- serious mechanical, spelling, and usage errors that obscure the message

1 A 1-response ignores the requirements of the assignment and/or is incomplete, inconsistent in content/organization, or so riddled with errors that it is unreadable.

Extension Activities

Comprehension Have pairs of students interview each other about one of the following events/situations that happened to them:

- funniest
- worst
- strangest
- most embarrassing
- etc.

Each student takes notes while listening, then writes a narrative describing what happened to the other person.

Analysis Because many short stories recount a single significant incident in a character's life, the Watermarks assignment is a natural lead-in for and personal connection to a short story/search for identity unit. For their reading assignments, as they did for their own experiences in this lesson, ask students to identify and describe the event the protagonist experiences and then to try to determine how the character was changed or affected by it.

Writing Domain: Analytical/Expository   Thinking Level: Comprehension
Grade Level: High School/College

Theme Explanation Using *Lord of the Flies*

Lesson

Students will write an essay explaining how specific parts of a novel (e.g. character, plot, setting, symbol) are used in *Lord of the Flies* to reflect a generalized theme statement.

Objectives

Students will exhibit the critical thinking skills necessary to find appropriate examples to support a given statement about a novel's theme.

Thinking Skills
Students' *KNOWLEDGE* is developed by asking them to:

- *DEFINE* key words and phrases;
- *LABEL* characters, symbols, and actions;
- *RECALL* events from the novel to provide examples;

Students' *COMPREHENSION* is developed by asking them to:

- *DESCRIBE* how the author develops his theme;
- *EXPLAIN* how the abstract ideas have specific forms;
- *IDENTIFY* examples and symbols of the author's ideas;
- *EXPRESS* their understanding of the theme.

Writing Skills
This lesson exercises students' ability to use specific examples to support a generalization and stresses the organizing of those examples into a form that has an introduction, development, conclusion, and clear transition between thoughts.

The Process

(Although this lesson uses a particular novel, the method used should be successful with any novel or short story to show students how an author develops his theme.)

This section, which is mostly at the *KNOWLEDGE* level, develops students' understanding of what happens in the novel, their recognition of some of the symbols in the novel, and their understanding that this is a carefully constructed novel.

Prewriting

Step 1

Ask students to begin reading **Lord of the Flies**

.

Step 2

If you have access to Peter Brooks' excellent film version of the novel (it is now available in videocassette), show the first 20 minutes of the film to help students visualize the characters and the setting. When students are finished reading the novel, or after they complete this lesson, show them the entire film. It will be an earned reward.

Step 3

After students read the first chapter, ask them whether they would vote for Ralph or Jack as the leader. Discuss their motivations for voting and discuss the possible reasons the boys had for voting the way they did.

One reason to vote for Jack might be his leadership experience as head of the choir. A vote for Ralph might be cast because, since he was the one to call all the boys together, he already appears as a leader.

Step 4

Share with students Golding's own words that "the whole book is symbolic in nature . . . " (Notes on *Lord of the Flies,* Capricorn Books, 1959.) Also, point out that many critics have commented on the rich symbolism of the characters, action, objects, even setting. For example, E.L. Epstein says in the critical note to the novel, "Mr. Golding's [novel is an] extremely complex and beautifully woven symbolic web." (Capricorn Books, 1959 edition.) Make sure students understand what symbolism means and then ask them to keep notes on what the different characters, events, and objects might symbolize. In class discussions of their reading, use their notes to develop their understanding of objects as symbols (the island, Piggy's glasses, the fire), characters as symbols (Piggy as the scientific, reasoning mind), and events as symbols (Simon's death.)

Students may understand a symbol better if they cluster one.

Sample Cluster:

As students suggest various meanings for *fire,* ask them *how* they thought of it. If you ask students, throughout the entire lesson, how they got their ideas, you will be helping them focus on the thinking process.

Here is a list of some of the symbols in the novel:

Character	**As . . .**
• Jack	• The military, authoritarian mind
• Ralph	• The common sense, moral mind
• the ''littluns''	• The ''great silent majority''
• Roger	• The sadistic mind

Object	**As . . .**
• The island	• Microcosm of world
• Fire	• Rescue from violence and barbarism; power; knowledge (see Prometheus myth)
• Conch	• Rules and social convention
• Piggy's glasses	• Source of fire, invention, science; next to Jack's knife, one of two man-made objects capable of help or danger

Event	**As . . .**
• The development of the ''Beast''	• Evil and man's dark side
• Dividing of the boys into groups	• Divisions of people
• Simon's experiences and death	• Religious image with Christ-like overtones

Step 5

As students progress through the novel, class discussions should be held about the changing relationships among the boys, the development of the idea of "the Beast," the increasing violence, and the questions of meaning or plot that arise.

Step 6

Sometimes shorter pieces of writing can act as prewriting. Following are a group of sentences which can be used for short compositions (1/2 page to 1-1/2 pages) that will give students additional practice in providing details. The idea is for the student to take the "telling" sentence and "show" what it says by adding detail, examples, and explanation. You need to pick the sentences from the text or write your own that are appropriate to student ability level, appropriate to classroom emphasis, and correspond to what has been read. Here are some "telling" sentences*:

Setting	The island was a paradise.
	When night fell, somehow the island changed.
	The setting of the island was a necessary part of the plot.
Character	Piggy was a good thinker.
	Being a leader, Ralph learned, was more difficult than he had imagined.
	Ralph and Jack were very different kinds of leaders.
Plot	Life on the island wasn't as much fun as the boys had imagined it would be.
	Everything would have been easier if adults had been on the island.
	The relationships among the boys changed during the story.
Writing Techniques	The fire was symbol.
	Golding used foreshadowing in the novel.
	The ending of the story was full of irony.
	The third-person point of view allowed Golding to tell the story more effectively.

A sample showing paragraph for the telling sentence "Piggy was a good thinker" might look like this:

Piggy was a good thinker. He thought about practical things like counting the number of boys on the island and getting their names. He knew how important keeping the fire going was to their rescue and reminded Ralph about it. He also

*For a description of showing, not telling, see the Glossary.

suggested that if the fire couldn't be kept on the mountain because of the "Beast," they could build a fire on the beach. Ralph realized that only Piggy had the genius to think of something original. It was Piggy who said the idea of a beast was impossible because if a beast were possible, then television and radio and other inventions wouldn't work. He seemed to sense that technology couldn't exist in a world controlled by magic. Although Piggy's body was soft and fat, his brain was strong.

These compositions can be shared in class and scored or graded orally, or at random, or cumulatively.

After the novel has been finished and the author's notes at the end of the book have been discussed, pass out the following prompt.

Prompt:

In William Golding's novel, *Lord of the Flies,* the theme is stated by the author as follows: "The shape of a society must depend on the ethical nature of the individual and not on any political system however apparently logical or respectable."

In its generalized form, that may be difficult to understand. Therefore, in standard expository format (introduction, development, conclusion), explain how selected events, characters, and writing techniques (use of symbols, metaphors, foreshadowing, etc.) express the theme.

Precomposing

Step 7

In preparation for writing, students need to understand some key words (e.g., ethical, political system) and organize their examples to develop their comprehension of Golding's theme.

Direct a student to look up the word "ethical" and then discuss its definition with the class.

Ethical *adj.* 1. In accordance with the accepted principles of right and wrong governing the conduct of a group.

Ethics *n.* 1. The study of the general nature of morals and the specific moral choices to be made by the individual in his relationship with others.

Write the phrase "ethical behavior" on the board and have students cluster or brainstorm in order to see specific examples of the abstract idea.

Make sure students understand the phrases "shape of a society," "ethical na-

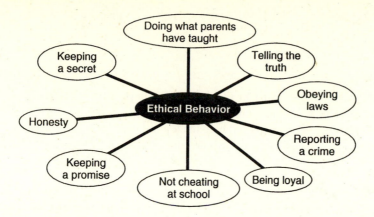

ture,'' and ''political system.'' Use definition, examples, discussions, or clusters to help make these clear as in the example above.

Step 8

The next step is to help students see the above words and phrases as they occur inside the novel. Have students make two lists, one headed ''Political Systems'' and another one ''Ethical Actions.'' Ask students to take incidents, characters, actions, or symbols from the novel and group them under the appropriate headings. For example:

Political Systems	Ethical Actions
• boys elect a leader • hold meetings with rules • establish different groups with different responsibilities • conch as symbol of order	• following the rules • taking responsibility for keeping fire lit • taking care of littluns • being a true friend • stealing fire

Start these lists in class in case further explanation is needed. The following day, students share their lists in groups and discuss the appropriateness of the items. Each student may expand his list with the ideas of other students in the group. Remind the students that what they are gathering are specific examples of the general idea Golding has expressed in his theme statement.

Ask students how they chose their examples. Once again, emphasize the thinking skills so that students who are having difficulty can see how other students arrived at their ideas. Most likely, they will also see that there are different ways to think about a problem.

Step 9

Before students put pen to paper to begin their composition, they may need some help in organizing their ideas and notes to formulate a plan to start writing.

The following questions should help them put their notes in perspective. (These questions can be discussed by the whole class or in groups, or responded to individually.)

- How do Golding's characters fit into his theme statement? (Possible answers: They represent the "individual," the "shape of a society," and the "political system" that emerges on the island.)

- How does the list of symbols fit into his theme? (Possible answers: They make the specific characters, objects, and situations more universal. They are one of the methods Golding uses to develop his abstract ideas in a concrete way.)

- How can the definition of terms (e.g., ethical) and the list of "political systems" and "ethical action" fit into the essay? (Possible answers: These are necessary to clarify and define terms used in the essay and to show specific examples of Golding's theme.)

- How can I use the "Showing, not telling" compositions in my essay? (Possible answers: These helped me understand the events and actions of the novel, as well as the ideas and techniques. Those that relate to theme may be utilized in the essay.)

With these questions answered, students should know that their job is one of organizing their material to help explain Golding's theme.

Step 10

Before students begin to write, create, with their help, a general expectations list of what their compositions should include in the areas of Fluency, Form, and Correctness. See the sample list below:

Fluency

- ideas and examples are easy to follow
- ideas are organized
- examples are appropriate
- sentences connect together
- language is effective or descriptive

Form

- paper has a title
- paper is written in paragraphs
- introduction, development, and conclusion are recognizable

Correctness

- spelling is accurate
- title of novel is underlined or in bold typeface
- quotes from book are punctuated correctly
- sentences are complete

Writing

Step 11

Students now begin to write their essays. Tell them to write an introduction that states Golding's theme and explains the purpose of their essay (i.e., to provide examples to explain the theme and how it was developed). Students may vary their beginnings as long as the above information appears before the body begins.

Two sample introductions are included below:

William Golding, at the end of his novel *Lord of the Flies*, states that his theme is based on the concept that ''the shape of a society must depend on the ethical nature of the individual and not on any political system however apparently logical or respectable.'' That is a very general statement and perhaps not very clear by itself. But if that theme can be examined through the actions of characters, through the development of plot, through setting and through symbols, then the generalizations of ''shape of society,'' ''ethical nature,'' and ''political systems'' can be more meaningful. We can then understand the novel better and make the abstract theme more concrete . . .

''The rules!'' shouted Jack. ''You're breaking the rules!''
''Who cares ?''
''Because the rules are the only thing we've got!''
''Bollocks to the rules! We're strong—we hunt. If there's a beast, we'll hunt it down. We'll close in and beat and beat and beat—!''

This exchange of words between the two boys Ralph and Jack in *Lord of the Flies* emphasizes the growing differences between them. Each sees a different way to prepare for a problem; each depends on a different way to resolve a problem. These differences create one of the major conflicts in William Golding's novel. They also give a practical expression of Golding's central theme: ''The shape of a society must depend on the ethical nature of the individual and not on any political system however apparently logical or respectable.''

It seems that rules do not create the society but, rather, the society depends upon how individuals respond to rules. Other examples of character's action, events, setting, and symbols in the novel will give a clear picture of how Golding's theme is developed throughout the novel . . .

The main body of the essay should consist of students' examples and discussion of how the examples reflect the theme.

You might suggest to the students that their conclusion can include their responses to Golding's theme and his manner of development.

Step 12

Before students divide into groups to share their first drafts, have them write a paragraph beginning with the lines ''What I really meant to say was . . .'' in which they summarize the underlying message of their papers. Divide students into response groups to share each other's papers. Have students check to see if the three parts of form are met (you might want to give them a check sheet) and respond, either orally or in writing. Students may then respond to problems of clarity, word choice, strengths, etc. Mechanical correctness need not be an issue at this time. At the end of the discussion, response groups should react to the writer's message by composing a brief summary that begins ''This writer seems to be saying . . .'' The student writer can then compare them to his/her own ''What I really meant to say was . . .'' statement to check if he/she has communicated successfully.

Step 13

Another approach to revising could be to have students share each other's papers, individually or in groups, and have them underline the main points of the paper and then identify the different kinds of examples as follows: C = character; Set = setting; P = plot; Sym = symbol. Discuss with the students whether it is more effective or not to use examples from a variety of sources, rather than focusing on just one, such as character. Students could also record in the margins the parts of the composition: introduction, body, and conclusion.

Groups may choose one paper to be shared with the rest of the class as a model of effective writing. Ask students whose papers were selected to describe HOW they put together an effective passage, HOW they changed their ideas around, etc. Students need to see the thinking process.

Step 14

At this time, guide students in a discussion to formulate an evaluation guide. This will be based on your earlier efforts at developing an expectations list. Divide the guide once again into the areas of Fluency, Form, and Correctness. If a rubric is to be used to grade the papers, make sure it reflects this guide. A sample rubric is included in the Evaluation section of this lesson.

Revising

Step 15

Students now have the opportunity to revise their papers as necessary. Their revisions should take into consideration the comments from the sharing time, the items in the evaluation guide, and the following questions:

- Have I stated the author's theme in the introduction?
- Have I provided specific and varied examples from character, plot, symbols, etc., to support the ideas in the theme?
- Have I provided a logical order to my explanation?
- Are my examples clearly explained?
- Are my examples appropriate?
- Have I used language aptly or descriptively?
- Do I have a conclusion?
- Does my conclusion express my ideas about the author's theme and how he developed it?

Editing

Step 16

Students will share their final papers with another student for final editing. This editing is for correctness in mechanics only. It is mainly proofreading. When the editing is completed, the papers are handed in for evaluation.

Evaluation

Step 17

Evaluation methods vary from teacher to teacher, from class to class, from assignment to assignment. Experience and research prove, however, that student writing improves when the evaluation method is understood by both teacher and student. This assignment has taken several steps to aid this understanding. A rubric is also very helpful in achieving understanding because it makes clear what the criteria for evaluation are. The following is a sample rubric for this lesson. It uses a conventional A-F grade scale but a numeric scale, such as 6-1, or a range of points, A = 90–100 for example, could easily be substituted. A rubric must be shared with students before they begin to write or when they begin to revise if it is to prove helpful. You may need to adapt it to what you have emphasized in your own classroom.

Rubric

A This is an essay that is clearly superior, well written, clearly organized, insightful, and technically correct. An A paper does most or all of the following well:

Fluency

- uses precise, apt, or descriptive language.
- varies sentence structure and length.
- moves from one explanation to another with appropriate transitions.

Form

- identifies the theme and gives a clear idea of the purpose of the essay.
- presents clear and appropriate examples from character, plot, symbols, etc., which support the development of the theme.
- organizes examples in a logical order.
- has an effective opening, development of ideas, and closure.

Correctness

- follows conventions of written English.

B This paper is a thinner version of the A essay. It may be less successful in some of the following areas:

Fluency

- uses some precise, apt or descriptive language but overall paper is not as vivid as the A paper.
- has some variation in structure and length.
- moves from one explanation to another but the transitions are not quite as smooth.

Form

- identifies the theme and gives a clear idea of the purpose of the essay.
- presents examples but they are less developed and less effective than those in an A paper.
- organizes examples in a fairly logical order.
- has an opening, development of ideas, and closure but not all sections of the essay are equally strong.

Correctness

- contains some lapses in the conventions of written English but none that interfere with the message.

C This paper, although still a learning experience for the student, is more superficial in development, less independent in thinking, or contains more problems in the conventions of written English. A C paper may exhibit some or all of the following:

Fluency

- employs less precise, apt, or descriptive language.
- uses repetitive sentence structure and length.
- transitions between parts of the essay are less apparent.

Form

- explains purpose of the essay less clearly.
- develops examples superficially and has fewer examples.

Correctness

- has problems in the conventions of written English which interfere with explanations.
- displays misunderstanding of some of the elements of the theme.

D This paper follows the assignment only in the most superficial manner or may be incomplete. It probably exhibits all of the weakness on the C paper and is difficult to understand or follow.

F This paper is completely off the track and has no applicable redeeming qualities.

Extension Activities

The techniques that this lesson has used to help students comprehend an author's theme and to see how he develops that theme can be applied to other novels and short stories as well. The thinking level of this lesson requires that either students develop a statement of the theme or that students be given a theme statement. The next step would be for students to be able to read a work of literature and discover the theme for themselves (*ANALYSIS.*) One final step might be for students to write a story themselves that has a well-developed theme (*SYNTHESIS.*)

The following are some other suggested extension activities:

Application

Prompt: Take one particular event from the novel, *Lord of the Flies,* and write it in the first person from the point of view of one of the characters, remaining true to the author's theme.

_____

Synthesis

Prompt: Imagine what one or more of the characters would be like twenty years from the end of the novel, *Lord of the Flies.* Based on the personality of the character and the novel's theme, formulate a plausible future and present it in a narrative form.

_____

3 Application

The Horrible Day

Lesson

Having listened to the story *Alexander and The Terrible, Horrible, No Good, Very Bad Day* by Judith Viorst, students will write an imaginative/narrative account of a terrible day in their lives.

Objectives

Thinking Skills
Students will function at the *APPLICATION* level of the taxonomy by *APPLYING* knowledge of Alexander's life to their own, *SELECTING* situations appropriate to the theme, and *SEQUENCING* these in narrative fashion.

Writing Skills
Students will write an imaginative/narrative account; they will be expected to use vivid examples and incorporate logical time frames into their stories (beginning, middle, end.) Their ideas are to be written in complete sentences, using capitals and periods where they are needed.

The Process

Prewriting

Prepare to read *Alexander and The Terrible, Horrible, No Good, Very Bad Day* (New York: Atheneum, 1972) to your students.

   Note: Use of an Alexander puppet while reading provides students with motivation for listening and responding.

   To motivate, ask:

- How many of you have ever had a terrible day?
- What kinds of things happened?
- What other words mean the same thing as terrible? (very bad, hideous, horrible, awful, horrendous, dreadful, shocking, ghastly, appalling, abominable)

   Then explain:
   Today, I'm going to read a story about a boy named Alexander who has a terrible, horrible, no good, very bad day. I'd like you to listen to find out what specific details make his day so bad.
   As you read the story, stop at the end of each sentence to discuss the specific details that made Alexander's day so terrible (i.e. ,''I went to sleep with gum in my mouth and now there's gum in my hair . . .''). Upon completion of the book,

ask, "Do you think that all of these things could have happened to Alexander in a single day?" Discuss the concept of exaggeration.

Prompt:

Now that you have heard about Alexander's terrible, horrible, no good, very bad day, you are going to write a story describing a terrible day in your life. You may choose to tell about awful things that have actually happened to you, or you may wish to imagine them. You will need to sequence these happenings, starting with those that begin in the morning, moving to midday, and ending with night. Your ideas are to be written in complete sentences, using capitals and periods where they are needed. Additionally, words need to be spelled correctly. It should be clear to your friends from your specific details and vivid descriptions (use at least three to five examples) why your day was so bad.

Note: Dictation may be appropriate for K-1.

Precomposing

1. Lead a class discussion, focusing on questions that begin at the knowledge level of the taxonomy and move upward. Individuals' responses should be noted on a blackboard or chart in the form of clusters or note taking.

   - What kind of terrible things have happened to you? (Name)
   - What other things might cause you to have a terrible day? (Describe)
   - Which of these things would happen . . . (Sequence)
     - early in the morning?
     - on the way to school?
     - at school?
     - after school?
     - at any time?

   Responses may be charted in the following manner:

Terrible Happenings				
Early in the Morning	**On the Way to School**	**At School**	**After School**	**Any Time**
• Sneezy, runny nose • Ran out of Cocoa Puffs	• Car broke down	• Split pants playing on jungle gym • Had to sit in corner	• Mom picked me up an hour late	• Dog ate library book • Pet frog died

2. Provide students with a frame for writing.

Sample Frame:

When I got out of bed this morning, _____

_____

_____

_____

I could tell it was going to be a _____ , _____ ,

_____ day. I think I'll _____

_____ .

On the way to school, _____ . When I got to school,

_____ . At (i.e., singing) time, _____ . Dur-

ing (i.e., lunch), _____ . In the afternoon, _____ .

It was a _____ , _____ , _____ ,

day. I think I'll _____ .

After school, _____ . It has been a _____ ,

_____ , _____ , _____

day. My _____ says some days are like that, even _____ .

Model the narrative on a blackboard or chart by filling in the frame as a class.
Use ideas from class cluster/chart.

Whole Class Model (Based on Charted Ideas):

When I got out of bed this morning, my nose was runny. I could tell it was
going to be an awful, dreadful, hideous, very bad day. I think I'll go back to
bed.

On the way to school, dad's car broke down. When I got to school, a girl
stuck her tongue out at me. At singing time, I didn't get to play an instrument.
During lunch, I opened my pail and found a bologna sandwich. In the afternoon, my pants split. It was an awful, dreadful, hideous, very bad day. I think
I'll go back to bed.

After school, my mom forgot to pick me up. It has been an awful, dreadful,
hideous, very bad day. My brother says some days are like that, even if you
stay in bed.

3. Once the frame has been filled out with general ideas, go back and emphasize the need for vivid description/specific detail. Revise the model. A sample follows:

Revised Class Model

When I got out of bed this morning, my nose was all runny. Tommy took the last Kleenex in the box so I had to use a paper towel. It hurt. I could tell it was going to be an awful, dreadful, hideous, very bad day. I think I'll go back to bed.

On the way to school, dad's Mustang broke down. Mom kept telling him to get that noise fixed. Too bad he didn't. When I finally got to school, Mindy Seymour stuck her tongue out at me. Girls are weird. At singing time, I was the only one who didn't get to play an instrument. I'd been hoping for the maracas all week. During lunch, I opened my pail and found a bologna sandwich. I hate bologna. In the afternoon, I played on the jungle gym. My pants split. I had to spend recess in the nurse's office while they got sewed up. It was an awful, dreadful, hideous, very bad day. I think I'll go back to bed.

After school, mom didn't pick me up. All the buses left and I sat on the curb by myself. She came an hour later. It has been an awful, dreadful, hideous, very bad day. My brother says some days are like that, even if you stay in bed.

4. Have individuals make their own clusters around "My Terrible Day." To organize these thoughts, students will number them in order/supposed order of their occurrence.

A sample cluster might look like this:

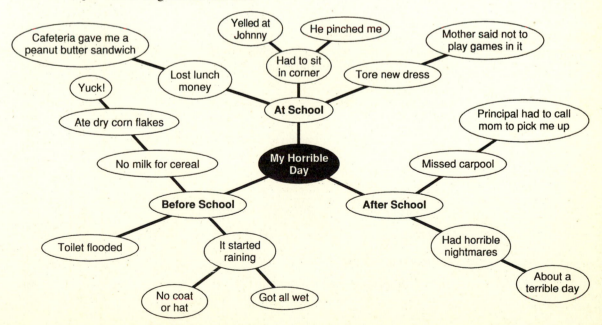

Writing

Students write individual narratives using clusters and frames.

Sharing

WHOLE CLASS SHARING—One student reads his/her piece. The others (responders) listen for vivid descriptions of a terrible day as well as appropriate sequencing of ideas. When the reader is finished, responders give oral feedback according to the following patterns:

- I like your description of _____ , particularly your use of the

  words _____ .

- I like the fact that you included the description of _____ at the

  - beginning of your story.
  - middle of your story.
  - end of your story.

Revising

Students will examine their papers for descriptions that have not been mentioned during sharing. They will work to see if they can improve the content of these, making them more vivid for their readers/listeners. Students will also reread for appropriate sequencing of at least 3 to 5 vivid descriptions. During this phase, the teacher may model by reading an exemplary student narrative.

Editing

Students edit in pairs for complete sentences and correct spelling.

Rewriting

After polishing, students will write final drafts.

Evaluation

The Scoring Guide below is based on:

- a vivid description of events in a terrible day
- sequencing thoughts from beginning to end of day
- complete sentences
- correct spelling

 Paper includes:
- at least 3 to 5 vivid descriptions (uses specific detail)
- clear sequencing, from beginning to end of day
- complete sentences (caps and periods)
- correct spelling

 Paper includes:
- 3 general descriptions (not as vivid/specific as a "smile" paper)
- some lack of clarity in sequencing
- few errors in capitalization, punctuation, and spelling

 Paper includes:
- less than 3 descriptions or weak descriptions
- poor sequencing of events
- many errors in capitalization, punctuation, and spelling

Extension Activities

Synthesis

Prompt: After completing your story about your terrible day, go back through your sequence of events and propose how one would avoid having such a terrible day.

_____

Evaluation

Prompt: Predict what kind of life you would have if nothing terrible ever happened to you.

_____

Personification of a Sound

Lesson

Following a science unit on the nature of sound, students will write a personification of themselves as a specific sound in which they describe their journey from sender to receiver.

Objectives

Thinking Skills
Students will function at the *APPLICATION* level of the taxonomy. They will be required to *DEMONSTRATE* their *KNOWLEDGE* of the nature of sound, the manner in which it travels, and the process whereby it enters the human ear. They must then *ILLUSTRATE,* through personification, the traveling patterns of a single sound.

Writing Skills
Students will write in the imaginative/narrative domain using paragraph form. They will be expected to utilize the narrative components of setting, characterization, plot, conflict, climax and resolution.

The Process

This assignment requires seven to ten days for thorough completion. Suggested time frame is noted.

Prewriting

Day 1

Review major science unit concepts on sound:

- What is sound?
- Where does sound begin? (Sources)
- How does sound travel?
- What characteristics describe sound? (Volume, pitch, tone)
- How do we sense sounds? (Sequence steps necessary to enter the human ear)

Day 2

1. As a class, cluster different kinds of sounds. A sample cluster might look like this:

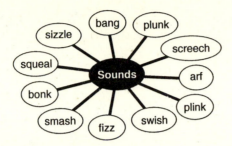

2. Select a few contrasting sounds from the cluster and discuss the qualities of each—for example, consider volume, pitch, tone, where sound may be heard.

3. Dramatize specific sounds. Direct students to stand and imitate particular sounds (i.e., a cat's purr, trumpet's blare, middle "C" on the piano . . .):

   • as it emerges from its source;
   • as it travels through the air;
   • as it enters an ear.

   (As an example, have the class imitate a cat's hiss. They might stand and move their bodies rapidly from side-to-side, as they imagine emerging from the cat's throat. They may describe the throat and what they see as they enter the back-yard. They might imagine bouncing off the barbeque pit, the lawn, and the prickly stucco wall of the house. You may want to set up a path in the class-room that represents the ear so students can concretely see and follow the path-way to their destinations.)

4. While the students are dramatizing their journey through the ear, ask the fol-lowing questions to stimulate their imagination:

   • Where are you? What kinds of things surround you? (Setting)
   • At what rate are you traveling? How are you moving?
   • What kinds of things are you running into?
   • What is your pitch? Volume? Tone?
   • How do you feel?
   • What kinds of problems are you having?
   • Where are you headed? (Destination)
   • In what fashion do you enter the ear? (Sequence: outer ear, ear drum, stir-rup, anvil, hammer, inner ear)

As students answer your questions, chart their responses on the board. You may want to save this to use as a word bank later:

Settings	Character Traits (volume, pitch)	Actions	How I Act (as the sound)
Kitchen: kitty litter box, refrigerator, counter, defrosting chicken *Backyard lawn*: fruitless pear tree, sprinkler, fence *Rooftop*: treetops, chimneys, shakes	loud soft blaring clear high low middle garbled	vibrate shake jerk wiggle bounce jump rumble roll fall move	quickly slowly lazily nervously fast quietly rapidly
Feelings	**What I Run Into**	**Problems**	**Destination**
fast dizzy nervous jazzed excited scared wonderful light-headed adventurous	windows signs body car	wind tries to sweep me away detoured down sewer	dog's ear tomcat's ear owner's ear

Prompt:

Day 3

You are going to personify/imitate a specific sound. You will describe yourself (characterization), where you live (setting), and recount a specific journey in your life as you move from sender to receiver (plot). During this journey, you will encounter some problems (conflict) which you will need to resolve. You must demonstrate your knowledge of sound in your narrative. Your paper should be organized into introduction (include characterization and setting), body (include conflict and climax), and conclusion (include resolution) and be written in paragraph form. Your narrative should appeal to your classmates as well as your teacher.

(*Note:* The teacher may wish to paraphrase and/or introduce this prompt in sections. This may be accomplished by dealing with each paragraph separately.)

Precomposing

Day 3

Each student picks his/her own sound and clusters in the following format:

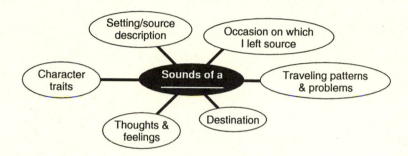

To guide the clustering, ask:

- What are your character traits? (Define)
- Where do you live? (Describe)
- What people are you related to or in the vicinity of? (Explain)
- Where do you travel on a given trip from start to finish? (Sequence)
- What kinds of problems do you encounter? (Illustrate)
- How do you feel? What do you think? (Apply, Dramatize)

Day 4—Review narrative format:

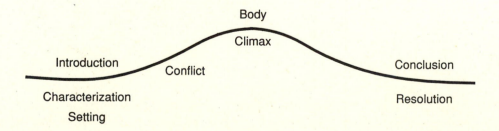

Provide students with the following framing exercise, and show how it incorporates the narrative form.

From the Diary of a ____(sound)____

I am the sounds of _____

_____(Describe characteristics of sound)_____

_____

I live inside _____

_____(Describe source/setting)_____

_____

I often take trips. One trip began when _____

_____

_____

Initially, _____

_____

Unfortunately, _____(Describe problem)_____

_____

I felt _____

I continued on _____

Eventually, I neared my final destination. _____

_____(climax)_____

At last, _____

_____(resolution)_____

Note: The lines (blanks) provided on this frame are intended only as a guide. They may be adjusted according to the content of the individual writer.

Model the narrative structure by reading the following entry from a sample student paper such as the one below:

Diary of a Cat's Meow

I am the sounds of a cat's meow. I live in the throat of an orange and yellow striped cat named Clyde. Around me are the larnyx, muscles, veins, flesh, blood, tendons, and spinal cord. Outside Clyde is the house which he lives in. The person I am closest to is Clyde. He uses me to tell his owner he is hungry. He also uses me to talk to other cats.

I often take trips. One trip began when Clyde saw a dog; therefore he hissed. Initially, I flew out of his throat and ricocheted off some molecules. Suddenly, the wind blew me into the street where a car knocked me from molecule to molecule. I hit the sidewalk and bounced up, hitting another molecule. I felt very, very dizzy. I continued on, bouncing around, high pitched. I vibrated through the grass and kept on bouncing around.

Eventually, I neared my final destination. I was in the dog's ear! I went to the outer ear, vibrating through the eardrum, hammer, anvil, and stirrup. I entered the inner ear and went to the brain. At last, the dog heard me and started barking at Clyde.

—Justin Johnsen

Day 4 & 5

Have students identify descriptions of the character (sound), setting (source), conflict, climax, and resolution. Record on the board.

Writing

Students write individual narratives using clusters and frames.

Sharing

Day 5—Small group (3 to 5 persons) sharing.

Responders should listen for the following:

- vivid descriptions of a specific sound's trip;
- flow in the sequencing of plot (introduction to include conflict and climax, and conclusion and/or resolution).

Provide students with charts to help them focus their feedback to the writer on specifics about what worked and what didn't. Also, the teacher should move from group to group providing specific feedback as needed.

Sample Chart

Character Traits	Setting of Source	Conflict	Climax	Resolution
cat's meow high pitched dizzy	orange & yellow striped cat	ricocheting off of molecules	entered dog's ear	the dog barked
	larynx, muscles, veins . . .			

Revising

Day 7

Students will incorporate ideas from sharing into their writing. During this phase, the teacher may model by reading an exemplary student narrative to the class.

Editing

Day 8

Students edit in pairs for mechanics and for paragraph form.

Rewriting

Day 9

Students write a polished final draft.

Evaluation

Papers can be evaluated by the teacher using a scoring guide such as the one that follows:

Highest possible score = 7.

Primary Trait Scoring Guide

For response to the elements of the prompt which call for a vivid description of a sound and its journey in logical sequence:

4 Narrative displays clear personification of sound and effectively describes setting, characterization, and plot in an appropriate sequence.

3 Clear personification of sound. Manages 2–3 narrative components well. Sequence may be a bit weak.

2 Personification may display some inconsistencies. Obvious weakness in 1–2 narrative categories, in description and/or sequencing.

1 Personification may display some inconsistencies and fails to deal effectively with 2–3 narrative components. Lacks sequencing.

Secondary Trait Scoring Guide

For response to the elements of the prompt which call for content knowledge and paragraph form:

3 Evidences sound knowledge of subject matter. Perfect paragraphing.

2 Evidences moderate knowledge of subject matter. Few or no errors in paragraphing.

1 Lacks knowledge of subject matter, and/or poor paragraphing.

Extension Activities

Synthesis

Prompt: Create an environment in which you would hear only the most pleasant of sounds.

Evaluation

Prompt: What's the most appealing kind of music? Defend your answer.

Writing Domain: Imaginative/Narrative   **Thinking Level: Application**
                                                           Grade Level: Intermediate

Should I Or Shouldn't I?
Unresolved Conflict

Lesson

Students will read and then write a brief narrative illustrating their understanding of the dilemma faced by the princess and the lover in "The Lady or the Tiger?" by imagining a similar unresolved conflict a teenager of today might face.

Objectives

Thinking Skills
Students will demonstrate *APPLICATION* level thinking skills by *IMAGINING, DRAMATIZING, FRAMING, IMITATING, TESTING OUT, USING* and *APPLYING* the insights they gained from studying "The Lady or the Tiger?" and applying it to a new situation.

Writing Skills

Students will write a narrative describing an unresolved conflict a teenager of today might face. Students will dramatize the conflict by sequencing the events which lead up to the point when the teenager makes a decision and will generally imitate some of the narrative techniques the author uses in writing "The Lady or the Tiger?" Students will use descriptive language and supporting details, and will pay attention to the overall grammar and mechanics of good writing.

The Process

"The Lady or the Tiger?" by Frank Stockton (in *Literature and Life,* Glenview, Ill.: Scott, Foresman & Co., 1982, 106–111.) is a short story which can be effectively used in the classroom to challenge students to do some creative thinking about decision making and the inherent problems involved in the process of choosing between alternatives.

The lesson can be organized as a series of activities spanning a 10 to 12 day period, or it may be used as a two to three hour writing assignment, depending on whether you are interested in presenting a mini-unit in this particular area of study or whether you merely wish to zero in on the writing skills segments. The process as outlined is flexible, allowing you to choose from the listed activities those best suited to your individual teaching style.

Prewriting

1. To prepare students to read "The Lady or the Tiger?" introduce the vocabulary words in the story which may be unfamiliar to them:

semibarbaric	impartial	retribution
progressive	incorruptible	tribunal
genial	emanated	devious

2. To set the stage for discussions pertaining to such personal values as friendship and distrust, love and hate, loyalty and disloyalty, as well as such concepts as semibarbaric and civilized, the class will cluster the individual pairs of words and/or concepts, illustrating these words and/or concepts by listing with examples. The teacher can act as recorder at the board.

Sample Clusters:

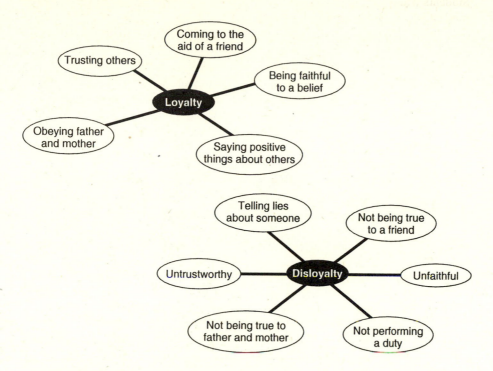

3. Read "The Lady or the Tiger?" aloud in class so all students have the same frame of reference. (You may elect to be the reader or you may select students to read.)

4. If available, show the film "The Lady or the Tiger?"* directing students to pay special attention to the questions raised during the discussion portion.

   As a group, consider the following questions which apply to both the written narrative and the film, since regardless of the medium, the story line remains the same.

   • What does the princess value?
   • What does the lover value?
   • Was the princess being disloyal to her father?
   • Do you feel the princess intended to be disloyal to her father?
   • How does the knowledge that the princess is described as "semibarbaric" influence your opinion about the decision you imagine she will make?

*The film "The Lady or the Tiger?" was produced in 1969 by *Encyclopaedia Britannica* (425 North Michigan Avenue, Chicago, Ill., 60611. Telephone: 1-800-558-6968.)

- If the lover can accept the fate that awaits him should the tiger leap from behind the door he opens, why can the lover be described as "semibarbaric"?
- Can you point out any examples of "semibarbaric" behavior in today's society?

5. Because it is necessary for students to realize that the resolution of this story is actually left up to the reader, continue the discussion, exploring the consequences for the princess and for the lover, based on the following questions:

- What alternatives does the princess face?
- What conflicts does the princess' lover face?
- Should the lover trust the princess?
- What will happen if the lover opens the door behind which the lady stands?
- What will happen if he opens the door behind which the tiger lurks?

6. To expand on the idea of considering the consequences of decision making, have students test out these conflicts by writing an ending for this short story in which they imagine the consequences.

   Using a form similar to the sample given below, have students individually chart the possibilities for the ending they will write to "The Lady or the Tiger?"

Character	Conflict	Possible Decisions/ Solutions	Consequences
Princess	1. Which door should the princess signal her lover to open? 2. _____?_____ 3. _____?_____	1. Have her lover open the door behind which the lady is standing. 2. _____?_____ 3. _____?_____	1. Risk losing him by having him marry the beautiful lady. 2. _____?_____ 3. _____?_____
Lover	1. Should the lover trust the princess and open the door she signals him to open? 2. _____?_____ 3. _____?_____	1. May choose door with tiger behind it. 2. _____?_____ 3. _____?_____	1. Will be killed by the hungry tiger. 2. _____?_____ 3. _____?_____

Note: Ask students to complete the chart by generating additional conflicts, possible decisions/solutions and consequences.

7. Other possible ''twists'' to suggest might be:

   • Is there a possible ending for this story if the princess later kills the lady, and when accused, must be tried by her father for the murder?
   • Is there a possible ending for this story that does not involve the opening of either door?
   • Is there a possible ending for this story if the lover is neither eaten by the tiger nor greeted by the lady?

Prompt:

Illustrate your understanding of the dilemma faced by the princess and the lover in ''The Lady or the Tiger?'' by imagining a similar unresolved conflict a teenager of today might face. Dramatize the conflict by writing a narrative. Sequence the events which lead up to the point where the teenager must make a decision and/or arrive at a solution in the order in which you imagine they occur. Leave the conflict unresolved, and, as in ''The Lady or the Tiger?'' let your reader complete the story in his/her own mind. Make your narrative as interesting as possible so that your reader will be left ''hanging'' and will want to know what happened.
   Within the frame of your narrative:

• Describe the character who must make the decision.
• Explain the conflict.
• Describe the relationship between the main character and any other characters involved, and show how this relationship might influence the decision of the main character.
• Imagine what the decisions/solutions are as well as what the consequences of each decision/solution might be.
• Test out the reasons why the character would be likely to choose or not choose each solution.
• Dramatize the conflict in the story by generally applying some of the techniques of narrative writing for organization, sequencing, character and plot development, the use of narrative details, descriptive language (vivid verbs, colorful adjectives, similes, metaphors, etc.) and the natural use of language or dialogue the author uses in ''The Lady or the Tiger?''
• Pay attention to the overall grammar and mechanics of good writing.

   (*Note*: You can become the character in your narrative and write from the first person ''I,'' or you can write about someone else from the third person ''he'' or ''she.'')

Precomposing

1. Students study the narrative ''The Lady or the Tiger?'' carefully to understand that it uses certain techniques common to all good narratives:

- The overall narrative is organized and follows a plan. Events are sequenced in the order in which they happened. The use of "flashback" (the telling of an earlier event that took place before the main events of the story) is also employed.
- The narrative creates, out of experience and imagination, events that make a difference to the main character or characters. The characters, in turn, do not merely summarize things that happen, but rather the events show meaning, some of which is stated and some of which is suggested.
- The plot is developed with many narrative details—specific actions that move the story along with interest.
- Descriptive as well as figurative language adds to the reader's ability to visualize the setting. The scenes become vivid from the details of action the author chooses.
- The narrative is realistic in style. The language or dialogue is natural and sounds the way the reader would expect the particular person to sound.

Students will orally cite particular passages or events from "The Lady or the Tiger?" to demonstrate that Stockton uses the techniques mentioned above.

2. Introduce additional vocabulary words that students might wish to use in their narratives, such as:

confront	circumvent	dilemma
retaliate	ignore	consequence

Add to this list any vocabulary words students may suggest.

3. To generate ideas for writing, students can engage in a narrative group activity, using one of the conflicts and consequences from the following sample chart, or one of the ones the class generates.

Conflict	Consequence
Should a student risk cheating on an exam or accept a failing grade	*if* it means not being nominated for the office of Student Body President?
In the event there is a divorce in the family, with whom should the child decide to live	*if* going to live with one parent means moving and leaving the friends and school in his/her area?
Should you sneak out to a party that you have been forbidden to attend	*if* it means either risking punishment by your parents or the disapproval of your peers?
(Add to this list with examples generated by the students.)	

With one student in each group acting as recorder, students can dramatize the conflict their imagined character will face and test out the reasons why the character would be likely to choose or not to choose a certain solution.

4. If time permits, have each group write up their narrative to share with the class. Have a member of each group read the paper to the class. Have the class comment on the effectiveness of the narrative, making suggestions for improvement as necessary.

5. Students should now develop their own list of possible conflicts and consequences which they might dramatize. Have them develop an individual *CONFLICT/CONSEQUENCE* chart similar to the one they worked on as a group.

6. After consulting their list, students should select the dilemma they wish to write about. The following activities will help them respond to each of the requirements in the prompt:

   - Put the name of their character in the center of a piece of paper and cluster all the descriptive words they associate with him/her.
   - Do a 10-minute freewrite describing their character's dilemma.
   - Put the name of their character in the center of another piece of paper and cluster all of the other people who are related to the character and his/her dilemma. Then, taking each person, form a new minicluster of ideas about how the relationship with this person might influence your character's decision.
   - Fill out a chart like the one below:

Character	Conflict	Possible Decisions/ Solutions	Why The Character Would or Wouldn't Be Likely to Choose Each Decision/Solution
Jim, football captain.	Jim's best friend took the final history exam one hour previously. Should Jim, who did not study, accept the answers from his best friend?	Accept the best friend's answers, risk being caught and being kicked off the football team. Take the test on his own and risk failing the exam.	Would not want to cheat because to be caught would reflect on his standing and would affect his status on the football team. Would be tempted to cheat to maintain GPA.

Writing

Students will write a rough draft of their narrative, paying particular attention to the requirements of the prompt.

Sharing

Before rough drafts are shared with a writing response partner, give each student a copy of the Primary and Secondary Trait Scoring Guides (see *EVALUATION* section.) Students should read each other's papers, checking to see whether all the points mentioned in the Primary and Secondary Trait Scoring Guides have been covered. The response partner should make any comments in the right- or left-hand margin of the paper. Each response partner should also write a written response to the paper he/she read, discussing the positive aspects of the narrative.

Students should note:

- Whether the character was adequately described;
- If the conflict was clearly described;
- Whether relationships with other people who might influence the character's decision/solution were discussed;
- If reasons why the character would be more or less likely to make a certain decision or choose a certain solution were alluded to;
- If the narrative events were sequenced in a way that was easy to follow;
- Whether the conflict was left unresolved; Whether the reader is left wanting to know what happened?

Students can also:

- Underline effective words and phrases;
- Make comments about whether they can identify with the dilemma;
- Point out where the dialogue does or doesn't sound natural.

A model rough draft and sample written comments are included in Figure 11:

Revising

Based on the annotated suggestions and the written feedback from their peer response partner, students will make conscious choices about what portions of the narratives to revise by adding, deleting, substituting or rearranging their story as they feel necessary.

Should I or Shouldn't I?

Good opening. You got my interest.

It looked like Bob, but I could not be sure. The girl with him, though, I could spot in a minute. It was Jane Thompson. She had just arrived from New York, and had immediately bragged she could get any boy in our 8th grade class. Now here she was with Mary's boyfriend. I turned the corner toward my Spanish class. Then I backed up to take one more look. It was Bob all right. His cropped blonde hair and his glistening smile were unmistakable. I would not have given it a second thought, but Mary and I had been best friends since first grade. And, she had been so excited about going out with Bob. She had had her eyes on him ever since school started. We followed him everywhere those first few weeks. We even managed to show up at his locker, across campus from ours, at the exact time he was there. Then it happened. He had said "Hello" to Mary and for the last seven months all I had heard was 'Bob this' and 'Bob that'. How could I tell Mary that Bob was now seeing Jane? She had been so happy. Maybe I would not have to tell her. After all, who was I to give her the news. And, I could have been mistaken. On the other hand, I was sure it was Bob and that kiss meant more than being friends. If I did not tell her everyone would be talking behind her back and she would be the last person to know. I could not let her look like a fool. But she would hate me at first for telling her. Could I risk losing her friendship? And then what about Bob? He had been so nice to Mary and even to me. I would hate to hurt him. But, how could he be so cruel to Mary? He had never said anything to her about breaking up or about wanting to see someone else. Could I tell Mary without talking to Bob first? As the tardy bell rang, I ran toward class. I knew I would have to do something, but maybe after lunch it would come to me.

New paragraph?

What kiss? Did I miss something?

Maybe you could combine these short sentences into one longer one.

Is it OK to begin a sentence with And? I can't remember the rule.

I really like this. I can identify.

It's really great the way you look at all the pros and cons.

Bob sounds like a creep. I wouldn't worry about hurting him.

Great. You left me hanging!

Dear Melanie,

I enjoyed reading your rough draft. It was so real! You used good description, like when you talked about Bob's "glistening smile." Your story was so interesting that I couldn't wait to get to the ending to find out what happened. Your story moved. There were no boring places. I did have one question. When you backed up to take a second look, did you see Bob kissing Jane? Most of all, I'm dying to know how you solved the problem. How did this story turn out?

Marie

FIGURE 11: Should I Or Shouldn't I?

Editing

Students will write the final copy of their narratives, proofreading for errors in grammar, sentence structure, and mechanics (spelling, punctuation, etc.).

Evaluation

Students will submit the final copy for teacher evaluation, based on the same Primary and Secondary Trait Scoring Guides.

Primary Trait Scoring Guide

Content

5–4 The writer does an excellent job with most or all of the following:

- Successfully demonstrates his/her understanding of "The Lady or the Tiger?" and applies insights gained from the literature by creating his/her own unresolved conflict
- Clearly describes a character who is faced with a dilemma, using precise and vivid language
- Explains the conflict in detail
- Explores the character's relationships with others that might influence the decision made or solution arrived at
- Imagines what the decisions and/or solutions are and what the consequences might be
- Tests out the reasons why the character would or would not be likely to make a particular decision or arrive at a particular solution
- Leaves the conflict unresolved in such a way that the reader is left hanging and wants to know what happened

3 A 3-paper follows the requirements of the prompt but is less impressive than a 4- or 5-paper. A 3-paper has some or all of the following characteristics:

- Creates an unresolved conflict but the similarity between the conflict and the dilemma in "The Lady or the Tiger?" is not entirely clear
- Character is described but not as vividly as in a 4- or 5-paper
- Conflict is explained but not in much detail
- The character's relationships with others that might influence his/her decision or solution are inadequately explored or not explored at all
- Writer imagines what the decisions made or solutions arrived at might be but does little to test out the reasons why one choice would be made over another
- Conflict is left unresolved

2-1 A 2–1 paper does not respond to all of the requirements of the prompt. A 2–1 paper:

- Creates a conflict that is unlike the dilemma in "The Lady or the Tiger?"
- Only vaguely describes the character
- Conflict is unclear
- Does not refer to the character's relationships with others
- Does not imagine or test out possible decisions/solutions and consequences
- Resolves conflict or presents an unresolvable conflict
- Paper is too unclear for the reader to wonder about what happened

Secondary Trait Scoring Guide

Style, Form and Correctness

4-3 A 4–3 paper uses very good to excellent narrative skills. A 4–3 paper:

- Sequences narrative events in a manner that is easy to follow
- Develops plot (i.e., the conflict/dilemma) clearly
- Uses precise, apt, or descriptive language in establishing setting, plot or characterization
- Provides ample narrative details to make the story line concrete
- Uses realistic, natural language and/or dialogue that is reminiscent of "The Lady or the Tiger?"
- Has few, if any, errors in grammar, spelling, or punctuation.

2-1 A 2–1 paper has some problems in style, narrative structure or correctness that make the paper far less impressive than those scoring a 4 or 3:

- Narrative sequence is difficult to follow
- Conflict development is poor; story line is unclear
- Provides only sketchy details
- Uses overly general language
- Dialogue, if any, sounds unnatural
- Has errors in grammar, spelling, and punctuation that impede the writer's message

---

Extension Activities

Synthesis   Have students exchange the first portion of their "Should I or Shouldn't I?" papers with a peer partner.

Prompt: After reading the dilemma which faces the character in your classmate's paper, speculate about what decision you think that person will make and write your own ending to the paper, resolving the conflict.

Evaluation

Prompt: Write a letter to the princess in "The Lady or the Tiger?" telling her what you think she should do. Evaluating the pros and cons of your advice, anticipate objections that the princess might raise, and overcome those objections, justifying your point of view with logical reasons.

Writing Domain: Sensory/Descriptive   **Thinking Level: Application**
                                                              Grade Level: High School

Your Romantic Childhood:
A Stylistic Imitation of Free Verse

Lesson

Students will imitate free verse by applying their own life experiences to the form and content of Walt Whitman's poem "There Was A Child Went Forth."

Objectives

Thinking Skills
Students will:

- *RECALL* early life experiences, *ORGANIZE* and *CATEGORIZE* them into chronological and subject groupings;
- *CHOOSE* the most effective memories to *APPLY* to the free verse form;
- *EVALUATE* rough drafts during revision by *ASSESSING* both form and content.

Writing Skills
Students will construct a free verse poem in imitation of Walt Whitman's "There Was A Child Went Forth" by:

- expressing their memories in vivid language;
- using grammatical structures and punctuation similar to Whitman's;

- emulating Whitman's tone;
- substituting their specific content for Whitman's;
- revising rough drafts to become polished products.

The Process

Prewriting

Step 1

Begin the lesson with a discussion of childhood memories. Share a few of your earliest recollections about people, places, things, or experiences. You might mention your very first memory, your room as a child, secret hiding places, games, happy or sad moments, school days, etc.

Then, ask your students to recall their earliest memory or a favorite time in their early childhood. Ask them to describe their memories in writing, telling them not to worry about correctness this time but to be as specific as possible. You might help them express vague memories by posing these questions:

- Where were you? What was it like?
- How old were you? What was that like?
- Who was there with you?
- What could you see, hear, taste, or smell?
- What were you feeling and thinking?
- Why do you remember this? (optional)

Ask volunteers to share their memories with the class or in peer groups.

Step 2

Explain that even such vague memories form part of the structure of our conscious self. In many ways, we are the product of what we can remember.

Begin a discussion about developmental influences. Ask the students, "What made you become the unique individual you are today?" Begin talking about the forces of Nature (Heredity) and Nurture (Environment) and ask, "Are you more a product of heredity or environment?"

Step 3

After this discussion, draw the conclusion that both heredity and environment are significant influences in each of our lives. Establish transition to the literature by explaining that some people, including our writers and other artists, find it important to share this concept through their art. The poet Walt Whitman certainly does this in his poem, "There Was A Child Went Forth" (reprinted later in this lesson).

Step 4

Before assigning the reading of the literature, you may wish to share with the class some of what we do know about the biography of Walt Whitman. Included is a brief biography you may wish to use or edit in response to the needs of your students and the demands of your curriculum. Of course, there are many readily available sources that will furnish you with more complete and in-depth information.

Tell the class that although we know quite a bit about Whitman's life, his poetry tells us even more about Walt Whitman, the human being.

Biographical Information
Walt Whitman (1819–1892)

Whitman was born in a rural village on Long Island, New York. His parents were semiliterate and taught him little more than a vague sympathy for political liberalism and a deistic faith shaped by Quakerism. While he attended only five or six years of formal schooling, he was a voracious reader of the nineteenth-century novelists, English romantic poets, "classics" of European literature, and the New Testament. His teachers saw him as a "dreamy and impractical youth."

He drifted through a series of jobs as an office boy, printer, and country school teacher, until he finally used his natural journalistic talent for a short time as an editor of a Long Island weekly newspaper. At twenty-two he was attracted to the Bohemian life of Manhattan so he went to New York City to work as a printer, editor and free-lance journalist, contributing essays, short stories and poems to many popular newspapers and magazines. At twenty-seven he became editor of *The Brooklyn Daily Eagle*, but after only two years he was dismissed because of his radically liberal political views.

After a brief visit to New Orleans, he returned to New York City to open a printing office and stationery store and began to write his greatest poetry. In 1855, he first published *Leaves of Grass*, a quite controversial collection that drew such varied reactions as R. W. Emerson's "extraordinary!" and John Greenleaf Whittier's "loose, lurid and impious!"

From 1857 to 1859, he edited *The Brooklyn Times*, but his real task was reworking *Leaves of Grass* and the publication of its second and third editions. When the Civil War began, he traveled south to Washington, D.C., and served as a volunteer nurse in military hospitals and as a government clerk. While living in Washington, he published *Drum Taps*, a collection of Civil War poems that he included in the fourth edition of *Leaves of Grass*. By its fifth edition, he began to see his work as a single poem to be revised and improved throughout his lifetime.

At the age of fifty-four, he suffered a paralytic stroke and moved to his brother's home in Camden, New Jersey. There, he spent the last nineteen years of his life being cared for by a group of devoted friends and revising his poetry. The final version of *Leaves of Grass* was published shortly before his death in 1892.

Source: *Anthology of American Literature, Part One: Colonial Through Romantic*, ed. George McMichael, (New York: Macmillan Publishing Co., Inc., 1974).

Step 5

Introduce the poem by teaching potentially difficult vocabulary from "There Was A Child Went Forth":

- *phoebe bird* (noun): bird found in the eastern United States; markings of gray, brown, yellow, and white.
- *esculent* (adjective): edible.
- *usages* (noun, plural): habits, established or common practices.
- *gainsay* (verb): deny, dispute.
- *facade* (noun): front or artificial appearance.
- *aureola* (noun): radiant, luminous light surrounding an object or area.
- *schooner* (noun): large ship with two to seven masts.
- *slack-tow'd* (adjective): attached or tied loosely.
- *astern* (adverb): at the rear or back of.
- *strata* (noun): layers or levels (plural of "stratum").

Step 6

Read the poem together orally in class the first time for general comprehension. This may become a homework assignment if time does not permit class reading.

There Was A Child Went Forth"
(from *Autumn Rivulets* by Walt Whitman)

There was a child went forth every day.	1
And the first object he look'd upon, that object he became,	2
And that object became part of him for the day or a certain part of the day,	3
Or for many years or stretching cycles of years.	4
The early lilacs became part of this child,	5
And grass and white and red morning-glories, and white and red clover, and the song of the phoebe-bird,	6
And the Third-month lambs and the sow's pink-faint litter, and the mare's foal and the cow's calf,	7
And the noisy brood of the barnyard or by the mire of the pondside,	8
And the fish suspending themselves so curiously below there, and the beautiful curious liquid,	9
And the water-plants with their graceful flat heads, all became part of him.	10
The field-sprouts of Fourth-month and Fifth-month became part of him,	11
Winter-grain sprouts and those of the light-yellow, and the esculent roots of the garden,	12
And the apple-trees cover'd with blossoms and the fruit afterward, and wood-berries, and the commonest weeds by the road,	13

And the oldest drunkard staggering home from the out-house of the tavern
      whence he had lately risen,   14
And the schoolmistress that pass'd on her way to the school,   15
And the friendly boys that pass'd, and the quarrelsome boys,   16
And the tidy and fresh-cheek'd girls, and barefoot negro boy and girl,   17
And all the changes of city and country wherever he went.   18

His own parents, he that had father'd him and she that had conceiv'd him in
      her womb and birth'd him,   19
They gave this child more of themselves than that,   20
They gave him afterward every day, they became part of him.   21

The mother at home quietly placing the dishes on the supper-table,   22
The mother with mild words, clean her cap and gown, a wholesome odor
      falling off her person and clothes as she walks by,   23
The father, strong, self-sufficient, manly, mean, anger'd, unjust,   24
The blow, the quick loud word, the tight bargain, the crafty lure,   25
The family usages, the language, the company, the furniture, the yearning
      and swelling heart,   26
Affection that will not be gainsay'd, the sense of what is real, the thought if
      after all it should prove unreal,   27
The doubts of day-time and the doubts of night-time, the curious whether
      and how,   28
Whether that which appears so is so, or is it all flashes and specks?   29
Men and women crowding fast in the streets, and if they are not flashes and
      specks, what are they?   30
The streets themselves and the facades of houses and goods in the windows, 31
Vehicles, teams, the heavy-plank'd wharves, the huge crossing at the
      ferries,   32
The village on the highland seen from afar at sunset, the river between, 33
Shadows, aureola and mist, the light falling on the roofs and gables of
      white or brown two miles off,   34
The schooner nearby sleepily dropping down the tide, the little boat slack-
      tow'd astern,   35
The hurrying tumbling waves, quick-broken crests, slapping,   36
The strata of color'd clouds, the long bar or maroon-tint away solitary by
      itself, the spread of purity it lies motionless in,   37
The horizon's edge, the flying sea-crow, the fragrance of salt marsh and
      shore mud,   38
These became part of that child who went forth every day, and who now
      goes, and will always go forth every day.   39

Step 7

Discuss the text for content. Following are some questions at various critical thinking levels that you may wish to use. This is not intended to be a complete list:

Knowledge

- The poem seems to be a series of lists of scenes and impressions of "a child." What images from the poem stand out for you?
- What plants, animals, people, and settings are described?
- What did the parents "give the child" in lines 19 to 21?
- What is seen in the streets, at the wharves, in the sky, and on the horizon?

Comprehension

- What feelings or attitudes do you get from the listing descriptions in the following sections:

  - lines 1–13
  - lines 14–18
  - lines 22–26
  - lines 27–29
  - lines 30–38

(Students might answer with feelings such as restful, safe, warm, homey, carefree, frightened, confused, angry, awestruck and fulfilled, or many others, depending on the passage and their understanding.)

- What does the poet say about doubt?
- What does the poet say about affection?

Application

- When have you felt any of the feelings you get from the poem?
- Can you name any other poem, story, or novel that expresses any of these feelings or attitudes?
- Can you name any character in literature, cinema, or television that might feel some of these feelings?

(Students may offer some farfetched responses. That's okay, but require them to tell why they answered the way they did.)

Analysis

- Reread the poem carefully. Point out the lines that mark distinct changes in scenes or feelings.
- Compare and contrast the way the poet characterizes his mother and father.
- What does Whitman mean by "the tight bargain, the crafty lure" in line 25?
- What does this poem imply or state about the effect of the environment on the individual?

(Students might say that the environment affects the mood or outlook of a person; for example, the pleasant natural images of plants and animals might develop a child's appreciation of nature, while the mean father might make the child wary or depressed.)

Synthesis

- Why would Whitman be moved to write this poem?
- Based on the feelings and ideas expressed in this poem, speculate about what you think Walt Whitman was like as a person.

Evaluation

- Which part of the poem did you like the best? Why?
- Which part of the poem did you dislike? Why?
- Would you recommend this poem to others? Why?

Step 8

After the students thoroughly understand the content of the poem, it is time to begin studying its form. Introduce the concept of free verse or *vers libre* with a definition and other examples. There are usually many free verse poems in contemporary literature anthologies available at all schools. The following descriptions taken from *Concise Dictionary of Literary Terms,* edited by Harry Shaw, (New York: McGraw-Hill, Inc., 1976, 122 & 285) may prove helpful:

free verse: Verse that lacks regular meter and line length but relies upon natural rhythms. Free verse is ''free'' from fixed metrical patterns but does reveal the ''cadences'' that result from alternation of stressed and unstressed syllables. Some writers and critics contend that free verse by its very irregularity provides added force to thought and expression. Conversely, Robert Frost once remarked, ''Writing free verse is like playing tennis with the net down.'' For further discussion, see *vers libre.* (122)

vers libre: A French term for free verse. Vers libre, also known as polyphonic prose, is distinguished from conventional verse by its irregular metrical pattern. Vers libre relies more upon cadence than uniform metrical feet and does not always follow the usual rhythm of poetry. Vers libre (free verse) is an ancient form; the Psalms and Song of Solomon from the Bible are in free verse. Much of the poetry of Walt Whitman and Carl Sandburg is vers libre, a form of experimentation that has contributed to freeing poetry from formal conventions of structure and subject matter. An example of vers libre and a statement of its purpose appear in these lines by Ezra Pound: (285)

> Go, little naked and impudent songs.
> Go with a light foot!
> (Or with two light feet, if it please you.)
> Go and dance shamelessly!
> Go with impertinent frolic.

Some examples in school anthologies:

- Stephen Crane, "The Wayfarer"
- Matthew Arnold, "Dover Beach"
- Karl Shapiro, "Auto Wreck"
- Gary Snyder, "Hay for the Horses"

Step 9

Now, question the students concerning the form of the poem. Following is a list of questions at various levels of critical thinking. It is not intended to be a complete list.

Form Questions

Knowledge

- Without looking at the poem again, what is the mark of punctuation most often used in the poem?
- How many sentences are there in the poem?

Comprehension

- Are there any end rhymes?
- Are there any examples of alliteration?
- Is there a consistent, fixed metric pattern throughout?
- Are there any repeated words or phrases?
- Are there any examples of parallel construction?
- What parts of speech are most prevalent?

Application

- Have you read any other poems in similar listing or free verse style? Name them.

Analysis

- What part of speech seems most important to the form and content of the poem? Why?

(Answers may vary. Some students may say that the noun is the most important because of the prevalence of naming lists, while others may say that adjectives or adverbs are most important because of the vivid description.)

- Compare free verse style to more traditional poetic form. How are they different and/or similar?

Synthesis

- Reconstruct two to four free verse lines from this poem into a more traditional rhythm and rhyme pattern.

Robert Frost's "Stopping By Woods On A Snowy Evening" and "The Road Not Taken" are good examples to use for traditional patterning.

Examples:

Lines 1–4 might become:

Every day a child went forth;
Each object he became.
Through days and years and cycles more
He came and went and came.

Lines 22–23 might become:

The mother worked so quietly to set the supper table,
Her clothing, self and all the rest as clean as she was able.

Evaluation of these reconstructions should be lenient and supportive, since students find this to be very difficult.

Evaluation

- What do you like about free verse form? Why?
- What do you dislike about free verse form? Why?
- How do the first four and the very last lines work together? Are they effective? In what way?

Step 10

Introduce the writing prompt.

Prompt:

One of Walt Whitman's poems, "There Was A Child Went Forth," records many of the personal impressions and memories that influenced him throughout his life. Just like Whitman, you have certain impressions and memories of scenes and people that make up your emotional and mental past and have contributed to your present personality and outlook.

Make his poem your poem by imitating his style and form—applying your life history to his structure. Start your poem by copying his first four lines exactly as they are written, but begin substituting your experience with line five. Use similar grammatical structures (noun for noun, verb for verb, etc.) as you write, and continue until the last line that should remain:

"These became part of that child who went forth every day, and who now goes, and will always go forth every day."

Precomposing

Guide the students through the following precomposing activities that will serve to generate content ideas for their imitations of Whitman's poem.

Step 11

The first precomposing activity should be a guided imagery that you will conduct. Direct the students to clear off their desks, put both feet on the floor and sink comfortably into their seats. Help them relax by telling them to take in a deep breath and then slowly exhale while they feel the tension in their bodies ease away. Have them breathe slowly and deeply two more times to calm and clear their minds as well. After they are relaxed, you may tell them that they might want to close their eyes for this exercise. It is often a good idea to dim the lights of the room, and it is not necessary for every student to close his eyes if it is uncomfortable. When they are ready, begin guiding them through different stages of their childhoods so they recall vivid memories of people, places, and things that will help them write their imitations. Speak clearly and slowly to keep them relaxed and focused.

You might begin like this:

''I want to take you on a journey back in time to a different place you once knew. I want you to clear your mind of the present and remember back to the days when you were a very small child. Imagine yourself as a child of two or three. (*Note:* Be sure to pause after each question so students have time to clearly imagine what you ask.)

- Where are you?
- What are you doing?
- Who are you with and how does it feel?

Now, take yourself to a little different time. Imagine you are four or five years old. Think of a place you would have been.

- What do you see?
- What do you hear?
- What can you smell or taste?
- What do you feel?
- Are you thinking about anything?
- What are you thinking?

Let your memory and imagination keep you there for a little while or take you to another place at the same age. (Pause a little longer so they can create the images.)

I want you to take yourself forward in time a little and remember what it was like in the days of primary school, first through third grades. Keep relaxed and imagine yourself at six years old.

- Where are you?   –
- Who is with you?   –
- What do you see and hear?   (Repeat these questions
- How do you feel?   as indicated below by *)
- What are you thinking?   –
- What do you want to do?   –

Let all these images sink in. (Pause a while, in addition to pauses after questions.) Now it is time to move on to second grade—in your seventh year. (Repeat questions.*)

You are getting a little older now and becoming a little more independent. Now you are in third grade—in your eighth year. (Repeat questions.*)

It's time to move ahead to fourth and fifth grades. You are becoming more of your own person and you are nine or ten years old. Place yourself in other locations and with other people you knew then. (Repeat questions.*)

For a moment, focus on yourself sitting in your seat here. Breathe deeply and try to relax a little more, letting the tension flow from your body. Clear your mind and allow yourself to go on. (Pause.)

Now take yourself back just a few years to when you were eleven or twelve years old. You would have been in the sixth or seventh grade, almost entering your teens. (Repeat questions.*)

Think of how it was to just turn thirteen—a very important year for most young people because it is their first official teenage year. Be thirteen again. (Repeat questions.*)

Now take yourself from that time of just turning thirteen through the months or years of your recent past. (Repeat questions.*)

Now try to think of your life as a whole. Of all the images you created in the last few minutes of this exercise, which ones seem most vivid or most significant? Let them sink in for a moment. (Pause.)

Now we are going to end this exercise. Take another deep breath and slowly open your eyes. Look around and feel you are here with us. Do not speak because I want you to remember all you just imagined. I want you to record those images on a chart that will help you plan your composition.''

Distribute the precomposing guide chart and give directions on how to fill in the chart. Keep students quiet so they can easily recall the information.

Precomposing Guide to Prepare Content Student Worksheet

Directions: Fill in the chart with places and people in your life. Quickly jot down those that immediately come to mind—whether they seem significant or not. (The students must complete the chart immediately after the exercise or their images may be lost.)

Your Age	Places		People
	Description	**Name of Place**	**Name of Identity of Person**
0–5 Years	1. 2. 3. 4.	1.* 2. 3. 4.	1. 2. 3. 4.
6–9 Years	1. 2. 3. 4.	1. 2. 3. 4.	1. 2. 3. 4.
10–12 Years	1. 2. 3. 4.	1. 2. 3. 4.	1. 2. 3. 4.
13 Years to Present	1. 2. 3. 4. 5.	1. 2. 3. 4. 5.	1. 2. 3. 4. 5.

*Note: Students may have only vague impressions of these early years. It is not necessary that they specifically identify places and people on the 0–5 year section of the chart.

After the students have filled in the chart, ask them to turn it over and record any other images they want to remember from the visualization exercise but couldn't fit into the chart or question format. The following questions may also be helpful:

- How would you describe how you feel most often?
- What words come to mind when you think of your neighborhood?
- What words come to mind when you think of your city or town?
- What do you see in the distance from your home?
- Describe your most vivid impression of the sky and the horizon as seen from your home or neighborhood.

Step 12

In order to gather information for the family portion of their poems, students need to respond to the following questionnaire. Please remind students that we are not here to pry into their private lives so they have the liberty of fictionalizing portions of the poem to protect their privacy. If they do not have a mother and/or father to write about, they may wish to use their idealized image of who that person would be or describe a man or woman they respect to use as a father or mother figure in their poem.

Family Questionnaire Student Worksheet

Directions: Fill in the necessary information as quickly as you can. Do not dwell too long on any answer. First impressions are often best.

List five words that describe your *mother*.

1. _____   2. _____   3. _____

4. _____   5. _____ .

When you first picture your mother, what is she doing? _____ .

How does she look? _____ .

How does she sound? _____ .

What smell or fragrance do you associate with her? _____ .

List five words that describe your father's personality or manner:

1. _____   2. _____   3. _____

4. _____   5. _____ .

List five nouns naming him (Example: car-fixer, jogger, teacher, etc.)

1. _____   2. _____   3. _____

4. _____   5. _____ .

Step 13

Orally review the general structure of the poem by content:

- lines 1–4   Copy as written
- lines 5–13   Impressions of natural settings
- lines 14–17   People in the daily environment
- line 18   May be copied as written for transition
- lines 19–21   Introduce family; may be kept as written
- lines 22–26   Describe mother and father
- lines 27–29   Personal inner states
- lines 30–38   Town, neighborhood, sky, horizon—
                  future
- line 39   Copy as written

Step 14

Model an example of your imitation. For instance, someone who pictures his mother working at an office might rewrite lines 22 and 23:

The mother at work efficiently managing the people in the office,
The mother with alert look, tailored her skirt and jacket, a fresh
fragrance falling off her person and clothes as she comes in

Reinforce the objective of actually substituting nouns for nouns, phrases for phrases, etc.

Example:

• Whitman's line 22:

     (noun) (prepositional phrase) (adverb) (verb)
The mother   at home   quietly placing

     (noun) (prepositional phrase)
the dishes on the supper-table,

• Imitation of line 22:

     (noun) (prepositional phrase) (adverb)   (verb)
The mother   at work   efficiently managing

     (noun) (prepositional phrase)
the people   in the office,

You may wish to distribute a model previously written by you or another student.

"There Was A Child Went Forth"

Eric Klein, Capistrano Valley High School

There was a child went forth every day,	1
And the first object he look'd upon, that he became,	2
And that object became part of him for the day or a certain part of the day,	3
Or for many years or stretching cycles of years.	4
The white snow became part of this child.	5
And the stockings and the green and silver Christmas tree, and the red and green gifts, and the songs of Christmas,	6
And the tall dark pews, and the room's eerie hollow echo, and the air's smell and the stranger's voice,	7
And the cozy warmth of the back seat or under the shelf under the TV,	8

And the world so beautifully coloring itself out there, and the warm inside,   9

And the Leggos with their bright varied shapes, all became part of him.   10

The rain storms of March and April were part of him.   11

Spring rose buds and those across the cool, dirty street, and the mysterious
houses of the neighbors,   12

And the preschool filled with children and the drive home, and gum
wrappers, and the windshield wipers up and down,   13

And the cheerful ice cream man driving home past the children on the street
where he had just been,   14

And the lady that'd knock on the door for his mom,   15

And the friendly neighbors that'd wave, and the mean neighbors,   16

And the cruel and the big mouthed boys, and the bright colored bigwheels
and bikes,   17

And all the changes of city and country wherever he went.   18

His own parents, he that had father'd him and she that had conceived him
in her womb and birth'd him,   19

They gave this child more of themselves than that,   20

They gave him afterward every day, they became part of him.   21

The mother at home busily cleaning the house with her rags,   22

The mother with dark hair unchanging her mind and complexion, a dull
color radiating from herself and her clothes as she moves around.   23

The father, big, all-knowing, understanding, strong, smiling, warm.   24

The argument, the big mean words, the long night, the hasty apology,   25

The family house, the yard, the fort, the garage, the blue and sparkling
pool,   26

Property that will not be taken, the knowing of who you are, the idea if
after all it should be imaginary,   27

The questions about the world and the questions about life, the curious
animals and how,   28

Whether those which seem so are real or are they all faces and figures?   29

People and machines working continuously in this world, if they are not
faces and figures, what are they?   30

The houses themselves and the lawns of grass and bushes along the streets,   31

Cars, parking lots, the smoke-filled waiting rooms, the faceless mannequins
at the department store.   32

The city in the hills seen from the bay at dusk, the boats between,   33

People, buildings and shops, the mimes performing in the streets and plazas
with crowds or alone thirty feet away,   34

The wilderness nearby peacefully running along the hillside, the little trees'
green-brown dots   35

The endlessly breaking waves, sandy wooden boardwalk, laughing,   36

The lines of bright rides, the endless line of horizon and blue and orange
water alone shining by themselves, the frame of stillness they gleam
silently in,   37

The world's edge, the burning redwood, the fragrance of charred
marshmallows and tree moss,   38

These became part of that child who went forth every day, and who now
    goes, and will always go forth every day.   39

(Eric was a first semester ninth grader at Capistrano Valley High School in Mission
Viejo, California, when he wrote this in the fall of 1984.)

Writing

Step 15

Allow students to begin writing the first draft in class so that you can help them.
Continue writing as a homework assignment. It is helpful to break the writing into
two parts. Line 18 serves as a good breaking point.

    When students return the next day with the first 18 lines complete, they may
have some questions, so allow a few minutes for discussion before they complete
the remaining lines in class or the next night as homework. Students should use
copies of the poem while they write to ensure close imitation. Their precomposing
worksheets should also be kept handy for immediate reference.

    You may need to remind female students to use feminine pronouns instead of
Whitman's masculine ones.

Sharing

Step 16

Note: Students should be familiar with sharing groups before this assignment.*

    When the first draft is complete, organize students into small groups of two to
five students. Write the group task on the board:

- Read your writing out loud to the group. (Two times is best.)
- *Readers*: Ask your *Listeners,* ''Does this sound like Whitman and yet still create
  a picture of my world?''
- *Listeners* will give the writer positive, supportive comments. Tell the writer
  what words and phrases are most effective and memorable.
- Optional Step: Ask the listeners what needs improvement in your poem. You
  may ask for general suggestions or about specific editing problems.
- Inform the teacher when your group is done.

    Plan ample time for this exercise and expect a noisy classroom. Supervise each
group by walking around the room and sitting in with each group for a couple of
minutes. Be visible, available, and supportive!

*For further reference, see Peter Elbow's *Writing Without Teachers* (New York: Oxford University
Press, 1973).

Revising & Editing

Step 17

Students may work individually or in pairs for this exercise. Each should have a legible copy of the rough draft to compare with the Revision Guide Frame. During the comparison of rough draft and guide frame, students will check for structural and mechanical imitation. Did the writer meticulously match Whitman's form? Student writers will then revise problem areas, keeping in mind that content and form are important in this assignment. If students work in pairs, they will be able to help each other and discuss the strengths and weaknesses of each section. Allow time and space for quiet conversation during this exercise.

Sample Revision Frame Guide

Note: Prepositions may differ from Whitman's. This is just a guide.

1   There was a child went forth every day,

2   And the first object s/he look'd upon, that s/he became,

3   And that object became part of him/her for the day or a certain part of the day,

4   Or for many years or stretching cycles of years.

5   _____ became part of this child.

6   And _____ and _____ and _____ and _____ and _____ , and the _____ of the _____ ,

7   And the _____ and the _____ , and the _____ and the _____

8   And the _____ of the _____ , and the _____ and the _____

9   And the _____ _____ing themselves so _____ below there

10 And the _____ with their _____ , all become part of him/her.

11 The _____ of _____-month and
_____-month became part of him/her.

12 _____ and those of the _____, and the
_____ of the _____,

13 And the _____ and the _____ and _____
and the _____ by the _____,

14 And the _____ing home from the _____
of the _____ when s/he had _____,

15 And the _____ that _____ed on his/her to
the _____

16 And the _____ that pass'd, and the _____,

17 And the _____ and _____, and the
_____ and _____,

18 And all the changes of _____ and _____
wherever s/he went.

19 His/her own parents, he that had father'd him/her and she that had conceiv'd
him/her in her womb and birth'd him/her,

20 They gave this child more of themselves than that,

21 They gave him/her afterward every day, they became part of him/her.

22 The mother at _____ _____ing _____
on the _____,

23 The mother with _____, _____ her
_____ and _____, a _____
_____ing _____ her _____
and _____ as she _____,

24   The father, _____ _____, _____,

_____-_____, _____

_____, _____,

25   The _____, the _____, the _____, the

_____,

26   The family _____, the _____, the

_____, the _____,the _____

and _____

27   _____ that will not be _____, the sense of

what is _____, the _____ if after all

it should _____ _____,

28   The _____ of _____ and the _____

of _____, the curious _____ and

_____,

29   Whether that which _____ _____

_____ _____, or is it all _____

and _____?

30   _____ and _____ _____ing

in the _____, if they are not _____

and _____, what are they?

31   The _____ themselves and the _____ of

_____, and _____ in   the

_____,

32   _____, _____, the _____, the

_____ at the _____,

33   The _____ on the _____ seen from afar at

_____, the _____ in between,

34   _____ , _____ and _____ ,

   the _____ _____ing on the _____

   and _____ of _____ or _____

   miles off,

35   The _____ nearby _____ _____ing

   down the _____ , the _____

   _____ _____ _____ ,

36   The _____ing _____ing _____ ,

   _____ _____ , _____ing

37   The _____ of _____ _____ ,

   the _____ of _____ away by

   _____ , the _____ of _____

   it _____ in,

38   The _____ 's _____ , the _____ing

   _____ , the _____ of _____

   and _____ ,

39   These became part of that child who went forth every day, and who now
   goes, and will always go forth every day.

Sharing & Revising

Step 18

During this second sharing group, students should help each other double-check
for appropriate application of content, imitation of style, and correctness before
handing in their poems for evaluation. Students should be given the opportunity
to rewrite before handing in their final drafts.

Evaluation

Step 19

The class may help you develop a rubric for evaluation or you may wish to use
the following as a guide.

Sample Evaluation Rubric

A This paper is clearly superior in form and content. It demonstrates all or most of the following:

- substituting and applying student's life history to Whitman's form
- using effective diction
- creating vivid images
- substituting grammatical structure for grammatical structure (nouns for nouns, verbs for verbs, etc.)
- using similar punctuation at similar points
- demonstrating control of language through coherent sentence structure and syntactical fluency
- demonstrating control of language through excellent mechanics (spelling, punctuation, capitalization)
- demonstrating neatness and legibility in writing or typing

B This paper is *good* or *very good* in form and content, but it may demonstrate difficulty in two or three qualities defined above. For example, it may contain images that are less vivid than an "A" paper or not be as syntactically fluent as the "A" paper. It *must,* however, substitute and apply the student's life history to Whitman's form and demonstrate control of language that is above average.

C This paper is average in form and content or may be especially strong in form or content and a little weak in the other. It *must,* however, substitute and apply the student's life history to Whitman's form and demonstrate at least adequate control of language.

D This paper is poor and would benefit from major revision. It displays weakness in content and form; however, it still *attempts* to apply the student's life to Whitman's form. The paper shows inconsistencies and weaknesses in most of the qualities defined under the "A" paper.

F This paper does not write to the prompt.

Extension Activities

Analysis

Prompt: Compare and contrast Whitman's free verse style in "There Was A Child Went Forth" with the free verse style of another poet.

(*Note:* Matthew Arnold's ''Dover Beach'' and/or Karl Shapiro's ''Auto Wreck'' are good pieces to use in this exercise.)

Analysis

Prompt: Compare and contrast Whitman's free verse style in ''There Was A Child Went Forth'' with the traditional verse style of another poet.

(Note: Robert Frost's ''The Road Not Taken'' and/or ''Stopping By Woods On A Snowy Evening'' are good pieces to use in this exercise.)

Synthesis

Prompt: Emulating Whitman's style, compose a free verse poem of your own on a topic of your choice. The poem should be at least fifteen lines and employ some repetition and alliteration. When it is read, there should be a feeling of a beginning, a middle, and an end.

Writing Domain: Analytical/Expository   **Thinking Level: Application**
Grade Level: High School/College

Birth Order Essay

Lesson

Students will write an essay on the subject of birth order and how it influences a person's character traits.

Objectives

Thinking Skills
Students will demonstrate *APPLICATION* level thinking skills by *ORGANIZING* the material gathered from class discussion, group debate and reading, and *APPLYING* their birth order findings both to themselves and others so they can *TEST* their validity.

Writing Skills
Students will write an analytical/expository essay demonstrating logical organization, using specific examples for support, containing sentence and paragraph transitions, and a clear-cut conclusion. Correct footnoting and bibliographic form is required, if used.

The Process

Background Information

This lesson should be assigned after students have become acquainted with each other, usually at least a month into the course. It takes about four one-hour sessions in-class and two weeks out-of-class. This assignment can be modified easily for students from 8th grade through college even though this particular version is geared to college students and presupposes previous instruction in essay writing.

As an introduction to this lesson, the teacher should share the following birth order theory with students:

> According to psychologists, being the first, last or middle in anything influences people in fairly predictable ways. This is particularly true of the order in which we are born in our families. Since the turn of the century when Freud's student Alfred Adler introduced the concept, psychologists have been exploring the ways in which birth order influences personality traits, and they have noticed that the oldest, only, middle or youngest children in any family will share certain common tendencies or what Adler called a "lifescript."

Oldest children

Because they are the focus of attention until the next sibling arrives, oldest children often carry the expectations and dreams of their parents on their shoulders. They tend to be serious, high achievers who work diligently to attain goals. Treated like little adults, firstborns are usually very responsible and conscientious. They thrive on being organized and in control. All the direct or indirect pressure to perform can produce overly compliant people-pleasers who take on more than they can do or fiercely individualistic perfectionists who are often critical of others. One thing all first borns share in common is that they are eventually "dethroned" by a sibling. Coming to terms with the new rival and reestablishing their dominance within the family structure is a major challenge for oldest children.

Only children

Only children manifest many of the traits of oldest children—sometimes even to extremes; and yet they will also always be the baby of the family. Like oldest children, only children are often perfectionists who have a clear sense of the "right" way to do things. Growing up in the center stage, as it were, and receiving intense personal attention from their parents and other adults, they *expect* to be taken seriously, are touchy about being excluded, and are often outspoken in their opinions. Because of their upbringing, only children are also likely to be more comfortable in the company of people who are much older or much younger than themselves. At the same time that they are frequently in the limelight, only children are also used to entertaining themselves, enjoy solitude, use time creatively, and learn to be self-reliant. Having had little opportunity to compete or to share while growing up, they may be uncomfortable with altercations or squabbling in later life and are either likely to hold back or go overboard on matters involving generosity.

Middle children

Middle children are just that—in the middle—born too late to get the special treatment of the firstborn and too early to "get away with murder" like the youngest child. Middle children are very hard to characterize because their personality is influenced to a significant degree by the sibling directly above them. They may be shy or extroverted, easygoing or driven, depending upon their sibling's traits. But, in general, middle children are likely to look outside the family unit for support. They often belong to a strong peer group, "run with the pack," so to speak, and are very loyal to their friends. One word for middle-borns is "contradictory." They tend to be very independent and to do their own thing, and yet they also have a strong need to belong. Of all the birth orders, they are the most private. They "play their cards close to the vest." And yet, they are also quite social and are often very popular.

Youngest children

"Last but not least" is an apt expression for youngest children. Determined to get their fair share of attention, and then some, youngest children often become the family entertainer and, later on, the class clown. Typically, they are rewarded for the cute and engaging things they do as the baby of the family; but they may also be dismissed with a pat on the head when the audience has had enough. Deep down, youngest children may secretly resent not being taken as seriously as their siblings. They can charm the birds out of the trees, but they can also be spoiled, rebellious and temperamental. Unlike oldest children, who tend to be overprotected in their formative years and can react by becoming very cautious, youngest children grow up in a more relaxed and even permissive atmosphere. Consequently, they are more likely to take a risk and to act on impulse. They are also less reliable and more easy-going than individuals in other birth order positions.

From *The Birth Order Book* and *First Child, Second Child* (sources cited below)

This brief synopsis is basically all the students will need to begin to apply birth order theory to their own lives and want to discuss its provocative premise. However, the students can find additional information at the library in the psychology section. Sources include:

Dr. Alfred Adler, *Understanding Human Nature* (New York: Fawcett Publications, 1959).
Helene Arnstein, *Brothers and Sisters,* (New York: E.P. Dutton, 1979).
Flora Davis, "First Born, Last Born, In between," *Mademoiselle* 89 (1983):115.
Dr. Lucille Forer, *The Birth Order and Life Roles* (Springfield, Ill: Charles C. Thomas Publisher, 1969).
Dr. Kevin Leman, *The Birth Order Book,* (Old Tappan; N.J.: Fleming H. Revell, 1985).
C. Schooler, "Birth Order Effects: Not Here, Not Now, " *Psychological Bulletin* 78 (1972): 175.

Dr. Walter Toman, *Family Constellation* (New York: Springfield Publishing Company, 1969).

Bradford Wilson and George Edington, *First Child, Second Child* (New York: McGraw-Hill & Co., 1981).

R.B. Zajonc and G.B. Marcus, ''Birth Order and Intellectual Development,'' *Psychological Review* 82 (1975): 74–88.

Prewriting

Following a brief overview of birth order theory, ask students to individually cluster their own personality traits. An example might be:

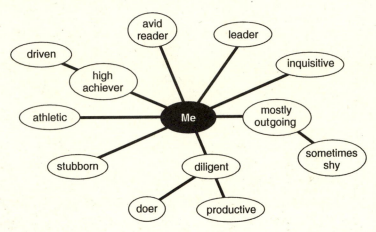

Then, break the class into three groups: 1. oldest and only: 2. middle; and 3. youngest. (Note: If you have enough only children, they can form a separate group.) Ask these groups to share the traits on their individual clusters and come up with a composite list of traits they share in common. Each group should report its findings to the class. The teacher can record these traits on the board. A sample chart might look like this:

Oldest & Only	Middle	Youngest
Self-reliant	Diplomatic	Entertaining
Perfectionist	Fun-Loving	Compassionate
Conscientious	Easygoing	Affectionate
Inflexible	Private	Humorous
Punctual	Gregarious	Sensitive
Studious	Black Sheep	Intuitive
Leader	Troublemaker	Dedicated

During the next week, the students will interview others outside class to obtain more material about birth order as well as to examine written material on the subject.

Brainstorm a list of possible interview questions with the class. Sample questions include:

- What is your birth order?
- What traits would you use to describe yourself?
- What is your profession? Why did you choose it?
- How do you perceive the benefits you derive as a result of your birth order? Drawbacks?
- Are there specific things you do because of the way your sibling(s) act(s)?
- Do your parents treat you a certain way because you're the oldest, only, the youngest, or middle child?
- Do you feel your birth order is important in the way others outside the family treat you? If not, why?

Using the groups' questionnaire as a point of departure and adding his or her own questions, each student should interview at least ten people (family members, friends, classmates) to test the validity of the birth order premise. They should be encouraged to take careful notes and perhaps even to tape-record their conversations.

(*Note:* Usually, in the course of these interviews, students will explain the birth order theory and ask the interviewee for his or her opinion about its relevance. However, some students prefer to keep the people they interview in the dark about the reason for their questions so they have a more unbiased sample.)

Prompt:

Many authorities feel placement in the family such as oldest, only, middle, or youngest child will influence a person's character traits. Your essay (of at least four double-spaced typewritten pages) dealing with this premise should explore how important or unimportant you feel birth order is in determining personality traits, based on your careful selection of data. You will need to identify in your introduction the characteristics of oldest and only, middle and youngest child. However, the main body of your essay should test the theory in relation to your own experience. Is it applicable to you, personally, and to the people that you have interviewed? How? Be specific. Bring in all other credible information you have gathered to test out your use of the premise. (Be sure to use footnotes if you cite information from secondary sources.) You will need to select applicable material and demonstrate what is relevant. If your findings refute the premise, discuss this in detail and present your conclusions accordingly. In drawing your conclusions, be sure you show how important or unimportant you feel birth order is in determining personality traits. Remember to apply your investigation data when coming to your conclusions.

Precomposing

As a result of their interviews, students will have gathered a great deal of data which they must analyze to determine whether or not it supports the birth order theory. To help them organize, you might suggest that they use the following chart to record their information:

Data That Refutes Birth Order Theory	Data That Supports Birth Order Theory

A sample chart might look like this:

Data That Refutes Birth Order Theory	Data That Supports Birth Order Theory
1. All the firstborns I interviewed, save one, were extremely gregarious and seemed happiest in groups of people, though researchers say the opposite should be true.	1. Interestingly, even though Susie and Sara, twins, were born only minutes apart, Susie, the firstborn, has all the text book qualities: academic, a leader, and somewhat conservative and traditional. Sara, on the other hand, is very like the typical middle child, preferring to follow, doing only enough to get by in school, and into whatever fad is popular with her friends. It would appear that these differences might have been set early on by the parents' attitude toward the girls because of the order in which they were born.
2. Seven out of the ten middle children I interviewed were leaders, either in their professions or in their community life; therefore, they should be firstborns.	2. I was amazed that all ten middle-borns said they were good negotiators. I wonder how many will become lawyers or diplomats.
3. All ten of the lastborns I interviewed were shy loners, preferring their own company and needing much private life. Why would this be? Should be firstborns or even sometimes private middleborns.	3. Eight of the ten youngest I interviewed displayed extreme sensitivity to animals' vulnerability and showed their inability to leave strays but instead chose to bring them home. How like the researchers' findings on the sensitive and compassionate natures of lastborns.
..... and so on	..... and so on .....

Students can now freewrite on the following questions:

- Do you think your birth order has influenced your personality traits? If so, why? If not, why not?
- Has your observation of interviews with other validated the birth order theory? If so, why? If not, why not?
- Students should now go back to their charts to select examples from interviews, reading and personal experience to support their opinion on birth order theory.

To facilitate the translation of the students' ideas into a structured essay, suggest that they write a microtheme (a mini-essay) on their topic. On a sheet of 8-1/2″ × 11″ paper have them write Introduction, Main Body, Conclusion.

	Birth Order Essay
◯	
	Introduction
	Main Body
◯	
	Conclusion
◯	

Under *Introduction,* have them sketch out an idea for how they will open their paper in a way that will engage their reader and explain how they will integrate the information on birth order theory. For example, will they begin with a quote from a secondary source, an anecdote, some dialogue, description, etc?

Under *Main Body,* have them outline the main points they intend to make, noting the specific examples they intend to use for support.

Under *Conclusion,* have them summarize their findings about the relevance or irrelevance of birth order theory.

Sharing

Students will meet in response groups of four for oral discussions to devise their own checklist of questions. The checklist should be written down by each student and kept for reference. The teacher will write the questions on the board, such as:

- Does the writer organize his material so that the information is clear?
- Does the writer apply the birth order theory to his or her own experience?
- Are the examples supportive of the point of view that birth order theory as discussed in class is valid or not?
- Is the language apt, precise or vivid enough to hold the reader's attention?
- Does the paper flow well with good sentence and paragraph transitions?
- Is the conclusion clear-cut and logically presented?
- Is the paper at least four pages long?

Before breaking into small groups to share their papers, it is helpful to critique a student model using the checklist. Putting the paper up on an overhead will make it possible for the teacher to record the comments of class members on the draft as in the example on the next page:

First Draft:

Birth Order Essay

Very effective to open with dialogue

The dimly lit, smoked-filled bar was alive with the chatter of the singles crowd on this warm summer night. A gregarious young blonde approached a dark-haired male, sitting alone on a bar stool, who seemed out of place in the midst of this very Southern California scene.

"Hi. My name's Susie. Are you a firstborn?" she asked.

Taken aback, he replied, "How did you know?"

"Oh, you seem kind of quiet and you definitely look like you'd rather be at home reading a good book. I'm a middle-born."

Good Transition

And so there seems to be another way to start a conversation besides, "What's your astrological sign?" Admittedly, the premise is a provocative one, but ever since the turn of the century when Alfred Adler gave the idea some credibility, there have been those psychologists who have also thought that perhaps birth order in the family might play a very important part in personality development. One of the most recent, extensive birth order studies was conducted by Edington and Wilson under the title First Child, Second Child and was published in 1981. These psychologists went beyond the first- and only-born, middle-born, and last born categories into the more delineated subcategories of oldest girl, youngest girl; oldest boy, middle girl, youngest girl; oldest girl, youngest boy, and so on. They found a certain amount of predictability within each category that seemed to take away the element of mere coincidence.

Maybe you should explain who Alfred Adler is.

Predictability about what?

Edington and Wilson?

After reading this book and after conducting our classroom discussion based on the three main categories, I was intrigued enough to do some research on my own. Luckily, I am from a family of three—oldest girl with two younger sisters, and I know many families of three or more who I chose to interview for my own individual study. Our classroom discussion gave me the basis to work from, and I formulated the questions I wanted to ask in order to come up with my findings. (See attached questions.)

Because I am the oldest, I was naturally more intrigued with this category. I interviewed ten oldest and only besides interviewing those who knew me well so that I could be more objective about myself. In class discussion we had found most in this group happiest in a leadership role that required conscientious fulfillment of specific goals. Eight of the oldest and only are clearly in roles of leadership from the executive president to the housewife who was chairman of three clubs to the student body president of a high school. These oldest are viewed by others as conscientious, task-oriented people—even workaholics—who seem to thrive on difficult tasks. Thinking back to my school days, I remembered my always being happiest in school when I was in charge. I, too, took my positions seriously and could not rest until the job was done. By doing so, I did not have to interact as much with people on a social basis but found I had a purpose. Not comfortable with nonstructure, I was most at ease when my job was defined. Almost all the people I interviewed felt the same way and when asked why they might prefer this role, conjectured that possibly they had received more focused attention from their parents to excel and accomplish at an early age. They were also rewarded for doing well and enjoyed the positive feedback. Most were good students and/or good athletes as well. Many were considered shy loners who needed much private time. Again, this group was the only one to ever have been alone, so they wouldn't have necessarily developed social skills. Therefore, the professions chosen reflected these traits as mentioned; the preponderance of firstborns and onlys who have been President of the United States and leaders of large companies is staggering. Sometimes this serious group is considered too inflexible, too rule-oriented, and too much in control. I was always told that I needed to ''lighten up'' and not take the burden of the world on my shoulders. However, when I thought back to my earliest childhood, I felt intense responsibility when I was caretaker for my two younger sisters in addition to being their role model by setting high standards

Instead of attaching questions, maybe you could intersperse them throughout the rest of the essay.

Could you quote from some of your interviews to make this information seem more personal and immediate and less like just a summary?

That word "thrive" works well here.

Do you need to provide documented support for this statement?

and leading the way. No wonder I was serious and tense. To this day, I have a hard time sharing and am sometimes accused of being stingy. For the first four years, I had it all and then my sisters usurped my territory and my toys. My best friend, also an oldest, (oldest seem to prefer the company of oldest) felt the same way when her younger brother was born. Edington and Wilson definitely corroborated my findings and found the firstborns and onlys to be the most consistent in their character traits as opposed to the other two groups. We can speculate that less variables are at work in the first group such as divorce, death, residence change, and so on.

Good example but maybe you could dramatize it.

Why? We don't follow. Can you elaborate?

When the next child comes along, naturally the parents are more relaxed, and this trait reflects itself in the middle child who is never alone. Therefore, she tends to be gregarious, flexible, and diplomatic. My middle sister entered the world without a time clock in contrast to the ever punctual and regimented me. Her sunny disposition delighted my parents though she rarely accomplished what she set out to do. Too many diversions presented themselves along the way and, of course, I was there to provide the foil by doing the necessary tasks. All people-related jobs seem to abound with middleborns such as personnel, sales, public relations, and communication. Depending on how many children are in the family and what kind of attention he or she gets, the middle child will vie for her attention in a positive or negative way. More black sheep of families come from this category than any other. My findings definitely supported this when I counted seven troublemakers out of the eleven interviewed. To make her mark in a family, often times the middle gets attention adversely, so that her parents spend much time in the principal's office. My parents certainly attested to this finding when they remembered how they got to know the principal on a first name basis. The middle children interviewed loved parties, having grown used to comraderie early on unlike their older siblings. All the early photos of my sister and me show a serious, rigid, older sibling standing ramrod straight next to a happy, relaxed younger sibling. What a graphic illustration of our differences.

Interesting, and effective use of the word "foil."

Should you be documenting where you got the information about the black sheep and also about the people-related jobs?

We thought it might be really effective to open this whole section of the paper with a description of this photograph.

Nice use of question.

But what about the lastborn? I found this category difficult to pigeonhole in that more discrepancies seem to occur, perhaps because of so many more group dynamics at this stage in the game. Generally, our groups in class found lastborns to be compassionate and nurturing. I, too, found that ten of

Reasonable assumption, but did your interviews bear this out?

twelve people I interviewed were drawn to children, animals, and underdogs. They told me stories of their bringing stray animals home, feeding beggars, and helping outcasts. My youngest sister was forever bringing home baby birds who had fallen out of trees and children whose parents were never at home. It would seem to follow that these lastborns, then, are good in social work and nurturing professions such as nurses, doctors, and ministers. However, their overabundance of sensitivity can get them into trouble by people who take advantage of their good nature. Many in this group emulate the firstborn by competing for the leadership role so they become goal-oriented and often very successful in their chosen field. My mother's friend, Ellen, is a good example of this combination of leadership and sensitivity. Having always followed her oldest sister around who had all the firstborn qualities, Ellen became a very successful professor and writer.

Good use of example.

Many times, the youngest strives for attention because he's the baby who can't do anything yet and so purposely performs antics to become the class clown. The entertainment field is filled with the lastborns who like to be on stage. My sister has always regaled the family gatherings with her funny stories and improvisations. When she was very small, she says it was her only way to make herself known in our busy group.

Effective use of question.

Thus, it would seem that the premise, at least in my research, in our class, and in the Edington-Wilson book, is substantiated. Birth order should be looked at in character development. So what, you may ask? Other than a conversation provoker, what good is it to know someone's birth order? I mulled this over and decided it actually helped me to understand why I and my friends sometimes do the things we do. And as Edington-Wilson pointed out, it helps explain why certain marriages work and others don't. A youngest boy will naturally feel more comfortable married to an oldest sister. The original order in the family has been maintained. When two oldest who are both used to leading marry, they will have many adjustments to make in competing for the boss position. Perhaps birth order knowledge is more pragmatic than at first supposed and may very well replace the horoscope chatter at gatherings. Edington and Wilson would be pleased even though Wilson would be the first to admit, "There is life after birth order."

Doesn't seem like the paper leads up to this point about marriage as the key conclusion of your research.

Nice way to bring opening back in.

Good use of quote.

Attachment

Interview Questions

1. What is your profession? Proposed profession? Why?

2. What do you enjoy doing most? Why?

3. What do you think of as your best qualities?

4. What do you think of as your worst qualities?

5. Do others see these in the same way?

6. Think back to an earliest childhood incident and tell me about it.

7. Do you feel birth order findings for your category to be relevant to your life? How so?

Once students have critiqued the model, ask them to break into peer groups and to silently read the papers of their group members, noting their individual comments, questions and suggestions in the margins. Each group should then select one of the first drafts which they feel is off to a particularly good start. Each group should read their chosen paper aloud to the whole class who will discuss 1. Why it is effective and 2. How it can be improved.

Revising

Students receive their own papers back, including the written feedback from their peers. Any questions raised by the response group need to be resolved. Students will take papers home for revision. A second draft will be shared in a one-to-one conference with the teacher. It might help to assign a piece of expressive writing, "What I Really Meant to Say Was . . ." that the students also bring to the conference. The teacher can then verify for the student whether or not his intended message came across clearly in the paper.

Sample "What I Really Meant to Say Was . . ." statements for the student model in the *SHARING* section of this lesson are included below:

"What I really meant to say was . . .
Even though people should not be categorized quickly like inanimate objects, the assumption that we all see things differently may be based on the way we've been raised—possibly birth order expectations. This awareness may help us understand ourselves and others more easily.

or

"What I really meant to say was . . .
More than anything I've read in the field of psychology, the study of birth order has given me some creditable insight into the interactions of siblings within the family and later on into their adult lives.

Editing

The students will edit with a partner for the conventions of written English. This task could be conducted in or out of class. The editing partner should sign the corrected essay. The corrected copy should be stapled to the earlier drafts and handed in on the due date.

Evaluation

An "A" essay truly excels, includes superior critical thinking skills, and:

- Has a well-defined premise
- Consistently develops an argument either for or against the validity of birth order theory and applies theoretical hypotheses to personal experience
- Effectively illustrates main points with specific examples
- Follows standard expository format—introduction, main body, and conclusion
- Has smooth transitions
- Uses apt, precise and/or descriptive language and ample sentence variety
- Uses proper format for documenting secondary sources
- Has few, if any, errors in the conventions of written English

A "B" essay falls short of excellence but is very good. It includes the following:

- Still has a well-defined premise
- Does not develop in as much depth and does not apply theorectical hypotheses to personal experience
- Follows standard expository format but the introduction, main body, and conclusion are not equally strong
- Examples are not as detailed as in an "A" paper
- Has some smooth transitions
- Has good command of the language but it is not as apt, precise or descriptive as in an "A" paper
- Uses proper format for documenting secondary sources
- Has a few errors in the conventions of written English but none that interfere with the message

A "C" essay is average. It includes the following:

- Establishes a thesis but fails to define it clearly
- Is not well organized and doesn't develop or apply theoretical hypotheses to personal experience in depth
- Makes points but fails to use adequate examples; doesn't elaborate with enough detail
- Has some semblance of standard expository format, but it may be difficult to tell where the introduction, main body, and conclusion begin and end
- Attempts transitions

- Has little sentence variety; ordinary word choice; some awkward jumps in thought
- Documents secondary sources improperly or fails to document information that clearly should be footnoted
- Has many errors in the conventions of written English but none that interfere with the message of the paper

A "D" essay is below average. It includes the following:

- Is impossible to find the thesis. If found, it may be impossible to figure out
- Organization is unclear
- Student does not develop ideas or apply theoretical hypotheses to personal experiences
- Has no examples to support assertions
- Does not follow standard expository format
- Disregards transitions
- Exhibits poor language skills
- Fails to consult secondary sources or even to cite first-hand interviews
- Has many problems in the conventions of written English that inhibit the reader's understanding of the essay

An "F" essay is failing. It contains all the weaknesses of a "D" paper and either misunderstands or fails to seriously attempt to address the assignment.

Extension Activities

Evaluation   Because students gather so much information in order to develop a premise for the birth order essay and because the subject matter is highly debatable, students tend to get very involved and may want to use the idea for a more in-depth research or "Personalized Research Paper." (See the last lesson under the *EVALUATION* section of this book.) In the past few years, most libraries have stocked their shelves with many sources by reputable authorities. A personalized research assignment might look something like this:

Prompt: After presenting what you know, assume or imagine about the effect birth order has on character traits, conduct a search of both first and second hand sources to test out your theory. Then, compare what you thought prior to your research with what you actually learned, draw some conclusions about the validity of the birth order theory and its relevance to your life, and assess the value of what you learned.

4 Analysis

Who Are You?

Lesson

Students will write analytical/expository sentences about a classmate based on an analysis of a cut-and-paste collage which each student will make about him/herself.

Objectives

Thinking Skills

In order to become more familiar with each other, students will work at the *ANALYSIS* level by *EXAMINING* a collage poster depicting another student and then *DRAWING CONCLUSIONS* about why the person chose those particular pictures to express him/herself following the guidelines set in the prompt.

The students will *LIST, SUMMARIZE, INTERPRET,* and *INFER* in order to *ANALYZE* the pictures and write about the collage artist.

Writing Skills

Students will write analytical/expository sentences about a classmate by analyzing a collage. The first sentence will tell whom the writing is about. The supporting sentences will describe that person's favorite color, thing, food, activity, and what frightens that person. Each of the supporting sentences will also suggest reasons for that person's preferences based on the writer's inferences from the collage. The last sentence will be a conclusion. Editing stress will be placed on capital letters and periods at the K-1 level. (A suggestion for paragraph format suitable for grades 2–3 is provided in the *EXTENSION ACTIVITIES* at the end of this lesson.)

The Process

This is an excellent activity to be presented over several days at the beginning of the year in order to facilitate the students and the teacher getting to know one another.

Prewriting

The prewriting phase consists of three components:

- motivating questions and discussion
- modeling how to make a collage
- making collages

Materials needed:

- A collection of magazines from which pictures will be cut
- An envelope for each student for storing pictures
- Paste
- Scissors
- 12″ × 18″ construction paper for collage backing
- Paper for writing sentences
- A photo of each student (or a self-portrait drawn by a student if a photo is unavailable)
- Teacher-prepared collage materials of him/herself for *COMPONENT TWO.*

Component One

During the motivational section of the lesson, the teacher's goals will be:

- to help students discover that they can get to know one another better;
- to demonstrate that we can communicate not only by talking and listening, but also through pictures and through writing and reading.

In order to reach these goals, the teacher will ask the students to name others whom they knew before the year started and then to state a neighbor's name and a favorite pastime. Following the question about a student's favorite pastime, the teacher asks those who already *knew* what the student's favorite pastime was to raise their hands in order to note how many students already knew the information. Additional questions may be asked:

- Does anyone know what someone's favorite color is in this class?
- Does anyone know what someone else's favorite food is in this class?
- Does anyone know what frightens someone else in this class?
- Who else is frightened by this?

After each question, the teacher asks those who knew the answer beforehand to raise their hands. Fewer hands will be raised as the questions become more difficult and the answers more subjective. During this time, the teacher will stress that students may have more to learn about each other in order to get to know one another better. The teacher, then, will ask students to describe experiences they may have had concerning how they felt about a person before they actually got to know him/her, how they felt after they had had the opportunity to get to know the person better, and how much the friendship was based on similar likes and dislikes.

With the use of pictures (of a tired person, a happy person, a sad person, a frightened person, etc.), the teacher will encourage students to make inferences about the feelings that are shown by the people in the pictures and to share their inferences with the class. The object of this exploration is to show students that information about someone or something can be gathered without requiring written words.

However, in order to emphasize that written words can give us more information, the teacher will use the same pictures and elicit various conclusions about the reasons for the facial expressions shown in the pictures. For example:

- This man is happy because. . .
- This girl is sad because. . .
- This boy is mad because. . .
- This woman is frightened because. . .

As each sentence is completed, the teacher will write student responses on the board. Finally, the teacher will explain that without reasons and words, we wouldn't know as much about the people in the pictures. Using the language experience approach, the teacher will emphasize that writing words and then reading them is a way to know more about a person.

Component Two

Beginning with a recent picture of him/herself, the teacher will model how to make a collage. Prior to this step, in order to save time, the teacher will have cut out pictures from magazines following the same guidelines that students will use—stressing the importance of choosing pictures which accurately reflect his/her personality.

The following student guidelines may be written on the board or charted as the teacher models them:

- Who is this picture of? (Paste a photograph—or draw a picture—of yourself on your poster.)
- What is your favorite color? (Paste five pictures of your favorite color on your collage.)
- What is something you like very much? (Find three pictures of this favorite item and paste them on your collage.)
- What foods do you like? (Find two pictures of the same food that you like to eat and paste them on your collage.)
- What do you like to do? (Find one picture of someone doing that activity and paste it on your collage.)
- What frightens you? (Find one picture of something which scares you and paste it on your collage.)

The teacher will then ask each question and model a response:

Question: Who is this picture of?
Teacher's Response: ''It's a picture of me.''

Question: What is your favorite color?
Teacher's Response: ''My favorite color is red. I have five pictures of red on my collage.''

Question:	What is something you like very much?
Teacher's Response:	"I like sailboats very much, and I have three pictures of sailboats on my collage."
Question:	What foods do you like?
Teacher's Response:	"I like to eat grapes, so I have two pictures of grapes on my collage."
Question:	What do you like to do?
Teacher's Response:	"I like canoeing, so I have a picture of a person canoeing on my collage."
Question:	What frightens you?
Teacher's Response:	"When I see polar bears, I get scared. I have a picture of a polar bear on my collage."

During modeling, the teacher will stress the importance of choosing pictures which actually reflect one's own personality.

Component Three

After the teacher has modeled how to make a collage, the students each will then make a collage. With magazines, scissors, and an envelope, students will cut out pictures following the guidelines stated above. When pictures are cut out, the student will place them in an envelope for safekeeping. Students will have the option of finding pictures in magazines at home to add to their collections, but each must have the designated number of pictures on the finished collage (1 picture of the student, 5 of a color, 3 of the same favorite thing, 2 of the same favorite food, 1 of an activity, and 1 of a frightening thing.)

The next day, students will paste their pictures onto 12″ × 18″ sheets of construction paper beginning with their own photo (or a self-portrait drawn if a photo is not available.)

When the collages are complete, put them on display around the room.

Using the following questions, the teacher will model how to interpret the pictures on the collage which he/she made. This interpretation is presented orally. (A second analysis of the collage will occur during precomposing. It will involve clusters and language experience frames elicited from the students for their writing.)

Questions:

Question:	Whose collage is this? Whom is this collage about?
Sample Response:	Ms. McCurdy.
Question:	How do you know that this is Ms. McCurdy's collage?
Sample Response:	Her picture is on it.
Question:	What is this person's favorite color?
Sample Response:	Red is her favorite color.

Question: How do you know that red is her favorite color?
Sample Response: She has five pictures of the color red on her collage.

Question: Why do you think she might like the color red?
Sample Response: It is the color of fire engines. Apples are red, etc.

Question: What do you think is Ms. McCurdy's favorite thing?
Sample Response: Sailboats.

Question: How do you know this?
Sample Response: She has three pictures of sailboats.

Question: Why do you think she likes sailboats?
Sample Response: They go in the ocean or on lakes. They go up and down over waves, etc.

Question: What food does Ms. McCurdy like?
Sample Response: She likes grapes.

Question: How do you know this?
Sample Response: She has two pictures of grapes on her collage and grapes are food.

Question: Why do you think she likes grapes?
Sample Response: Grapes are sweet. Green grapes don't have seeds. Grapes are juicy, etc.

Question: What does Ms. McCurdy like to do?
Sample Response: She likes to go canoeing.

Question: How do you know this?
Sample Response: There is one picture of a person canoeing.

Question: But there is one picture of polar bears on her collage. Just because there is only 1 picture does not necessarily mean that she likes to do something. So why do you think canoeing is what she likes to do?
Sample Response: Polar bears are animals. Canoeing is something people do, etc.

Question: What frightens Ms. McCurdy?
Sample Response: Polar bears frighten her.

Question: How do you know?
Sample Response: There is one picture of polar bears.

Question: Why do you think that polar bears frighten her?
Sample Response: The polar bears look scary. Their teeth are showing, etc.

Question:	Does this picture frighten you?
Sample Response:	Yes, because the bear looks mean and hungry.
Question:	Looking at the collage, is there something on it that Ms. McCurdy likes that you like too?
Sample Response:	I like the color red.
Question:	Do friends sometimes like the same things?
Sample Response:	Yes.
Question:	Would you like Ms. McCurdy as a friend?
Sample Response:	Yes, because we both like red.

Assign each student a partner. Partners will be responsible for writing about each other by analyzing their partner's collage.

Prompt:

Now that you have a picture collage of your partner that shows who your partner is, what your partner likes, and what frightens him/her, you are going to write seven sentences that tell other people about your partner. We will put your sentences up next to your partner's collage. Then we can all learn more about the people in our class by reading about them and looking at the pictures, too.

- The first sentence tells whom the collage is about.
- The next sentence tells what his/her favorite color is and why you think he/she might like this color.
- The third sentence tells what his/her favorite thing is and why you think he/she might like it.
- The fourth sentence tells what his/her favorite food is and why you think he/she might like that food.
- The fifth sentence tells what he/she likes to do and why you think that he/she likes to do that activity.
- The sixth sentence tells what frightens him/her and why you think he/she may be frightened by it.
- The last sentence is an ending sentence that tells why you might like this person for a friend.

Begin every sentence with a capital letter and end it with a period.

Precomposing

Analyze the collages using the same questioning techniques and guidelines as during prewriting when the teacher modeled drawing conclusions about his/her collage. The difference between this step and the prewriting is that the teacher will now write sentence frames on the board and the students will provide answers. The teacher can use a collage from a student in another class as a model while students look at their partner's collage and relate the pictures to him/her.

The teacher will ask the questions one at a time and encourage students to cluster for inferences about why the partner might like (or be frightened by) the picture representations. As the students provide sentences, the teacher will write them on the board as frames for the students to copy. (For K-1 classes, the students may dictate their answers.)

Each sentence required in the prompt will be presented individually with the writing step following the precomposing. One or two sentences only will be covered in a day's lesson. For example:

Question: Look at your partner's collage. Whose collage is it? What is your partner's name? Think of a sentence that you could write that would tell everyone who read it whom the collage is about.

Sample response: This is *Dana's* collage. This collage is about *Dana*.

Writing

Students will choose one of the sentences from the board and write (or dictate) it on their papers. During this time, the teacher will circulate around the room to give assistance when requested.

Precomposing

Next, have the students analyze their partner's favorite color, again utilizing the questions from prewriting. With the teacher continuing to model the procedure, the students will work on their analyses.

Question: What is this person's favorite color?
Sample Response: *Dana's* favorite color is *blue*.

Question: Why do you think Dana likes blue?

In order to think about the reasons someone may like blue, the teacher will model a cluster on blue and then instruct the students to cluster on the color represented on their partner's collage. Students may use words or pictures in their clusters. (The inferences which students make do not have to be their partner's reasons for liking the color.)

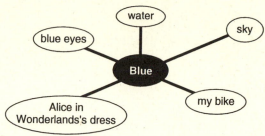

The teacher will write the following frame on the board and model how to fill it in after clustering on the sample collage:

_____ is _____'s favorite color because it is

_____ .

Sample Response: *Blue* is *Dana's* favorite color because it is *the color of the sky.*

Writing

Students will copy the frame and fill it in with information from the collage on which they are working and also from their own clusters which provide inferences for the color preference.

This recursive procedure will be followed as students write each sentence in accordance with the requirements of the prompt.

Precomposing

Sample sentence frames:

_____ likes _____. _____ are

_____ .

Sample Response: Dana likes bikes. Bikes are fast.

_____ tastes _____. I bet that is why _____

likes _____.

Sample Response: Cake tastes sweet. I bet that is why Dana likes cake.

_____ likes to _____ because _____

is/are _____ .

Sample Response: Dana likes to go to the movies because movies are exciting.

_____ frighten _____ . _____

are _____ .
Sample Response: Ghosts frighten Dana. Ghosts are in a haunted house.

_____ is my new friend because we both like _____ .
Sample Response: Dana is my new friend because we both like movies.

Sharing

As this may be the students' first experience in sharing, the teacher may choose to model how to share and re-read the writing for revision by providing guided practice before the students undertake independent sharing and revising. Thus the teacher will make two copies of the chart for each student. One will be filled out by the author, the other will be filled out by the sharing partner.

- The teacher will pass out one copy of the following chart to each student who will use it along with his/her own writing.

Your name _____

Author's name _____

Directions: Fill in the blanks and write yes or no in the boxes	Does Each Sentence:	
	begin with a **Capital Letter?**	end with a **Period?**
Name of person written about _____		
Favorite color _____		
Favorite thing _____		
Favorite food _____		
What does the person like to do? _____		
What frightens the subject? _____		
Why might the author and the subject be friends? _____		

Why do you like this sentence? _____

What was your favorite sentence? _____

- Using a piece of writing based on the sample collage, the teacher will model how to use the chart for sharing by comparing each item on the chart with the actual written sentences. (The sharing chart may be written on the board for this group exercise.)
- The teacher will read the first sentence aloud, and then read the first item on the chart. Next, the teacher will fill in the chart by writing the name of the person written about on the blank. Following this, the teacher will check that sentence for capital letters and periods and fill in the boxes with yes or no responses.
- Each sentence will be compared with its corresponding item on the chart in step-by-step fashion with the teacher's guidance for the students in a group setting as they complete the chart based on their own writing.
- Once the students have had guided practice reviewing their own writing with the chart, the students will have independent practice sharing their writing with their partner (about whom the collage was analyzed.) The teacher will pass out new copies of the chart to each student. By sharing their pieces of writing and utilizing the chart, students will read each sentence (written by his/her partner) and complete the chart in a step-by-step manner. Then the chart and writing will be returned to the author.

(*Note: The accuracy of the inferences is *not* the intent of this lesson. However, if a partner disagrees vehemently with a reason, both students may need to review the collage for a correct interpretation of the pictures. This sharing provides the students with the opportunity to get to know each other as well as to share and revise their writing.)

Revising

At primary grade levels, the teacher may need to guide the students through the revision process. Again, the teacher may model how to interpret the chart in order to promote revision.

- During this step, the teacher will apply information from the chart directly onto the sample draft by crossing out and adding information as needed reinforcing that neatness is not necessary, nor the objective yet, in this step of the writing process.
- After revisions have been made, the students will write their final copy.

Editing

Students will meet with their partners to check their final writing for capitalization and periods.

Evaluation

Primary Trait Scoring Guide

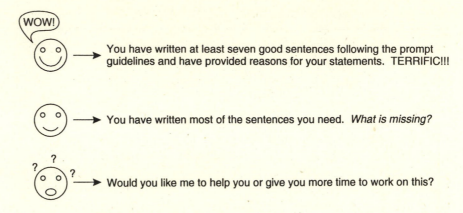

You have written at least seven good sentences following the prompt guidelines and have provided reasons for your statements. TERRIFIC!!!

You have written most of the sentences you need. *What is missing?*

Would you like me to help you or give you more time to work on this?

Secondary Trait Scoring Guide

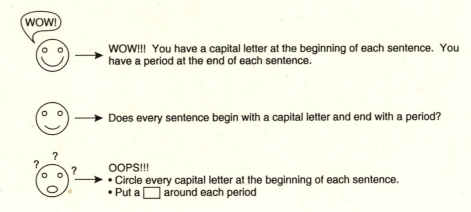

WOW!!! You have a capital letter at the beginning of each sentence. You have a period at the end of each sentence.

Does every sentence begin with a capital letter and end with a period?

OOPS!!!
• Circle every capital letter at the beginning of each sentence.
• Put a ☐ around each period

Extension Activities

The following steps will enable teachers to adapt this lesson for a higher elementary grade level with emphasis on paragraph structure.

1. Use the chart below with sentence frames and colored pencils to give students an opportunity to begin to recognize paragraph structure.

Color Green	Color Blue	Color Red
Beginning Choose 1 sentence.	**Middle** Choose at least 3.	**End** Choose 1 sentence.
This collage is about ____. This is _____'s collage.	_____ is _____'s favorite color because it is _____. _____ likes _____. _____ is/are _____. _____ tastes _____. I bet that is why _____ likes _____. _____ frighten _____. _____ are _____.	_____ is my new friend because we both like _____. I like _____ because he/she likes _____.

2. Students will write their first drafts using colored pencils which correspond to the colors on the paragraph chart in order to emphasize the parts of the paragraph. With this technique, they will organize their sentences into a paragraph.

3. Students will count the number of sentences in each color to make sure that they are following the chart correctly.

4. Students will revise their writing depending upon the feedback they receive during sharing.

5. Students will write their second draft without using colored pencils.

6. Students will check each other's work for correct paragraph organization.

7. The teacher will adjust prompt and rubrics to fit his/her class requirements concerning the paragraph.

It's All in the Way You See It

A Lesson on Different Perspectives

Lesson

Students will analyze Thanksgiving from varying perspectives.

Objectives

Thinking Skills
Students will *EXAMINE* what happens on Thanksgiving, *ANALYZE* it from three points of view, and *DISTINGUISH* elements significant to each separate perspective.

Writing Skills
Students will write three analytical paragraphs in which they support each main idea with at least three details. They will add a fourth paragraph comparing and contrasting the three points of view and explaining why they vary.

The Process

Prewriting

Explain to the class:

Our point of view is the way we see or view something. It is based on our experience and our perceptions of what we see, hear, taste, smell, touch, and feel. Through these exercises, you will see that there can be many different opinions/ points of view concerning one topic.

1. Pass out dittoes with the figures on the next page or make a transparency to go on the overhead projector. Discuss each figure individually, asking the following questions:

   - Figures 1 & 2: What figure do you see? Explain?
                     Can you see another figure? What?
                     What do you have to do to see another figure?
   - Figure 3:   Which line is the longest? How can you tell? Why does one seem longer than another?
   - Figure 4:   Are the crosses getting larger or smaller? Observe and explain how either answer could be correct.

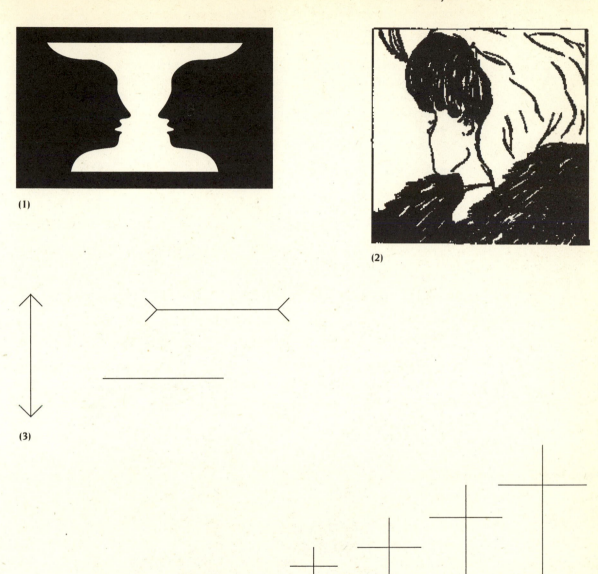

(1)

(2)

(3)

(4)

Explain: What we see is based on our particular point of view or perspective. Two people looking at the same object may often see very different things. To see another person's point of view, we have to shift our perspective.

Note: Answer key is at the bottom of the last page of this lesson (following EXTENSION ACTIVITIES).

FIGURE 12: Perspective Figures

2. Direct students to think about one subject: a baseball game.

- What specific people would have feelings/opinions about a baseball game? For example, who might really like it or dislike it? (Possibilities are a fifth-grade Little Leaguer, a member of the Dodgers, a homeowner who lives next door to a baseball diamond, the baseball, and home plate.)
- Choose three of the suggested points of view. As a class, cluster the feelings and/or opinions about baseball for each of the chosen individuals.

Sample Clusters

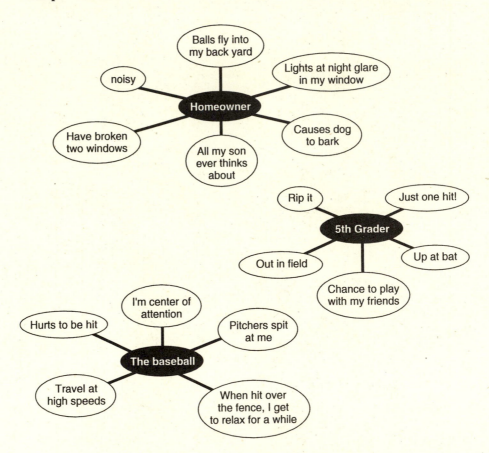

- In partners, have students share their three different perspectives. After reading their cluster to each other, students should choose one of the clusters and work together to add more ideas to it. They should consider:
  - What would the particular "personality" see? Hear? Feel? Do (both physically and emotionally)?
  - When they have expanded the cluster, students should continue working in partners to write a paragraph showing a baseball game from that personal-

ity's perspective. Remind them to be sure to use "I" and to speak in the language they think that personality would use.

3. Match partners with other pairs who have chosen different personalities to portray. Create groups of six to share three points of view.

    Direct each group to discuss and write the following:

    - After you have listened to all three perspectives, answer the following questions:
      - What can you conclude about the differences in points of view?
      - Can you see any similarities?
      - Why do you think the perspectives vary as they do?

4. Select one group's answers and put them on an overhead to model possibilities for drawing conclusions. Ask the class if there are any other similarities, differences and conclusions they can draw from the three perspectives.

Prompt:

Examine Thanksgiving from three different perspectives: a mother who is cooking Thanksgiving dinner, a turkey who will be served for Thanksgiving dinner, and you who will eat the dinner. Use first person point of view ("I"). Write a paragraph from the point of view of each of those "personalities." In other words, become the mother, the turkey and then yourself and explain in each personality's voice how each feels about Thanksgiving. In each of these paragraphs, be sure to include the main feeling you have about Thanksgiving from that personality's perspective, and use at least three details to support your feeling. In a fourth paragraph, compare and contrast the three perspectives and explain why these vary. Arrange your paragraphs to best show the perspective you feel is most significant. Also, include a title that ties the various perspectives together.

Precomposing

1. Pass out three sheets of blank paper and crayons for drawing. Ask students to picture Thanksgiving day in their minds and ask the following questions:

    - Where do you see your mother? What is she doing? Focus in on one specific thing she does for Thanksgiving and draw her doing that thing.
    - Where do you see the turkey? What is happening to it? Draw what is happening to the turkey on a second piece of paper.

- Where do you see yourself? What are you doing? Draw yourself at Thanksgiving on a third piece of paper.

2. Have students share their drawings with a partner, and then brainstorm sensory words in a cluster on each picture. For each picture, they should consider:

- What is the main subject of your picture?
- What does the main subject look like?
- What objects surround the main subject of your picture? You may list more objects than you draw.
- What other sights, sounds, smells, tastes and textures do you associate with your picture?

For Example:

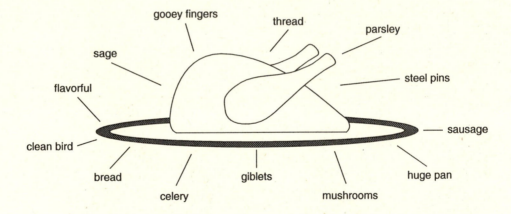

3. In new groups of three, have students role-play each of the personalities they have drawn and clustered. One plays the turkey, one the mother and one the child. Each speaker uses the voice of his character, expressing his feelings about Thanksgiving and explaining why he feels that way. During the role-play, each character speaks, one after the other. After each has a say, the characters may dialogue with each other. This role play will help students focus attention on the varying perspectives.

4. Pass out a chart for students to list perceptions of each personality (both positive and negative). Explain to students:

- Pretend you are each of the following personalities. List some of the good and bad points you would experience at Thanksgiving.

Perspectives		
Mother's	**Turkey's**	**Mine**
+ • I love to entertain • Happy time to be with my whole family	• Farmer S. has treated me well all these years • I'm glad to serve his family	• Yeah! • Vacation • Good food! • I get to make turkey baskets out of construction paper • Get to play with cousin
– • Too much work • 20 people for dinner is nerve-wracking • No fun to clean house • Baste turkey for five hours—eat it all in 20 minutes	• Have to hide in yard to save my life • I live in confinement for years only to be slaughtered	• Have to see all the relatives • Have to get dressed up
Conclusion: What can you conclude about the differences in perspectives? Why do you think the perspectives vary as much as they do?		

Writing

Transposing ideas into actual paragraphs is often a frightening step for inexperienced writers. To build confidence along the way, try breaking the process into parts.

1. Ask students to begin with the picture/cluster and chart of the personality they like the best. Using however much information they want from these idea lists, they are to write a paragraph from the perspective of the personality. If they think of more details as they write, it's okay to add them in also.

2. After they've written the first paragraph, have the students pause to take a look at it and answer the following questions for themselves:

   • What kind of personality is portrayed in the paragraph? List two adjectives that describe what he/she/it is like.
   • What words, phrases, or ideas in your paragraph best show these traits?
   • How does the subject feel about Thanksgiving?
   • What details in the paragraph best show that feeling? List them.
   • What detail least shows that feeling? List it.

- Add a sentence to any weak details that will make them show your subject's feelings about Thanksgiving more clearly.

Sharing

Allow students time to share orally this first paragraph with their original partners. Response partners will look for the same qualities in another's paper that they have just seen in their own.

A sample paragraph might look like this:

Boy, I just can't wait until Thanksgiving! I've seen pictures of turkeys everywhere celebrating this holiday. So, I know I must play a key role. Maybe I'll be the guest of honor in Farmer Brown's house. Gee, it makes my mouth water just to think of the delectable bread stuffing and tangy cranberries. Wonder what Mrs. B. will serve for the main dish. Main dish. Hmm. *MAIN DISH*!! Wait . . . Am I the *MAIN DISH*? Oh, how I dread Thanksgiving. There won't be anything for me to be thankful for. I better go find a secret place in the barn to hide. Maybe they'll forget about me and serve ham.

The goal is to compare what the writer thinks he is saying with what the reader is getting. By sharing their two perspectives, the writer may find new additions or deletions he wants to make in the paragraph.

Revising

Time should be allowed for writers to make any changes that they think are necessary at this point before they go to their next paragraph. They may also want to come back and to make more changes later when all their paragraphs are drafted.

Writing

1. Before students write their next paragraph in which they form the next personality's perspective, ask them to note somewhere on their picture/cluster sheet what they want the next paragraph to do:

   - What do you want to show with this personality?
   - Will this personality be a contrast to the first? Or will it be sympathetic to the first?

2. When they have thought about the purpose their paragraph will have, they should be able to begin writing. For their next two paragraphs, have students follow the same *WRITING, SHARING, REVISING* steps they began with the first paragraph.

Sharing

Once the three perspective paragraphs have been written, have students work with a new partner. This time, as they listen to their partner's paragraphs, responders should listen for conclusions they can draw about the three perspectives. Then, as a pair, they answer the following questions:

- How does each personality feel about Thanksgiving?
- What role does each character play in Thanksgiving?
- What similarities and differences do you see in perspectives between the mother and turkey, mother and child, and the child and the turkey? Chart these.

Personalities	Similarities	Differences
Mother and Turkey		
Mother and Child		
Turkey and Child		

- How do the similarities you found between any two of the personalities relate to their role in and their feelings about Thanksgiving?
- How do the differences you found between any two of the personalities relate to their role in or feelings about Thanksgiving?
- What can you conclude from your chart about why these three perspectives vary the way they do?
- Whose perspective do you like the best? Why?

Writing

From this sharing, as well as the conclusions they drew in answering the questions about the three perspectives, students should be able to write their fourth paragraph. Suggest that this paragraph include a general statement and a couple of more specific statements that explain it.

Revising

Now that the students have all their paragraphs written, their next step is to decide how they want to order them most effectively. The comparisons and contrasts they have written about in their fourth paragraph may help them decide on the arrangement. You might ask them to consider these questions:

- Where should the turkey go—before or after the mother?
- Should the perspective you like best begin your piece or end it?
- Where should the comparison and contrast paragraph go—in the beginning? In the middle? At the end?

As a last step in completing their piece, students should give their paper a title that is appropriate to the overall effect they want their perspectives on Thanksgiving to have on their readers.

Optional activity: As a class, brainstorm some catchy titles for this assignment. Examples might be: A Day in a Life; Let's Get Stuffed; Thanks for Giving, Turkey, etc.

Editing

Students should write their final piece in class.

Before they write, do the following spelling checks:

1. Ask students to circle any words they feel might be spelled incorrectly in their papers. They raise their hands for any words they are unsure about. As you call in each student and hear the problem word, refer him to someone in class who can spell it, or send him to a dictionary with a partner, or spell the word correctly on the board. The student corrects the spelling and continues to check his/her paper. Keep going until all hands are down and thus all words have been edited.

2. Ask students to check their paragraphs. You might say, "You have four paragraphs in your paper. How many indentations should you have? (4) Check them. If you do not have four, find where you forgot to indent and draw an arrow to remind you to do so in your final draft."

3. To check sentencing, ask students to trade papers with a neighbor. Direct the partner to put a question mark in the margin near any statement that is not clear. When they trade papers back, the writer should check each questioned sentence to make sure it says what he/she wants it to.

4. As students write their final draft, remind them to write neatly and legibly.

5. After editing the piece, students may want to illustrate each point of view with new sketches of each personality they portrayed.

Evaluation

The following scoring guide can be used either for teachers who grade by the point system or by those who want to average the total points together and determine a letter grade.

Perspectives

1	2	3	4	5
I don't hear clear perspectives		I hear some of the personalities better than others.		Yes, I hear 3 clear personalities. Your piece shows distinct perspectives.

Voice

1	2	3	4	5
Let your characters each tell their stories in their own words.		Be sure to stay inside the speaker and use ''I.'' The differences between each personality's voice are not completely clear.		Yes, effective and accurate. Each character spoke personally and in a natural, believable language.

Feeling

1	2	3	4	5
The main feeling of each character is not clear.		The main feeling of each personality is reasonably clear.		The main feeling of each personality is very clear.

Detail

1	2	3	4	5
Use more concrete details to support feelings. Name things. Photograph with words.		Some good use of details. Look at your cluster. Did you use the best details to support feelings?		You put me there! Choice of details to support feelings is excellent.

Comparison/Constrast Paragraph

1	2	3	4	5
Your comparison/contrast ¶ is too vague to make your point clearly.		I don't quite see precisely why the perceptions vary.		You make an interesting comparison and contrast that clearly explains why the perspectives vary.

Placement of Paragraphs

1	2	3	4	5
You don't seem to have any reason for placement of ¶.		Try placing one of your paragraphs somewhere else.		Your placement effectively portrays the contrast in perspectives.

Proofreading

1	2	3	4	5
Spend more time. Check spelling and handwriting.		Only a few errors. Neat and readable.		No errors. Good work.

FIGURE 13: Scoring Giude

Extension Activities

Evaluation

Prompt: Try to persuade someone else, through debate, of your perspective on a topic such as one of the following. Consider the differing perspective of the people you are trying to persuade, anticipate what objectives they would raise to your perspective, and overcome their objections with logical arguments.

- Assigned areas during recess
- Cafeteria lunches
- Homework
- Need to learn a particular subject
- Chores
- Allowance
- Bedtime
- Access to television

ANSWER KEY to second page of lesson:

Figure 1:   vase/pedestal
two faces

Figure 2:   side view of pretty woman; choker around neck
more frontal view of ugly woman; large nose

Figure 3:   All lines are the same length.

Figure 4:   It depends on your perspective.

Writing Domain: Analytical/Expository   **Thinking Level: Analysis**
                                                              Grade Level: Intermediate

Pac Man or Kick the Can?

A Comparison of Growing Up Now With Growing Up During the Depression

Lesson

Students will write a multi-paragraph analytical/expository essay comparing growing up during the Depression with growing up today.

Objectives

Thinking Skills
Based on an analysis of toys and/or games, students will *ANALYZE* childhood
during the Depression and childhood today by writing an essay in which they:

- *EXAMINE* one or more toys and/or games of the Depression;
- *DESCRIBE* one or more toys and/or games that they enjoy;
- *CHARACTERIZE* each type of childhood;
- *COMPARE* the two types of childhood;
- *CONTRAST* the differences between them;
- *DRAW CONCLUSIONS* about growing up in each period of history.

Writing Skills
Students will write an analytical/expository paper using:

- logical organization;
- topic sentences;
- examples;
- details;
- transitions;
- concluding sentences.

The Process

This lesson should be scheduled late in the school year after sentence structure and
paragraph structure have been taught and practiced. It may encompass seven or
more class periods in a social studies or an English class.

Prewriting

1. The lesson asks the students to interview one of their grandparents or someone
   who lived during the Depression, and, using information gathered in their
   interviews and classwork, to plan and write a three-paragraph comparison of
   childhood during the Depression with childhood today.

   Explain the prompt (see next section) and assign due dates for interview
   results worksheets.

2. Present an introductory lecture on the Depression (1929–1939), stressing the
   problems of unemployment, poverty and hunger generated by this worldwide
   economic crash and the responses to these conditions by the people and the
   government. Two good sources of information are William Manchester's *The
   Glory and the Dream* (Boston: Little, Brown and Co., 1973) and James

Agee's book *Let Us Now Praise Famous Men* (Boston: Houghton Mifflin, 1960).

3. Since students will be gathering data based on personal interviews, discuss interview sources, manners, and methods. This outline can be given to the students or they can take notes on a fill-in-the-blank worksheet containing the information.

- Sources
  - Relatives
  - Neighbors
  - Convalescent home
  - Parents' friends or grandparents' friends

- Manners and methods
  - Be polite.
  - Be yourself; be natural.
  - If responses bring other questions to mind, ask them.
  - Listen attentively.
  - Don't get stuck on questions; not every one must be answered.
  - Take notes or tape your interview or take a friend who can take notes with you.

4. Before students conduct their interviews, allow them to practice introducing themselves and asking questions. The following guidelines will help the students get off to a good start with their interviews:

- Interview introduction:
  - Before you start the interview, introduce yourself (if you need to) and find out the person's name.
  - Explain that you are collecting information for a paper you will write for your history/English class.
  - Describe the topic of the paper.

5. Choose a student to interview as a demonstration for the class. Pass out the list of interview questions included below so that students can follow along as you conduct your interview.

- Interview questions:
  - Where did you grow up? Was it more rural or urban?
  - Describe your neighborhood.
  - How many brothers and sisters do you have?
  - Did you have a lot of friends in your neighborhood?
  - Which word best describes how you lived?
    well-off   average   below average

- How did you spend your free time as a child?
- Did you work or do odd jobs?
- What chores were your responsibility at home?
- Do you remember your childhood as a happy time?
- What do you think the main differences are between growing up when you were a child and growing up today?

- Questions About Toys
  - What kind of toys did you have?
  - Did you make them or buy them?
  - Where did you get the materials?
  - How did you make them?
  - Were your toys important to you?
  - Did you use your imagination to play with them?
  - What was your favorite toy? Describe it.

- Questions About Games
  - What types of games did you play?
  - Name the games you played as child. (Example: Kick the Can)
  - What things did you need to play the game(s)? (Example: A stick and a ball)
  - Was the game based more on rules, objects, or your imagination?
  - How many kids played?
  - What are the rules?
  - How long did a game take?
  - Was it fun?

Model taking notes during this interview by jotting things down on transparencies projected by an overhead.

6. After you model the process, students should practice interview questions and note taking in pairs:

- Ask students to write down the results of their practice interviews:
  - List their own toys/games and list their partner's toys/games in two columns.
  - Mark the items that are the same.
  - Using the models which follow, write five one sentence statements about the similarities and differences between the lists.

(*Note: Because of the age level of the students, some questions on the interview sheet will have to be phrased in present tense. If you can arrange for someone from the community who grew up during the Depression to come in and share their impressions with your class, that would be even better.)

Models:

We both like to _____. Neither of us enjoy _____.

I like to _____, but _____ likes to

_____.

_____, _____ , and _____ are

the three things we have in common.

7. To help students get a better idea of what life was like during the Depression, do a guided imagery exercise:

- Turn off the lights,
- Slowly read the following narrative, pausing between each sentence to allow students to create an image in their minds:

Close your eyes and picture yourself as a twelve-year-old growing up on the outskirts of a large town in Indiana. Your family has a small wooden farmhouse with a screened front porch. Other houses are close by, but there is wide open space around them. There are wide, flat, green fields of grass extending for miles, interrupted only by a few trees and farmhouses. The sky above is clearer than you've ever seen before, and the air smells clean. The late afternoon sun is not too warm, but the moisture in the air makes you feel restless.

You are in your backyard helping your mother take clothes off the line when you see some of your friends playing in a field. Your mom says it's okay for you to join them, so you run over to play Kick the Can. Two girls are standing next to a base with a tin can on it. ''Hey, you're it,'' one of your friends yells from behind a tree. The other kids are all hiding and you have to find them all to make someone else ''it.'' As you start to look, a boy runs up from behind you, kicking the can off the base. The two girls run away to hide since they are free. You play until the sun goes down.

Dusk has fallen. The fireflies are blinking on and off like tiny lightbulbs in the darkness. A few of the kids walk down the road to go home.

One of them turns around and yells back to the group, ''Hey, you wanna take that cart we made down to the railroad station tomorrow? We can get the coal that drops off the cars and try to sell it.''

''No, I'm gonna ride my bike over to the golf course on the other side of town and see if I can caddy,'' one member of the group replies.

You remember that you promised your sister you'd pick blueberries by the stream tomorrow. But one boy says he'll go.

You head for home with a couple of your friends. After a dinner of turnips and bread, your parents turn the radio on to listen to a mystery show called ''The Shadow.'' You skip it tonight so you can meet at your friend's house to make a toy lantern. You take a shoe box and a candle with you. You cut windows in the box and line it with newspaper, tie a string to one side, put your candle in the box and go outside. Even though it's evening, you feel the sticky wetness in the air. You light the candles and start walking up the road to nowhere, talking about fishing and picking blueberries, pulling your shoe box lanterns on strings. It's been a fun day, but tomorrow you'll have to work.

8. Discuss the guided imagery exercises:

   • Ask the students to share what they pictured as you read the guided imagery narrative.
   • Then, ask them to discuss how they felt about what they pictured.
   • Finally, cluster words that come to mind which capture what growing up on that farm in the outskirts of Indiana might be like.

   A sample cluster might look like this:

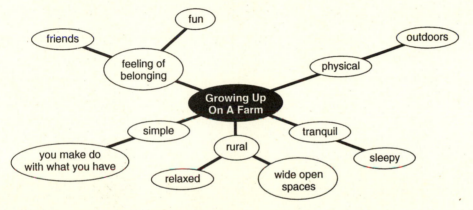

9. Discuss and interpret one toy of the Depression era:

   • Bring a sample toy (a doll, a slingshot, or a top are possibilities).
   • Ask questions on all levels of critical thinking:

Sample Questions:

• What is it? (*KNOWLEDGE*)
• What does it do? (*COMPREHENSION*)
• What is it made of? (*KNOWLEDGE*)
• Is it handmade or machine made? (*APPLICATION*)
• Do you have a similar toy? (*APPLICATION*)
• Have you ever made a toy? (*KNOWLEDGE*)
• Would you rather have a handmade or machine made toy? Why? (*EVALUATION*)
• If this were the only toy a person had, what would it tell you about that person? (*ANALYSIS*)

- Did it take more time or money to make it? (*EVALUATION*)
- Which is more important? (*EVALUATION*)
- If you were going to invent a toy using the same materials, what would you make? (*SYNTHESIS*)
- After students have answered the questions listed above, put students in groups of three to four and ask them to draw some conclusions about what their answers to the questions they used to examine the toy tell them about what childhood might be like during the Depression. Ask each group to report their conclusions to the whole group and record these on the board. Then, ask students to think about the toys and games described by the person they interviewed and to draw some conclusions about what those toys and/or games tell them about what childhood might be like during the Depression.

Prompt:

Using the results of your interview and your classwork, write a paper in which you:

- Describe one or more toys and/or games of the Depression era, making reference to your interview.
- Describe one or more toys and/or games you enjoy.
- Discuss the similarities and differences between the two types of toys and games.
- From your study of toys and games and from your class notes on the Depression, draw conclusions about and compare and contrast what it was like to grow up during the Depression with what it is like growing up now.

Precomposing

10. Students should gather the following work together before they begin this stage:

    - notes from the interview,
    - interview results worksheet,
    - list and statements from the practice interviews,
    - statements written after the guided imagery exercise,
    - notes on the Depression from various sources, such as lecture and reading.

11. Students will use all of the above to plan their essays. They will also construct a map, a graphic outline on white paper, as a composing guide. The map can be any shape, but it should distinguish the primary and secondary ideas. If they wish, students can label the map to show what parts will go in each of the paragraphs of their paper.

Figure 14 shows a sample map:

Kick the Can	Pac Man
• Similar to Hide & Seek except you have to find all the other players.	• Electronic game in which you move a lever to manipulate a visual image of "Pac Man."
• Materials are a tin can and a base.	• Pac Man eats dots to get points.

Similarities of Games

- Both involve strategy.
- Both involve some sort of movement.
- Both have obstacles that must be overcome.
- Both are fun and challenging.

Differences of Games

running around	vs	staying in one place.
physical	vs	visual
simple materials	vs	complex machine
played with a group	vs	played alone or with a partner
outdoors	vs	indoors

Conclusions About Growing Up During The Depression And Now

- Electronic games are now available, whereas they were not then.
- Technology has made life easier today but also more complex.
- Life is lived at a much faster pace now.
- Activities were more oriented around the home and family then, whereas now we go outside our neighborhoods for entertainment.

FIGURE 14: Sample Map

Writing

12. After students map their plan for writing, they write their first drafts. Discuss the sample paper pointing out its strengths and weaknesses. Then, analyze it using the Response Sheet (see the *SHARING* section). Have students point out how the paper fulfills or does not fulfill each of the items on the Response Sheet chart. Emphasize the conclusions drawn and the transitions used in the paper. (You may elicit a list of transitional words at this point in the lesson, such as whereas, in contrast to, in conclusion, etc.) Here is a sample first draft of a student paper:

Pac Man or Kick the Can Model

Growing up during the 1980s seems very different from growing up during the Depression. But not everything is different. I learned about the differences between these two time periods and about the similarities when I interviewed my grandmother, Mame Anderson.

Grandma's favorite toy was an orange rag doll with black button eyes that her aunt made for her. Grandma named her doll Peggy and took her everywhere. She pretended to feed her, put her down for naps, and tucked her in every night. Peggy was like a member of the family. There may not be as many homemade dolls today, but girls still like to collect dolls. My grandmother would not have been able to afford the Barbie or Cabbage Patch dolls that sell for high prices in the stores today. Because she grew up during the Depression, her family had to struggle to get by. When Grandma grew up, they didn't even have TV! How surprised she would have been if Peggy could talk or even tell stories like many of the dolls do today. But Grandma had conversations with Peggy all the same. She just imagined them. And she and Peggy sat on the big, overstuffed couch in the living room and listened to their favorite radio show every evening. When she talks about her childhood, Grandma smiles. They were hard times, she says, but also happy times.

In contrast to my grandmother, my favorite possession is my skateboard. A skooter was probably the closest thing that kids had during the Depression. I ride my board—which is a Santa Cruz board with red kriptonic wheels and a black deck with blue tape—every day for fun and for transportation. When I ride it, I feel independent. I can enjoy it alone or ride with my friends. We try out different stunts like 360's which are complete circles, and axel drop-offs, which is when you stand on a low brick wall and then turn the board around and drop off the wall and land on the board. Although I like all kinds of computer games that Grandma could never have even dreamed of as a child, it's really my skateboard that I'll remember when I'm her age and I look back. I am sure that kids during the 1930s experienced the same feelings about wanting to express themselves, take risks and have a good time.

In conclusion, I think the difference between my grandmother and myself has to do with her being a girl and me being a guy rather than because we grew up during different times. Maybe kids are kids no matter when they grow up.

Sharing

13. Students work in groups of four or five. The writer reads the paper to the group. Other students in the group each make one positive comment about the paper and record it on the response sheet shown below. Then the content, format, and mechanics are evaluated; a recorder checks off the items on the response sheet. This sheet can be used for both initial and final drafts. (It should be noted that teachers will not be able to respond to all first drafts.)

Response Sheet

The responses of other students and the teacher will help you revise and edit your paper. Make sure that your response group completes this form before you rewrite to help you make sure you have fulfilled the requirements of the prompt. (*Note:* Your teacher will probably not be able to read all first drafts.)

This paper is worth a total of nine points. Content means the ideas you are communicating in your paper and it is worth five points. Format includes paragraph structure, neatness, and margins and is worth two points. Mechanics is also worth two points and it includes spelling, capitalization, punctuation, and grammar. Your conclusions about the similarities and differences of childhood during the Depression and childhood today are the most important part of your grade.

What we liked best: _____

_____

What we think needs to be worked on: _____

_____

Are there any parts of the paper that are unclear? List. _____

_____

_____

Do you have any questions about what the author is saying? _____

_____

_____

Teacher's comments: _____

_____

_____

FIGURE 15: Response Sheet

Response Sheet					Page 2 of 2
Content	(5 points)	**Omitted**	**Needs Work**	**Good**	**GREAT!**
• Identifies and describes a Depression toy/game					
• Identifies and describes a toy/game you enjoy					
• Describes childhood then and now					
• Indicates similarities					
• Indicates differences					
• DRAWS CONCLUSIONS					
Format	(2 points)				
• Topic sentences					
• Details					
• Transitions					
• Margins					
• Legibility					
Mechanics	(2 points)				
• Title					
• Indents paragraphs					
• Spelling					
• Capitalization					
• Grammar					

Writer's notes for revision: (You may use back of this paper.)

FIGURE 15: Continued

Revising

14. After sharing in groups and teacher conferencing (whenever possible) and using feedback from the response sheets, students make revisions and work on their second drafts. They may share again in pairs and use another response sheet for response to later drafts. Students will make decisions about what to add, delete, substitute or rearrange. (*Note:* At this point, you may wish to return to the sample student paper or select a paper from the class to discuss and model possible strategies for revising the first draft.)

Editing

15. Students recheck the response sheet and edit after checking each item.

Evaluation

16. The teacher evaluates according to the following rubric. The paper is worth a total of 9 points: with Content = 5 points; Format = 2 points; and Mechanics = 2 points.

Primary Trait Scoring Guide

Content

5 A 5-paper compares and contrasts and draws conclusions about childhood during the Depression and childhood today by giving examples of one or more toys/games and analyzing the similarities and differences of each.

4 A 4-paper only makes one comparison or contrast and draws one conclusion and otherwise fulfills the same criteria as a 5 paper.

3 A 3-paper only discusses the toys/games and does not compare or contrast or draw conclusions about the two eras.

2 A 2-paper does not discuss the differences of the toys/games in each era.

1 A 1-paper does not provide sufficient detail about the toys/games or does not give one example from each era.

Secondary Trait Scoring Guide

Format

2 A 2-paper

- has topic sentences,
- contains details,

- uses transitions,
- has neat margins and handwriting.

1 A 1-paper omits three of the elements of a 2-paper.

0 A 0-paper omits four of the elements of a 2-paper.

Mechanics

2 A 2-paper has a title, indents paragraphs and has a minimum of mechanical, grammatical, or spelling errors.

1 A 1-paper does not have a title, does not indent paragraphs, or has a noticeable amount of mechanical, grammatical, or spelling errors.

0 A 0-paper does not have a title, does not indent paragraphs, and has an abundance of mechanical, grammatical, or spelling errors.

Extension Activities

Analysis

Prompt: Compare and contrast another aspect of the Depression with life now. Some possible choices are education, nutrition, housing, chores, etc.

Synthesis

Prompt: The Depression took place more than 50 years ago. Based on the differences between the past and the present you noticed from your interview and research, predict what it will be like to live 50 years from now. Then, create a toy or game that might be used in the future.

Evaluation

Prompt: Write a paper in which you compare growing up in the Depression with growing up now. What value do you see in each period? Give reasons why you would rather have grown up in the 1930s or why you'd rather be a child today.

Character as Onion
An Analysis of Character Delineation

Lesson

Students will write an essay analyzing how Ibsen reveals different aspects of Nora's character in **A Doll's House** through her interactions with others in the play.

Objectives

Thinking Skills
By *EXAMINING* and *COMPARING* the roles of Dr. Rank, Christine Linden, and Nils Krogstad and by *CHARACTERIZING* their relationship with Nora, students will be able to *CHOOSE* the significant words and actions which reveal Nora to the audience and to *ANALYZE* how each minor character reflects separate layers of Nora's personality.

Writing Skills
After selecting and sequencing significant quotes and incidents which reveal their changing perceptions of Nora's personality, students will write an expository essay (introduction, main body, conclusion) in which these words and actions are examined and interpreted.

The Process

Prior to this lesson, students will have had practice in analyzing the function of minor characters in fictional works and in drawing inferences from the words and actions of characters. This assignment will probably take place late in the semester.
 Reading the play and writing the essay will take about three weeks.

Prewriting

1. A useful prewriting activity to set the stage for reading the play and focusing in on the prompt that students will be asked to write about might be a 15-minute writing exercise about a time when your first opinion of someone proved invalid—examining what caused the change in your viewpoint. Groups will share, with one or more papers from each group to be read aloud to the whole class.
 Discussion will follow which addresses the following:

- What are significant acts or words which cause us to make misjudgments?
- How does someone undo a bad first impression?
- How does someone undo a good first impression?

2. Next, assign roles in the play to students who will then read the play aloud in the classroom.

   Reading Logs: Throughout the reading of the play, students will be instructed to keep a log of significant words and actions occurring between the major and minor characters. In addition, notes should be made about what these words and actions reveal about the major characters and how the student's perceptions of the characters change as the play progresses.

3. Halt reading of the play to discuss significant words or actions by any of the characters as well as to discuss stage directions.

4. You may put a diagram such as the following on the board with examples contributed by the class from their reading logs:

Words	What They Reveal
"my lark," "my squirrel" Act I	Torvald considers her a plaything.
"Oh that was too bad of you." (N. to D. R.) Act II	Nora's attitude toward men's roles.
"I almost felt as if I was a man." (N to C. R.) Act I	Dissatisfaction with her role.
Actions	**What They Reveal**
Hides macaroons. Act I	Nora is childlike
Plays with T's buttons. Act I	Wheedles like a child.
Shows D. R. her stockings. Act II	Provocative.
Dances the tarantella. Act III	Desperation.

Students should add pertinent information from the board to their own reading logs.

5. At the end of each act, put the names of the characters across the top of the chalkboard and have the class contribute their ideas about the characters' chief attributes. Students should add pertinent information from the board to their own reading logs.

Sample Attribute Lists:

Krogstad	Christine	Rank
desperate	strong	self-pitying
determined	determined	generous
arrogant	hypocritical	understanding
threatening		
etc.	etc.	etc.

6. Introduce the metaphor of character as an onion in which the layers of characteristics which make up the whole personality can be successively peeled away to reveal its deeper aspects.

   Nora's interactions with the other *dramatis personae* serve to give substance to these aspects, so their interactions must be examined, compared, and differentiated. It is most useful to do this by using the end of each act to characterize the audience's view of Nora:

At the end of . . .	Nora is . . .
• Act I	silly, spendthrift, woman-child
• Act II	desperate, frightened, cornered
• Act III	strong, loyal, self-sacrificing
• Act IV	determined, in control

Her character has been peeled away, layer by layer, to reveal a whole, complicated woman.

Prompt:

Ibsen reveals Nora's depth of character in *A Doll's House* by showing interactions with others in the play. By analyzing these interactions, show how each reveals a different aspect of Nora's character and how each contributes to the audience's view of her as a total personality.

   Your essay should be written in standard expository form and must include:

- An introduction to the audience's perception of Nora's outer layer (end of Act I), supported with specific acts and words;
- A brief description of the minor characters, showing how each contributes to the audience's understanding of Nora;
- A discussion, using material quoted from the text, of how significant words or acts reveal successive layers of Nora's character;
- A conclusion describing the audience's perception of Nora at the end of the play, reflecting back on the growth of their understanding of her as a whole character.

Precomposing

The following activities generate further data and help clarify the form for the subsequent essay:

1. Ask students to recall orally the names and relationships of major and minor characters.

2. Then, discuss the minor characters by clustering their characteristics.
    Sample Cluster:

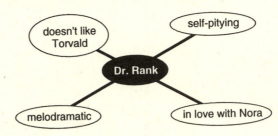

3. Ask students to list what each character contributes to the audience's knowledge of the major characters.
    For example:

Christine Linden

- Says Nora was a spendthrift in school.
- Acts as a confidante over Torvald's illness and Krogstad's demands.

Dr. Rank

- Reveals that Nora thinks about serious matters.
- Reveals Nora's attitude about men.
- Reveals Nora's attitude about her situation.

4. Students will imagine the play without one of the minor characters—Ellen, the maid, for instance—to show how even very minor characters reveal major character attributes.
    (For example, without Ellen, Nora has no role model of someone who has given up a child for someone else to raise; furthermore, Ellen has raised Nora, an important consideration when Nora considers her own departure.)

5. Students will then show how the audience's attitude toward Nora changes by sequencing the inferences about her from the most superficial outer layers to the core she reveals at the end.

6. After reviewing their logs, students will write a succinct statement about their final perception of Nora and the main causes of this perception.

The teacher will walk around the room helping students to formulate their statements. These statements will become the thesis statement.

7. By the end of the discussion, the following critical thinking skills will have been explored:

   - Repeat key phrases and recall key actions of major and minor characters. (Knowledge)
   - Recognize and explain how these words and actions affect our perceptions of the characters. (Comprehension)
   - Sequence the events which support and illustrate our changing understanding of Nora and Torvald, Nils and Christine. (Application)
   - Interpret the importance of the minor characters by showing how their presence peels away Nora's mask of childlike diffidence and dependence. (Analysis)
   - For synthesis and evaluation, see the *EXTENSION ACTIVITIES* at the end of this lesson.

8. The teacher will review the prompt with students to show how the insights gained in the precomposing stage can be incorporated into the final essay.

9. Before the students begin to write, the teacher may want to share a sample introduction to give them a sense of how to lead-in to the topic:

Sample Introduction:

Character As Onion

At the beginning of the play, Nora Helmer enters her house rosy from the cold, eyes sparkling with excitement, getting ready for Christmas festivities. After generously tipping the porter for bringing in a small tree, she forages her pockets for her cache of macaroons, a treat specifically forbidden by her husband, Torvald. During the first act, the audience's impression of Nora as a shallow, frivolous doll is further supported by her wheedling and begging her thrifty husband for more money, playing hide and seek with her children, and monopolizing the conversation with an old school friend, Christine Linden, with prattle about Torvald's new job. The bad impression deepens when she reveals she has secretly borrowed money to go on a trip, the sole mitigating factor for this being that the trip is necessary for her husband's health. This Nora scarcely seems a promising subject for a serious play. But through the interaction of Nora with the minor characters in the drama, she is revealed as a complex, deeply troubled woman whose surface does not even hint at the person we understand her to be at the end of the play.

Note: The teacher may prefer to withold the model introduction for use in the *SHARING* or *REVISING* stages of the process.

Writing

Students will compose a first draft at home, sketching the perceptions of Nora's personality and using information generated in the prewriting and precomposing stages of the lesson.

Sharing

Using writing groups, students will share their rough drafts. They should address themselves to the following considerations:

- Was the writer's attitude toward Nora at the end of Act I clear?
- Were the inferences supported by significant quotes?
- Were the sketches of the minor characters and their contributions to revealing Nora's character convincing?
- With what specific words or actions was the character revealed?
- Was the evidence for the revelation convincing? Full?

After giving and receiving oral feedback, students will exchange papers, and fill out the following Response Sheet.

Character as Onion   **Response Sheet**

Author's name _____

	Well Done	Adequately Done	Needs Work
Introduction focuses on Nora's outer layer; supports with specific acts and words.			
Minor characters are described and their contributions to audience's understanding of Nora are discussed.			
Uses material quoted from the text to show significant words or acts reveal deeper layers of character.			
Conclusion describes character at the end of the play and reflects back on the growth of their understanding.			

What I liked best about your paper was:

One thing I think you could improve is:

Responder's name _____

Revising

Students will revise their papers using the suggestions made by their peer group and the Response Sheet filled out by a classmate.

Editing

Students will edit for the conventions of written English, paying particular attention to the rules for quoting from a text.

Evaluation

6 Excellent grasp of Nora's complexity as revealed by her interaction with the minor characters. Clearly responds to all aspects of the prompt.

- Strong introduction focusing on audience's perception of Nora's outer layer (Act I) supported by specific acts and words
- Clearly shows how minor characters contribute to the audience's understanding of Nora
- Ample use of textual material to support how words or acts reveal the successive layers of Nora's character
- Well thought-out conclusion describing audience's perception of Nora at the end of the play, reflecting back on the growth of their understanding of the whole character
- Is written in standard expository form
- Quotes from the text correctly and accurately
- Has few, if any, errors in the conventions of written English

5 Good concept of Nora's complexity, but may skip some of the facets of her personality by not using significant examples. A few unimportant mechanical errors.

- Reasonably strong introduction focusing on audiences's perception of Nora's outer layer (Act 1) supported by specific acts and words
- Shows how minor characters contribute to the audience's understanding of Nora but not as clearly as a 6 paper
- Some use of textual materials to support how words or acts reveal the successive layers of Nora's character
- Reasonably well thought-out conclusion describing audience's understanding of the whole character
- Is written in standard expository form
- Quotes from the text correctly and accurately
- Has few, if any, errors in the conventions of written English

4 Reduces Nora's complexity to two or three examples of her interactions with the minor characters and generalizes from too few examples. Tends to be unconvincing and poorly supported. Some careless errors in editing or proofreading.

- Contains an introduction focusing on audience's perception of Nora's outer layer (Act 1) supported by specific acts and words which is not as strong as a 6 or 5 paper
- Does not show how Nora's interaction with minor characters contribute to the audience's understanding of Nora as clearly as a 6 or 5 paper
- Inadequate use of textual material to support how words or acts reveal the successive layers of Nora's character
- Conclusion does not contain an in-depth perception of the complexity of Nora's character
- Is written in expository form (introduction, main body, conclusion) but not all three sections are equally strong
- Some minor problems in quoting from the text accurately
- Some errors in the conventions of written English but none that obscure the writer's message

3 Analysis generalizes without convincing support and depends on cause-effect actions rather than complex or ambiguous relationships. Emphasizes one minor character to the neglect of others.

- Overly general introduction focusing on audience's perception of Nora's outer layer (Act 1) which is not fully supported by specific acts and words
- Emphasizes minor character's interaction with Nora to the exclusion of others
- Inadequate use of textual material to support how words or acts reveal the successive layers of Nora's character
- Relatively weak conclusion describing only a superficial perception of Nora at the end of the play, failing to reflect back on the growth of understanding of the whole character
- Written in some semblance of expository form but the transition from introduction to main body to conclusion may be unclear
- Does not quote from the text at all or quotes only rarely to support ideas
- Has errors in the conventions of written English which distract the reader

2 Consists mainly of plot summary, attributing change in our perception of Nora to her change. Any paper with major stylistic faults.

1 Consists of plot summary—what happened to Nora. No grasp of the effects of words or actions on character delineation. Slovenly mechanics.

0 No paper submitted, or no evidence that the process was followed.

Extension Activities

Analysis

Prompt: How does Browning reveal the character of the narrator in "My Last Duchess"? Is his manner similar to Ibsen's?

_____

Synthesis

Prompt: Choosing another work—*Hamlet,* for instance—show, citing specific examples, how Shakespeare reveals depth in his characters using significant words and actions.

_____

Evaluation

Prompt: Using the character-as-onion concept, explore how our understanding of Torvald's character in Ibsen's *A Doll's House* evolves throughout the play.

_____

Writing Domain: Sensory/Descriptive
Analytical/Expository

Thinking Level: Analysis
Grade Level: High School/College

Obviously Short, Probably a Democrat: A Lesson on Making Inferences

Lesson

After noting down both clearly observed and inferred information, the student will write a character sketch of a classmate.

Objectives

Thinking Skills
Students will practice ANALYSIS by drawing *INFERENCES* in a real life situation.

Writing Skills
Students will use sensory/descriptive skills to *CHARACTERIZE* a classmate based on obvious, factual information as well as on what is intuited or *INFERRED*. They will select a paragraph structure which shows how facts and inferences are related and include transition to emphasize those relationships.

The Process

Sometimes we have difficulty distinguishing between what is implied in a text and what is more clearly stated. For example, I may infer one thing about a character, and you may infer something quite different. Of course, the important issue is, how the inference was made. Since authors will probably be unable to attend your class to address such questions (try getting James Joyce to lecture these days), the first part of this lesson allows you, the instructor, to be the ultimate authority. Your students will be asked to infer things about *you*.

This lesson could be adapted for most grade levels. Three class periods are necessary for the complete lesson.

Prewriting

1. Ask the class to write two lists on a sheet of paper, spending about six or seven minutes doing so. List #1 should include at least three things that are obvious about you. This example might be given: Today my teacher is wearing pants.

   List #2 should include at least three things the student thinks might be true about you, but without being totally sure. There should be some reason for these inferences, although students should be encouraged to make some wild guesses as long as there is some basis for guessing. This example might be used: Mr. Schneider is the kind of person who feels lonely at parties.

   Items on the list should be one word, a phrase, or a sentence.

   Students should be told *not* to put their own names on their papers, thus encouraging them to say whatever comes to mind. Assure the class you will not know who wrote which list.

2. After six or seven minutes—longer, if you feel it's necessary—the lists are turned in and redistributed to the class so that it is unlikely any student has his own paper. If the student receives his own paper, he should trade.

3. Ask the class which list was easier to prepare. Ask why.

4. Now, begin with the "obvious" list. Ask volunteers to read their lists, especially if there is something particularly interesting on the list. Write down and number each item on the board.

   Note: If people don't volunteer, merely choose students at random, or go up and down rows.

Your OBVIOUS LIST, compiled from group discussion, might look something like this:

1. Short	11. Not very tall
2. A teacher	
3. Dark hair	12. Brown hair
	13. Black hair
4. Wears glasses	
5. Age 25–30	6. Age 35–40
	7. Over 40
8. Needs dental work	
9. Reads a lot of books	
10. Has dimples	
14. Good sense of humor	

When writing on the board, write similar choices across from each other—for example: "short" and "not very tall." Discuss the similarities and differences and the connotations implied.

When appropriate, ask, "Is this really obvious?" "Does this really belong on the 'obvious' list?"

Consider issues such as this: If someone writes "brown hair" and another writes "black hair," ask how one would find out which is correct. If someone writes "dark hair" and another writes "brown hair," you might ask if one phrase is more useful as a description than the other.

5. Do the same as above, but with the second list. Since students will not be reading their own lists, they should all be encouraged to answer the question: Is this inference a good one? Is there any reason to think it is true? For example, if someone says, "He is a Democrat," ask the class if that was ever stated explicitly or revealed clearly in any other way. If not, what was ever said or done to imply that the person is a Democrat? If someone answers, "The instructor was critical one day of nuclear weapons," ask if that is enough to characterize someone as a Democrat.

   When appropriate, ask if an item on this list really belongs on the first list:

Your INFERRED LIST might look like this:	
1. Married	11. Single
2. Likes classical music	
3. Hates to dance	
4. Feels lonely at parties	
5. Does great with the girls (or boys)	
6. A Democrat	
7. Prefers serious conversations to small talk	
8. Has a hairy chest	
9. Got good grades in school	
10. Likes to write	

6. After discussing the inferred list, ask the class, "What have you learned by doing this lesson so far?" You might get responses such as these:

- Some things which we take as obvious are not obvious after all.
- We often make inferences without really good reasons.
- Some inferences are based on stereotyped reactions.
- Some inferences seem right, even though it's hard or impossible to state why.

Prompt:

Observe a classmate and list what is obvious and what might be inferred about that person. Then, draw some conclusions about him/her and write a 1- or 2-page character sketch. Be sure to include detailed, descriptive information from both of your lists. Suggest your reasons for drawing certain conclusions about your fellow student. In your sketch, avoid a simple A-B paragraph structure, one paragraph merely listing a few obvious details, a second paragraph merely listing a few inferred details. Instead, sometimes show how various details are related and include transitions to emphasize relationships.

Note: These lists and sketches will be shared with other people in your class.

Precomposing

1. Break the class into groups of two.

2. Have each student silently prepare two lists about the other person, one "obvious" and one inferred.
   Stress that there should be at least five items on each list, but even more would be helpful. (See Prewriting Step #1 for models.)
   Give about 10 minutes for this part of the lesson.

3. Ask for volunteers from the class to read their lists and lead a discussion on the appropriateness of what is listed as obvious and inferred. Are the obvious items really obvious and are the inferences reasonable? If the inferences are not reasonable, are they interesting, appropriate, or useful anyway?

   At this point, the person about whom the lists are written should not comment about the reliability of the inferences.

4. Various models can be introduced at this point to aid the student in the composing of his character sketch.

   First, caution the students about sequencing their paragraphs in an A-B fashion—a number of obvious details and a number of inferences. That would be a sort of prose copy of the original lists. The reader wants to see the reasons for the inferences. Emphasize that simple details can sometimes imply interesting things about a person. Point out that transition words can help show relations between ideas.

   • Read an example of a sketch from a previous semester. Ask the students what makes the sketch successful.
   • Give students who want one a framing exercise one such as this; point out that it is a workable yet fairly predictable structure for this assignment:

(*Student's name*) is definitely a _____ kind of person. You get that feeling when you observe _____ and _____. I heard him (or her) say this in class yesterday, _____," and that makes me believe _____. I think it may be hard to get to know (*name*) because _____. I would guess that one thing that (*name*) would enjoy is _____. I say that because _____ _____. That's another reason I think that _____.

5. Put 10 items from each list written about you (the instructor) in the *PREWRITING* phase back on the board, and brainstorm a paragraph based on some of the information.

6. Give your students the following model to discuss in class:

   Cathryn looks like a professional dancer. She's tall—about five-ten—and has long, shapely legs, and she moves with a certain grace and dignity. Sometimes she wears a rose leotard, a short, plaid shirt, and grey warm-up socks to class. I guess she'd be a jazz dancer, really; she doesn't have that emaciated look or far-off expression associated with ballet dancers.

   I think she would be a good friend to have because she smiles when you look at her and she has warm, "accepting" eyes. Of course, good friends need more than that, but that's a good start.

One thing I think Cathryn lacks, however, is self-confidence. In class she looks like she understands what's going on and she writes down all the important things the teacher says, but she never says anything in discussions unless she is asked. I think her responses are always intelligent or funny—she has a great sense of irony—but she usually prefaces her remarks with something like, "This is probably dumb, but . . ." On the other hand, maybe she is being ironic when she says she's dumb. Maybe someone taught her that girls aren't supposed to act smart, especially pretty ones. I've heard of cases like that. Now I wish I knew the answer to this. I wish I knew Cathryn better.

7. These are a few questions to ask about the above model:

- Which things in the paragraph are obvious, which inferred?
- Are some of the inferences reasoned out more than others? Which are reasoned out well and which not as well?
- When the writer says that Cathryn's remarks are always intelligent or funny, is he making an inference or stating the obvious? Would an example or two of what she said help make the point any better?
- Thinking about Cathryn in this way has led the writer of the paragraph to state something in his last sentence. How does this work as a conclusion? Do you like it?
- Why?
- What transitional words are helpful in this paper?

Writing

In class, students write their first drafts, observing their group partners once again if desired.

First drafts can be finished at home, although you should request that students not share their inferences yet with the person they are writing about.

Sharing

Students share in peer groups of three to four people, reading the character sketches aloud. It will be helpful to have copies made for the entire group. Have response aimed at use of detail (from the "obvious" list) and quality of inferences. In other words, some inferences might be valued for reasonableness, others more for cleverness or imagination. Have students point out phrases that are exciting because of diction, metaphor, or other stylistic devices. Students should be encouraged to discuss inferences that are purely intuited, according to the writer of the draft. For example, a student might say, "I can't explain why, but I think Fred is spaced out." Searching for reasons why might lead to an interesting analysis.

Revising

Students revise by adding or refining details or by formulating reasons for their inferences.

Peer group comments should be helpful in revising, as should looking over the original two lists the student made.

The student should also revise with an eye toward form and structure.

Editing

Peer groups help edit the writing to conform to standards of correctness. This may lead some to a further revision.

Evaluation

Either peer or teacher evaluation may be used. The following 6-point rubric is suggested:

6–5 A character sketch that draws on both descriptive details and analytical conclusions or inferences.

- The student makes particularly perceptive observations and especially interesting and well thought out inferences
- The author clearly distinguishes between fact and opinion and explains in most instances how one leads to the other
- The author avoids a simple A-B structure and uses transitions to suggest relationships between ideas
- Paper follows the conventions of written English with only isolated, minor grammatical problems

4–3 A 4–3 paper does most or all of the following:

- Shows strong descriptive ability without being as analytical as 6–5 papers
- Gives reasonable inferences, although perhaps not as well thought out or as interesting as higher scored papers
- Has a clear sense that facts lead to inferences, although perhaps fewer transitions are used to show relationships
- Contains problems in the conventions of written English but only rarely in a way that lessens the clarity of ideas

Note: Stylistically exciting papers should get the higher score (''4'').

2 This paper makes an attempt to follow the prompt, but:

- The writer has failed to observe enough details or to show enough reasons for his inferences

- The paper may show elements of A-B structure—a few details followed by a few inferences
- Grammatical problems may seriously affect the clarity of the paper

1 • The writer has failed to make any observations of worth or any inferences based on analysis
   - The paper may be stricken with grammatical problems

Extension Activities

Comprehension

Have the class do a freewriting exercise expressing how they felt about the experience of writing their character sketches in class. A focus might be: What did the other person infer about me that surprised me?

Application/Analysis

Write two lists about someone in your family, a list of what's obvious and another list. The second list could be of inferences, or it could be a list of things you would like to know but don't know yet about the person. For example, you might want to know how much money your mother makes at her job, or how your mother and father met. In discussion of the lists, decide how one can find out the answers to such questions.

Analysis

Ask the class to list what is obvious and what can be inferred about a character in a story you are reading. What is clearly stated by the author or characters and what is implied? Students can then write a paper discussing the information in those lists.

5 Synthesis

A Mountain of Stories

Lesson

Students will write a narrative essay using the Story Mountain as a frame for their story.

Objectives

Thinking Skills
Students will demonstrate *SYNTHESIS* level thinking by *IDENTIFYING, INVENTING, CREATING* and *SEQUENCING.*

Writing Skills
Students will write an imaginative/narrative paper using the Story Mountain formula.

The Process

Prewriting

The Story Mountain involves writing a narrative according to a formula that involves rising and falling action. As the hero goes up the mountain, problems are encountered and overcome. Just when it seems as if the hero has reached a peak where all is going well, another problem arises and all seems lost. Some goals are never achieved and the story can end here. But the journey can also take an upswing as the hero resolves this new problem and reaches his goal.

The following Story Mountain Explanation outlines the steps of the Story Mountain journey.

Story Mountain Explanation   Table A

Step 1	What the hero wants—goal.
Step 2	The first problem encountered in the story.
Step 3	How that first problem is overcome.
Step 4	Here, it looks like all is well. The main character is well on his way to getting what he wants.
Step 5	Another problem arises.
Step 6	Now, it seems like the main character will never get what he wants.
Step 7	How the hero gets what he wants, or how the hero does not get what he wants—goal.

This lesson follows the preceding discussion and explanation of the use of the Story Mountain as a way of framing a story.

In order to further introduce the concept of the Story Mountain, explain to the class:

"Today we will be writing a story based on the use of the Story Mountain. So far, we have discussed what the Story Mountain is and now *as a group* we will create a story on the board using that format."

Then, ask particular students to give responses to the components of the Story Mountain as you write them down on the board. The following is a copy of the Story Mountain and its components.

Story Mountain Formula

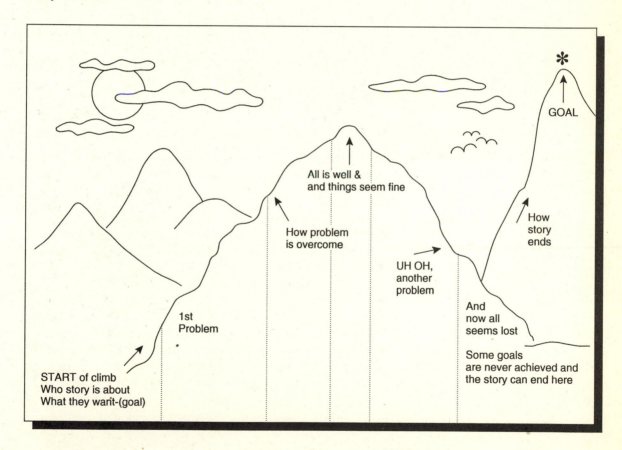

The graphic on the next page demonstrates a Group Story Mountain about a boy named Don who wants to go to the movies.

Group Story Mountain

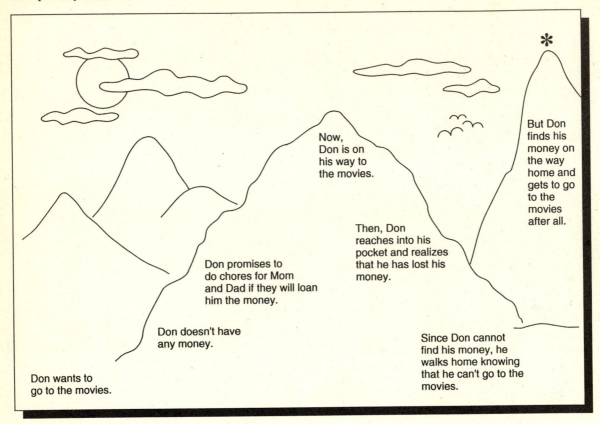

Don wants to
go to the movies.

Don doesn't have
any money.

Don promises to
do chores for Mom
and Dad if they will loan
him the money.

Now,
Don is on
his way to
the movies.

Then, Don
reaches into his
pocket and realizes
that he has lost his
money.

Since Don cannot
find his money, he
walks home knowing
that he can't go to the
movies.

But Don
finds his
money on
the way
home and
gets to go
to the
movies
after all.

Prompt:

Now that we have written a Story Mountain story as a group, I want each of you to create and write your own Story Mountain story. Your story should follow the Story Mountain format, clearly identifying the subcomponents and sequencing them in the correct order. Your ideas should be written in complete sentences using capitals and periods where appropriate. Your story will be read to your classmates.

Precomposing

1. To assist students in choosing their own goal and obstacles, as a class, list some possible goals and problems encountered

Examples:

- Miss Piggy wants to go out dancing, but she needs a partner.
- Bill wants to buy a pet but has no money.
- Sue wants to play outside but it's raining.
- Spot wants to be the mascot for the fire station, but the firemen want a dalmatian and not a cocker spaniel.

Have students brainstorm in small groups to add to this list. Then, ask each group to shape their goals and obstacles. Record these ideas on the blackboard or on chart paper.

2. After the students have chosen their topics, have them fill in the subcomponents using the list in Table A. For example:

Example

Step 1	This is a story about Don who decides to go to the movies.
Step 2	The problem is that Don does not have any money.
Step 3	Don promises Mom and Dad that he will do some chores if they will lend him the money.
Step 4	Now, Don is on his way to the movies.
Step 5	Then, Don reaches into his pocket and realizes that he has lost his money.
Step 6	Since Don cannot find his money, he walks home knowing he can't go to the movies.
Step 7	But Don finds his money on the way home and gets to go to the movies after all.

Note: Students can also map their story steps on a Story Mountain to make sure that it has rising and falling action. A blank story mountain is appended to the end of this lesson.

Sample Story Frame:

When the students have finished with their subcomponents, hand them the following frame:

This is a story about _____

who wants _____ . The problem is _____

_____ . _____ decides to

_____ . Now, _____

_____ . Then, _____

_____ . Since _____

cannot _____

he/she _____ . But _____

_____ .

For K-1 students, each of the seven steps can be framed out on a separate page with a space at the top to add a comprehension drawing.

This way, the story is seven pages long and adds a visual hook for the non-reader to use to remember the sequence and content of the story.

| **Picture** |
| This is a story about (name) who _____

_____

_____

_____

1 |

As students learn the sequence, the frame can be expanded greatly to include other features of a story. Things that can be added are setting, dialogue, more problems and richer description. Students can use the frame as a point of departure to understand sequence and then should be exposed to other variations.

For example, students in grades 2–3 can begin with their Story Mountain skeleton and add specific details to the frame. Here are additions for the story of Don:

Don example

Step 1	This is the story of Don who decides to go to the movies. *Don lives in an apartment with his Mom near the movie theater and sees that the newest "Star Trek" movie is playing there.*
Step 2	The problem is that Don doesn't have any money. *Gee, I'd like to see the movie, Don thought to himself, but it costs $2.00 to get in and I don't have it.*
Step 3	Don promises Mom and Dad that he will do some chores if they will lend him the money. *"Mom and Dad, I'll do any chores that you want if you'll loan me $2.00 to go to the movies."*
Step 4	Now, Don is on his way to the movies. *Don crunches through the autumn leaves as he walks down the sidewalk to the movies.*
Step 5	Then, Don reaches into his pocket and realizes that he has lost his money. *"Oh no! My money's gone," says Don.*
Step 6	Since Don cannot find his money, he walks home knowing he can't go to the movies. *He shuffles down the street and sees something green beneath a pile of autumn leaves.*
Step 7	But Don finds his money on the way home and gets to go to the movies after all. *"Oh boy," he says happily as he picks up two crisp dollar bills from the pile of leaves. "I can't wait to see the show."*

The students may leave their Story Mountains as is at this point, or with help from the teacher, can combine their steps and additional details into a more unified narrative. (*Note:* Students may want to switch from present to past tense in this version.)

Example:

Once upon a time, there was a boy named Don who lived in an apartment with his Mom that was near a movie theater. He saw that the newest "Star Trek" movie was playing there. Gee, I'd like to see that movie, Don thought to himself, but it costs $2.00 to get in and I don't have it. Then, Don thought about asking his Mom and Dad to lend him the money.

"I'll do any chores that you want," he promised, "if you'll loan me $2.00 to go to the movies."

Now, Don was on his way to the movies. He crunched through the autumn leaves as he walked down the sidewalk to the movie theater. Then, Don reached into his pocket and realized that he lost his money. ''Oh no! My money is gone,'' he said.

Since Don could not find his money, he walked home knowing that he couldn't go to the movies. But, as he shuffled down the street, he saw something green beneath a pile of autumn leaves. He leaned down and picked up two crisp dollar bills from the pile of leaves.

''Oh boy,'' Don said happily. ''I can't wait to see the show!''

Writing

This is first draft writing that stresses fluency, sequencing, and clarity in the story formula.

Sharing

In small response groups, the students will read their rough drafts and listen for the sequences and the story clarity. As they listen, they will fill in the Story Mountain Sharing Sheet. This sharing sheet gives the writer feedback on how well his Story Mountain sequence can be identified by a listener. As the writer reads, listeners identify parts of the Story Mountain and fill in the Sharing Sheet. (Please see sample Sharing Sheet on the following page.)

Students can also give verbal feedback using the following model:

I like the part of your story where ————————————— .

I don't understand the part where ————————————— .

Story Mountain Sharing Sheet

Step 1	What the character wants. ————————————————
Step 2	First Problem. —————————————————————
Step 3	How problem is solved. —————————————————
Step 4	Plateau—All is well. ———————————————————
Step 5	Uh oh, another problem. ————————————————
Step 6	All seems lost. —————————————————————
Step 7	How story ends. —————————————————————

What I liked:

How the paper can be improved:

Revising

Students incorporate the feedback they received from their classmates, concentrating on the correct sequencing of the story as well as the overall cohesiveness of the story. Students can refer to the Primary Trait Scoring Guide (under *EVALUATION*) for the fluency and form requirements of the assignment.

Editing

Students can meet with sharing groups, work in pairs, or conference with the teacher to edit their work for complete sentences, capitals, periods, and spelling. Students can refer to the Secondary Trait Scoring Guide (under *EVALUATION* for correctness requirements).

Evaluation

Students and/or teacher can score papers according to primary and secondary traits.

Primary Trait Scoring Guide

4 Greatly enjoyed climbing your Story Mountain. A story that was easy for me to follow.

3 Enjoyed climbing your Story Mountain. Most of the steps in the sequence were easy to follow.

2 Climbing your Story Mountain was a little difficult. I couldn't follow all the steps in the sequence.

1 I couldn't climb your Story Mountain. I couldn't follow any of the steps in the sequence.

Secondary Trait Scoring Guide

3 Paper made correct use of sentences, periods, capitals, and spelling. Minor errors.

2 Paper had some errors in sentences, periods, capitals, and/or spelling.

1 Paper had many errors in sentences, periods, capitals, and/or spelling.

Extension Activities

Synthesis

Divide students up into groups of seven. Have each person write only one part of the story. Example: One person writes the premise, another the first problem, etc. Students, as a group, can then illustrate the story.

Story Mountain

Writing Domain: Sensory/Descriptive   **Thinking Level: Synthesis**
Grade Level: Elementary

Darwin Redone:

Creating a New Species

Lesson

Students will write a three paragraph encyclopedia entry describing an animal they have invented based upon a synthesis of the characteristics of three common animals.

Objectives

Thinking Skills
Students will:

- *RECORD* information about three common animals based on observation and research;
- *CLASSIFY* the animals according to a scheme they have devised based on physical characteristics;
- *CREATE* a new animal based upon a synthesis of the characteristics of three common animals;
- *DRAW CONCLUSIONS* about the animal they have created based upon their observations.

Writing Skills
Students will:

- write a three-paragraph encyclopedia entry;
- use vivid sensory/descriptive language;
- employ concrete details;
- use similes and/or metaphors;
- employ correct spelling, punctuation and usage.

The Process

Students have a difficult time with the concepts of classification and speciation. This lesson is designed to provide practice in the skills of drawing conclusions based on given information in a manner that allows for freedom from the rigid scientific boundaries of predetermined speciation. Students are allowed flights of fancy as they create their own animal. Students have already completed lessons in encyclopedia research and the use of similes and metaphors.

Prewriting

1. As a class, brainstorm a list on the board or on butcher paper of four-legged land animals (25 to 30 usually works best):

dog	sheep	zebra	wolf
cat	goat	giraffe	rhinocerous
elk	hamster	bear	antelope
deer	rat	koala	wildebeast
skunk	mouse	opossum	horse
chipmunk	rabbit	raccoon	elephant
cow	lion	aardvark	coyote

2. Students, as a group, organize the animals, looking for common elements related to appearance, habitat, behavior, etc. Make a list of five or six common elements.

   Example:

   - domestic milk-givers
   - hibernating
   - carnivorous
   - house pets
   - antler bearing
   - tree-dwelling
   - burrow-dwelling

3. List the chosen common elements students come up with, allowing room for lists in columns. Ask each student to select an animal from the brainstorming and write his choice under the appropriate column.

milk-givers	hibernating	carnivorous	house pets	etc.
cow goat	bear	lion bear coyote	dog cat	

4. To reinforce the classification process, students tell why they have put that animal in whatever category. Students quickly recognize that some animals may fall into more than one category. This cross-referencing may mean that the category is too general and must be made more specific scientifically. Students and teacher discuss the difficult nature of describing categories of increas-

ing differentiation (genus, family, species) necessary to scientifically classify plants and animals. For the purposes of the lesson, students are asked to assume that the broad range of genus applies; so an animal may fall into two categories.

5. Students choose three animals—each one from a different column above. The animals chosen must not appear in more than one column. (Example: cow, lion, dog.)

6. Students should consult an encyclopedia to generate information about their three chosen animals. Consulting these entries, such as the one on the zebra below, will also serve as a model for the encyclopedia entry they will be writing:

Zebra is a striped, horselike animal found wild in Africa. It stands 4 to 5 feet (1.2 to 1.5 meters) high at the withers. The zebra differs from all other members of the horse family because of its startling color pattern. It has alternating white and black or dark brown stripes arranged in exact designs. These stripes run all over its body, meeting diagonally down the sides of the head. The lines may appear even on the zebra's long ears, short thick mane, and down its tail to the tuft of hair. The lines help to hide the zebra from its enemies. The zebra's chief foe is the lion. Some kinds of zebras live on open grassy plains, and some live in rough mountains. Zebras are grazing animals. They live in small bands, each of which is led by a stallion. Zebras are savage fighters. They are difficult to tame and train to work. They are sometimes tamed in

*Graphic by Sheryl Palmer.

South Africa because they appear immune to *nagana,* a disease that attacks most domesticated animals in Africa. Nagana is carried by the tsetse fly (see TSETSE FLY).

Great numbers of zebras once lived over most of the eastern part of Africa, from southern Egypt to Cape Colony. They were killed for their meat and hides. Their meat is said to have an excellent taste and their hides are used to make a tough leather. Some kinds of zebras are nearly extinct, but others are numerous.

Scientific Classification. The zebra belongs to the horse family, *Equidae.* It is classified as genus *Equus.* The three species of zebras are *E. zebra, E. bontequagga,* and *E. grevyi.*

From *World Book Encyclopedia:* Vol. 21 (Chicago: World Book Inc., 1984) 493–494.

In order to ensure that students generate the kind of information they will need to write their own entry, provide them with the following list of questions:

- What is the animal's scientific name?
- What are its colors, size and shape?
- What does it eat?
- What kind of living space does it need?
- Does it hibernate?
- How many babies does it usually have?
- Who are its enemies/predators?
- What is its relationship to mankind?

7. Students draw or trace a picture of each animal they have read about. Students write answers to the questions about each animal at the bottom of the page below the picture. Stress the use of complete sentences.

Prompt:

Imagine you have discovered an entirely new animal no one else knows exists. The animal has some characteristics of each of the three animals you chose to research. An encyclopedia publisher has personally asked you to send him information about this animal. Your job is to write three paragraphs that will do the following:

- Give the animal scientific and common names.
- Describe what the animal looks like (size, color, shape, etc.)
- Draw conclusions about where it lives, its eating and sleeping habits, offspring,

and its enemies. (*Note:* Conclusions should be logically related to the physical description of the animal.)

• Discuss the relationship of your animal to mankind.

Accompany your encyclopedia entry with an illustration of the animal. Your description of your animal should be so vivid that your reader can reproduce your illustration strictly from the mental picture created by your words. Use similes and metaphors, if you can, to help your reader picture your new creature by comparing it to something else. You are responsible for correct paragraph form, spelling, punctuation and usage.

Precomposing

1. From their research, students make a list of the important characteristics of their new animals. They cross out on their lists any remarkably different characteristics and keep the ones they want to play with. (Examples: Students may choose to eliminate size as a difference if they have chosen a cow, a cat, and a mouse. They may choose to make the animal whatever size they fancy. Students may choose to keep a characteristic such as deer antlers even though the other two animals don't have antlers, because it makes a more interesting animal.) Students may wish to become more creative with the animals by giving them an unusual color or habit. As long as the characteristic can be described, it can be allowed.

Cow	Cat	Mouse
• very large	• small	• very small
• horns	—	—
• 4 legs	• 4 legs	• 4 legs
• hide	• fur (long to short)	• fur (short)
• long tail	• long tail	• long tail
• eats grass	• eats meat	• eats garbage
• raised and used by man for food	• kept as pet	• looked at as a pest
• brown/white/black	• multicolored	• gray/brown
• slow and lumbering	• quick on its feet	• darts and scurries

2. Students draw a picture of their animal, including each of the characteristics they have chosen from their three animals. Pictured next is *Felibovine rodenta*, commonly known as comotause—a synthesis of cow, cat and mouse:

Comotause

Students should conceal their drawings from classmates for the time being.

3. Using his/her own drawing, have each student write a description of the animal's appearance. The description must use precise, descriptive language so that the reader can picture the animal. Remind students that similes and/or metaphors may help create an image in the reader's mind. (Example: When Comotause hunts beetles, roaches or grasshoppers, it creeps quietly and slyly, always watching its prey and waiting for the right moment to spring suddenly and pounce, just as a cat does when stalking a mouse.)

4. Next, ask the student to create a scientific name for the new animal from all the letters in the three scientific names or from the complete names of the original animals. The more "Latin" the name sounds, the more believable the name becomes. Students may make a game of listing as many combinations of letters of the names or combined names as possible from the original scientific names.

   Students may repeat the process with the letters of the common names. Example: COW*CAT*MOUSE might become SUTACOO or MEASTAW or COMOTAUSE.

*Graphic by Sheryl Palmer.

5. Based upon the drawings and the listed characteristics, students decide upon the animal's behaviors. (For example, an animal that has horns probably fights others of its kind for territory or females, or uses the horns to drive away predators. If the animal has short legs, it probably lives on the flat lands, while a long-legged animal would live in a marshy area or in the mountains. An animal that makes great leaps would live in a forest or desert and not in a marsh. A small animal would need protection from predators like a disguise, an unpleasant odor, stickers, or fast feet.) Students need to consider what the animal eats and what animals might be its predators.

Writing

The following structure is helpful for students who may be unsure about how to organize their information into the three paragraph essay form.

Top of paper: Give scientific name and common name.

Paragraph 1:

• Describe what the animal looks like and where it lives.

Paragraph 2:

• Describe the animal's eating and sleeping habits, offspring, its enemies, etc.

Paragraph 3:

• Discuss the animal's relationship to mankind.
   • Is the animal destined to be domesticated like the cow?
   • Will the animal threaten farms or ranches?
   • Is the animal likely to become a pet?

The following student model may also be useful as a review:

Scientific Name: *Felibovine rodenta*
Common Name: *Comotause (Cow-Cat-Mouse)*

The Felibovine rodenta, or comotause, is a small animal about the size of a mouse. It is completely gray except for the brown horns on its head that resemble the horns of a milk-cow. It has bright green eyes that glow in the dark, short silky fur, and the four-inch-long body of a house cat. Unlike the rest of its body, its long tail is hairless and shiny. Comotause curls up into a ball and wraps its tail around itself when it sleeps. Speaking of sleep, comotause uses its horns to dig burrows in the fields or woodlands to make its bed or it sleeps in old mouse holes or abandoned gopher holes. But its favorite spot is a cozy corner of a drawer or a breadbox in someone's nice, warm kitchen.

Like its cousins the cat and mouse, comotause is a carnivore. Actually, it eats large and small insects. When comotause hunts beetles, roaches or grasshoppers, it creeps quietly and slyly, always watching its prey and waiting for the right moment to spring suddenly and pounce, just as a cat does when stalking a bird or mouse. It can use its horns to pin an animal down, trap it in its claws, or hold it in its mouth. Comotause also uses its horns to defend itself against its primary enemy, the house cat. The house cat is especially partial to baby comotauses, and since comotause adults usually have only one or two offspring, they are very protective of their young.

The comotause is very beneficial to man. It eats pests that people don't like, doesn't take up much room, and is very tame. It would be cheaper to keep comotause in the house than a cat that likes canned food, and safer to keep comotause in the house than insecticides. Also, comotause makes a funny noise when you pet it that makes people laugh—"mooeow."

Sharing

Students exchange their first drafts with response partners. Response partners should draw a picture of the new animal based solely on the author's written description.

Each response partner should give feedback to the writer about what parts of the description helped or hindered him/her in drawing the picture. After comparing his drawing with the writer's, the response partner can also underline parts of the description where his or her drawing does not match the writer's.

Revising

Using the response partner's feedback (comments and drawing), students should revise their encyclopedia entries with an idea of enhancing the descriptive language.

Sharing

Students again exchange their second drafts with a peer partner. This time, each partner is to play the role of the encyclopedia publisher who requested information on the new animal the writer has discovered. Partners should write a brief note to the writer regarding whether their information is complete enough to include in the next edition of the encyclopedia. Partners should look for and comment upon the following components of the essay:

- Scientific and common name of animal;
- Physical description of the animal;

- Description of where it lives, its eating and sleeping habits, offspring, and enemies;
- Discussion of the relationship of this animal to mankind.

After receiving their letters from the publisher, students should make any necessary additions, deletions, substitutions or rearrangements to their essays.

Editing

Students exchange papers a final time to read for mechanics and the conventions of standard written English. Students make corrections wherever necessary and then rewrite the paper for the final time, using ink, best handwriting, and observing margins. Students include their original drawings as part of the essay.

Evaluation

The following scoring guide may be used to assess the final written product:

Scoring Guide

Thinking Skills

5 A 5-paper will:

- Give the animal a scientific and common name which logically stems from the names of the chosen animals from which it derives.
- Describe what the animal looks like so that a reader could accurately draw it.
- Describe where the animal lives, its eating and sleeping habits, offspring, and its enemies in a way that is consistent with the physical description of the animal.
- Discuss the relationship of this animal to mankind.
- Overall, give enough in-depth information that the reader, role-playing an encyclopedia editor, could include the animal in his next edition.

4–3 A 4–3 paper will:
(*Note:* A 4-paper will handle the criteria described below slightly more effectively than a 3-paper.)

- Give the animal a scientific and common name, but one that does not relate as logically to the three animals from which it derives.
- Describe what the animal looks like, but not concretely or vividly enough for the reader to draw it accurately.

- May leave out or gloss over one of the following topics:
  - where the animal lives
  - its eating and sleeping habits
  - offspring
  - enemies
- Description of habitat and habits may not fit logically with what the animal is like physically.
- Refer to the animal's relationship to mankind but not really discuss it.
- Overall, does not give the reader, role-playing an encyclopedia editor, enough information to include the animal in his next edition.

2-1 A 2-1 paper will:

- Fail to give the animal either a scientific or common name.
- Not describe the animal well enough for the reader to even attempt to draw it.
- Fail to adequately explain where the animal lives, its eating and sleeping habits, offspring, and enemies.
- Neglect to refer to animal's relationship to mankind.
- Overall, give so little information that the reader, role-playing an encyclopedia editor, would definitely decide not to include the animal in his next addition.

Writing Skills

5 A 5-paper will:

- Include three well-detailed paragraphs in proper form.
- Employ rich sensory/descriptive language that helps the reader to mentally picture the animal.
- Utilize one or more similes and/or metaphors to help the reader compare what the animal might look like to something else.
- Contain only minor errors in spelling, punctuation, and usage.

4-3 A 4-3 paper will:

- Include three reasonably well-detailed paragraphs in proper form. (*Note:* A 3-paper may consist of two well-developed paragraphs.)
- Employ enough sensory/descriptive language that the reader can at least partially picture the animal.
- Contain few, if any, similes and metaphors to help the reader compare what the animal might look or act like to something else.
- Contain errors in spelling, punctuation and usage but none which interfere with the author's message.

2-1 A 2-1 paper will:

- Not be written in paragraph form. (May be all one long description without paragraphing.)

- Fail to employ enough sensory/descriptive language for the reader to picture the animal.
- Neglect to make use of similes and/or metaphors to help the reader compare what the animal might look like to something else.
- Contain major errors in spelling, punctuation and usage, which interfere with the author's message.

Illustrations:

2 Essays should be accompanied by illustrations. Illustrations which closely match the description in the encyclopedia entry should receive 2 points.

1 Illustrations which do not closely match descriptions should receive 1 point.

0 Papers turned in without illustrations should not be awarded points.

Extension Activities

Comprehension

Collect the descriptions and drawings and compile a book of the "Fantasy Zoo."

Application

Make a stuffed toy animal that resembles your fantasy animal.

Analysis

Compare and contrast your new animal with the three original animals you worked with.

Synthesis

Create a comic strip in which your animal is a family pet and create a series of cartoons showing the animal's difficulties in adapting to the house.

Evaluation

The climate of the continent is changing and a new ice age is on its way. Predict the survival rate of your new animal. Judge how can it adapt to withstand the cold weather.

Evaluation

Crossbreed your animal with another common animal. Predict the description of the new offspring.

"Thank You Ma'am":
Speculating About the Ending of a Story

Lesson

Students will speculate about an outcome and then compose an ending for the story "Thank You Ma'am" by Langston Hughes.

Objectives

Thinking Skills
Students will function at the *SYNTHESIS* level by *SPECULATING* about an ending of a story based upon facts from the story, *FORMULATING* that speculation as an ending, and *COMPOSING* that ending.

Writing Skills
Based on their understanding of the story, students will employ the composing and crafting skills of narration, showing, not telling description, and dialogue writing to complete the story, "Thank You Ma'am."

The Process

Prior to this lesson, students will have had practice in Rebekah Caplan's technique of showing, not telling.*

Prewriting

1. *Clustering:* Ask students to create a cluster of specific incidents from their lives which come to mind around the phrase, "I knew it was wrong, but I did it anyway." Assure them that their clusters will remain confidential. A sample cluster might look like this:

---

*Please see the Glossary for a description of the showing, not telling technique.

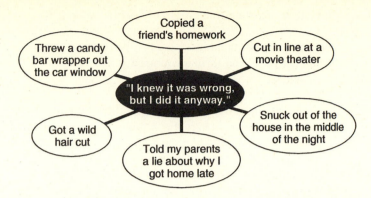

2. *Charting:* After students have completed their clusters, ask them to choose three of the incidents and to record them on the chart below. As they record, ask them to respond to the following questions for each incident:

- What did you do even though you knew it was wrong?
- Why did you do it?
- How did you feel about it afterward?
- Did your feelings about what you did cause you to take any actions? If so, what were they?

A sample chart might look like this:

What	Why	Feelings	Actions
Stole something from the store.	To see how it felt.	Felt guilty. Wished I hadn't done it.	Took it back and left it on the counter when no one was looking.
Cut off my pigtail.	Thought it would be funny.	Was embarrassed later.	Tried to tape it back on with scotch tape.
Short-sheeted my friend's bed.	For a joke.	Thought it would serve him right for playing practical jokes on me.	Apologized. Then put a lizard in his bed the next day.
Copied my friend's homework and turned it in as mine.	Didn't get mine done.	First relief, then had second thoughts.	Resolved to do my own homework next time.

3. *Sharing:* Then, divide students into groups of four and provide each group with a blank *WHAT/WHY/FEELINGS/ACTIONS* chart. Each of the four students should select one of his/her three incidents that he/she would feel comfortable sharing with his/her peers and form a composite chart comprised of one incident from each student.

4. *Showing, not telling:* Collect these composite charts and distribute them so that each group has another group's chart. Each group member should now select one of the four incidents from the chart the group received to dramatize through showing, not telling. (*Note:* More than one student can select the same incident.) The goal of this exercise is to empathize with another person's experience and to vividly describe what that person did, why he/she did it, how he/she felt about it afterwards and what actions he/she took as a result. Since these incidents come from classmates but the specific students are not identified, students will have to speculate to create a fictional account of what they believe might have happened.

    Showing, not telling paragraphs should illustrate the telling sentence, "He (or she) knew it was wrong, but he did it anyway." A sample student model is provided below:

The Clock

This never would have happened if our math teacher didn't get sick. Eric and I went to our math class and for the first time we arrived there before the bell sounded. When we arrived, I noticed that we had a sub, but I don't think Eric did because he was too busy talking to some blonde. But when Eric did notice that we had a sub, he got a gleam in his eyes and a funny grin on his face. I knew he was up to something, but, at the time, I wasn't sure what. I casually walked over to my desk, keeping my eye on Eric. I noticed Eric was still standing at the door as if he were thinking, but that would be impossible because Eric never thinks. As I kept watching Eric through the corner of my eye, I saw that he had come out of his trance and back to the real world. Eric then ran over to me so fast I thought a dog was chasing him.

    "What is it this time, Eric?" I asked.

    "Why don't we play a trick on the sub?" he said, with that same devilish gleam in his eye.

    What Eric wanted to do was, near the end of the period when the sub wasn't looking, go over to the clock and set it forward so that we could get out early. Eric told me that all I had to do was go over to the sub and distract him in anyway possible so Eric could do the dirty work. The sub was teaching the class but, of course, I wasn't paying attention, because I was too busy worrying about the clock. After the sub was done with his lecture, he went and sat down at his little desk with a picture of George Washington and started to read *Time Magazine*. Then, Eric stood up and started coughing. I figured that that was the signal so I took my math book up to the teacher. While I was walking to the teacher, I saw Eric start to go over to the clock. I told the teacher, ''I don't understand problem number 7.'' The sub started explaining it to me but, of course, again I wasn't listening. I was too busy watching Eric carry the desk, with all the colorful pieces of bubble gum stuck to the bottom, over to the clock. He stood up on the chair, slowly reached his pudgy hand up to the knob of the clock and turned the big hand of the clock ten minutes ahead. Then, he slowly stepped down and put the desk back where it was. The sub finished explaining the problem and then asked me if I understood. I said, ''What, oh yah.'' Then I went and sat down.

The sub went back to reading his magazine and then looked up at the clock. He noticed that it was time for us to go home, so he said, ''O.K. see you guys later.'' Everyone was laughing as they left. As Eric and I were leaving, I told him, ''You shouldn't have done that.''

Eric said, ''I knew it was wrong, but I had to do it anyway. You know I can't resist a good practical joke.''

''Well, next time don't count on me to be an accessory to the crime,'' I said.

''Oh, there won't be a next time. I'll be nice and give the next substitute we have a break.''

But I could tell from that devilish gleam in his eye that the temptation would be too great. Although he knew it was wrong, he just might do it again.

5. *Reading:* The preceding activities are designed to set the stage for the introduction of Langston Hughes' short story, ''Thank You Ma'am,'' and to help students to identify with the main character. Read the following portion of ''Thank you Ma'am'' aloud. Assign parts in the story so that it reads like a play.

Thank You Ma'am

She was a large woman with a large purse that had everything in it but hammer and nails. It had a long strap and she carried it slung across her shoulder. It was about eleven o'clock at night and she was walking alone, when a boy ran up behind her and tried to snatch her purse. The strap broke with the tug the boy gave it from behind. But the boy's weight and the weight of the purse caused him to lose his balance. Instead of taking off full blast, the boy fell on his back on the sidewalk and his legs flew up. The large woman simply turned around. She kicked him square in his blue-jeaned sitter. Then she reached down and picked the boy up by his shirt front. She shook him until his teeth rattled.

After that the woman said, ''Pick up my pocketbook, boy, and give it here.''

She still held him. But she bent down enough to let him to stoop and pick up her purse. Then she asked, ''Now ain't you ashamed of yourself?''

Firmly gripped by his shirt front, the boy said, "Yes'm."

The woman said, "What did you want to do it for?"

The boy said, "I didn't aim to."

She said, "You lie!"

By that time two or three people passed, turned to look, and some stood watching.

"If I turn you loose, will you run?" asked the woman.

"Yes'm," said the boy.

"Then I won't turn you loose," said the woman. She did not release him.

"Lady, I'm sorry," whispered the boy.

"Uh-hum! Your face is dirty. I got a great mind to wash your face for you. Ain't you got nobody home to tell you to wash your face?"

"No'm," said the boy.

"Then it will get washed this evening," said the large woman. She started up the street, dragging the frightened boy behind her.

He looked as if he were fourteen or fifteen. He was thin. He wore tennis shoes and blue jeans.

The woman said, "You ought to be my son. I would teach you right from wrong. Least I can do right now is wash your face. Are you hungry?"

"No'm," said the boy. "I just want you to turn me loose."

"Was I bothering you when I turned that corner? asked the woman.

"No'm."

"But you put yourself in contact with me," said the woman. "If you think that contact is not going to last a while, you got another thought coming. When I get through with you sir, you are going to remember Mrs. Luella Bates Washington Jones."

Sweat popped out on the boy's face, and he began to struggle. Mrs. Jones stopped, jerked him around in front of her, put a half nelson about his neck, and continued to drag him up the street. When she got to her door, she dragged the boy inside, down a hall, and into a large room at the rear of the house. She switched on the light and left the door open. The boy could hear other roomers laughing and talking. Some of their doors were open, too; so he knew he and the woman were not alone. The woman still had him by the neck as they stood in the middle of her room.

She said, "What is your name?"

"Roger," answered the boy.

"Then, Roger, you get to that sink and wash your face," said the woman. Then she turned him loose—at last. Roger looked at the door—looked at the woman—looked at the door—and went to the sink.

"Let the water run until it gets warm," she said. "Here's a clean towel."

"You gonna take me to jail?" asked the boy, bending over the sink.

"Not with that face. I would not take you nowhere," said the woman. "Here I am trying to get home to cook me a bite to eat, and you snatch my pocketbook! Maybe you ain't been to your supper, either, late as it be. Have you?"

"There's nobody home at my house," said the boy.

"Then we'll eat," said the woman. "I believe you're hungry—or been hungry—to try to snatch my pocketbook."

"I want a pair of suede shoes," said the boy.

"Well, you didn't have to snatch *my* pocketbook to get some suede shoes," said Mrs. Luella Bates Washington Jones. "You could of asked me."

"Ma'am?"

The water dripping from his face, the boy looked at her. There was a long pause. A very long pause. After drying his face, and not knowing what else to do, the boy dried it again. Then he turned around. The door was open . . .

> Langston Hughes
> Anthologized in *Literature and Life*
> (Glenview, Ill: Scott, Foresman and Company, 1982)

6. *Showing, not telling:* Give students the telling sentence, "He knew it was wrong, but he did it anyway." Ask them, once again, to practice writing a showing description to bring this sentence to life. But, this time, the "he" they should write about is Roger in Langston Hughes' story. In order to ensure that students don't simply summarize what they have just read, ask them to use quotes from the text and to add showing details of their own to dramatize the statement.

A sample showing, not telling description might look like this:

Long after most boys would be in bed—11 o'clock to be exact—Roger was out on the street looking for a likely target for a purse snatching. But he was no match for the "large woman with a large purse" that he singled out. Just one tug from her and he fell head over heels in the street. She grabbed him by the shirt front, kicking and struggling, and "shook him until his teeth rattled." *Oh boy, I've really gotten myself into it this time,* he thought to himself. People were already beginning to stare at him and to shake their heads. "Sweat popped out on his face." He was so flustered that he couldn't think clearly enough to come up with a good excuse to talk his way out of the mess he was in. He tried suggesting that he "didn't aim to" steal her purse, but she didn't buy it. So his next step was to apologize. "I'm sorry," he whispered. But no dice. So, after she refused to turn him loose, he began to struggle. However, struggling only caused this Mrs. Luella Bates Washington Jones to tighten her grasp. He knew it was wrong, but he did it anyway. And now he was beginning to regret wanting those blue suede shoes. He wondered what would happen next.

Prompt:

Compose an ending for the Langston Hughes' short story "Thank You Ma'am" following the lines "The door was open . . . ." Your ending should:

- reflect both a close reading of the story and your ability to make inferences about:
  - what each character does;
  - why Roger and Mrs. Jones do what they do;
  - how he/she is feeling about what has happened;
  - what actions each might take as a result.

- logically weave together the actual story and your ending for the story;
- rely on showing, not telling as a means of vividly conveying information;
- demonstrate an understanding of narrative structure;
- use dialogue as a means of revealing character development;
- display your understanding of the conventions of written English (spelling, punctuation, grammar)—especially those dealing with proper dialogue form.

Precomposing

1. *Rereading:* Ask students to silently reread the portion of ''Thank You Ma'am'' which the class previously read aloud.

2. *Quick-writing:* Then, they should speculate about how the story will end and compose an ending, that begins at the line ''The door was open . . .'' This should be a quick-write (5 minutes) in which each student narrates as rapidly as possible the ending option he or she thinks will be most appropriate for the story. When completed, these quick-writes should be put aside and referred to later.

3. *Character Analysis:* Ask students to go around the class counting off 1, 2, 1, 2, 1, 2, etc. All the students with the number 1 will analyze the character of Roger. Those with the number 2 will focus on Mrs. Jones. Pass out three differently colored markers to each student.

Roger

Using the markers, students with the number 1 should silently reread the story, focusing on Roger. Each time they come to a direct quotation by Roger, they should underline it in one color. Each time they come to something Roger does, they should underline that in a second color. Each time they find something told about Roger by the author or another character, they should underline it in the third color.

Then, they should use this information to fill out the Character Analysis Chart for Roger:

What Roger Says	What Roger's Comments Tell the Reader	What Roger Does	What Roger's Actions Tell the Reader	What Others Say About Roger	What These Statements Tell the Reader About Roger
Example: "I didn't aim to."	Roger did aim to steal her pocketbook. He is either really ashamed of what he did or he is trying to talk his way out of what he did. Maybe both things are true.	**Example:** Struggles to get away from Mrs. Jones.	Roger is nervous about what Mrs. Jones is going to do with him. His impulse is to escape from her clutches.	**Example:** "Ain't you got nobody at home to wash your face?"	Roger's face is dirty and he's also very thin. There's probably no one at home to take care of him.

After the students analyzing Roger have completed their individual charts, put them into groups of three or four to discuss the following questions.

- What did Roger do?
- Why did he do what he did?
- How did he feel about it afterward?
- Based upon his feelings in the remainder of the story, what kind of action do you think he will take?

Mrs. Jones

While the students assigned to study Roger are completing their task, those who counted off as number 2 should be completing the same process with Mrs. Jones.

Using three different colors of markers, students assigned to study Mrs. Jones should silently reread the story, focusing on Mrs. Jones. Each time they come to a direct quotation by Mrs. Jones, they should underline it in one color. Each time they come to something Mrs. Jones does, they should underline that in a second color. Each time they find something told about Mrs. Jones by the author or another character, they should underline it in the third color

Then, they should use this information to fill out the Character Analysis Chart for Mrs. Jones:

What Mrs. Jones Says	What Mrs. Jones's Comments Tell the Reader	What Mrs. Jones Does	What Mrs. Jones's Actions Tell the Reader	What Others Say About Mrs. Jones	What These Statements Tell the Reader About Mrs. Jones
Example: "You ought to be my son. I would teach you right from wrong."	Mrs. Jones still seems to have a maternal feeling toward Roger even though he tried to steal her pocketbook.	**Example:** Takes Roger home to make him a bite to eat.	Rather than blame Roger, she looks for a motive behind what he did. She decides he must be hungry to steal from her.	**Example:** She was a large woman with a large purse. The purse had everything in it but a hammer and nails.	Mrs. Jones is a large, imposing and determined lady. You don't mess with Mrs. Jones.

After they have completed their individual charts, break the students who analyzed Mrs. Jones into groups of three or four to discuss the following questions:

- What did Mrs. Jones do after Roger tried to snatch her pocketbook?
- Why did she react the way she did?
- How did she feel about what happened?
- Based upon her feelings, what kind of action do you think she will take in the remainder of the story?

4. *Sharing Character Analyses:* Now, pair up each student who analyzed Roger with a student who was assigned to study Mrs. Jones. Give each student five minutes to share with a partner:

- what each character did;
- why Roger and Mrs. Jones did what they did;
- how he/she is feeling about what has happened;
- what actions each might take as a result.

5. *Silent dialogue:* Keep students in the same pairs—one who analyzed Roger and one who focused on Mrs. Jones. Direct them to look at the portion of "Thank You Ma'am" given to the class to read and to note the places where Roger and Mrs. Jones talk to each other. Then, ask the pairs to compare the sections of the story written in dialogue form with the other portions of the narrative. As a class, make a list or cluster of "what's different when we write dialogue." A sample cluster might look like this:

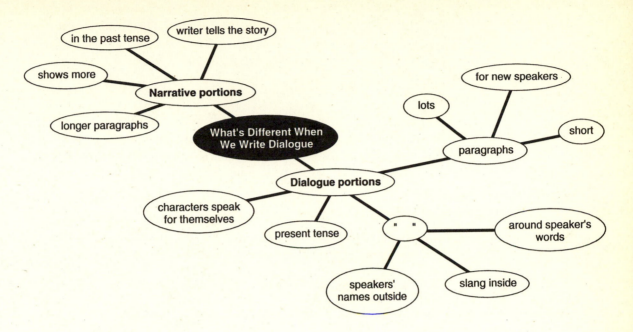

Then, give the pairs a chance to practice writing dialogue in the roles of the characters they have just analyzed. They can begin their conversation with the end of the portion of the story they have just read . . . "The door was open . . ."

They may choose from the following dialogue starters below or select any other option that seems plausible to them:

To begin with Mrs. Jones:

- "You eyein' that door pretty hard, boy. You fixin' to run?"
- "What you hungry for, son? I'm going to make you a meal you won't forget."
- "I was young like you once, boy. I know what it's like to want something that isn't yours."

To begin with Roger:

- "You sure you ain't gonna take me to jail, Ma'am?"
- "Ok, I'll wash my face. What you got to eat?"
- "You turned me loose. Does that mean I can go if I want?"

Advise students that the goal of this exercise is not to complete an ending to the story, but simply to experience being in the role of one of the characters and to share their insights into what that character might say with their partner. Once students finish their silent dialogues, have them read them aloud to see if they sound like Roger and Mrs. Jones.

Writing

Have students go back to their quick-write endings of ''Thank You Ma'am'' and see if their first impression of how the story would end still seems appropriate now that they have taken a closer look at the characters. They can also use their dialogues and character analysis charts in composing their endings to the story.

Revising

1. *Critiquing Models:* Have students read and discuss the following sample endings to ''Thank You Ma'am,'' focusing on how each is effective and how each can be improved. You may wish to put these student models on an overhead and to record the students' comments as in the first example provided below:

Effective to show what Roger is thinking. Seems like what would be on his mind.

The door was open. Now's my chance to get out of here, he thought to himself. Maybe I can sneak out when she goes to fix dinner. But she seems like such a nice lady. It wouldn't be right to just run away after I promised. Besides, she must trust me a lot to bring me in her home and open her arms out to me. She has even offered me a free meal. Nobody's ever done that before. But what if she calls the cops on me. Then I'll be sitting up in jail feelin' like a fool for not runnin' away when I had the chance havin' no one to blame but me. Still, if I run away, I could probably never come back here in this neighborhood because she'd catch me and turn me in for sure.

←

Maybe some dialogue could go here between these two paragraphs that would lead to Roger's next thought.

Doesn't look like I've got much of a choice but to stay here anyway. I got no place to go, so I might as well take a chance and stay. After all, if she can trust me, I should be able to trust her. She seems to be real lonely like me. Must be sad to live in this place all alone. Yes, I'll stay here and keep her company for a little while.

The tense of the ending changed here.

Mrs. Luella Bates Washington Jones gives the young boy a bath and feeds him. After they have eaten, Mrs. Jones gives the boy a pair of her husband's old shoes but they are too big and she tells him that he will grow into them. Then she gives him some money to get him through the week. The young boy learns a valuable lesson about people and never steals a purse or anything again.

—Marcus Mumford

This is all telling instead of showing. The writer should turn this from a summary into a narrative.

*   *   *

The door was open. He dashed out. As he ran down the flight of stairs, one thought crossed his mind—over and over again. Why does this stranger care so much about me? He became very curious as to why a perfect stranger would care about a kid who has just stolen their purse.

Just as Mrs. Jones stepped out of the kitchen and into the living room, she saw him sitting on the couch. He was breathing heavily and in a deep sweat.

She asked, ''Good heavens, boy what in God's name is wrong with you?''

''Nothin' Ma'am. I guess it's the heat.''

—Shelly Register

*   *   *

The door was open. Roger thought, *Should I try to get away? Naw, she might catch me. Then she'll be sure to take me to jail.*

''Boy, why you looking at the door like that? I done turned you loose and you want to get sneaky?''

''No'm.'' said Roger. ''I was just thinking about the suede shoes.''

Mrs. Jones went over to her stove and started filling the two plates she had with food.

''Come and sit down, Roger.''

''Yes'm.'' They both ate in silence chewing and savoring the food. Roger finished his food first and in a flash ran through the door and to the outside. He stopped outside her window and said, ''Thank you, Ma'am, but I gotta go home.'' Then he was gone.

Mrs. Jones sat in her chair thinking over what had happened in the last half hour, and it dawned on her that she'd never see that boy again—Well, at least the boy said thank you.

—Pam Barnes

After critiquing the sample student models, students can break into groups of three and discuss what is effective and what needs to be improved in their own endings.

2. *Revising Checklist:* Individually, or in pairs, students can also review their ending using the following checklist. This will ensure that what they have written meets the requirements specified in the prompt (See Figure 16).

Figure 16: Revising Checklist   **"Thank You Ma'am"**

This story ending:	Great	Good	Needs Work
Reflects a close reading of the story			
Makes inferences about: • what each character says • why Roger and Mrs. Jones do what they do • how he/she is feeling about what has happened • what actions each might take as a result			
Logically weaves the actual story ending with writer's ending for the story			
Relies on showing, not telling as a means of vividly conveying information			
Uses dialogue as a means of revealing character development			
Demonstrates an understanding of narrative structure			
Displays a knowledge of the conventions of written English (spelling, punctuation, grammar), especially those dealing with proper dialogue form			

Note: This checklist could also be used for teacher/student conferences.

Editing

Students should exchange papers with a new partner and check each other's work for proper dialogue form. Some guidelines for checking correctness follow:

Compare the dialogue places in the story ending with those in the printed version.

- Do they look alike?
- Are they different? Where? Underline these parts.
- Is there a paragraph change for each speaker change? Use a ¶ symbol to signal your partner that he/she needs to indent.
- Are the exact words—and only the exact words—of the characters in quotation marks? If not, move them/add the quotation marks.
- Are punctuation marks used appropriately with question marks?
  - Periods always go inside.
  - Commas always go inside.
  - Question marks and exclamation points vary.
- Are speaker identifications set off from what they say by commas? If not, add them/move them.
- Is the tense right?
  - Narration is in the past tense.
  - Dialogue is usually in the present tense.

Partners should also mark any errors that they notice in spelling, punctuation, grammar, and sentence structure.

Evaluation

The following scoring guide may be used for self, peer or teacher evaluation.

Scoring Guide: ''Thank you Ma'am''

Reading/Thinking: Check if this paper

☐ reflects a close reading of the story

☐ displays the writer's ability to make inferences about the story based on facts from the story

☐ reflects an understanding of what each character does, why Roger and Mrs. Jones do what they do, and how he/she is feeling about what has happened

☐ uses facts and inferences from the reading of the story to speculate about what actions each character might take as a result—(based upon their understanding of what has happened, why it has happened, and how he/she is feeling about it).

☐ Reading/Thinking Subtotal
4 points possible

Thinking/Writing: Check if this paper

☐ logically weaves together the facts and inferences that the writer gleans from the actual story with what he or she speculates about the story's ending

☐ relies on showing, not telling, as a means of vividly conveying information

☐ relies on dialogue as a means of character development

☐ displays an understanding of narrative structure

☐ Thinking/Writing Subtotal
4 points possible

Writing/Editing: Check if this paper

☐ uses paragraph change to show each speaker change

☐ encloses the character's exact words—and only his or her exact words—in quotation marks

☐ displays knowledge of how to use punctuation in conjunction with quotation marks:

- periods inside
- commas inside
- question marks inside a direct quote or outside if whole statement is a question
- exclamation marks inside a direct quote or outside if whole statement is an exclamation

☐ sets off speaker's identification from what he or she says with commas

☐ sets dialogue in the present tense

☐ sets narration in the past tense

☐ Writing/Editing Subtotal
6 points possible

☐ **Total Score**
14 points possible

Extension Activities

Analysis

Provide students with Langston Hughes' ending to "Thank you Ma'am." The remainder of his story is printed below:

He would make a dash for it down the hall. He could run, run, run, **run!**

The woman was sitting on the daybed. After a while she said, "I were young once and I wanted things I could not get."

There was another long pause. The boy's mouth opened. Then he frowned, not knowing he frowned.

The woman said, "Um-hum! You thought I was going to say, *but, I didn't snatch people's pocketbooks!* Well, I wasn't going to say that." Pause. Silence. "I have done things, too, which I would not tell you, son, I neither tell God, if He didn't already know. Everybody's got something in common. So you set down while I fix us something to eat. You might run that comb through your hair. Then you will look presentable."

In another corner of the room behind a screen was a gas plate and an icebox. Mrs. Jones got up and went behind the screen. The woman did not watch the boy to see if he was going to run now. She didn't watch her purse, which she left behind her on the daybed. But the boy took care to sit on the far side of the room, away from the purse. He thought she could easily see him out of the corner of her eye if she wanted to. He did not trust the woman not to trust him. And he did **not** want to be mistrusted now.

"Do you need somebody to go to the store?" asked the boy. "Maybe to get some milk or something?"

"Don't believe I do," said the woman, "unless you want sweet milk yourself. I was going to make cocoa out of this canned milk I got here."

"That will be fine," said the boy.

She heated some lima beans and ham, made the cocoa, and set the table. The woman did not ask the boy anything about where he lived, or his folks, or anything else that would embarrass him. Instead, as they ate, she told him about her job in a hotel beauty shop, what the work was like, and how all kinds of women came in and out. Then she cut him a half of her ten-cent cake.

"Eat some more, son," she said.

When they were finished eating, she got up and said, "Now, here, take this ten dollars and buy yourself some suede shoes. And, next time, do not make the mistake of latching on to my pocketbook nor nobody **else's** because shoes got by devilish ways will burn your feet. I got to get my rest now. But from here on, son, I hope you will behave yourself."

She led him down the hall to the front door and opened it. "Good night! Behave yourself, boy!" she said, looking out into the street as he went down the steps.

The boy wanted to say something more than, "Thank you, ma'am," to Mrs. Luella Bates Washington Jones. Although his lips moved, he couldn't even say that as he turned at the foot of the stairs and looked back at the large woman in the door. Then she shut the door.

Prompt:

You have just read Langston Hughes' ending to "Thank you Ma'am." Compare and contrast his ending with the ending you wrote. What parts of your stories are alike? How are they different? What ending do you like the best and why?

Application

Turning Your Ending of "Thank You Ma'am" Into a Screenplay/Drama

1. You have learned that short stories often contain dialogue. *Dialogue* is a term used to refer to conversation between characters. Dramas have dialogue, too, but there are different conventions for writing dialogue in a drama. A *convention* is an agreed-upon way of writing something.

2. Look at two or three scenes from plays. Now, look back at the dialogue cluster and checklist for writing dialogue in the lesson we have just completed. Use these as a model to make a cluster and checklist for dramatic dialogue.

3. Compare your checklists. How are they alike? How are they different? Complete a Venn Diagram for dialogue. Model the one below.

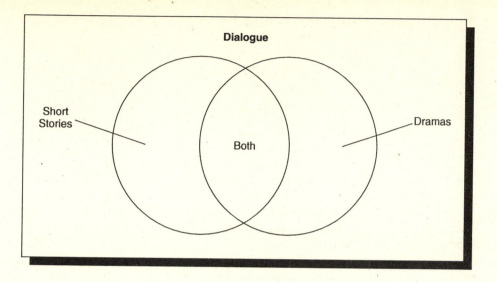

Dialogue

Short
Stories

Dramas

Both

Prompt:

Now, using a scene as a model and referring to your *CHECKLIST FOR DRAMA DIALOGUE,* adapt your ending of the story, ''Thank You Ma'am'' for production. When a writer changes the *genre* or kind of writing from a novel or short story to a drama, we call him a ''screenwriter.'' When you have completed your adaptation, you will be a screenwriter too.

4. Find some partners.

5. Assign jobs. You'll need a stage crew, a prop crew, a costume crew, a cast, and a director.

6. Get your jobs done. For the stage crew, that means creating scenery. For the prop crew, it means finding tables, chairs, and other props and setting them up and taking them down. For the costume crew, it means finding clothes, shoes, and jewelry for the characters. For the cast members, it means memorizing and rehearsing lines.

7. Produce your play for an audience.

After the Storm:
A Continuation of *The Old Man and the Sea*

Lesson

Students will compose an imaginative/narrative extension to *The Old Man and the Sea* by Ernest Hemingway, paralleling the story of Christ.

Objectives

Thinking Skills
After *ANALYZING* the novel for religious parallels with the story of the Crucifixion, the students will *IMAGINE* and *FORMULATE* a continuation of the novel. They will *PROPOSE* events which are in keeping with the established characterization and the Hemingway Code, as well as with the symbolic parallels they have found.

Writing Skills
Students will write a narrative sequel to the story with dialogue and with sentences which show instead of tell. They will organize events in order to create symbolic and structural parallels in their ending. In addition, they will use word choice, tone, and point of view in keeping with those of the novel, as well as transitions and supporting details.

The Process

This lesson should be used to reinforce an understanding of the religious symbolism in *The Old Man and the Sea* and to give students an opportunity to apply one kind of symbolism to their writing—in this case, to a continuation of the novel. In conjunction with this lesson, therefore, students will have read or will be in the final days of reading the book and will have received at least a basic knowledge level lecture and handout on the Hemingway Code, plus a lecture on the tone and point of view of the story. (See the cluster in the *PREWRITING* section for aspects of the Code.)

In this particular lesson, it is frequently necessary to go back to the knowledge level in order to build on several concepts that are essential to prepare students to respond to the prompt.

1. First, you will build on the students' knowledge of the novel and of the Hemingway Code.

2. Next, you will build the students' knowledge about the story of the crucifixion of Christ.

3. Then, you will help the students see how the plot of the novel and the story of Christ are similar.

4. Next, you will help them understand how the elements of the Hemingway Code parallel the characteristics of Santiago and how both of them emulate the characteristics of Christ.

5. Only then can the students begin to see how they might extend the story.

In addition, you must spend about 10 minutes daily reviewing the material previously covered to provide a greater familiarity and to allow for greater student success. Question, quiz, discuss or use any other techniques with which you are comfortable. Just be sure to review the following information briefly each day in a variety of ways:

- The Hemingway Code
- The characters and plot of the novel
- The timeline information

Also, it would be helpful to review showing, not telling* skills. This lesson will require several days of in-class time.

Day 1

Prewriting

Have students complete a chart about the characters in the novel. First, have them list the characters, label main and secondary characters with M or S, and then record all of the details they can recall about each one: physical information, personality, and motivations for their actions.

Next, with the whole group, cluster the characteristics of the Hemingway Code.

*See "showing, not telling" in the Glossary.

Character Chart				
	Santiago (M)	Manolin (S)	Pedrico	(etc.)
Physical Information	thin and gaunt deep wrinkles on back of neck strong (etc.)			
Personality	humble simple (etc.)			
Motivations	to catch a big fish to not give up (etc.)			

Example:

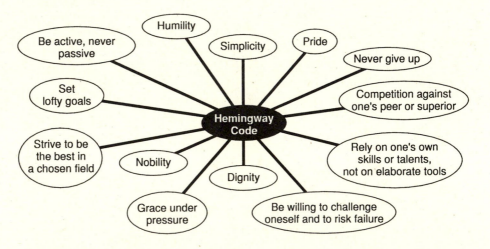

Day 2

Give students a worksheet, such as the one on page 303. Encourage them to locate specific details in the book and to restate the information as thoroughly as possible on the worksheet. Leave ample room for their answers.

The Old Man and the Sea Worksheet

Directions: Locate specific evidence stated in the book to answer these questions. RESTATE the information in your own words. Be thorough; do not leave anything out. Identify the page numbers on which you find your answers so that you can return to them quickly at a later time, if necessary.

1. Tell what Manolin thinks of the old man. Pages _____
2. What do the boy's parents think of Santiago? Pages _____
3. What do the other fishermen think of Santiago? Pages _____
4. Describe the old man's personality and his character. Pages _____
5. Explain what the old man thinks of Joe DiMaggio. Pages _____
6. What does the old man think of the boy? Pages _____
7. What does Santiago think of the fish? Pages _____
8. How does the old man live? Describe his house. Pages _____
   Describe the contents of the house. Pages _____
   Describe the old man's clothing. Pages _____
   Describe his boat. Pages _____
   Describe his fishing gear. Pages _____
9. Tell where the old man chooses to fish and the reasons he gives for that choice. Pages _____
10. Explain the odds against Santiago successfully bringing in the marlin.

After these questions have been completed, discuss the answers in class. Encourage students to fill in any details that they might have missed.

Day 3

Draw a blank timeline on the board and hand out a duplicate one for the students. Have students sequence in detail Santiago's actions from the time he lands on shore to the end of the book. Include Manolin where necessary.

Example:

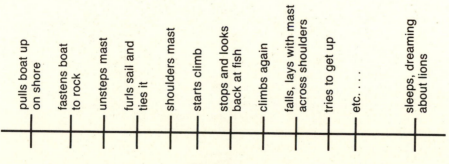

Santiago . . .

Note: Students may find it helpful to construct a timeline on a wall or bulletin board in your classroom. Use yarn for the line and colored index cards for each action. Tack the cards at the correct intervals *above* the line. When you reach the *second time line* in this lesson, use *different colored cards* and tack them *below* the same line or *below* a parallel line so that the students can see the parallel actions.

Ask your students how many of them know, at least partially, the story of Christ. Be very aware of those students whose backgrounds are such that they have little or no knowledge of the story. (For your reference, go to the last two chapters of any of the first four books of *The New Testament* and to the fifth book.) Conduct a careful discussion based on these two items:

• Recall as much of the story of the persecution, crucifixion and resurrection of Jesus Christ as you can.

• What happened after the resurrection?

Have your students record this information in their notes for later use.

Day 4

Next, divide your class into groups of three to five students and give them a handout of questions to research:

Interview/Research Questions

Directions: Answer all questions with as many facts and details as you can.

1. Who are Christ's tormentors?
2. How is He persecuted?
3. What happened the night that the Romans took Jesus Christ into custody?
4. Does He ever want to give up? When?
5. What is placed on His head? When?
6. How is His forehead cut?
7. Who has He chosen to carry on His work?
8. What are disciples?
9. What was Peter's occupation?
10. What occupation did the other disciples have?
11. Tell about Christ carrying the cross to Cavalry.
12. What happens along the way?
13. In what position was He while on the cross?
14. What happens while He is on the cross?
15. What is the weather like after the crucifixion?
16. How many days passed from the burial to resurrection?
17. What is the resurrection?
18. Did anyone visit His grave?
19. What happened to Christ after the resurrection?
20. What happened to the disciples after the resurrection?
21. Did you find out any other information that might be useful? What?

The groups are to collaborate in researching the answers. Suggest these sources of information:

- Parent or guardian
- Clergyman
- Another teacher
- A knowledgeable classmate or friend
- The Bible
- Other books about the story of Christ
- A children's picture Bible

Day 5

Select one member of each group to report the results of their work to the whole class when they have finished. Their assignment is to accomplish two tasks which they are to talk through and then to document for later use.

Task 1:   Restate the story of Christ in your own words, incorporating all parts contributed by the class. Be sure you understand what happens *after* the resurrection.

Task 2:   Explain Christ's motivation, personality, and ethics. What had he hoped to accomplish?

Following the group work, ask one group reporter to begin telling the story. Classmates are to add any details that have been omitted. Divide the tasks so that each reporter gets a chance to speak. For example, Task 1 can be divided chronologically into 1.) persecution and background; 2.) crucifixion and resurrection; 3.) after the resurrection—immediately and within a few weeks.

If you feel that it is necessary, you may begin the story and let the students provide details and the time sequence.

Repeat the timeline exercise of *DAY 3,* only this time have the students sequence in detail the events leading to and following the crucifixion of Christ. Include the disciples where necessary.

Arrange this information on a wall time-line parallel to the Santiago one. (*Note:* Expect the Christ line to be much longer.)

This is a critical step in the thinking process. Begin by referring students to the body of information they have gathered so far. By a show of hands, determine which students feel knowledgeable about the Hemingway Code, the characteristics of Christ, and the characteristic of Santiago. Then, group students so that each group has at least one person knowledgeable in each of these three areas.

In their groups, students are to reexamine and compare the information in these areas. They are to analyze and chart the similarities that they find.

Day 6

Have groups share their charts in class discussion.

Sample entry on chart of similarities:

Elements of the Hemingway Code	Characteristics of Santiago	Characteristics of Jesus Christ
Pride in simplicity, at least on surface	A man of simple life style; not complicated on surface	Praised simple pleasures, simplicity in living, simple, basic moral ideas
Never gives up	Had gone 84 days without catching a fish	Many doubted His ability, but He kept proving it to them; accomplished what He set out to do
Humility	Knew he had attained humility but was too simple to wonder when he had attained it; knew there was no disgrace in being humble; doesn't speak of his greatness	On the eve of His arrest, washed the apostle's feet to teach them a lesson in humility

Prompt:

Near the end of Ernest Hemingway's *The Old Man and the Sea,* Manolin talks with Santiago about the two of them fishing together again. At first Santiago says, "No, I am not lucky." Manolin insists, and Santiago responds by listing what "we must get" in order to go out again. He also speculates that the village will experience three, maybe more, days of heavy winds during which no one will be able to fish. When Manolin leaves to get food, newspapers and medicine, the old man rests.

Your assignment is to write a continuation of the story, projecting Santiago and Manolin beyond the end of the book.

You now have two choices:

- Begin your story at that point, imagining what occurs during the next three days, the days of the storm; or
- Begin your story early on the fourth day. Imagine that, at the end of three days, the winds die down and Manolin has a good lance and a knife and has everything ready to go out again.

Refer to your Christ timeline. From the period after the crucifixion, select one event with which you can draw a parallel in your own story.

Use your timelines, notes, and charts. Remember that your characters must behave according to the Hemingway Code, and the story must parallel that of Christ in a realistic way. Your continuation needs only contain one major event. You must write your narration as if it were a continuation of the novel. Be careful to show what happened instead of just telling your reader. Use dialogue, as Hemingway does, to further the action of your event. Limit your ending to no more than five typed pages.

Day 7

Precomposing

Now that your students have discovered some existing parallels between the story of Christ and *The Old Man and the Sea,* you will need to help them prepare for their sequels by providing some questions for their consideration. A full class discussion is probably the most effective arena for this planning session. In addition, a handout similar to the chart below may assist the students in recording their ideas.

Christ's Story	Your Possible Ending

To stimulate discussion, ask students such questions as the following. Allow students time to write down their ideas before you give the next question.

Option: You might want to try a guided imagery during which these questions are posed to the class.

- What occurrences after the crucifixion might you use as a parallel for your story?
- What happened to Christ?
- What did Christ's followers do?
- Imagine what Santiago might do next.
- What might Manolin do while Santiago rest and heals?
- Manolin and Santiago talk of going out together after the winds die down and after Santiago is healed and rested. Do they?
- What could happen after the three days of heavy breeze?
- Does Santiago go out again?

- Does Manolin go out with him?
- Does Manolin go out alone?
- Does Manolin continue to fish from one of the large boats that stays in close to shore?

After the group discussion, give your students overnight to write a one paragraph statement about what they intend to do. In this paragraph, they should address the following concerns:

- Which event associated with Christ is to be paralleled and why that event was selected;
- Which character(s) will be involved;
- Where the action will occur;
- What Code characteristic(s) their ending will show;
- Briefly, how they will make the parallel;
- Why that ending is a believable extension of Hemingway's novel.

Day 8

Next, have students sequence or outline their endings. Respond to these papers, and return them to the students the next day. Your main concern should be whether the ending is well thought out, parallel, and believable.

A sample sequence might look like this:

- Santiago eats with Manolin.
- Manolin goes fishing alone.
- Santiago goes out in his own skiff to check on Manolin.
- Their boats are separated by a strong current, and Manolin tries to row against it.
- Santiago is able to reach Manolin again.
- Santiago teaches Manolin more about how to fish and how to handle the sea.
- Santiago assures Manolin that he will always be with the boy to help and to guide him.
- Santiago's boat disappears into the fog.

Give further help in planning, if necessary. Students need to develop a clear strategy before they begin to write.

Day 9

Focus on some oral and written exercises to help your students *show* the story, *not tell* it. Select portions of the book rich in dialogue and in showing statements, and model how telling sentences can be made into showing ones.

Examples of showing, not telling:

- The boy told the old man to rest while he went to the drugstore for medicine for Santiago's hands. (Telling)

  "Rest well, old man. I will bring stuff from the drugstore for your hands." (Showing)

- The old man wanted to catch up on all the news so he asked for all the newspapers he had missed. (Telling)

  "Bring any of the papers of the time that I was gone," the old man said. (Showing)

- The boy was worried about the old man and saddened by what had happened. (Telling)

  As the boy went out the door and down the worn coral rock road, he was crying again. (Showing)

Next, model some possible transition sentences, and have students suggest some of their own. These will be useful between the novel and the student's ending and between segments of the continuation itself.

Examples of Transition Sentences:

- The boy tucked the old army blanket carefully around the old man's shoulders as the day cooled and he waited.
- The old man stirred reluctantly from his dream and looked at the boy on the chair. He loved the lions playing on the beach and he loved the boy.

  "Did you bring the papers?"

  "Yes, and I have stuff for your hands."

- When the old man woke again it was cool and the sky was losing its light.

  "I am hungry now."

  "I brought the medicine and papers. While you read, I will bring some food."

Day 10

Writing

Allow some in-class time for students to work on this assignment, but expect the majority of the work to be done at home. Give three to five days until the first draft is due. Using those drafts, conduct the following sharing session.

Three to five days later

Sharing

Use read-around groups* of four or five, and allow students to select the best papers in each group. Ask students to identify the major qualities of the top papers. From their input, create a primary trait scoring guide.

*See "read-around groups" in the Glossary.

Goals

- Make the narrative *sound* like the story (showing, not telling).
- Use dialogue to further the action of the sequel.
- Make the ending plausible and not too long.
- Be sure the created ending is parallel to the events following the crucifixion and the storm.
- Be sure that Santiago and Manolin act in a manner consistent with the Code and with their personalities.
- Introduce no new characters of any significance. (Static characters similar to Pedrico, the other fishermen, or the tourists at the end of the novel may be acceptable.)

With response partners, encourage students to make written comments about any inconsistencies that they find between the Code, the Christ parallel, and the extension. A response form will help partners respond efficiently.

Response Form

The Christ parallel I see in your ending to the story is . . .

_____

_____

_____

This is how I see your parallel:

your ending	original story

Response partners should also comment on each aspect of the ending as addressed in the *Goals* list above.

Revising

Before students revise:

- Direct them to reexamine the Hemingway Code and their notes on the story of Christ;

- Suggest that they use dialogue to further the action in at least one part of their extension if they have not already done that;

- Remind them to show, not tell the story.

Editing

Students should edit with particular attention to use of quotes in dialogue form and to use of Hemingway-like style and vocabulary.

Evaluation

Score papers using the primary trait scoring guide previously created. A sample guide might look like this:

6 A 6-response is an excellent paper which completely and effectively addresses all aspects of the assignment. It will have all or most of the following:

- Excellent organization and content
  - Event has imaginative, effective parallels to events following the crucifixion
  - Description of the event shows and doesn't just tell
  - Characters are consistent with code
  - Sequence of events is quite clear
  - Use of effective dialogue to further action
- Appropriate vocabulary
- Appropriate sentence structure
- Mastery of mechanics, spelling, and usage

5 A 5-response applies to a paper which is a thinner version of a 6. It includes all aspects of the assignment, but with less depth or expression. It will have:

- Good organization and content
  - Christ parallel is effective and consistent
  - Description of the event shows and doesn't just tell
  - Characters are consistent with code
  - Transition between ideas but not as smooth as a 6-paper
  - Dialogue is used to carry action
- Less mature vocabulary
- Appropriate sentence variety
- A few errors in mechanics, spelling, and usage but none that interfere with the message

4 A 4-response includes all aspects of the assignment, but may be weak in development of organization or content. It will be adequate but less mature and will have:

- Basic organization, but not fully developed in one or more of the following ways:
  - Christ parallel not as clearly identified
  - Description adequate but possibly unimaginative, containing less detail and more telling than showing
  - Characters are consistent with code
  - Some transition but sequence of events is less clear
  - Some explanation of the event but less emphasis on its significance
  - Less use of dialogue
- Adequate vocabulary
- Less appropriate sentences
- Some errors in mechanics, spelling, and usage but none that interfere with the message

3 A 3-response is a lower half paper whose writer has ignored part of the assignment, treating the subject superficially. Errors interfere with content. A 3-paper:

- Addresses prompt but is not fully organized
  - Events are not clearly parallel and sequence is unclear
  - Little description or flat description
  - Few transitions, unclear sequence
  - Characters are inconsistent with code
- Less appropriate vocabulary
- Little sentence variety
- Several errors in mechanics, spelling, and usage which interfere with the message

2 A 2-response is assigned to poorly written papers which present some content. Error dominates paper. Paper has:

- Little organization
  - Little or no description
  - No transitions
  - No explanation
  - No parallel to Christ
  - No consistency of characters with code
- Inappropriate vocabulary
- Inappropriate sentences
- Serious mechanical, spelling, and usage errors that obscure the message
- Problems with legibility

1 A 1-response ignores the requirements of the assignment and/or is incomplete, inconsistent in content/organization, or so riddled with errors that it is unreadable.

Extension Activities

Evaluation   Pair your students with a different partner. Have students judge their partner's projection. In a written commentary, evaluate the choice of events and actions on the basis of their consistency with the Christ story and the Hemingway Code. Students must support their assessments with specifics from the partner's paper.

Student Model

Time passed, and the boy grew hungry. He went down to the Terrace. Pedrico was there. He asked about the old man, but Manolin did not reply. He had tears in his eyes. He got some food from Martin and hurried back to the old man's shack. The sky was dark and looked threatening.

I wonder if I should wake him while the food is still hot, the boy thought. No, I shouldn't. He had a hard trip. He deserves to rest.

Outside it was beginning to rain, and the wind was blowing. "He was right," the boy thought. "The *brisa* is here." The boy set the food on the table and sat down again.

When the old man awoke, Manolin was asleep. He noticed the food on the table and he ate it even though it was cold. The sound of the old man eating awakened the boy.

"Where did you get the food from?" the old man asked.

"I got it from Martin. He said that any one who brings in a fish that size deserves a good dinner."

The boy watched the old man eat. When he was done, Manolin got up to leave.

"I missed you," he said again.

"I missed you, too," replied the boy.

He hurried down the road to his home. It was night time, but there were no stars out. The rain clouds had covered them all up.

When the old man woke in the morning, it was still windy outside. "I wonder if I should go out today," he thought. "The great DiMaggio would not let bad weather keep him from playing." He was about to step outside when Manolin appeared.

"You weren't going to go out today, were you?"

"I am a fisherman, and the wind isn't that strong."

"You need to rest yourself. Look at your hands."

"They do not bother me. I caught the fish with a cramp in my hand. They will not bother me now."

"I will not let you go out. You are an old man and you need your rest. Sit down and tell me about the catch."

The old man was about to protest again except Pedrico had appeared in the doorway.

"Thank you for the head."

"You are welcome," the old man said.

"How do you feel?"

"I feel fine," he said with a strange look in his eye. "My little fisherman here will not let me go out today."

"He is right. I think that the storm may get worse, and you need a rest."

The three went inside and sat down. There wasn't much room left. They talked about the old man's outing. Outside it was still windy, and the rain still fell.

Pedrico left after a while. He came back with some lunch and coffee for the old man and the boy.

"Thank you again for the fish head," he said as he went out the door.

"You're welcome," the old man called out after him. He felt good inside. He was finally able to give Pedrico something in return for everything he had gotten from him.

Manolin spoke first, "Many people thought you were dead."

"But the important question is whether you ever thought that I was dead."

The boy was ashamed to speak, "I thought about it three times. I was trying to think logically, but I couldn't make myself believe it. Inside, I knew you would come back."

The two sat in silence. The only sound was the steady rain pounding against the walls of the old man's shack. The wind was nearly blowing it sideways. This time the old man spoke first. "I have never spent so long inside, but I suppose that I can't go outside right now."

"You are right. You have been inside ever since you got back. But do not worry, I am sure that the weather will clear up tonight."

"The wind was already beginning to blow when I came into the harbor."

"That was two nights ago. This is the third night that the weather has been bad."

"It is getting late. You should be getting home."

"But I do not want to go home now," the boy said. "I like being with you."

"Your parents are probably worried and you might go out fishing with him tomorrow. You have not had *salao* with him."

"You had luck in catching the fish."

"But I could not bring him home. I am not lucky."

"I will convince my father that you are lucky. Then he will let me go out with you."

"Then you must get home now and get some sleep," the old man said.

The boy got up. "You are well today. Would you like supper?"

"No, I do not need it," the old man replied.

"I will go now, but I am going out with you tomorrow."

The boy left. The old man took off his trousers and rolled them up with his newspaper inside them. I must get some new papers soon, he thought. I would like to know how DiMaggio is doing. He lay down on his bed, using his trousers as a pillow and he pulled the blanket over himself. Outside he could hear that the rain was still falling. It was only a light rain, and the wind was not so hard.

He was asleep in a short time, and he dreamed about the lions.

He woke when he smelled the land breeze. It would be nice to go out fishing again, the old man thought. He unrolled his trousers and put them on. He walked outside. Anxiously he walked down the pathway to get the boy.

by Denise Lew

A Letter From the Heart of Darkness

Lesson

Students will write a letter as though they were Marlow in Joseph Conrad's *Heart of Darkness* to any plausible person describing and reflecting upon their experiences in the Congo.

Objectives

Thinking Skills
Students will utilize synthesis level thinking skills:

- to *IMAGINE* they are Marlow;
- to *EMULATE* his character and personality;
- to *CREATE* a letter;
- to *SPECULATE* about Kurtz.

Writing Skills
Students will write in the practical/informative domain by creating a letter from Marlow to another person. Students will use imaginative/narrative skills to convey events of the journey. The skills to be emphasized are:

- writing a friendly, fluent letter
- using correct letter form
- utilizing descriptive word choice
- selecting details and events
- emulating Marlow's point of view
- emulating Conrad's style.

The Process

In order to successfully complete this assignment, it is important that the students read *Heart of Darkness* carefully and clearly understand the setting and plot of the story. The following activities, discussion, and writing assignments will involve the students in an in-depth study of the characterization of Marlow and Kurtz and the major themes of the book. Teachers may need to condense these activities and steps to fit their respective schedules.

Prewriting

The activities and discussion questions in this section of the writing process help the students discover the subject and become more familiar with those aspects of the book that will lead them to the synthesis level of critical thinking.

Activity

Step 1. Write the word *DARKNESS* on the board. Ask students to list all the words, ideas, or associations that come to mind as they think about *DARKNESS*. Give them three to five minutes and then cluster* with the class. A sample cluster might look like this:

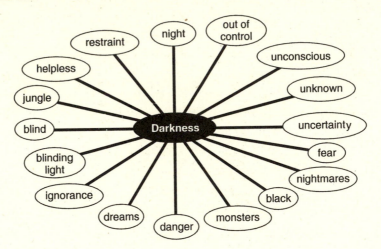

Step 2. Assign groups of five to six students to cluster one or more of the following terms in relation to the book.

- Heart
- Journey
- Light
- Unknown
- The Company

- Ivory
- Noble Cause
- Black
- (Primordial) Forest
- The Natives

Then, have each group share their cluster on the board or an overhead. Allow other groups to add their ideas to the clusters.

Alternate Activity for Step 1. Ask each student in the class to pick a partner. Explain that every class member will have an opportunity to experience a journey

*See the Glossary for a complete definition of clustering.

as well as to become the guide for a journey. Pass out one blindfold to each pair of students, and ask them to choose which role they prefer to assume to begin with. Once the students have selected their respective roles, the guide should assist his/her partner in putting on the blindfold. It is the guide's responsibility to lead the blindfolded person out of the classroom. Each guide will be given a map of the route planned by the teacher so that each person will experience senses of smell, texture, taste, and the sensation of ascending and descending, the feeling of an open space versus a closed-in space, changing temperatures, and any other aspect of the journey that the instructor feels is important. Obviously, there should be two routes so that when the students change partners the guide will not have knowledge of the journey. No conversation should take place during this journey. However, students can communicate through body language. After approximately 5 to 10 minutes (depending on how much time is available for the activity), the students should stop and switch roles.

Alternate Activity for Step 2. When students return to the classroom, write the words *JOURNEY INTO THE UNKNOWN* on the board. Ask them to put these words in the center of a blank piece of paper and to cluster (in single words and short phrases) all of the images, associations, and feelings associated with their journey in a circle around the stimulus phrase. Tell them, at the point in their clustering that they feel ready, to describe what it was like to be blind and to venture into the unknown. They can use any form of writing they choose: stream of consciousness, poetry, complete but disconnected sentences, or chains of sentence fragments, a formal paragraph, etc. A sample cluster is provided below:

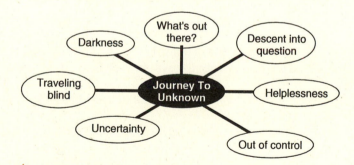

Step 3. Cluster with the class *HEART OF DARKNESS*. Students should see the relationship here to their previous clusters.

Step 4. Have students write in their learning logs about their overall impressions of *Heart of Darkness* (10 min.)

- Have them share their responses and discuss them.
- Then, have them compile a response to be shared with the large group.

Step 5. After students have had an opportunity to cluster and do some expressive writing about *Heart of Darkness,* begin a discussion of the novel with the following types of general questions:

- Did Marlow know what he was getting into when he ventured into the heart of darkness?
- Compare his illusions with the reality of the journey.
- If you had to divide this novel into three parts, how would you do it?
  - up to the arrival at the Congo
  - the descent: company station and Inner Congo
  - the return

Step 6. Ask several students to make a statement about the meaning of the novel. Record these on the blackboard and then group them thematically. For example, students might say:

- The novel is about man's inhumanity to man and his lust for power and possession.
- Kurtz is in the heart of darkness and lost because he has no restraint.
- Marlow learns about his capacity for evil through his journey to find Kurtz, a lost soul.
- The evil (greed) of the company is exposed through Marlow's journey to find Kurtz.
- The dual nature of man is brought to light through the revelations Marlow makes about Kurtz.
- The novel is about a journey into the darkness that is potentially within each of us.

List all statements on an overhead and display them the next day. Allow students 15–20 minutes to write in their logs expanding on their own statement or another they like.

- Have students pair and share responses.
- Have each partner respond in a brief essay on the student log entry in his/her partner's log.

Prompt:

Imagine that you are Marlow, the protagonist of *Heart of Darkness,* and compose a letter describing your experiences in the Congo from his point of view. Write the letter as if you (Marlow) were at some point in your journey from the Central Station to the end of the story. Before composing the letter, decide to whom the letter should be addressed: your aunt, the doctor, your employer, a friend who has just been hired by the company and plans to make the same trip, or any other plausible person. Your letter should:

- Describe the physical nature of the Congo,
- Discuss the psychological effect of the Congo on you,
- Speculate about the nature of the man, Kurtz, who has gradually become the focus of your journey.

Note: In writing your letter:

- Don't create any imaginary events.
- Stick to the text closely.
- Use description and narration.
- Be sure you indicate where you are now.

Precomposing

After a discussion of the prompt, students need to focus more closely on the elements of the prompt and the relationship of the text to the demands of the prompt.

1. Activity—Timeline/Map

The following activities are designed to help students become aware of the setting of the text and the geographic nature of the text. See Figure 17.

Step 1. Give each student an outline of a timeline chart like the one on page 320. Have them complete it for homework.

Step 2. Group students to add to their chart and then do a class chart. A sample chart is provided on page 321.

Step 3. Hand out a map of the Congo or Africa. Have students place Outer, Central, and Inner Stations on the map. You may also want them to put in major events. This will only be an approximation, but should prove effective to bring geographic constraints into focus.

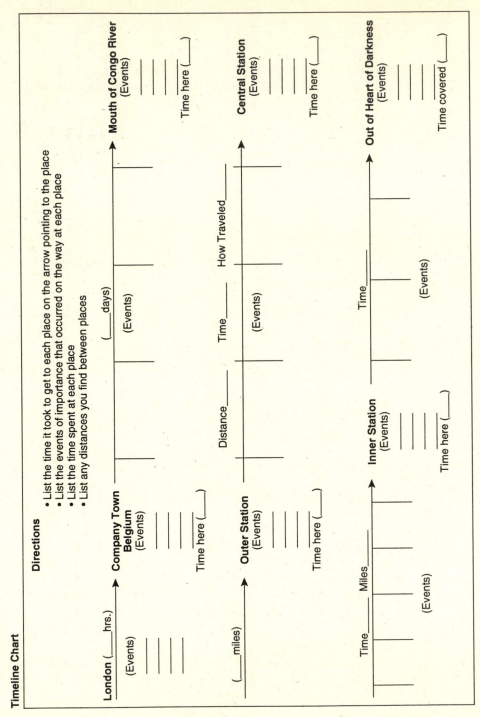

Figure 17. Timeline Chart

Partial Timeline of the Journey and List of Events

London 48 hrs.

- Gets job through Aunt

Company Town Belgium

- Whited Sepulchre
- Two women in black
- Company President
- Doctor
- Goodbye to Aunt

30 days

Mouth of Congo River

- Seagoing steamer
- Captain a Swede
- Swede hanged himself

30 miles

Outer Station
(10 days here)

- Black people like ants
- Blind sunlight
- Decaying machinery/ blasting cliff
- 6 chained natives
- Grove of death
- Dying black man with cloth around neck
- Bookkeeper
- Hears about Kurtz

- Weary pilgrimage
- Called at more places
- Trading places
- Ship fires into jungle
- Sees jungle
- Monotony

200 mile walk in 15 days

- Litter-bearers run away
- Carry companion
- Fainting white companion
- Meets white man drunk

Central Station

- Meets brickmaker
- Learns ship sunk
- Meets manager
- Learns more of Kurtz
- Out building burns
- No rivets

2 months more than 800 miles

- Marlow throws away shoes
- Helmsman killed
- Attacked 8 miles from station
- Find books
- Hunger
- Natives dancing
- Black cannibal workers
- Pilgrims on board
- Manager goes along
- Description of river & jungle

Inner Station
(24 hrs.)

- Meets Harliquin (Russian)
- Kurtz's hut with heads turned inward
- Hole in hut
- Meets Kurtz
- Kurtz crawls away

Down river 1 month 1/2 time

- Central Station again
- Manager tries to get papers
- Regains awareness
- Marlow ill
- Kurtz dies
- Kurtz gives papers to Marlow
- Kurtz ill

Out of Heart of Darkness

- Nursed back to health by Aunt
- Company rep tries to get papers
- Cousin of Kurtz visits Marlow
- Marlow visits Kurtz's Intended
- Marlow lies

Figure 17. Con't.

Step 4. Discuss the nature and attributes of the Congo River and the Belgian Congo jungle. The following information may be helpful: It would help to show a movie or slides if possible. (How about ''The African Queen''?)

Surface of Africa

The Kongo, like the Nile, rises in the lake region of middle Africa. One branch of the Kongo forms the outlet of Lake Tanganyika. Other branches flow from smaller lakes farther south.

East of the lake region rise two volcanic peaks, Mts. Keia and Kilimanjaro, the highest mountains in Africa, though they are not quite so high as Mt. McKinley.

There are rapids and falls in the Kongo river at the place where it descends from the plateau to the narrow coastal plain. These falls prevent vessels from going far inland from the sea, but small steamers have been carried overland past the falls and now navigate the upper river, where they find an open waterway for thousands of miles along the great trunk stream and its branches.

Step 5. Discuss what Marlow's references to maps, below, tell us about his attraction for the Congo:

''But there was in it one river especially, a mighty big river, that you could see on the map, resembling an immense snake uncoiled, with its head in the sea, its body at rest curving afar over a vast country, and its tail lost in the depths of the land. And as I looked at the map of it in a shop window, it fascinated me as a snake would a bird—a silly little bird.'' (p. 11)

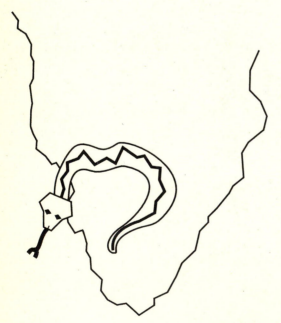

. . . ''a large shining map, marked with all the colors of the rainbow. There was a vast amount of red—good to see at any time, because one knows that some real work is done in there, a deuce of a lot of blue, a little green, smears of orange, and, on the East Coast, a purple patch to show where the jolly pioneers of progress drink the jolly lager-beer. However, I wasn't going into any of these. And the river was there—fascinating—deadly like a snake. Ough!'' (p. 15)

*Note: All quotes are from the Bantam Books edition of *Heart of Darkness* and *The Secret Sharer* (Garden City, N.Y.: Doubleday & Co., 1978).

2. Activity

   Step 1. Have students select the place on the journey from which they will write their letter.

   Step 2. Have them select three to five major events they wish to include in their letter.

   Step 3. Brainstorm and list possible audiences for the letter with the class. The list might include:

   > The Aunt
   > A London Friend
   > A Seaman Friend
   > Kurtz's Intended
   > Company President
   > The Reader
   > Girlfriend
   > The Company Board
   > The Bookkeeper
   > The Manager (after return to Belgium)
   > A Minister
   > The Doctor
   > Marlow's First Command

   Step 4. Have students select an audience and explain in a learning log entry why they have selected this person.

   Step 5. Have students cluster the person to whom they are addressing their letters. The cluster should include character traits that are real or consistent and plausible in relation to the text and Conrad's style.

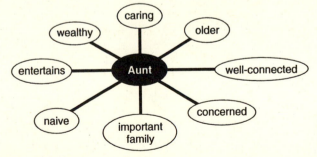

   Step 6. Have students write a character sketch of the person who is to be the audience for their letter. Share the sketch with a partner and discuss appropriateness of the character.

3. Activity—Learning About Marlow

   Step 1

   - Have students do a textual search for quotes that explain Marlow's character.

- The quotes may be kept in a reading/learning log, dialectical journal, or on 3″ × 5″ index cards.

Sample quotes might include:

6   "He was the only man of us who still 'followed the sea.' The worst that could be said of him was that he did not represent his class."

6   "He was a seaman, but he was a wanderer, too . . . "

7   "But Marlow was not typical (if his propensity to spin yarns be excepted) . . ."

10   "Now when I was a little chap I had a passion for maps."

44   "You know I hate, detest, and can't bear a lie, not because I am straighter than the rest of us, but simply because it appalls me."

Step 2. Have students do a similar search on Kurtz. Because Marlow's character is tied so closely to Kurtz, much of his personality is revealed as Marlow tells his audience (the readers and men on the ketch on the Thames) about Kurtz.

Sample quotes might include:

29   "On my asking who Mr. Kurtz was, he said he was a first-class agent . . ."

29   "He is a very remarkable person."

30   "Oh, he will go far, very far . . . He will be somebody in the Administration before long."

113 "But his soul was mad."

Step 3. Have students do a Venn Diagram to compare and contrast Marlow and Kurtz. A sample might look like the one below:

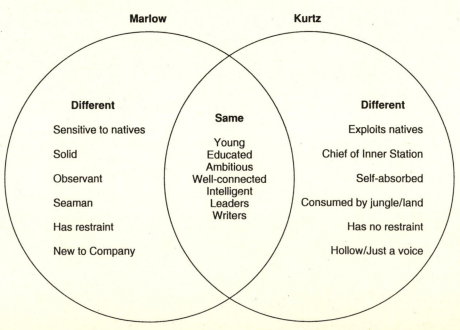

Marlow   **Kurtz**

Different   **Same**   **Different**

Sensitive to natives   Young   Exploits natives
                              Educated
Solid   Ambitious   Chief of Inner Station
                              Well-connected
Observant   Intelligent   Self-absorbed
                              Leaders
Seaman   Writers   Consumed by jungle/land

Has restraint   Has no restraint

New to Company   Hollow/Just a voice

Step 4. Students should write about the relationship between Kurtz and Marlow in their learning log. It will help them understand Marlow better and why he becomes so obsessed with Kurtz. Students may wish to share their concepts and ideas.

- The teacher could discuss the duality of Marlow and Kurtz here.

4. Activity

Step 1. List additional characters on an overhead or the board who have been affected by the Heart of Darkness. They might include the following:

Fresleven	The Russian
The Bookkeeper	The Manager
The Swede	The Brickmaker

Step 2. Assign a character to each group and have them list the effect of the Congo on the character:

Bookkeeper:

- kept perfect books
- dressed neatly
- businesslike
- ignored natives
- lost in his books

Step 3. Have each group share its finding and allow discussion about the effects of the Heart of Darkness. Then have students write about how they would feel if they saw the noble cause and the Company as Marlow saw it.

- This should help them become more subjective and think more like Marlow.

Step 4. Have students share this effort in groups and select one from the group to be read to the class. Give students time to discuss how Marlow felt and how they would react in his place.

5. Activity
Before students are ready to write the first draft of their letter, they need to explore the style of Conrad as he gives voice to Marlow.

Step 1. Have students complete a chart of some of Conrad's stylistic techniques: descriptive words/phrases, character development, imagery, symbols, repeated words and phrases.

Descriptive Words/Phrases	Character Development	Imagery
• dark places • gloom • exquisite brilliance • benign immensity • unstained light • marked ominously • lurid glare • growing regrets • longing to escape • powerless disgust • monotonous grimness	• He was a seaman. • He was a wanderer. • Marlow was not typical. • I had a passion for maps. • It's queer how out of touch with truth women are. • A queer feeling came to me that I was an imposter. • I always went my own road and on my own legs where I had a mind to go. • I, Charlie Marlow, set the women to work—to get a job. Heavens!	• monstrous town • dark places of the earth • immense snake uncoiled • plain as an umbrella-cover • large shining map • knitted black wool feverishly • a blinding sunlight • a sudden recrudescence of glare • boiler wallowing in the grass • decaying machinery • flies buzzed in great peace

Symbols	Repeated Words and Phrases
• darkness • heart • maps • snake • noble cause • light (blinding) • grass • black • door of darkness • white worsted cloth • chains • buzzing flies • stick of sealing wax • pail with a hole	• mournful gloom • brooding gloom • gloom to the west • touch of that gloom brooding • queer • monstrous • monotonous • "The horror! The horror!"

Step 2. Do a class chart so that students will have a chance to expand their own chart. You may find that you will add categories (use of color, similes, etc.).

Step 3. Have each student write for 15 minutes describing a place, event, or character in Conrad's style using some of the words and phrases. Have students share in response groups.

Step 4. Hold a class discussion and present some stylistic techniques Conrad uses in diction, sentence structure, usage, punctuation. Take the following quote and analyze it for your students:

The earth seemed unearthly. We are accustomed to look upon the shackled form of a conquered monster, but there—there you could look at a thing monstrous and free. It was unearthly, and the men were—No they were not inhuman. Well, you know that was the worst of it—this suspicion of their not being inhuman. It would come slowly to one. They howled and leaped, and spun, and made horrid faces; but what thrilled you was just the thought of their humanity—like yours—the thought of your remote kinship with this wild and passionate uproar. (59)

Step 5. Assign each group (five to six students) one of the following quotes. Have them examine the quote for stylistic techniques. Then, have them report to the class what they have discovered about Conrad's style from their examination. Direct them to look for descriptive words and phrases, showing, not telling, rhetorical devices, word order, sentence structure, tone, humor, understatement, irony or sarcasm, etc.

- In a very few hours I arrived in a city that always makes me think of a whited sepulchre. Prejudice no doubt. I had no difficulty in finding the Company's offices. It was the biggest thing in town, and everybody I met was full of it. They were going to run an over-sea empire, and make no end of coin by trade. (14)

- From that structure came out an impression of pale plumpness in a frack-coat. The great man himself. He was five feet six, I should judge, and had his grip on the handle-end of ever so many millions. He shook hands, I fancy, murmured vaguely, was satisfied with my French. *Bon Voyage.* (15)

- Watching a coast as it slips by the ship is like thinking about an enigma. There it is before you—smiling, frowning, inviting, grand, mean, insipid, or savage, and always mute with an air of whispering, ''Come and find out.'' This one was almost featureless, as if still in the making, with an aspect of monotonous grimness. The edge of a colossal jungle, so dark-green as to be almost black, fringed with white surf, ran straight, like a ruled line, far, far away along a blue sea whose glitter was blurred by a creeping mist. The sun was fierce, the land seemed to glisten and drip with steam. (19–20)

- I came upon a boiler wallowing in the grass, then found a path leading up the hill. It turned aside for the boulders, and also for an undersized railway-truck lying there on its back with its wheels in the air. One was off. The thing looked as dead as the carcass of some animal. I came upon more pieces of decaying machinery, a stack of rusty rails. (23)

- You know I am not particularly tender; I've had to strike and fend off. I've had to resist and to attack sometimes—that's only one way of resisting—without counting the exact cost, according to the demands of such sort of life as I had blundered into. I've seen the devil of violence, and the devil of greed, and the devil of hot desire; but, by all the stars these were strong, lusty, red-eyed devils, that swayed and drove men—men, I tell you. But as I stood on this hillside, I foresaw that in the blinding sunshine of that land, I would become acquainted with a flabby, pretending, weak-eyed devil of a rapacious and pitiless folly. (25)

- He was a common trader, from his youth up employed in these parts—nothing more. He was obeyed, yet he inspired neither love nor fear, nor even respect. He inspired uneasiness. That was it! Uneasiness. Not a definite mistrust—just uneasiness—nothing more. You have no idea how effective such a . . . a . . . faculty can be. He had no genius for organizing, for initiative, or for order even. That was evident in such things as the deplorable state of the station. He had no learning, had no intelligence. His position came to him—why? Perhaps because he was never ill . . . He had served three terms of three years out there . . . Because triumphant health in the general rout of constitutions is a kind of power in itself. (34–35)

- Going up that river was like traveling back into the earliest beginnings of the world, when vegetation rioted on the earth and big trees were kings. (55)

Step 6. Have students write 3–5 sentences using two or three of Conrad's sentence structure techniques. You (as teacher) might want to see these so that you can extend the activity if several students are not catching on.

Step 7. Have students record in their learning logs several techniques that will benefit them when they write the letter.

Writing

Using an informal outline/writing plan, students write rough drafts of their letters. Redirect students to the prompt so that they address all its requirements.

Sharing

Share a model of a letter—one written by a student or one which you have written. A sample student model is included below.

14 Southing Court
West Knightsbridge
London, England

The Reverend John Alter
222 East Kensing Court
Leveringham, England

My Dear Reverend Mr. Alter,

In answer to your query, I must say no, the last words of Mr. Kurtz as he died on my ship were not the name of his intended. I did lie, I confess to you, only in order to preserve the memory for the beautiful, distraught lady, for what he did say would not have given any comfort whatsoever. In that year of the journey, I saw into the abyss of greed and avarice, and felt the fascination of the abomination.

I observed the peeling of the crust of civilization under the steamy intensity of jungle life, and was profoundly shaken and changed by the totality of the experience. You, who are a close counselor to the late Mr. Kurtz's intended and former friend of the man himself, should know the astonishing facts, or what I perceive to be the facts, and my deep feelings about the somber experience. From that position, you may then choose to reveal the actual words to the lady, or to let the lie I told stand.

I did not know Mr. Kurtz when I manipulated my way to become a part of the Company that had called him some two years earlier. My first hearing of his name and reputation came from an accountant with whom I became acquainted while I spent my sentence of waiting for materials to continue my trade and journey. At first, the mention of Kurtz's name meant nothing, but as my informant badgered me with questions about my involvement with the Company, the name Kurtz began to be linked inseparably with my own purposes. I heard of how he collected more ivory than anyone, and how he dealt with natives to find their secrets, and the man began to draw me into his sinister net. I began to feel the need to meet this specter, to see into his power, to comprehend the unknown that lay ahead for me.

In that station where I waited, that world of raw ambition and base emotion, I saw sights that changed all perspective. There were black men dying, treated more callously than animals by those who came in the name of civilization. I felt their pained, shining eyes following me, and their glistening skin touching me, clutching at my very heart, until I became desensitized by their plight of agony. I moved as a machine when we finally steamed up the river farther and farther into the very source of human emotion. As the engine of the steamboat throbbed and wheezed, fear became a tangible part of my total body. It was the meal I ate, the prod that pushed me to the inmost reaches of the continent. The dense jungle on both sides of the darkly troubled, steaming river was living and breathing with eyes watching constantly; and fear was the controlling thread that gave continuity to day and night.

As we neared the station, the steamboat snagging its way up the treacherous narrows of that vein of the river toward the inmost core of the Company's influence, we were suddenly showered with lances, arrows thrown from the shore by spidery bronze arms raised above the bush. The door to the pilot house was open, allowing a great stick to enter and kill my dark helmsman immediately in front of me. His warm blood filled my shoes and the cabin, and his limp body fell mightily on my feet. In my desperation to rid myself of this burden, I dragged the body outside and pushed it over the side into the rolling river waves, and we limped along, closing in on the churning center of our quest.

Foreboding filled my being as we neared the inner station, but the urge to see the man in charge, drew me magnetically. I took the glass, sighted through the cold metal eyepiece to see—to see—the station, with its fence of poles standing about as sentinals. And, as I looked ever and ever more closely, I began to feel a new fear, a horror beyond dread. What seemed to be knobs atop the fence poles were something else indeed, human skulls, piked to face the inner station itself! Rebels, I was told. Those were the skulls of natives who had rebelled—against

Kurtz? Against the Company? Against me? And, who had nailed them there so carefully? This was a nightmare within a nightmare. Then, as through the haze of fear, I saw him, an ivory skeleton, an apparition from a lower world, a disease-ridden living corpse, but with an occult power to blind the heart of the purest to his way. His voice, his unbelievable deep, resonant voice, with its hypnotic message to all who heard, chilled me utterly. I, too, became a slave, a conspirator, an ally to the base nature of the primitive spirit. I saw into this heart of darkness.

We knew he could not last long on this earth, disease riddled as his body was, but we loaded him aboard the steamboat and encouraged him all the same. All that he had seen and done wracked his frail body with convulsive seizures, and I shook alongside as he cried out. When he could not go on, he spoke but two words, "The horror! The horror!" and I heard, I knew.

I must tell you, nothing about me is the same, and when the fevers rise again in my body, as they do rather regularly, I can see again the oily darkness of that river, the overhanging vines that caught at our vessel as we pulsed along. I can hear the silence, and the scream of the whistle and the panic it wrought. I can feel the throbbing heat, the fear laden waiting, the sinister rising of primitive tides in my own body and mind. "The horror! The horror!" is only a breath away.

I trust you to use your best judgment as to whether to tell the lovely mourner the actual words spoken at death, and I trust that I will be forgiven for my small lie.

> Your obedient servant,
> Charles Marlow
> (Written by Nancy Illo)

Ask students to critique the model using the following questions as a guideline.

- Is the letter written from Marlow's point of view?
- Is the Congo described vividly?
- Does the language emulate Marlow's character?
- Is the identity of person to whom the letter is addressed clear?
- Are the effects of the experiences on Marlow explored?
- Does the writer speculate about Kurtz's personality and the relationship between Marlow and Kurtz?
- Does the letter conform to the conventions of form, usage, and mechanics?

Then, ask students to apply the same questions to their own first drafts in small peer response groups.

Revising

Students will revise their letters to make sure they meet the requirements of the prompt, according to the information received during sharing.

Editing

Students will edit their papers for the conventions of written English (spelling, punctuation, grammar, sentence structure, etc.) and make any necessary corrections.

Evaluation

Papers may be holistically scored from according to the following rubric or graded by the teacher.

Sample Rubric

9–8 A paper that is clearly superior—well-written, clearly organized, insightful, and technically correct. A 9–8 paper does most or all of the following well:

- demonstrates that the writer has clearly assumed the character of Marlow
- displays insight, originality, and/or critical thinking in approaching the topic
- employs correct, friendly letter style; is addressed to a plausible audience
- employs precise, apt, or descriptive language to capture the person, place or event described
- includes:
    - description of the physical nature of the Congo
    - discussion of the psychological effect of the Congo on Marlow
    - speculation about the nature of Kurtz
- utilizes narrative techniques to sustain the reader's interest
- has few, if any errors, in mechanics, usage and form

7 A thinner version of the 9–8 paper—still impressive, cogent, and interesting, but less well-handled in terms of organization, insight, language, or form. A 7-paper has fewer supporting details in description and narration and does not convey as intense a feeling of the personality and character of Marlow.

6–5 These scores apply to papers that are less well-handled than 7, 8, or 9-papers. A 6–5 paper may be less thought-provoking, not as well organized, less interesting, and not as clear in purpose. A 6–5 paper will contain some errors in mechanics, spelling, etc. A 6–5 paper will exhibit some or all of these characteristics:

- demonstrates that the writer has an understanding of the character of Marlow
- displays a clear understanding of purpose of prompt
- utilizes proper form and displays some critical thinking skills

- employs appropriate language but is not as effective in capturing the nature of the character, place, or event described
- includes some statement of the nature of Kurtz's personality
- contains some errors in mechanics, usage, and form

4–3 These apply to papers that maintain the general idea of the writing assignment, but are weak in content, thought, language facility, organization, or the conventions of written English. A 4–3 paper will exhibit these characteristics:

- writer is not immersed in the character of Marlow
- displays little insight, originality, or critical thinking in approaching the topic
- does not appear to be written in letter form
- writer does not use descriptive or narrative detail to a specific purpose
- language is overly generalized
- fails to speculate about Kurtz
- has many problems with conventions of written English

2 This score applies to a paper that strays from or misinterprets the writing assignment and compounds the weaknesses of 4–3 paper. A 2-paper does several of the following:

- demonstrates that the writer does not understand how to assume the character of Marlow
- is muddled so that the reader has trouble following the writer's thoughts
- lacks insight, originality, or critical thinking skills
- contains very few details and is written in generalized prose
- fails to speculate about Kurtz
- has serious errors in the conventions of written English that obscure much of the intended message

1 This score is used for any paper which does not follow the writing prompt or fails to respond to the complete purpose of the prompt.

Extension Activities

Synthesis

Prompt: Imagine that you are the person to whom the letter you have just written (as Marlow) was addressed. Write a reply to Marlow, in the voice of your character (i.e., Marlow's aunt, a fellow seaman, Kurtz's Intended, etc.) in which you speculate about what Marlow must have learned as a result of his experience and offer some advice regarding any future journeys Marlow might undertake.

Evaluation

Prompt: At the close of *Heart of Darkness,* Marlow remarks of Kurtz's dying words ("The horror! The horror!"), "It was an affirmation, a moral victory paid for by innumerable defeats, by abominable terrors, by abominable satisfactions. But it was a victory!"

Evaluate this statement carefully, decide upon your own interpretation of what Kurtz meant by "The horror! The horror!" and write an analytical/expository essay in which you either agree or disagree with Marlow's proclamation of Kurtz's death as a moral victory. Justify your point of view with specific references to events from the text.

6 Evaluation

Writing Domain: Analytical/Expository

Thinking Level: Evaluation
Grade Level: Primary

How Does Your Cookie Crumble?

Taste Testing as a Prerequisite to Evaluating

Lesson

Having taste-tested and examined the qualities of cookies, students will write a paragraph rating and evaluating one of them.

Objectives

Thinking Skills
Students will progress through all levels of thinking before functioning at the *EVALUATION* level by *JUDGING*, *RATING*, and *EVALUATING* their favorite cookies.

Writing Skills
Students will write an expository paragraph that utilizes a main idea and three supporting details.

The Process

Although this lesson can be adapted for younger students, it will work best with grades 2-3. It may take three or more class periods to complete. Before starting, the teacher needs to collect the following materials:

- Three types of cookies (every student will need one of each)
- Napkins
- Blank grid forms (to be written on board or dittoed and passed out—see *STEP 2* for sample)
- Blank paper
- Crayons and pencils
- Examples of maps (see Step 4 for samples)
- Milk and cups (optional)

Prewriting

Step 1. Brainstorming (Knowledge and Comprehension)

Explain to the students that they will be giving their opinions as to what makes a good cookie. Before they can do this, however, you want them to tell you everything they know about cookies. As they make suggestions, cluster them on the board or write them out in list form. (See example below.)

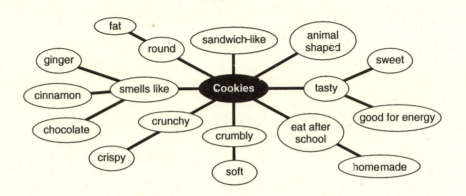

Note: The teacher may have to help students with some of these vocabulary words. Leave the list on the board if you have extra space or transfer it to butcher paper and leave this up as a resource bank through the remainder of the lesson. New vocabulary can be added as needed.

Step 2. Organizing (Application and Analysis)

- After brainstorming, help students sort the random information about cookies into categories.
- Some categories they might come up with are:

smell	advertising
taste	brands
texture	shape
uses	

- Now, ask students to select at least three of the general categories they have listed and to arrange the specific information from the cluster on a grid like the one on page 337.

Qualities	Name of Cookie		
Texture			
Crunchy			
Crispy			
Soft			
Chewy			
Crumbly			
Taste			
Sweet			
Chocolatey			
Buttery			
Shape			
Round			
Pinwheel			
Animal-shaped			

Step 3. Experiencing (Application and Analysis)

- At this point, pass out three cookies (one of each kind) to the students. Concretely experiencing cookies (i.e., eating them) will help them better analyze and evaluate qualities of the cookies.
- Have the students write the names of the cookies they will be sampling across the top of their grids.
- Next, have them check the appropriate squares for qualities they have determined for the cookies they taste. New information not already provided on their grids can be added as needed.
- The chart for this activity might look like the one on page 338.

Note: It will help students in filling out the grid to see one modeled on the board.

Qualities	Name of Cookie		
	Oreos	Chocolate Chip	Animal Crackers
Texture			
Crunchy	✔		
Crispy			✔
Soft			
Chewy		✔	
Crumbly		✔	
Taste			
Sweet	✔	✔	✔
Chocolatey	✔		
Buttery			
Shape			
Round	✔	✔	
Pinwheel	✔	✔	
Animal shaped			✔

- After the chart has been filled in, it might be helpful to do some verbal modeling of the sentences that will be used later in the lesson. For example, have the students use the information on the grid to respond to the statements

  - I like Oreos because . . .
             or
  - I like Animal Crackers because . . .

- Next, present the prompt.

Prompt:

You will select one of the cookies you have taste-tested and evaluate it in a paragraph. Use complete sentences and give logical reasons for your choice.

- In the first sentence, you will name the cookie and rate it as either great, good, OK, or bad.

- In the next three sentences, you will explain why you gave it the rating that you did

---

Precomposing
Step 4. Mapping (Application and Synthesis)

In order for the students to begin to make the transition from checks on a grid to actually writing about their subject:

- Explain to the students that they are going to create a map of one of the three cookies they have just tasted.
- Pass out sample maps such as the ones below and give the students the following directions:

You will be selecting one of the cookies and drawing the idea it suggests to you on your own paper. When you are finished with the drawing, add in the qualities you checked on the grid.

Chocolate Chip

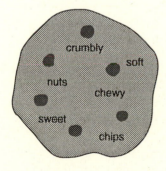

Oreo

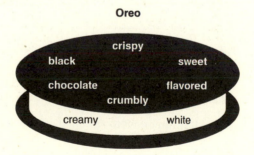

After illustrating and experiencing the cookies in this way, the students should be ready to write.

Writing

The response to the prompt may be written or dictated by the children. An open-ended frame such as the one below can be used:

I think (name of cookies) are (great, good, OK, bad).

Reason 1 _____

Reason 2 _____

Reason 3 _____

To help students generate logical reasons for and specific details to support their choice, you might ask some prompting questions such as:

- If you liked the taste, what about the taste appealed to you?
- If you liked the package, was there something on it that caught your eye?
- Was there something special about the shape that you liked?
- Did the cookies smell especially good? What was the smell like?

(*Note:* These questions can also be phrased in the negative for those who wish to write about a cookie they didn't like.)

If some children are having difficulty developing a paragraph, you may want to provide several focused frames to use as a point of departure:

I think (name of cookies) are (great, good, OK, bad).

1. They have _____

2. _____ is another reason _____

3. Best of all, _____

I think (name of cookies) are (great, good, OK, bad).

1. I can't resist the _____

2. Also the _____ reminds me of _____

3. But of all the reasons why _____ are my favorite, the most

important is _____

(*Note:* It is important to remind the students to eliminate the 1, 2, 3, numbering on their final draft.)

Finally, to encourage children to experiment with various ways to present their preference for a cookie, provide at least two models for discussion—one which uses a frame provided by the teacher and one which does not.

I think Oreos are great! They are crispy and chocolatey on the outside and have a creamy white filling on the inside. Their round shape is another reason why they're my favorite. Best of all, you can pull them apart and lick off the filling. Yum!

I think Animal Crackers are especially good. Where else can you get pink and white horses and cows and pigs all covered with sprinkles to eat one after another? Plain old vanilla wafers and even chocolate chips can't compete with these tasty little critters. The little box with the handle is great for carrying around, but I'd rather have a whole big bag.

Sharing

The first draft that the students write in response to the prompt can be shared with the whole class, in small groups, or with peer partners. The following questions will help them evaluate each other's work:

- Has the writer given the cookies a rating from great to bad?
- Are there three reasons provided explaining why the cookies are great, good, OK, or bad? Are they good reasons?
- Is each reason a complete thought and a complete sentence? If not, what should be added?
- Are there other good reasons you can think of that the writer didn't mention? If so, what are they?

Revising

Based on the responses from their peers, students may revise their papers by adding to or changing their reasons.

Editing

The teacher should circulate around the room to make sure the students have followed the frame and are using correct sentences.

Evaluation

You may use an evaluation rubric such as the following:

 3. Defends the cookie's rating with 3 supporting reasons. Uses logical reasons in complete sentences.

 2. Gives the cookie a rating but only defends it with one or two reasons. The reasons are not all in complete sentences.

 1. States a personal opinion about the cookie but gives no logical reason to support it. The sentences are not complete.

Extension Activities

Evaluation   To move the students to higher levels of evaluation based on the same demonstration lesson, one or more of the following prompts can be given:

Prompt: Rank your three cookies from best to worst and justify your ranking with specific reasons.

Prompt: Pretending that you are a judge of a cookie ''taste-off,'' write your choice of the best cookie and explain why. Be sure to compare and contrast the qualities of the cookies to demonstrate that one cookie is the best.

Prompt: After tallying the preferences of your classmates, predict which cookie will sell in the stores and explain why. In addition to taste, smell, shape, etc., also consider packaging. (*Note:* The teacher will need to explain the term packaging.)

Prompt: Write a note to your mother in which you persuade her to buy you your favorite cookies the next time she goes to the grocery store. Be sure to give reasons that will convince her to buy you what you want.

Persuasive Letters

Lesson

Predicting possible reactions and meeting them with logical arguments, students will write a letter designed to persuade a specific audience to do something.

Objectives

Thinking Skills
Students will function at the *EVALUATION* level by *PREDICTING* and *PERSUADING*.

Writing Skills
Students will be expected to write a persuasive letter which contains a well-supported-argument directed toward a particular audience.

The Process

Prewriting

1. As a class, ask students to brainstorm *WHO* they have persuaded in the past, *WHAT* they have tried to persuade them to do, *HOW* they tried to persuade them, and what the *RESULTS* were on the following chart:

Example:

Past			
What	**Who**	**How**	**Results**
take me to the movies	big brother	beg	was mad but took me anyway
let me take skating lessons	Mom	pant & whine	said, "No"
stay all night	friend	asked politely	stayed
buy me a bike	parents	cry	didn't buy it

2. Ask students to describe and explain orally their situation (*WHAT, WHO*) to the class. Discuss the *HOW* and *RESULTS* columns.

3. Ask the class if anyone has ever tried writing a letter to persuade someone. If nobody has, suggest it and explain that letter writing can be a very effective tool for persuasion because it gives you time to plan your argument.

Prompt:

Choose one thing that you would like to persuade someone to do. Write a letter to persuade your chosen audience. Your letter should show that you have done the following:

- clearly stated what you want and why;
- used a tone suited to your audience;
- predicted two possible objections your audience might have;
- met those objections with logical arguments;
- followed the standard letter format of greeting, body and closing.

Precomposing

Focusing

4. Students may work in pairs, in groups, or individually. Ask students to choose one thing that they would currently like to persuade someone to do (*WHO, WHAT*) and enter the information in the first two columns of the chart below:

Who	What	Possible Objections of Audience	Possible Arguments of Persuader
Mom	Let me take 3 friends to Farrell's for my birthday.	1. It's too expensive. 2. 3.	1. I'll help pay with my allowance. 2. 3.

Oral Persuasion

Experimenting with Tone

5. Introduce the concept of tone by presenting students with this situation:
   Suppose you were certain that you had put an audiotape of your favorite musical group in a special spot in your bedroom and it's not there. After searching your room thoroughly and feeling frustrated, you must set out to

question the following people about whether they've moved, misplaced or taken your tape:

- a person who cleans house
- your mom
- your kid brother or sister
- a neighborhood friend who is always "borrowing" things without asking
- What words and tone of voice would you use to inquire about the where-abouts of your tape with each specific audience?
- How would your language and tone differ depending on your relationship with each person?
- Choose a word or words to describe a tone you might use with each audience (i.e., respectful, humorous, accusing, sarcastic, angry, etc.)

Explain to students that tone is something you use in writing as well as in speaking. The same accusing tone one might verbally use when asking a neighborhood friend, who is always "borrowing" without asking, if they have taken a favorite tape can also be conveyed in writing through precise word choice.

Oral Persuasion and Predicting Objections of Audience

6. Ask students to brainstorm the characteristics of their chosen audience which might help them choose the appropriate tone. Enter the list on the chart as shown.

Who	What	Possible Objections of Audience	Possible Arguments of Persuader
Mom	Let me take 3 friends to Farrell's for my birthday.	1.	1.
		2.	2.
Characteristics		3.	3.

7. Ask two students to role-play the situation they chose during the Focusing Stage (see Step 4) in front of class. Ask the students to identify which person is the *AUDIENCE* and which person is the *PERSUADER*. Before the role-play begins, brainstorm characteristics of the *AUDIENCE* which might influence their reactions. (For example, if a student wanted to persuade his mom to let him buy a boogie board, it would help the partner role playing his mom to anticipate her objections if he knew that she had earlier refused to let her son buy a skateboard because she was afraid he might fall and hurt himself.) *PERSUADERS* can experiment with different tones in attempting to persuade the chosen *AUDIENCE*. Discuss which tones the *PERSUADER* used that were most effective and why.

8. Students should enter the *POSSIBLE REACTION OF AUDIENCE* and *POSSIBLE ARGUMENTS OF PERSUADER* on the chart:

Who	What	Possible Objections of Audience	Possible Arguments of Persuader
Mom **Characteristics** • likes bargains • cheerful • hates driving • worries • doesn't listen • always says, "I want you to be happy" • always says, "Get to the point"	Let me take 3 friends to Farrell's for my birthday	1. It's too expensive 2. 3.	1. I'll help pay with my allowance. 2. 3.

Transition from Oral Persuasion to Written Persuasion

9. Help students make the transition from oral role-play to written expression by conducting the following activity:

   • On a lined sheet of paper, the *PERSUADER* should ask the *AUDIENCE* to do what he/she is trying to persuade him/her to do.

   Example: Mom, will you let me take three friends to Farrell's for my birthday?

   • The *AUDIENCE* should read the question silently, then write a response according to his/her first possible reaction and return it to the *PERSUADER*.

   Example: No, Farrell's is too expensive.

   • The paper is to be passed back and forth in this manner until the *AUDIENCE* is convinced or the *PERSUADER* gives up.

- The *PERSUADER* should then read over the dialogue and enter new *POSSIBLE REACTIONS* and *POSSIBLE ARGUMENTS* on the chart.
- Now, have the students switch roles and do the exercise again so that both students' charts are complete.
- Enter more *POSSIBLE REACTIONS* and *POSSIBLE ARGUMENTS* on the chart.
- Ask students to put a star next to two objections they think their audience is sure to make.

Who	What	Possible Objections of Audience	Possible Arguments of Persuader
Mom **Characteristics**	Let me take 3 friends to Farrell's for my birthday.	1. "It's too expensive" ★ 2. "I don't know where Farrell's is." ★ 3. "I don't have time."	1. "I'll help pay with my allowance." 2. "There is a Farrell's only 2 blocks from school." 3. "You don't have to come."

10. Review the prompt and proper letter format with the class. Discuss possible opening statements they could use on their letters. It is helpful if you list them on the board.

    Example of Proper Letter Format

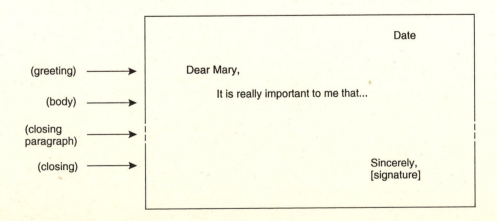

11. Read a model to the class emphasizing the structure followed. Students may use their own structure but should include the following:

- What is wanted
- Reasons why
- Two possible objections
- Reasons to overcome the objections
- Closing summary

[date]

Dear Mom,

This year I would like to have my birthday party at Farrell's with three of my best friends. I've always wanted to go to Farrell's because they sing ''Happy Birthday'' and play the big drum if you tell them it's your birthday.

I know that you probably will think that it will be too expensive, but it really won't be because I will pay for my friends' ice cream with my allowance. You won't need to give me any extra money because my ice cream will be free just because it's my birthday. That's why everyone likes to go to Farrell's on their birthday.

You might not know where there is a Farrell's and be worried about driving with kids in the car. Guess what? There is a Farrell's just two blocks from the school. We could walk and meet you there.

I hope you will think about my idea and say ''yes.'' The only thing I really want for my birthday is to have a party at Farrell's. Please let me know what you decide.

Love,
Molly

Discuss reasons why students might follow a different structure than Molly did. Why might it be a bad idea to start out with what is wanted and why? When might it be more useful at the end of the letter?

Could you combine two objections and arguments into one paragraph? When? How?

Could Molly's closing paragraph be used to begin the letter? What changes would have to be made?

Writing

Students write their letter referring to their lists of *POSSIBLE REACTIONS OF AUDIENCE* and *POSSIBLE ARGUMENTS OF PERSUADER*.

Sharing

Students share letters and help each other decide whether or not the letter will persuade the intended audience. Partners should underline what is wanted in **blue** and the reasons why in **yellow.** They should underline the objections of the audience in **red** and arguments to overcome objections in **green.** Partners should also discuss whether or not the tone is appropriate for the audience. Optional: Partners may indicate a preliminary primary trait score. (See *EVALUATION* section of lesson.)

Revising

Based on the feedback received, students should revise letters to make them more persuasive. They should consider the following questions:

- Is what I want clearly stated?
- Have I stated the reasons why I want it?
- Do the words I chose create the right tone for my audience?
- Did I include two possible objections?
- Are my arguments against those objections persuasive?
- Is my closing paragraph effective?

Editing

Students may edit their own letters or exchange them with a friend. The Secondary Trait Scoring Guide should be used as a reference. (See *EVALUATION* section below.)

Evaluation

Primary Trait Scoring Guide

3 This letter clearly states what is wanted and why, anticipates objections and meets them with logical arguments. It probably would persuade your audience because the arguments are presented in a suitable tone.

2 Although the tone is appropriate and this letter presents persuasive arguments, it does not anticipate the possible reactions of your audience, or it anticipates reactions, but does not meet the objections with logical arguments. It might persuade them, but then again it might not.

1 This letter would probably not persuade your audience since it is not presented in a tone suited to your audience and/or does not anticipate possible reactions or meet them with specific arguments.

Secondary Trait Scoring Guide

2 This letter follows proper letter format, is neat and easy to read and has no errors in spelling, mechanics, or usage. A letter like this is a pleasure to receive. Your audience will be impressed with your writing skills.

1 This letter follows most of proper letter format but is not as neat and easy to read. It has a few errors in spelling, mechanics, or usage. If your primary trait score is high, your audience still *might* be persuaded.

0 This letter is not neat or easy to read. It has many errors in spelling, mechanics, or usage. Even if your primary trait score is high, your audience probably would not do what you want them to since they might not be able to read it or even want to read it.

Extension Activities

Application   Deliver the final letter to the audience it was intended for. Ask your audience to write back and tell you if you persuaded them with your arguments.

Application

Prompt: After reading Mark Twain's novel, *Tom Sawyer,* explain how Tom persuaded his friends to whitewash the fence for him. How would you characterize the tone he used with his friends? Why do you think his approach to persuasion was effective?

Evaluation

Prompt: Choose a real audience at home or at school and try to convince them of something by writing a letter or composing a speech. You might try convincing:

- the teacher to give the class an extra recess.
- the principal to allow the class to raise money for a special field trip.
- the custodian to take you as a morning helper.
- other classes to write letters and send art to homebound children or a children's hospital.
- a community club to sponsor an activity at your school.
- students at your school to write letters to Congressmen about endangered species legislation.
- students at your school to write letters to Congressmen stating their position on the nuclear arms race.

Writing Domain: Analytical/Expository

Thinking Level: Evaluation
Grade Level: Intermediate

The Laws of Probability

Lesson

Students will write a letter which demonstrates the comprehension, analysis, and evaluation of the results of an experiment based on the laws of probability. They will use that information to persuade a friend that his or her claim that heads always comes up more often than tails when you flip a coin is invalid.

Objectives

Thinking Skills
Students will:

- *CONDUCT* experiments;
- *RECORD* observed data;

- *ANALYZE* data;
- *EXTRAPOLATE* from data;
- *FORMULATE* a theory;
- *PERSUADE* a friend that the laws of probability invalidate a claim she/he has made.

Writing Skills
Students will:

- describe experiments;
- interpret data;
- explain the laws of probability;
- use persuasive language;
- use friendly letter form;
- follow the conventions of written English.

The Process

The following experiments are designed to demonstrate to students that some occurrences in their lives are not completely arbitrary, but are governed by mathematical laws—in this lesson, the laws of probability.

To implement the lesson, allow six or seven days of instruction time though they need not be consecutive. Materials needed include pennies, dice, and four-sector spinners.

Note: Because this lesson focuses on writing across the curriculum, it would be helpful—although not absolutely necessary—to involve the mathematics teacher at your school in its implementation. We are indebted to Larry Chrystal, Director, UCI/California Mathematics Project, for his help on this lesson.

Prewriting

1. Coin Flip Experiment
    Divide the class into pairs. Provide each pair with a penny. One student flips the coin, one records the outcome on the following Recording Sheet:
    Figure 18 is a sample.

Coin Flip Experiment

Date _____

Group _____

Recording Sheet

Flips (F)	Heads (H)	Tails (T)
1	X	
2		X
3		X
4	X	
5	X	
•	X	
•	X	
•		X
•		X
50 Total	22	28

Recording Sheet

Flips (F)	Heads (H)	Tails (T)
51	X	
52	X	
53	X	
54		X
55	X	
•		X
•		X
•	X	
•		X
50 Total	27	23
100 Grand Total	49	51

FIGURE 18: Coin Flip Experiment Charts

After each 25 tosses, have students stop and take and make notes of their observations on this Note-Taking/Note-Making Chart. After 50 tosses, have partners switch roles.

Note Taking	Note Making

After 50 flips, (1–50)
 	
   ratio: H/F = 22/50
   ratio: T/F = 28/50
 	
After 2nd 50 flips, (51–100)
 	
   ratio: H/F = 27/50
   ratio T/F = 23/50
 	
Overall Ratio, (1–100)
 	
   ratio: H/F = 49/100
   ratio: T/F = 51/100
	For this experiment, the ratio was 22/50 for heads. It was not 25/50.
	
	The more we flipped the coin, the closer it got to a ratio of 50/100.

Theory: As number of events increase, the ratio of heads and the ratio of tails to the total number of flips approaches 1:2.

To start them thinking about what kinds of observations to make, you might ask specific questions on this first experiment:

Note Taking	Note Making
1. What is the ratio of heads to the total number of flips after the first 25 flips? H/F: 14/25 What is the ratio of tails to flips after 25 flips? T/F: 11/25	1. What observation can you make about this? *Heads seem to fall more often than tails.*
2. What is the ratio of heads to the total number of flips after the first 50 flips? H/F: 22/50 What is the ratio of tails to the total number of flips after the first 50 flips? T/F: 28/50	2. What observation can you make about this? *Now, tails are occurring more often than heads.*
3. What is the ratio of heads to the total number of flips after the second 50 flips? H/F: 27/50 What is the ratio of tails to the total number of flips after the second 50 flips? T/F: 23/50	3. What observation can you make about this? *The ratio is even closer, although heads came up more often than tails.*
4. What is the overall ratio of heads to the total number of flips after 100 flips? H/F: 49/100 What is the overall ratio of tails to the total number of flips after 100 flips? T/F: 51/100	4. What observation can you make about this? *The more often we flipped the coin, the more even the ratio got.*

Note Taking	Note Making
5. What can you predict about future flips?	5. *Maybe if we did it again, heads would win. If we continued, though, it would eventually come out 1:2.*

What theory can you conclude from your note taking and note making?

As the number of flips increases, the ratio of heads and the ratio of tails to the total of flips comes closer and closer to being 50 percent for each. In other words, there is a 1 out of 2 chance that either side will come up.

2. Four-Sector Spinner

   Note: Spinners should be constructed or purchased previous to teaching the lesson. If spinners are not available, the teacher may wish to construct them.

Tag Board Circle

Brass Fastener
Pushed through at center dot and bent loosely at the back.

uncolored

red

green

blue

Divide class into groups of three. Provide each group with a four-sector spinner. One student spins, one reads, and one records and notes on the Recording Sheet. After 20 spins, have students switch tasks and record, take, and make notes on the next 20 spins.

With this experiment, have students note the ratios as well as the percentages of colored and uncolored spins.

Here is a sample of what a Recording Sheet and a partial Note-Taking/Note-Making Chart might look like:

**Four-Sector Spinner Experiment
Recording Sheet**

Date _____
Group _____

	Spins	Uncolored		Red	Green	Blue
	1				X	
	2					X
	3	X				
	4			X		
	5					X
	•				X	
	•				X	
	•					X
	•			X		
Subt.	20	4		6	5	5
	21	X				
	22					X
	23	X				
	24			X		
	25			X		
	•				X	
	•				X	
	•	X				
	•					X
Subt.	20	7		3	6	4
Total	40	11		9	11	9

Note Taking	Note Making

After 20 spins:
 	
Ratio of colored/total possible:
  16/20 = 4/5
Percentage: 4/5 = 80%
Ratio of uncolored/total possible:
  4/20 = 1/5
Percentage: 1/5 × 100 = 20%
 	
After Second 20 spins:
 	
Ratio of colored/total possible:
  13/20
Percentage: 65%
Ratio of uncolored/total possible:
  7/20
Percentage: 35%
 	
After 40 spins:
 	
Ratio of colored/total possible:
  29/40
Percentage: 72.5%
Ratio of uncolored/total possible:
  11/40
Percentage: 27.5%
	(Students should make observations in this column based on the notes they took in the left-hand column.)

Theory: As the number of events increases, the ratio of uncolored and colored sections approaches 1:4 and 3:4 respectively. (There is a 1 out of 4 chance that the spinner will fall in any given sector).

3. One-die toss experiment

Divide the class into groups of two. Provide each group with a die. One student tosses the die, one records the outcome. The first student tosses the die 30 times, while the second records, takes and makes notes on a chart similar to those from other experiments.

After 30 tosses, the students should change roles and record, take and make notes for 30 additional tosses. Before students toss a second 60 times, ask them to predict what the percentage will be for each number in the next 60 tosses.

Ask students:

- What was the percentage of appearances of each number?
- Did the percentage change from your first 30 tosses?
- How did it compare with your prediction?
- Predict what you think the percentage will be for each number if you tossed the die 1000 times.

4. Group Findings

After conducting their experiments, students meet as a class to report their findings and to display their data on charts around the room. The class collectively analyzes all the data gathered and relates it to their individual findings. For example, they might see the following from the coin toss:

Class Chart

Group No.	No. of Flips	No. of Heads	No. of Tails
Group I	100	49	51
Group II	100	47	53
Group III	100	50	50
Group IV	100	51	49
Total	**400**	**197**	**203**

This approach enables them to formulate a theory of probability deduced from the outcome of all the experiments. To do this, students should regroup into their original pairs or triads for the coin flip, spinner and die tosses. Then, as they study the data of the class chart, they should test the theory they had originally posed against the additional data they see from the whole class. If they find a revision of their theory necessary, they should do so.

Prompt:

A friend of yours says that whenever she/he is asked to flip a coin, she/he *always* chooses heads because it's common knowledge that heads come up almost every time. Write a letter to your friend using what you have just learned about the laws of probability to clearly explain why you doubt her/his claim. Don't just tell your friend that she/he is wrong. Describe your experiments and explain how you arrived at the conclusion which invalidates her/his assumption about heads coming up more often than tails. In other words, your job is to use logical evidence, based on the experiments you conducted, data you collected, and theory you formulated to *persuade* your friend that your conclusion is correct. After reading your letter, your friend should be able to tell you why, based on the laws of probability, her/his belief that heads will come up more than tails was unfounded.

Your letter should be written in standard friendly letter format, be at least two paragraphs in length, use persuasive language, and include transition words to tie your argument together.

Precomposing

1. Laws of Probability Worksheets

To help students generate ideas for their letter, provide worksheets which will enable them to review their learning experiences. Students will need to refer to their Recording Sheets, Note-Taking and Note-Making Charts and group findings in order to complete their worksheets on each of the experiments they conducted.

Sample Worksheet

Name _____

Date _____

Period _____

Laws of Probability Worksheet

Type of Experiment: _____

Description of Experiment: _____

_____

_____

_____

What I Observed: _____

_____

_____

What I Concluded: _____

_____

_____

_____

_____

2. Listing Relevant Information

Ask students to make a list of what information they will need to use from their worksheets in order to convince a friend that the laws of probability refute her/his claim that heads will come up more than tails. Remind students to refer to the prompt as they complete this list.

(*Note:* It might be helpful to suggest to students that even though they should focus on the laws of probability as they relate to the flipping of a coin, they may wish to demonstrate how the laws of probability also apply in their other experiments as a way to strengthen their case.)

3. Freewriting

To facilitate the transformation of this list into a friendly letter, ask students to write for ten minutes using the following first line/last line frame:

(Date.)

Dear Joe (or Jane),
I know that you believe that whenever you flip a coin heads will come up more often than tails. However, . . .

So, as you can see . . .

Sincerely,
(Signature)

4. Sharing

Ask students to share these freewrites in groups of four to generate additional ideas for their letters as well as to see how students can use the same data in different ways to persuade their reader to accept their point of view.

5. Transition Words

Provide students with the following chart on transition words and discuss the ways in which transition words can be used to develop a logical persuasive argument:

Transition Words

To mark an addition:
    and, furthermore, next, moreover, in addition, again, also, likewise,
    similarly, finally, second, in the same respect, just as . . . so, con-
    comitant with, interestingly
 	
To emphasize a contrast or alternative:
    but, or, nor, neither, still, however, nevertheless, on the contrary, on
    the other hand, conversely, despite, aside from, although, even though
 	
To mark a conclusion:
    therefore, thus, in conclusion, consequently, in consequence, as a
    result, in other words, accordingly, hence, subsequently, in summary,
    in the final analysis, finally, ultimately, in retrospect
 	
To introduce an illustration or example:
    for example, for instance, thus, hence, significantly, that is, again

For practice, they may wish to insert appropriate transition words into their freewrites.

6. Persuasive Writing

Ask students to review the opening lines to the two sample letters below and to discuss which one would be more likely to persuade their reader and why:

Dear Sarah,

Your claim that heads will come up more than tails is completely invalid. How can you say it's common knowledge? According to the laws of probability, you are dead wrong. My experiments prove that you can't possibly be right.

Dear Rick,

You know, up until last week, if you had flipped a coin and asked me to pick heads or tails, I would have picked heads too. I guess, like you, I just had a hunch that heads would come up more often than tails. But in my class we've been conducting experiments and learning about the laws of probability. Let me tell you about what we did so that I can explain why what you believe in is mathematically unfounded...

Hopefully, the students will conclude that *what* you say will affect your reader differently depending on *how* you say it. In order to be persuasive, they must decide what kind of approach will be most likely to convince their reader and to select the language they use accordingly.

Writing

Students can use their freewrite as a point of departure for writing the first drafts of their letters. Remind them to review the requirements in the prompt.

Sharing

1. Peers

    Divide students into pairs and ask them to exchange each other's papers. The students should role-play the person to whom the letter they read was addressed and write back to the author. They can use the following three opening lines to begin to respond or create a response of their own:

    - Ok, I'm convinced. Now, I understand that . . .
    - What you said sounds reasonable but I still don't . . .
    - I don't buy it. If I'm so wrong, why did the coin come up heads four out of the five times I tossed it? Also . . .

    These letters should go on to point out the strengths or weaknesses in the writer's argument.

2. Trusted Adult

    Because all the students in the class will have participated in these experiments, they may understand a fellow student's explanation of the laws of probability even if it isn't clearly stated. As a double-check, ask students to give their paper to a parent and to have that parent paraphrase what they have understood about the laws of probability from the letter.

Revising

Students should revise their letters based upon feedback from peers and from a parent. The following self-checklist will also help them shape a second draft:

Writer's Checklist

- Have I addressed my friend in the kind of language that will be most likely to persuade her or him?
- Have I described the experiments I conducted and data I collected?
- Have I used this information to explain my conclusion about the laws of probability?
- After reading my letter, could my reader paraphrase why, based on the laws of probability, her/his belief was unfounded?
- Is my letter in standard friendly letter form—date, greeting, body, closing?
- Is it at least two paragraphs in length?
- Did I use transition words to logically develop my argument?
- Does my letter conform to the conventions of written English, i.e., correct spelling, punctuation, grammar, sentence structure?

Editing

Before submitting their papers for evaluation, have students meet in pairs to proof-read each other's work. Have them check for correctness: friendly letter form, paragraph and sentence structure, spelling, punctuation, and grammar.

Evaluation

Primary Trait

Content

4 A 4-paper:

- Addresses friend in language designed to persuade her or him thoroughly.
- Describes experiments conducted and refers to data collected.
- Uses information about experiments to explain the laws of probability as they relate to flipping a coin; may refer to laws of probability as they relate to die or spinner as well.
- Allows the reader to easily and correctly paraphrase why her/his claim was incorrect.

3 A 3-paper:

- Generally addresses friend in language designed to persuade her or him, but not as convincingly as the 4 paper.
- Describes experiments conducted and refers to data collected reasonably well, but not in as much detail as the 4 paper.
- Uses information about experiments to satisfactorily explain the laws of probability.
- Allows the reader to pretty clearly paraphrase why her or his claim was incorrect after reading the letter one or more times.

2 A 2-paper:

- Does not address the friend in language designed to persuade—may accuse or have an ''I told you so'' tone.
- Superficially describes experiments conducted and data collected.
- Does not use information to explain the laws of probability; may assume reader knows what they are.
- Lacks clarity and the reader cannot paraphrase why his or her claim was incorrect.

1 A 1-paper fails to respond to the assignment.

Secondary Trait

Form and Correctness

3 A 3-paper:

- Is written in standard friendly letter form—date, greeting, body, closing.
- Is at least two paragraphs in length.
- Uses transition words effectively to logically develop a persuasive argument.
- Has few errors in the conventions of written English—spelling, punctuation, grammar, sentence structure.

2 A 2-paper:

- Is written in standard friendly, letter form; one element like the date may be omitted.
- Is at least two paragraphs in length.
- Uses some transition words to logically develop a persuasive argument, but not as effectively as a 3 paper.
- Has some errors in the conventions of written English, but none that seriously hinder the writer's message.

1 A 1-paper:

- Is not written in friendly letter form.
- Is less than two paragraphs in length.
- Does not use transition words.
- Has serious problems in the conventions of written English.

Extension Activities

Application/Evaluation

Prompt: You have just written a letter to persuade your friend that her/his claim that heads come up more than tails when you flip a coin is mathematically impossible. But how often do people actually use the laws of probability when they choose heads or tails? Do you think people are likely to select heads and/or tails on the same 1:2 ratio that will actually come up when a coin is flipped, or will they have a tendency to choose one side of the coin over another? Conduct an experiment to research this question. Ask 100 people in your school to predict whether heads or tails will come up when a coin is flipped, and then flip the coin to see what actually comes up. Before conducting your experiment, predict what percentage of people you believe will select heads and what percentage will select tails. Then,

- keep a tally of how many people pick heads and how many people pick tails;
- compare your tally of how many people correctly predict the side of the coin that actually comes up and how many choose incorrectly;
- determine what the probability is that a person will accurately predict whether heads or tails will come up when the coin is flipped.

Describe the experiment you conducted and the data you collected. Compare the laws of probability with what you actually discovered about the percentages of people that select heads and tails. If people do not select heads and tails in the same ratio that it comes up when the coin is flipped, analyze and evaluate what factors you think influence which side of the coin they select.

Writing Domain: Analytical/Expository

Thinking Level: Evaluation
Grade Level: High School

Justifying a Decision:
A Character Evaluation from *The Crucible*

Lesson

Students will take the point of view of a character at a definite point in time in Arthur Miller's *The Crucible* and write an expository evaluation justifying a major decision.

Objectives

Thinking Skills
Through reacting to a series of real-life situations and *COMPARING* them to *The Crucible*, students will develop a set of standards by which they can *ASSESS* a character's point of view. By empathizing with the character and *EMULATING*

him, students will portray that point of view and *JUSTIFY* the character's actions and decisions.

Writing Skills

In their papers, students will offer thoughtful, relevant reasons for their judgment about why a character acts as he/she does, and will argue these reasons convincingly. They will organize their papers coherently, selecting their support through evidence, anecdotes, or examples exhibited in the play.

The Process

Prewriting

This lesson focuses on one aspect of teaching *The Crucible*. Information about consistency of verb tense, vocabulary, Puritanism, and McCarthyism will also be taught before and during the reading of the play.

1. To prepare the class to read this play aloud, pass out books and explain the plot, the various characters, and their roles. Assign (by reading ability and interest) parts to be read aloud. Students should be allowed three days to study their parts beforehand to be sure they know the character and can read fluently. (As an incentive to preparation, you might allow a grade for oral reading.) If there is time this day, discuss Miller's use of a Puritan situation as the framework for exploring his attitudes about McCarthyism.

2. Prewriting/prereading exercises during the three days of preparatory reading will focus on real life situations that will prepare the students for the attitudes they will encounter in the characters. In each, ask students to write before sharing experiences. Begin by posing the following problem:

   - Think of a time when your decision to do something you were strictly forbidden to do resulted in your getting caught.
   - Write a description of that incident, focusing on the moment you were caught. Using the present tense, begin your incident at that climactic moment. You may use narration, dialogue, monologue, or any combination of these.
   - After you describe the climax, explain how you got yourself out of this trouble and justify your escape techniques.

   (While students share experiences in general class discussion, on the board the teacher can cluster methods of getting out of trouble.)

(Later, these papers may be used as a basis for studying consistent verb tenses.)

3. Think of someone you resent. Write an interior monologue (stream of consciousness) reacting to that person's words or actions and explaining your antagonism to that person.

    (Students work in small groups and voluntarily share papers. They also discuss what puts people on the defensive.)

4. Describe a situation where you got carried away in a crowd and ended up doing something you wouldn't have done had you been alone. Justify this atypical behavior by explaining the pressures that led to it.

    (In class, discuss mob psychology and where we see it working in life: Jonestown, religious cults, anti-Russian fervor . . .)

5. Preceding the reading of each act of the play, offer situations students can relate to easily. For example:

- For Act II, to understand the relationship between Elizabeth and John Proctor—
    - Think of a time when you've hurt someone you love. What did you do to regain her/his affection? How carefully did you plan your actions and comments? How long did it take for things to become normal again?
    - Have you ever lost trust in someone you love? How did your behavior with that person alter? How were you able to regain that trust?

- For Act III, where the power of hearsay and rumor abound—
    - Think of a rumor you have heard recently. At the moment of your hearing it, what did you believe? Who had control—the rumor spreader or the one being rumored about?
    - How can you stop a rumor that has damaged your reputation?
    - Would you lie—or go against some firm belief you hold—to save the one you love?

- For Act IV, when John Proctor has to decide to die in truth or live a lie—
  - Can you think of any situation or idea that is important enough to you that you would die for it?

6. The difficulty in writing this paper lies in choosing a particular point in time to focus on and in moving back and forth from that point in time smoothly.

To facilitate consistency in verb tenses, use papers written during the reading of the play to practice. Here are some samples:

Sample 1. Change any verb tenses and sentence problems to make this paragraph consistent.

As I am coming through my bedroom window at 3:45 A.M., my mom was sitting there on my bed asking me where I was—and she wasn't asking in a polite manner. Well, at that time, I am just in shock. I froze, thinking of how I snuck out of my window to go out with my friends after my mom said I couldn't. But they were going to a party and I didn't want to be left out. Finally, I spoke up and said, "I couldn't sleep so I went out into the garage and cleaned it up." Being that I cleaned it up earlier without her knowing, I would have been in trouble for disobeying her, but she believed me.

Sample 2. Revise this story to begin at the point that the narrator arrives back home. Use the present tense to begin the tale. Include dialogue and go back to the past to explain earlier actions.

One night my friend was spending the night and we decided to steal the car. What happened was, we woke up in the middle of the night and climbed out of my window, took the car, and went driving around. We didn't even have our licenses.

Well, while I was gone my boyfriend called for me on the telephone. My mother came into my room to get me and I wasn't there. She got furious so she waited up for me in my bedroom. As I got home and was climbing back in the window, there I saw her with a very blank look on her face. I got in trouble that night. But the next morning I lied to her. I told her that my friend's car broke down in the middle of nowhere and she was all alone, so she called me to come get her. My mother believed me, and everything was back to normal.

The Revision of Sample 2:

Just a few feet more . . . God, I hope this drainpipe holds up . . . There! I made it! I ACTua . . . Um—"Hi, Mom." Oh, no! I can't believe she's been waiting up for me.

"Hello, Young Man. I don't suppose you'd like to tell me where you've been tonight."

What can I tell her? She won't like hearing that my friend and I stole a car, drove around and then took off, without even our licenses. Oh well, she'll calm down. Tomorrow morning I'll tell her my friend's car broke down or something, and everything will be all right.

Prompt:

Underlying his criticisms of the actions of his witch-hunters in *The Crucible,* Arthur Miller has a sense that each of these people of Salem was living life the best way he could in the world as he saw it. Virtually every character reaches a point where, from some personal sense of inadequacy, he panics. Some exploit this panic to give themselves power—to rise up in righteous indignation over others and attempt to destroy them in the artificial name of goodness. Others, to appear in control, try to become a part of the fanatical crowd and condone the manipulation of power. Still others, the stronger, overcome their personal fears and sacrifice themselves for what they consider a higher value. This examination of fear and the ways we handle it is the idea that makes Miller's play a universal one— more than merely a historical account of the witchcraft delusion of Salem, Massachusetts, or merely a sociological attack on paranoia.

Select from *The Crucible* a character you can best understand or most sympathize with. Write an evaluation, in the character's *own voice,* of the choice he made. Show in detail the moment of decision and the character's psychological and emotional responses to that moment. The assumption you must write from is that the character behaved in the best way he possibly could. Thus, you must assess his fears and motivations to judge why his actions were perfectly justifiable in terms of his values.

You may decide on any form of writing (a letter, journal, confession, testimony) and write to any audience (like a relative, another character in the play, a person outside the play, a court, a priest, God) you think most appropriate to your character. Do your best to find appropriate words for your character to utter. You may quote him, at his moment of decision, but write his justification in your own view of his language.

Your audience and form of writing will help determine at what point in the character's development you want to begin. However you structure your approach, be sure that you describe the dilemma your character faced, present the alternatives he chose between, identify the decision he made, and give several reasons to justify that as his best decision.

Precomposing

1. Analyzing Characters

As the play is being read, give students the following chart to fill in at the end of each act:

Character	One Major Problem In This Act	Decision	Reason To Justify Decision
Abigail Williams	To lie about conjuring or to tell the truth	She lies.	She avoids punishment. No one knows why she was conjuring.
John Proctor			
Elizabeth Proctor			
Mary Warren			
Reverend Parris			
Francis Nurse			
Rebecca Nurse			
Giles Corey			

2. Practicing The First Point of View

To give students practice in writing as a character, choose significant incidents from each act as the students read. Then, after each act has been read and discussed, assign the incident as a focal point for an interior monologue. Direct students to get inside the character's mind and show his or her physical and emotional response to the moment of the incident. Their writing goal is to let the reader see and feel the character's emotions without ever naming them.

Here are some examples of possible incidents from Act III:

- Mary Warren being accused by Abigail;
- Abigail when John calls her a harlot;
- Abigail when she turns on Mary Warren;
- John when he hears Elizabeth lie;
- Elizabeth when John says he confessed the truth;
- Hale when he leaves the court.

The climax of each act can be used to show the reactions of various characters.

The following student sample shows John watching Elizabeth in the courtroom:

Oh, please, Elizabeth, tell the truth. Don't try to save my name. You know that Abigail was a whore and that I committed lechery.

I hope she doesn't give in to Danforth. He knows Mary is telling the truth. Why is he still doubtful? Why is he putting so much pressure on Elizabeth?

Please tell the truth, Elizabeth. Come on, Elizabeth!

No! Don't say that! Tell the truth! Tell him she's a harlot and admit you threw her out for that. Danforth, don't pressure her so! She's done nothing wrong. Elizabeth, don't break. Tell the truth. You never lie. Don't start now, don't try to protect me.

Oh no! Why did you do that, Elizabeth? I confessed already. He knows! I'm dead.

And this student takes the same moment from Elizabeth's point of view:

Where is John—I can't find him in the crowd! There he is; John, why is your back turned? Alas! Abigail has turned away also.

Mr. Danforth is telling me not to look at John—Danforth looks repulsive now, this witchcraft madness has brought coldness and suspicion to his face. But why am I called to stand before this court? These people, packed together in this hot room to watch a play that decides whether people live or hang— Why for am I called before them?

He is asking me why I sent her from my service. John! Look at me! Give me a sign of what I am to say!

Am I to tell him the truth? Which will help, my husband? The truth or a lie?

"She were—"

John, turn around! Am I to lie to save you? Why won't they let me look at him? These people, they're staring at me with their mouths agape, entertained and shocked at my helplessness. The birds are singing outside and I am trapped.

Did John turn from me, he asks. Am I to disclose this thing that has been tormenting me since that wench went away? Lord, help me—help me save my husband. I see now how much I love him. I do forgive him, but I am now supposed to reveal his unfaithfulness to me. I can *not*!

I've got to look at John's eyes—*Why* may I not!! Danforth's hard, cold hands are holding my head away from him—He demands an answer—I will not admit John's mistake to the judge and these accusers of innocent people. Dear God, I pray forgive me for lying.

"No . . . no he is not a lecher." *Wait*!—was not that the answer I was to give? Why is there such a commotion? John—you told me to say the truth? "Oh God!" John! You already confessed!?

3. Focusing On A Character

   After the play has been read thoroughly and has been discussed, and students have selected the characters they want to portray, pass out a ditto with the following kinds of questions to help students understand the characters' motives and justifications:

   - What does your character think of himself?
   - What is he most afraid of ?

- What does he think of the people of Salem?
- How is he a good Puritan?
- What decision does he face?
- What several alternatives/choices does he have?
- Why does he choose as he does? (Deciding not to choose is also a choice.)
- How does he believe his choice is right?
- Does he consider the consequences when he chooses?
- How do these consequences seem fair to him?
- Is his choice consistent with his personality or values? In what ways?

Once each student has answered these questions for his character, the class can break into small groups according to characters (Proctors with Proctors, etc.) to review answers, to compare notes in preparation to write, and to add any other information they feel is important.

Writing

To demonstrate how to get started, show a few models of the beginnings of past papers. Here are a couple of samples: (Point out that each paper opens at a particular point in time and establishes the character's dilemma and personality.)

1. This opening shows Mary Warren's confusion about whom she should stand up for—her friend Abby, or her employer, Elizabeth:

> They arrest Elizabeth for witching Abby just now. I don't know Abby anymore. She accused Elizabeth of being a witch in the court. I know Elizabeth. She wouldn't do anything like that. About that puppet too—Abby saw me sewing it in the court, and now she says that Elizabeth made it to use to witch her.
>
> —Miemie Win

2. This paper is a journal entry in the diary of Thomas Putnam, two months after the witch-hunts of Salem. He reveals how he has manipulated the people of Salem.

> The trials are over, and the accused are hanged. Their land is up for sale on the morrow and I shall purchase it. Giles Corey has his just reward. He will threaten me no longer.
> As I look back at the trials, I realize what fools the townspeople are. It was so easy to accuse my enemies of being witches and make those idiots believe me.
>
> —Jim Ruga

Sharing

Break the class into small response groups (3 people) of unlike characters (Proctors with Abigails, etc.). Direct each group to look for the following aspects:

Setting

- From what point in the play is the character offering his explanation?
- If the explanation is begun before the play ends, does he take into consideration the consequences?
- Are the verb tenses accurate enough to show a clear time sequence?

Decision

- Is the moment of decision clearly shown?
- Would the circumstances be clear even to someone who has not read the play?
- Are the alternatives he chose between clearly explained?
- Are the motives (feelings behind the decision) clear?
- Do you fully understand what the decision was and why it was the best possible one to make?
- Does the writer avoid apologizing or making excuses for the decision?

Style

- Does the writer choose words appropriate to the character?
- Is the writer able to establish a character's attitude and language traits and stick to them throughout?
- Does the writer ever break character?

Revising

Taking suggestions from the response group, students will revise their original drafts by adding and deleting where they decide necessary. (This can be done in one class period.)

Editing

In pairs, students check each other's second drafts concerning these areas of grammar:

- consistency of verb tense
- spelling
- clear pronoun reference
- complete sentences

Rewriting

The final draft can be neatly handwritten or typed at home.

Evaluation

Use a read-around-group* to enable all students to read and judge all papers.

Day 1

Break the class into evenly sized small groups. (Allow only students with finished products to participate.) Instruct students to skim for the following traits:

- How clearly does the writer explain the choices of the character?
- How well does he justify the decision as being the best one of the character could make?
- How well does the writer maintain the character's point of view?

Day 2

Chart the groups' selections of best papers. Read the most frequently selected papers to the class and establish a scoring rubric.
    A sample rubric might look like the following:

Sample Rubric

6 This is a paper that is clearly superior, well-written, carefully organized, insightful, and technically correct. It does all or most of the following well:

- Maintains the character's attitude, point of view, and language traits throughout the whole paper
- Shows in detail and with depth of perception the moment of decision and the character's psychological and emotional responses to that moment
- Justifies the character's decision as the best possible one he could make—doesn't apologize or excuse the decision
- Moves through time easily and with appropriate verb tenses
- Varies sentence structure and length
- Demonstrates mastery of the conventions of written English (punctuation, capitalization, pronoun reference, agreement, spelling)

5 This paper includes all aspects of the assignment, but is a thinner version of the 6. It is still well-written, carefully organized, and technically correct. It does all or most of the following:

*For details, see read-around-groups in the Glossary.

- Establishes the character's attitude, point of view, and language traits, but may not be able to maintain them consistently
- Shows in detail and with clear (although perhaps implied) perception the moment of decision and of the character's psychological and emotional responses to that moment
- Justifies the character's decision as the best one he could make, but may begin or end with a regret.
- Moves fairly easily and with appropriate verb tenses
- Varies sentence structure and length
- Demonstrates competency in the conventions of written English

4 This paper includes all aspects of the assignment, but examines only some in depth. It may exhibit some of the following:

- Identifies the character's attitude and point of view but is unable to use characteristic language traits (writer speaks in his or her own voice)
- Reverts occasionally to plot summary rather than consistently analyzing the moment of decision
- Shows some understanding of the psychological and emotional responses of the character to the moment of decision
- Offers excuses for the character's decision
- Has trouble maintaining consistency of verb tenses
- Uses static sentence structure and grammar that is occasionally unconventional

3 This paper ignores part of the assignment or treats the subject in a superficial fashion. It exhibits *all* of the weakness of the 4-paper and:

- Identifies the character's attitude and point of view but is unable to use characteristic language traits (writer speaks in his or her own voice)
- Uses plot summary instead of analyzing the moment of decision
- Shows little understanding of the psychological emotional responses of the character to the moment of decision
- Has trouble maintaining consistency of verb tenses
- Uses static sentence structure and unconventional grammar

2 This paper represents an attempt to write the assignment, but is so poorly written and exhibits such serious defects in organization, depth, and mechanics that it is difficult to understand.
OR
The paper may use only quotes from the play, demonstrating no awareness on the part of the writer.

1 This paper is written *about* the character rather than *as* the character and thus ignores the requirements of the prompt.

Extension Activities

Note: These Extension Activities will promote further study of *The Crucible*.

Evaluation

Prompt: Should John Proctor have lied and lived or told the truth and died? Write a paper that justifies your answer not only in terms of your own values, but also in terms of what you know about the situation of the play.

Synthesis

Prompt: Imagine the life Elizabeth leads when she later remarries. How might she behave differently toward her new husband? Would she have learned anything from her relationship with John? Write a paper that speculates about both the consistencies and changes she might experience in this new marriage.

Synthesis

Prompt: Using the interior monologue you wrote in reaction to someone you resent, create an exterior monologue of what you might say to him/her if you had the chance.

Model Paper #1: Abigail's Prayers

Are you there, Mother? It's me Abby. How's Father? I talked to John today. Oh Mother, I know John loves me now and more than ever. After yours and Father's deaths, I felt lost until John came along. Oh, how I love him; I must save him from Elizabeth, I must. Help me, Mother. Please, help me. She's a witch. She's very wicked. I must tell everyone about her to save John. She's bewitched him on the inside into thinking that he loves her, but on the outside his soul is just dying for affection. That is why he came to me. Oh, Mother, I really love him, I really do. Well, I must go now and I'll talk to you tomorrow. Bye.

    Hi, Mother, I'm back. I went to court to confess and tell about all the bad people that I seen conjuring with the Devil. They must be hanged, Mother, or confess to what they have done. They're full of wickedness, and I must stop them. And with my power to sense witchery, I will stop them. I'll do anything to save John and myself.

Mother, last night at supper I was stabbed with a needle in my stomach and I fainted. But, Mother, I know who it was who did this to me—it was Elizabeth. She keeps poppets in her home. I know, I've seen them. She has tried to kill me with her poppet. She stuck a needle through the poppet's stomach to get to me, and Mother, it did get to me. I must go to the authorities with this now. So I must close for now. Bye.

Oh, Mother, I'm lost! I'm lost! Oh, my John, I have lost him! For he is such a good man that he mustn't live in shame, so he will be hanged tomorrow, and it's all because Mary Warren has called Witch on him. She has said that he be-witched her, but Mother, he didn't. It was Elizabeth, not John. But there's no proof of it, so John must hang, and it is too late to save him. But at least I know that he is away from Elizabeth.

Oh, Mother, I am going to leave, escape town. I must go to where I am wanted and to where I'll feel secure. Somewhere. Anywhere. As long as I am wanted. So I guess this is goodbye. So good-bye. I love you.

—Lisa Martinez

Model Paper #2: Proctor's Decision

My Dearest Brother William,

This is John. Salem has gone mad. I write this from behind the bars of the town jail where I stand sentenced to hang for witchery. I, along with many of our up-standing citizens, have been condemned to hang because of the vindictive accu-sations of a faction of the community.

I pray that you do not face the same predicament and that the situation in your Andover has not deteriorated to this degree. We hear word of rebellion in Andover, but nothing can be taken for certain, much less in this prison.

Even my dear wife, Elizabeth, is jailed for witchery, and her pregnancy alone keeps her from execution. Rebecca Nurse, whom I'm sure you remember, is also condemned to hang.

I know not what be of the boys now, as I have seen naught of them nor Elizabeth for these months. I am sure that Elizabeth has arranged for them to be well-kept, most probably with Rebecca Samuels.

I realize this must come as some surprise to you, to hear of your own brother sentenced to hang for witchery. For that reason, I shall recount the happenings of the past months.

First, although this grieves me deeply, there is something I must admit to you. Otherwise I could not expect you to understand my emotions and indecision in this matter.

I have sinned. I have committed lechery, and the girl has been trying to kill Elizabeth so she would have me to herself. This witchery gibberish started because she and her friends were conjuring spirits to kill Elizabeth. They were found and proceeded to name whomever they claimed to see in company with the Devil. Elizabeth, of course, was named.

An expert in matters of witchcraft, Reverend John Hale, was called in to advise the authorities. I must give Hale credit for his attempts to restore some semblance of sanity to this township. He has now realized that this has been a prodigious hoax set up by these girls. Unfortunately, the authorities see his advice only as an attempt to overthrow the courts. Even a petition submitted to vouch for a good character of the accused was considered a threat.

I should probably tell you how I came to be accused. I persuaded one of the girls, Mary Warren, my servant, to admit that it were pretense that the girls saw witches. But she sensed that the judge was not convinced, and when the girls turned against her, she turned against me, accusing me of doing the Devil's work. I was thus jailed.

I now must decide whether I live or die. I do know not what life would be like with the disgrace of knowing I had lied to save my own skin. What is John Proctor worth? I know not.

Yet I feel that my death would lessen the deaths of Rebecca Nurse and the others. They are dying as saints. I would die as a sinner.

However, I do not think that I could so sacrifice my honor for my life. I have two young boys; I would not have them raised with a liar for a father. How could they be taught right and wrong with my example before them?

My death could also help to bring the end of this madness. Rebellion can not be far off in this township; perhaps my execution could bring it about.

These are the reasons why I have chosen my death. I felt you should know this, William. I could not leave this world in such a way without giving you an explanation. When my children are grown, please show them this letter. Perhaps it will help them to understand.

Goodbye, William. I love you.

John Proctor
—Mike McMahan

Writing Domain: Analytical/Expository/
Imaginative/Narrative

Thinking Level: Evaluation
Grade Level: High School/College

Out of a Genuine Need to Know: Personalizing the Research Paper

Lesson

Students will write a personalized research paper on a topic of their choice.

Note: This lesson is an adaptation of Ken Macrorie's innovative I-Search paper. See *The I-Search Paper: Revised Edition of Searching Writing* (Portsmouth, N.H.: Boynton/Cook Publishers, Heinemann, 1988).

Objectives

Thinking Skills
This three-part assignment takes students through all of the levels of Bloom's taxonomy, culminating in *EVALUATION,* as they:

- *RECOUNT* what they *KNOW, ASSUME,* or *IMAGINE* about their topic;
- *TEST* and enhance that knowledge through research of primary and secondary sources;
- *ASSESS* what they learned in the process of searching and comment upon the *VALUE* of their discoveries.

Writing Skills
The lesson also taps all four domains of writing. It:

- reinforces sensory/descriptive skills such as the use of precise, vivid language and rich, sensory detail;
- stresses imaginative/narrative elements such as sustaining story-line, sequencing events, transition, and pacing;
- draws upon the clarity and coherence of practical/informative writing;
- introduces the footnote and bibliographic form that is required in many analytical/expository papers.

The Process

Although this version of the Personalized Research Paper is geared toward college students, the assignment can be adapted to all levels of the curriculum, elementary through college, and modified accordingly. We have chosen to share it as the culminating lesson at the evaluation level because it calls for a critical assessment of the student's own learning process. In addition, it provides training and practice in conducting research—consulting both primary and secondary sources—and in properly documenting those sources. Prior to this lesson, students will have written papers in all four domains of writing: sensory/descriptive, imaginative/narrative, practical/informative, and analytical/expository.

Prewriting

Give students time to "discover" their topic. One week prior to handing out the prompt, explain to your students that they will have an opportunity to write a personalized research paper that should focus on a topic *that they genuinely need to know about.* Ask them to keep a pocket notebook handy and to record every question they have during that week that they genuinely need to know the answer to. Provide a list of questions like the one that follows just to get them started thinking:

1. Is there something that you would like to do in your free time (i.e., skydiving, gourmet cooking, playing racquetball, volunteer work) that you need to know something more about?

2. Are you saving up to buy anything (i.e., camera, microwave, home computer, motorcycle) that you need to learn how to operate?

3. Are you beginning to think about what you want to do when you graduate (i.e., get a particular job, travel, pursue an advanced degree) and about which you need more information to make a decision?

4. Do you think you might like to move to another city or country someday? How much do you know about where you would like to relocate?

5. Do you have any concerns about health (i.e., pros and cons of popular diets or exercise routines, dangers from smoking, drinking or drugs, the individual risks when a disease runs in the family) that you would like to explore?

6. What do you fear the most? Would you like to know why?

After the students have a week to reflect about the kinds of things, they might need to know, pass out the following prompt, discuss it, and answer questions that arise.

Prompt:

Description

The Personalized Research Paper is designed to teach the writer and the reader something valuable about a chosen topic and about the nature of searching and discovery. As opposed to the standard research paper where the writer usually assumes a detached and objective stance, this paper allows you to take an active role in your search, to experience some of the hunt for facts and truths firsthand, and to provide a step by step record of the discovery process.

Topic

The cardinal rule in the Personalized Research Paper is to select a topic that genuinely interests you and that you need to know more about. Topics written by previous students have included: *Not Exactly the Brady Bunch: Understanding and Resolving the Tension in Step Families; Reaching Out to Orange County's Invisible Poor; Diabetes: What's the Prognosis? Auuuggghhh! An Exploration of Stress and Burn-out;* and *Should I Invest in the Silver Market?* The important point is that *you* choose the topic you will investigate rather than having the instructor select a topic or even provide a number of options.

Format

The Personalized Research Paper should be written in three sections:

- What I Know, Assume, or Imagine
- The Search
- What I Discovered

What I Know, Assume, or Imagine

Before conducting any formal research, write a section in which you explain to the reader what you think you know, what you assume or what you imagine about your topic. For example, if you decided to investigate teenage alcoholism, you might want to offer some ideas about the causes of teenage alcoholism, provide an estimate of the severity of the problem, and create a portrait of a typical teenage drinker, etc.

The Search

Test your knowledge, assumptions or conjectures by researching your paper topic thoroughly. Conduct first-hand activities like writing letters, making telephone calls, initiating face to face interviews, and going on field trips. Also, consult useful second-hand sources such as books, magazines, newspapers, films, tapes, etc. Be sure to record all the information you gather. If you were pursuing a search on teenage alcoholism, you might want to do some of the following: make an appointment to visit an alcohol rehabilitation center, attend a meeting of Alanon or Alcoholics Anonymous, consult an alcoholism counselor, or interview your peers, as well as check out a book on the subject, read several pertinent articles, or see a film.

Write your search up in a narrative form, relating the steps of the discovery process. Do not feel obligated to tell everything, but highlight the happenings and facts you uncovered that were crucial to your hunt and contributed to your understanding of information using formal form when appropriate.

What I Discovered

After concluding your search, compare what you thought you knew, assumed, or imagined with what you actually discovered, assess your overall learning experience, and offer some personal commentary about the value of your discoveries

Note: The three-part format of this paper can be organized explicitly—for example, set off with subheadings—or implicitly.)

and/or draw some conclusions. For instance, after completing your search on teenage alcoholism, you might learn that the problem is far more severe and often begins at an earlier age than you formerly believed. You may have assumed that parental neglect was a key factor in the incidence of teenage alcoholism, but now find that peer pressure is the prime contributing factor. Consequently, you might want to propose that an alcoholism awareness and prevention program including peer counseling sessions be instituted in the public school system as early as sixth grade.

Bibliography

Attach a formal bibliography listing the sources you consulted at the close of the report.

Precomposing

Once the students are aware of the specifics of the prompt, the following activities will help them to zero in on a topic and plan their compositions:

Phase One. Selecting A Topic

Look at two or more models of Personalized Research Papers and discuss how they fulfill the requirements of the prompt. (Consult Ken Macrorie's *The I-Search Paper* for samples your students can relate to. Once you have a set of your own student papers, you can use those as models for future classes.)

Ask students to take out their ongoing lists of questions they have been compiling over the past week and:

- Label the questions according to two categories:
  GN = genuinely need to know and
  MC = mildly curious about.
- Eliminate all the MCs.
- Prioritize the remaining GNs according to importance.

Give students one additional week to select topics from their lists of top priorities. Advise them that the availability of primary and secondary research sources should be a consideration in making their decisions.

Phase Two. Planning for the Process and the Product

After the students have selected their topic and checked to make sure research sources are available, they should write up an abstract (not to exceed one page in length), in which they explain *what* their topic is, *why* they have chosen it, and *how* they intend to go about searching and writing. A sample abstract is provided below:

Abstract for Personalized Research Paper on Procrastination

For almost as long as I can remember, I've had this nasty habit of procrastinating—postponing until tomorrow what could easily be completed today. This is especially true of the way I handle written work (like papers for this class, for instance), which has established due dates and a reader with high expectations.

I'd like to take a close look at why I procrastinate and suffer all the anxiety caused by putting things off until the last minute. Maybe I can learn something that will not only make my behavior more understandable, but will enable me *to do something about it!* Then I'll hire myself out as a consultant to all my fellow procrastinators.

Speaking of fellow procrastinators, I'll start by interviewing my friends and also try to make an appointment with a counseling psychologist. Maybe talking to a time management consultant would be useful too. I've checked at the library in the reader's guide to periodicals, and it looks like *Psychology Today* is my best bet for secondary sources. I didn't see any entire books on the subject, but maybe I can also find a chapter in a couple of books.

Have students share these abstracts in peer groups so that they can exchange ideas about their topics.

Students are not only good at helping each other clarify and refine their ideas about what they're planning to do and why, but they serve as valuable resources. A student wishing to investigate whether she should train to become a nurse practitioner, for example, may find that another student knows and can arrange for an interview with someone in that profession.

While they are sharing, call students up for individual conferences. The main thing students seem to need help from the teacher on at this point is narrowing their scope.

During the same class session, pass out the rubric for the assignment (see the *EVALUATION* section of this lesson) so students have a list of the criteria for the Personalized Research Paper.

Writing

The paper should be written in three progressive stages. The amount of time allotted for completion of each section will depend on the teacher and his/her time constraints. Included below is a sequence of steps from conception to completion that assumes a maximum amount of time (one week for prewriting, one week for precomposing and three weeks for writing). It is understood that some teachers may choose to collapse or skip some of these steps to condense the time-frame.

Sharing

Since this paper is written in stages, it is important to enable students to receive both oral and written feedback on their work throughout the writing process. To ensure that they are off to a good start, provide them with an opportunity to share the What I Know, Assume or Imagine section of their papers prior to conducting their research. To prepare them to give and receive feedback, you may want to introduce a student model (from Macrorie's book or from another class) for the group to critique. Section I of a Personalized Research Paper on procrastination (see *PRECOMPOSING* for the abstract of this paper) is provided below.

After reading the model, use the response sheet which follows it as the basis for group discussion.

Model

Procrastination

I can remember as far back as sixth grade, setting out at the last minute to finish up homework that could have easily been completed days before. How I dreaded high school classes that required a massive, five-page report at the end of the semester. Of course, these grueling writing sessions had to begin the night before they were due, much to the chagrin of my mother (who usually wound up typing!). With college came a new experience—The "All Nighter" Writing Marathon! What fond memories I have of analyzing forest images from Frost's poetry for my English I class at 3:15 AM no less! Even today, I have never ceased to lose that keen sense of "putting off until tomorrow" anything that holds in my mind major significance. (Many of my writing attempts for this class attest to this theory!)

I'm not without ideas as to why I—and I believe others—procrastinate. I say others because I know I am not alone at this well-developed craft . . . I've met a few in the course of writing those "all nighters." I believe we who put off do so because there is a bit of perfectionist in us. We can't sit down and put just anything on paper without having every detail worked out to our mind's satisfaction. I'd like to believe that, in a sense, we are smarter than the average person, but that we can't or don't always show it. Maybe we're so overly concerned with the minute details we tend to belabor every word or phrase that spills out on paper. There must be some sort of "procrastination mentality" that haunts us. I'm very curious to find out how other fellow procrastinators react to and cope with our syndrome. I'd like to kick this nagging habit, if I could . . . or at least cope with it more effectively. And what do the experts say on the subject? What solutions do they offer? I'm so excited I can't wait to start my research . . . that is, after I clean the house, grab a snack, go to the store for a few groceries, talk to . . .

Bruce Lubliner
Education 118
Writing and Critical Thinking
University of California, Irvine

Response Sheet

To the author of _____ : **Based on Section I, your Personalized Research Paper looks like it will . . .**	**Very much so. Great start!**	**Probably. Good start so far.**	**Possible. Hard to tell. Shaky start.**	**Not likely. Doesn't look too promising.**
• be a genuine learning experience for writer and reader.				
• be really interesting to read.				
• demonstrate that you will take an active role in your search.				
• be well organized.				
• offer specific examples to support the topic covered.				
• convey you own ''voice'' or style as a writer.				
• be well written in terms of word choice and pacing.				
• What we liked best about the What I Know, Assume, or Imagine section of your paper was: • One thing we thought you could work on improving was:				

Then, ask students to exchange Section I of their papers with another group. Individual group members should silently read and review each paper and then discuss their reactions with the group. Assign a group recorder to indicate the groups' collective response for each paper on the Response Sheet above. (*Note:* Encourage students to offer detailed comments rather than just to check boxes.)

When the papers have been returned, have students read their drafts aloud to their peer group and get their responses. While they are sharing, ask students who received ''Shaky start'' and ''Doesn't look too promising'' responses to conference with you so that you can assist them in refocusing their opening remarks.

Precomposing

Once students have completed the What I Know, Assume, or Imagine section of their papers, they should begin collecting data for The Search. The abstracts they wrote to explain the *what, why,* and *how* of their chosen topic can be used as an action plan. To enable students to make maximum use of firsthand sources, you may want to role-play an interview or share another student model which incorporates interviews and/or field trip material. Also, suggest that students record information from secondary sources on 3″ × 5″ cards and note all necessary references. *Note: During this class session, also take time to teach or review proper footnote and bibliographic form and to orient students to library research. This will prepare them to write The Search section of their paper.*

Prior to writing The Search portion of the paper, some students may want to retrace their data collecting journey in a narrative sentence outline form such as the one below on the silver market:

My Search on the Silver Market

1. I started out by posing the following questions: What is silver? What factors contribute to the price fluctuations in silver? Is silver a speculative investment or is it a real investment? Do I need a large amount of money to buy silver? What are various ways to invest in silver?

2. Then, I set out to answer these questions, one by one:

   - I looked up a definition of silver and found out not only what it is but that it's very rare.
   - My discovery of silver's rarity led me to the next phase of my search. Its price fluctuates with supply and demand.
   - To answer my question of whether investing in silver is speculation, I read a book called *Crisis Investing.*
   - Then I went to Rare Coin Galleries, Inc., in Orange to see if I could make an investment with a small amount of money. Tom MacDonald, a salesman there, helped me make a decision.

3. Upon completing my interview with Tom, I made my decision to invest. I bought 100 ounce silver bullion at the price of $8.25 an ounce plus 80 cents commission fee (for a total of $9.05 per ounce) plus $95 in commemorative coins.

4. I was set. All I had to do was sit back and rake in the dough.

5. It's only been a week since then and silver has already dropped to $8.00 an ounce. Stay tuned for what I learned from all this.

Writing

Students then complete Section II, The Search, and bring it to class for sharing.

Sharing

Direct the sharing this time to shift the focus from content to form. Is the narrative describing the search easy to follow, interesting, and informative? Are both first- and secondhand sources consulted? If time allows, talk the group through another student model that is particularly well structured. The Personalized Research Paper entitled ''A Matter of Identity'' appended to this lesson could be used for discussion purposes.

Precomposing

As a final precomposing step, ask students to compare the What I Know, Assume, or Imagine section with The Search portion of their papers. These questions might be helpful:

- How accurate were your original assumptions?
- What new information did you acquire?
- What did you learn that surprised you?
- Overall, what value did you derive from the process of searching and discovery?

Writing

Students write Section III, What I Discovered, and bring it to class for sharing.

Sharing

Ask peer group members to paraphrase what they have learned from each member's paper. Then, shift the focus of the peer groups—this time to correctness. Stress proper footnote and bibliographic form.

Revising

Because students are getting ongoing feedback on their paper they will, most likely, be revising as they go. Direct their attention now to the total product. The following list of questions should help them re-see what they have written:

- Has the process of searching and writing been a genuine learning experience for you? Do you feel you have taught the reader something valuable?
- Does your topic lend itself to investigation and discovery? Have you taken an active rather than passive role in your search?
- What special insights do you think you have offered on your topic?
- Is your paper structured, either implicitly or explicitly, according to the three-

part format designed in the explanation of the assignment? Which of the three sections do you feel is the strongest and why?

- Have you included both firsthand and secondhand research? Did you include footnotes and a bibliography?
- Does your paper have continuity (does it hang together and follow logically)? How did you tie the different sections together?
- Have you supported your main points with ample use of examples?
- What techniques have you used to make your paper interesting?
- Do you feel your own "voice" as a writer has come through in your paper?
- Do you feel you experimented with different sentence patterns and lengths?
- Have you proofread your paper carefully and checked for correct spelling, sentence structure, grammar, punctuation, etc.?
- Overall, are you pleased with your paper? What are its strengths?
- What still needs improving?

Final Editing/Rewriting

Students polish their final drafts.

Evaluation

Papers will be scored by both the students and the instructor according to the following rubric:

Scoring Guide for the Personalized Research Paper

9–8 A paper that is clearly superior—well written, clearly organized, insightful, and technically correct. It does the following well:

- Paper is a genuine learning experience for the writer and the reader
- Paper displays evidence of all levels of critical thinking and offers special insight into the topic discussed
- Topic lends itself to investigation and discovery
- Paper is written in three sections. (Format may be explicit or implicit)
  - What I Know, Assume or Imagine (prior to the search)
  - The Search (testing knowledge, assumptions or conjecture through documented research)
  - What I Discovered (comparing what you thought you knew with what you learned and offering commentary and conclusions)
- Author takes an active role rather than a passive role in the search
- Writer uses research effectively as a supplement to, but not as a substitute for, his or her own ideas
- Paper conveys a clear sense of the author's "voice" or style
- Writer uses precise, apt, or descriptive language

- Main points of the essay are well supported with examples.
- The writer uses ample transitions between ideas, paragraphs, and sections.
- Writer varies sentence structure and length.
- The Search portion of the essay is properly documented with footnotes in correct form.
- Paper includes references to a minimum of two primary and two secondary research sources.
- Paper includes a formal bibliography.
- Writer generally uses effectively the conventions of written English.

7 This is a thinner version of the 9–8 paper—still impressive and interesting but less thoroughly researched, more loosely organized, less insightful and/or not as informative as the 9–8 paper.

6–5 These scores apply to papers that are less well handled than 7, 8 or 9-papers. A 6–5 paper may be less interesting and informative, more superficially researched, less insightful or contain problems in the conventions of written English. It will exhibit some or all of the following characteristics:

- Paper is a learning experience for the writer and reader but the paper is less informative than a 7, 8, or 9-paper; thus the lesson is less valuable.
- Paper does not display as much critical thinking or insight as 7, 8, or 9-paper.
- Paper is written in three sections but they are not equally complete or well-handled.
- Author does not really seem involved in his/her topic.
- Writer may rely too heavily on the research rather than using it to augment his/her own thoughts.
- Paper does not convey a clear sense of the author's ''voice'' or style.
- Main points of the essay are well supported with examples.
- The three sections of the report are not tied together effectively with transitions.
- Language is not as descriptive as a 7, 8, or 9-paper.
- Sentence structure and length could use some variation.
- Writer uses very few footnotes, indicating that little research has been conducted; bibliography is sketchy.
- Paper does not directly refer to at least two primary and two secondary research sources.
- Some problems in the conventions of written English, but none that seriously impair the message.

4-3 These scores apply to papers that maintain the general idea of the writing assignment but are weak in content, thought, language facility or the conventions of written English. A 4–3 paper will exhibit some or all of these characteristics:

- Paper is not a genuine learning experience for the writer or the reader.
- Paper demonstrates little or no evidence of critical thinking.
- Paper is not written in three sections or sections do not follow the guidelines set up in the assignment description.
- Writer either has relied too heavily on research or has conducted little, if any, research.
- Discussion is overly general or superficial.
- Main points are not supported with examples.
- Writer's ''voice'' does not come across.
- Language is vague and imprecise.
- Research sources are not documented in bibliography or footnotes.
- The reader may have a problem understanding the paper.
- Paper has serious problems in the conventions of written English.

2 This score applies to papers that do not follow the writing assignment and contain weaknesses of the 4–3 paper.

1 This score applies to a paper that is completely off track and has no redeeming qualities.

Note: An extremely well-written paper may receive a point higher than it would on the basis of content alone. If a paper has serious problems in the conventions of written English that impair the writer's message, it can receive up to a two-point deduction.

Extension Activities

Evaluation   If your students have had previous experience with holistic scoring of the work of their peers, you may want to consider assigning this final task:

Prompt: Carefully examine your Personalized Research Paper and compare your written product with criteria listed on the scoring guide. Then assess the strengths and weaknesses of your paper and rate it on a nine-point scale. Begin your self-evaluation, ''After carefully examining my Personalized Research Paper, I feel it warrants a score of _____.'' Justify your score by answering (with a commentary—not a simple yes or no) the questions for revision you used earlier to rethink and re-see your paper.

A Matter of Identity

"Just relax and be yourself. Keep looking at the camera. When you are not talking to the guest, you must be looking at the camera. You can look at the monitor and fix your make-up before you start, if you like. But, afterwards, you must address the camera. That's your audience."

I stare at the camera. *What a responsive audience!* I reflect sarcastically to myself; but I nod my head approvingly. The atmosphere is encouraging. I am supposed to interview a Lebanese musician whom I greatly respect and whose work I enjoy. So, too, the director and the camera man are old friends of mine. As a matter of fact, it doesn't seem like an audition at all. It's more like a rehearsal session.

I look at the monitor and my dark eyes, enhanced by the black Arabic eyeliner on them, look back at me assuringly. My eyes have always given me confidence in my appearance. I run my fingers through my hair, fluffing it over my ears. It looks great—soft, thick and healthy. My hair has never failed me. Every hair dresser who has touched it has commented on its quality. My mouth looks fine, although it feels heavier than usual with this much lipstick on. Ordinarily I lick it off; I cannot do that now. I concentrate on my mouth for a couple of seconds. I've been told "it's too big," especially when I laugh. But I don't care. I have a beautiful set of teeth that compensate for that.

Having given myself the "once-over," I practice one of my best camera-ready smiles. As my lips curve, the tip of Arabic nose dips down right into the middle of my smile. *I knew it,* I muse to myself, constricting my smile, *I knew my nose would get into it!* I study my nose; it sits there otherwise unobtrusively. But when I smile again, I can only watch as it dominates my face. Feeling uneasy, I take the tip of my nose between my fingers and press it back and then up. I peer askance at myself in the mirror, considering the adjustment, and reevaluate my smile, then my head to check my profile. *Of course it looks better . . . or maybe it doesn't,* I think ambivalently. It's as though I've seen my nose for the very first time. Yet I cannot remember ever not seeing it. I feel ridiculous because here I am manipulating it as if it were some newly discovered piece of my anatomy—and a not very attractive one at that. *Don't make too much of it,* I tell myself.

Momentarily, I try to think of some of the positive remarks that people have made about this nose of mine: "It is distinctive"; (*so is a rhino's horn*); "It's got character"; (*maybe it is a character*); "It suits your face"; (*perhaps it should be wearing a suit*); "It's . . . er, . . . typically Arabic"; (*sure, just like a camel's hump*); "At least it's not bigger than a breadbox!" (*but it couldn't fit inside a breadbox either*). Nothing seems reassuring, as I force it closer to my face.

"You surely would look gorgeous that way," says the director who has been watching me all this time. I burst into laughter.

"You really think so? *I'm not so sure.* I think I like my nose the way it is," I respond, trying to conceal my ambivalence.

"C'mon, Intisar, I don't think you like it *that* much. Look at your profile. It would make a lotta difference if your nose were a little shorter and lacked that

Arabic bump. You know, TV is a helluva sensitive medium. People out there focus on your face continuously. And the nose seems to be a focal point, you know what I mean? Now, a nose like yours could . . . , er . . . , kind of get in the way, you know what I mean? You could have them focus on your eyes instead by getting an ordinary nose. I got an idea: why don't you consider having a nose job for this opportunity?''

''I really don't know. I am not sure,'' I reply candidly as I turn to start the interview.

Two days later, the director called concerning the test.

''. . . You did wonderfully, Intisar. Presence, personality, voice, diction—all in all just fine. But like I said last time, your nose at some points, gets all the attention. You been thinking about my suggestion? I'm telling you, it would be a guaranteed opportunity.'' I manage to give a diplomatic but noncommittal response to his query; and we end up discussing everything *but* my nose.

I have to admit to myself that I have been thinking about what the director said, but not without lots of ambivalence. My nose has been functioning well for thirty-three years, except for the usual colds and sinuses. It has never affected my confidence, nor has it interfered with my activities. The truth is, however, that I do not like it. I have been always sarcastic about it, wishing I could change it. Yet the idea of nose surgery—cutting bones and removing cartilage, and I don't know what else, frightens me. I wish there were some kind of physical exercise that could fix it up—pressing, pushing, rubbing, molding, anything but *surgery*.

The job as a hostess on a cultural program for Arab-American TV is still available to me in January, just six months from now. I must make a decision: cosmetic surgery, a new opportunity, perhaps a new career or my life (including my nose) as it is.

A week passed after the telephone call, and I was still reflecting on the psychological aspect of cosmetic surgery and consulting with my closest friends. Although I have not been completely satisfied with the look of my nose, I have accepted it as part of my personal as well as my ethnic identity. Would my decision now, in favor of cosmetic surgery, offend my sense of identity and stigmatize me as an inferior person who's complying with other people's aesthetic criteria! One friend, who thinks that my nose is ''distinct,'' does not favor unnecessary cosmetic surgery. He argues that Asian girls who have operations on their eyes to make them look bigger and ''rounder'' are only deceiving themselves. And black women who straighten their hair are admitting a sense of inferiority.

I think, if that is the case, then we should question the validity of our use of makeup, our interest in fashions or hair styles, and anything we do that may change our very natural appearance. But in so doing, would we be denying every culture part of its aesthetic aspect, its standards of beauty? And would we also be denying human beings the right to share their aesthetic standards? Certainly, undergoing cosmetic surgery shouldn't require or be accompanied by any special apologies; it should be accepted as a means to improve an individual's appearance when she/he has the choice. Nevertheless, when it comes to cosmetic surgery, there is a great deal of risk, and one should take into consideration the possibilities of an unsuccessful surgery, the potential hazards associated with the surgical procedure. Accordingly, I started my search for reliable and factual information, even though I was still ambivalent about surgery.

Dr. Michael J. Watanabe, a plastic surgeon at Saddleback Medical Center, recommended that I start my inquiry by reading his group's medical publications, which answer the most frequently asked questions about nasal surgery. He also recommended that I plan on a consultation visit whereby an appraisal for my case would be specific and personal.

According to *Cosmetic Surgery,* one of the medical booklets, aesthetic rhinoplasty is performed to reduce the overall size of the nose: to reshape a tip, or remove a nasal hump or to improve a poor angle between the nose and the upper lip. One or all of these changes can be made during a single operation. This booklet had an encouraging and realistic tone. While not denying the overall risk of undergoing any surgery, it assures the reader that the surgical procedures have been repeated successfully thousands of times and are dependable when executed by experienced, competent cosmetic surgeons. It attributes the yearly increase in the number of individuals who undergo cosmetic surgery to the social and economic influences which place emphasis upon appearance. This includes ''younger people seeking peer acceptance and older people facing their own challenge in maintaining positive attitudes for an extended time.''[1] In my case, I am thirty-three years old and would be risking a perfectly well-functioning nose for the sake of a new career opportunity! Would it be worth it? Well, I didn't know. I hadn't learned enough about the surgical procedures yet. I might be more decisive if I did.

Surgery of the Nose, another medical booklet, exemplifies and illustrates the procedures of the different kinds of rhinoplasty. I examined the illustrations casually, with a mirror in my hand, comparing them to my nose, trying to appraise my own case. But as I started reading, I became more apprehensive:

> On the surgeon's recommendation, the patient may be operated on in the surgeon's office, in an outpatient facility, or may be admitted to a hospital. The surgery may be performed under a local or general anesthetic. . . .In most nasal surgery an incision is made inside the nostrils, through which the surgeon can cut, trim, and manipulate the cartilage and bone to reshape the nose and alter its external appearance. A hump is removed by using a sawing instrument or a chisel and then bringing the nasal bones together to form a narrower bridge.[2]

This is frightening! I tell myself, staring down at the words—cut . . . trim . . . sawing . . . instrument . . . chisel . . . bridge. . . . This sounds more like carpentry, with my nose being the project. I touch my entire nose—protectively. The ''hump'' that I found so offensive in the monitor three weeks ago is hardly there now. It's not big at all. I grab the mirror and peer into its magnifying side. Even that side agrees with me. *Well,* I ponder to myself, *why a hump removal? I don't need that. Maybe what I need is just reducing the size of the nasal tip and improving the angle between the nose and my upper lip!* I continue reading.

Removing cartilage reduces the size of a nasal tip and provides better contour. . . . To improve the angle between the nose and the upper lip, the nasal tip is elevated by trimming the septum through the incisions in the nostrils. . . . Following surgery, a splint composed of tape and a plastic or plaster overlay is applied to the nose to maintain bone and cartilage in the new shape. Nasal packs are inserted to protect the septum.[3]

This sounded less frightening to me. But I became anxious to find out about the postoperative recovery. The medical publications were too general. I felt I needed a firsthand narrative from someone who had actual experience. So I called Marcia Smith, one of Dr. Watanabe's patients, who agreed to share her experience.

Although she is not completely recovered yet, Marcia believes she has had a satisfactory result. Her surgery consisted of correction of a deviated septum, hump removal, reduction of tip, and angle improvement. All this was done in the surgeon's office, and under local anesthetic. Marcia, thirty-eight years old now, regrets the fact she did not benefit from cosmetic surgery fifteen years ago.

"I always thought about it," she told me, "but never knew it was so easy. I went into the office at 7:00 AM and at 12:30 PM I was home. I had the packing in my nose for one day. I stayed at home one week. The second week I went back to work."

"You sound like you just had fun, Marcia! What about the cast and the pain?" I inquired with astonishment.

"Oh, the cast was on for two weeks. But it is not as uncomfortable as you might think, and the medication takes care of all the pain. However, it is *very* important to adhere to the postoperative instructions. I was restricted from activities that raise the blood pressure like jogging, swimming, or even bending, for about four weeks."

"Didn't the swelling bother you? They say it persists for months?" I asked.

"Yes, this is the hard part of it. As a matter of fact, it has been three months now and my nose still feels numb and is a little swollen, but it is not noticeable after the first two weeks; besides, I had no bruising around the eyes," she answered me assuringly.[4]

Despite the fact that Marcia's story was—and still is—heartening, the particulars of her case are different from mine. She apparently never accepted her nose and was, in that sense, convinced that she should undergo surgery. As for me, even as ambivalent as I am, I don't think I rejected my nose. Whether it is viewed as socially acceptable or not, it remains *my* nose. It does what it's supposed to do. And the more I've thought about cosmetic surgery, the more I equate it with a violation of the unique characteristics of my nose. Noses such as mine may someday become fashionable—even ideal. I think I'll just accept my own standards which means accepting *all* of me.

That week, the director called to know what my final decision was. With a new found confidence resulting from my search, I said, "No nose job—opportunity or not." He groaned but was unsurprised: "I knew it. I knew you wouldn't go for that. But I thought I'd give it a shot. Anyway, come over next week and bring your nose with you for rehearsal.''

By:
Intisar Najd[5]
Education 102C: Methods of Teaching
English in the Secondary School
University of California, Irvine

Notes

1. *Cosmetic Surgery II* (Plastic Surgery Publications, Inc.: N.J., 1977),8.
2. *Surgery of the Nose, Rhinoplasty* (American Society of Plastic and Reconstructive Surgeons, Inc.: Chicago, Ill., 1984),6.
3. *Surgery of the Nose,* Rhinoplasty, 6.
4. Phone interview with Marcia Smith, patient of Dr. Watanabe, Mission Viejo, California, Wednesday, June 12, 1985.
5. This student paper was also printed in Ken Macrorie's book, *The I-Search Paper* (Portsmouth, NH: Boynton/Cook Publishers, Heinemann, 1988), 197–202.

PART THREE

Making Thinking/ Writing Your Own

1 What About the Affective Domain?

Knowledge. Comprehension. Application. Analysis. Synthesis. Evaluation.

Problem solving.

Thought.

Intellect.

In designing the Thinking/Writing lessons in this book, we found ourselves preoccupied with the cognitive domain. We examined cognitive psychology, learning theory, composition research, the writing process, and taxonomies for thinking in order to build what Arthur Applebee called "instructional scaffolds" which enable students to think at higher levels.[1]

A basic question seemed unanswered. What happened to affective concerns—feelings, interests, attitudes, and values? It appeared as if much of basic humanness had been ignored. In attempting to stretch student thinking, were students being approached as if they were data-crunching computers? As Alice Brand has pointed out, "Understanding the collaboration of emotion and cognition in writing is both fundamental and far-reaching. It is in cognition that ideas make sense. But it is in emotion that this sense finds value."[2] We were reminded of the collaboration of emotion and cognition in writing when reviewing Sondra Perl's concept of "felt sense"—the need for a writer to feel an emotional and physical attachment to a piece of writing during the composing process.[3] We wondered how we could systematically incorporate affective concerns into the stage process that underlies each Thinking/Writing lesson scaffold. How could students' feelings, interests, attitudes, and values be as fully developed as their thoughts and minds?

Because humans work as a unit of brain/mind, heart/feelings, it is impossible to separate the cognitive from the affective. Martin Scheerer wrote, "Behavior may be conceptualized as being embedded in a cognitive-emotional-motivational matrix in which no true separation is possible. No matter how we slice behavior, the ingredients of motivation-emotion-cognition are present in one order or another."[4] With an eye toward a more integrated approach to the cognitive and affective domains, we resolved to revise and enrich our lessons with activities that would motivate learners to invest themselves in thinking and writing in a more personal way. To our surprise, most of what we consciously intended to add was already inherent within the existing Thinking/Writing model.

For example, one tenet of the Thinking/Writing model is that thinking and writing are developmental. They are dynamic rather than static processes that evolve with the experience base of the learner. One of the best ways to structure a scaffold that provides thinking experiences for students is to use their own feelings, interests, attitudes, and values as a springboard—in other words, to use the affective as a bridge to the cognitive. In many of the lessons, this often takes the form of personal experience writing. The "Watermarks" lesson invites students to step back into their memories to write a narrative about an important event (a symbolic watermark) that made a lasting impression on their lives. Similarly, "A Rose Colored Life by Any Other Name" asks students to recall a significant event in their life which turned out differently than they expected and to compare the actual event with the way they had played it out in their imagination. In "Justifying a Decision," students move toward an understanding of a character in Arthur Miller's play *The Crucible* through a series of freewrites at the end of each act which enable them to explore their own actions, reactions, and decisions and to connect their personal experiences to the drama. "The Birth Order Essay" takes yet another approach as students are asked to apply birth order theory (the theory that the order in which you are born into your family has a significant and predictable influence on your personality traits) to their own lives.

Jerome Bruner suggested that student interest is heightened when students are able to manipulate concrete data during a discovery approach to learning. This idea that thinking is progressive and that we more readily make cognitive leaps when we move from concrete to abstract is also embodied in many Thinking/Writing lessons. For example, "On the Nose," invites students to explore their sense of smell to reawaken memories of a significant place in their lives. "How Does Your Cookie Crumble?" encourages students to use their five senses in analyzing cookies, establishing criteria for judging them, and writing an evaluation which defends that judgment. Again, in "Laws of Probability," students conduct a series of experiments such as throwing dice, tossing coins, and spinning a top to formulate a theory about the laws of probability.

Building in an audience and purpose for writing often results in building high interest for students. "Persuasive Letters" lesson introduces youngsters to the sophisticated concept of argumentation as they choose an audience they would like to persuade to do something, address that audience in a suitable tone, anticipate the objections of that audience, and overcome those objections with logical reasons. As the children carefully craft letters such as Molly's persuasive address to Mom to let her take three friends with her to Farrell's Ice Cream Parlor for her birthday, writing becomes an authentic means of communication. Research also takes on a more personal dimension in the Personalizing the Research Paper lesson as students are asked to consider one thing they have a genuine need to know about—whether it is why they procrastinate, what the effects of violent television on young children are, how to invest in the silver market, and so forth. They then explore what they know, assume, or imagine about that topic. This includes conducting first and second hand research on the subject, comparing what they discover with their original assumptions, and valuing what they have learned. This kind of open-choice paper has a far greater affective and cognitive pay-off for students than the numerical score or letter grade they might receive on the final product. It represents a personal investment in an important issue in their lives.

Implicit in the Thinking/Writing model is the concept that all of the steps in the process must take place within a supportive, positive environment. In building a conducive environment for fostering growth in writing, it is necessary for the teacher to treat the class as "a community of writers," to use Donald Graves' term.[5] The teacher's success in building this positive feeling tone or "community of writers" in the class is a crucial factor in creating a climate for learning to write well. Teacher attitude is central to this community feeling. We view the student as a writer, with certain expertise and something important to say. We arrange for our students to write to different audiences. Many of our students work together in peer response groups or in other small group activities which reflect mutual trust, commitment, honesty, cooperation, and support. This sharing stage is instrumental in generating a spirit of cooperation within the classroom rather than a spirit of competition. The affective commitment of writing and sharing with or for an audience can also enable a writer to gain the insight he or she needs to take a step back in the revising process and maintain the cognitive detachment to translate his or her writing from writer-based to reader-based prose.[6]

Even within the most supportive of atmospheres, there will always be some degree of anxiety over performance and evaluation. Familiarizing students with the evaluation criteria (rubric) when the writing assignment or prompt is given not only helps ease student anxiety, but clarifies the nature of the thinking and writing task. Practice in thinking/writing skills—initially through concrete and experiential activities and then through more abstract activities—also builds student confidence and reduces anxiety over performance and evaluation. Furthermore, structured revision activities offer students the chance to learn from and redirect early efforts during the lesson, before the finished written piece is evaluated. Finally, placing more emphasis on the process of thinking and writing and on progress over time rather than on each individual product helps students view their development as writers as ongoing and their efforts as cumulative.

In short, successful teaching of writing combines the cognitive and affective domains. David Krathwohl, Benjamin Bloom, and Bertram Masia compared the use of both domains to a person trying to climb a wall using a pair of parallel ladders, each with rungs too wide to scale in a few easy steps. They wrote, "One ladder represents cognitive objectives and behaviors, the other the affective. The ladders are built so that the rungs of one ladder fall between the rungs of the other. The attainment of some complex goal is made possible by alternately climbing a rung on one ladder, which brings the next rung of the other ladder within reach. Thus by alternating between affective and cognitive domains, one may seek a cognitive goal using the attainment of a cognitive goal to raise interest (an affective goal). This permits achievement of a higher cognitive goal, and so on."[7]

Thinking/Writing, with its emphasis on student experience, feelings, interest, choice, attitude, and peer groups in a positive environment capitalizes on this affective/cognitive model. Perhaps the best evidence of the model's success comes from students—such as the three cited below—who have studied in classes where Thinking/Writing lessons are used consistently.

> Overall, I grew up in this class. I wrote with my heart and in this class. I developed pride in what I wrote.
>
> —Stella Madrigal

> I have liked my English class this year. It was fun and I learned a lot . . . All the time I was learning, I was having fun. Maybe that's why I learned so much.
> —Nichole Phillips

> I believe I learned most whenever we did things like groups and presentations because they were exciting. A person can't help but to be alert and learn when excited.
> —Peter Phan

Thinking/Writing fosters success in writing—which, in itself, can be one of the most affective of experiences.

Notes

1 Arthur Applebee and Judith A. Langer, "Instructional Scaffolding," *Language Arts* 60 (February 1983): 168–175.

2 Alice G. Brand, "The Why of Cognition: Emotion and the Writing Process." *College Composition and Communication* 38 (December 1987): 443.

3 Sondra Perl, "Understanding Composing," *College Composition and Communication* 31 (December 1980): 363–369.

4 Martin Sheerer, "Cognitive Theory," *Handbook of Social Psychology: Vol. 1* (Cambridge, MA: Addison-Wesley, 1954): 123.

5 At numerous conferences and workshops, Donald Graves has stressed the importance of building "a community of writers." This concept is described in his book *Writing: Teachers and Children at Work* (Portsmouth, N.H.: Heinemann Educational Books, 1983.)

6 Sheridan Blau, "Competence for Performance in Revision," in *Practical Ideas for Teaching Writing as a Process,* ed. Carol Booth Olson (Sacramento: California State Department of Education, 1987): 156–157.

7 Benjamin Bloom, et al., *Taxonomy of Educational Objectives: The Classification of Educational Goals. Handbook II: Affective Domain* (New York: David McKay, 1956): 60.

2 Thinking and Writing About Thinking/ Writing

This Explorer Journal assignment was interesting and hard because there weren't exact instructions like with math problems. You have to decide on almost everything. Also, it was hard to skim through books and decide which part to use. It was interesting because it is fun not only to burn paper, but to put yourself in the situation of your explorer. It would have been easier if I had had more books though. Sometimes I got confused because my explorer went on a lot of journeys and I never knew which was which. I thought it wasn't fair that on number six I got a 13 when I had pictures, neat writing, and burned paper.

Nina—Fourth grade

Joel wanted to see more "showing, not telling details" in my story. Sometimes, though, it is much better to tell. Often, in casual writing, we tell. When a book or story is told in first person like mine is, its point is to think like that person. Usually one doesn't talk or think in a show not tell method. So, here it is better to tell as the first person sees things.

Karli—Eighth grade

The dialectical journal provided me with a relatively easy method by which I could get my initial thought formalized. Generally, this is a difficult step that requires much trial-and-error. But I now find that I can allow my thoughts to lead wherever they might—and still be able to find a "theme" within.

Arthur—12th grade

How do I transform my thoughts into writing? Hmm. . . I grasp on to one thing, a symbol, a moment, a color, a feeling. I feel and think with the camera eye. Then I mull and stew, compare it, contrast it, synthesize, humanize my symbol, hopefully twist it into a new shape or feeling, different from the trite. From there, I knock it out without thinking; then I go over and over and over it, rewrite. Mostly, if it is good, the guts are out on the page. My first write is 80% good or basic stuff; then a lot of throwing out goes on. Finally, I edit, but it is a two week process. I live inside of it. Sometimes, I go into great pain—and I know it because it is part of the process. But when I really write something good, the child in me feels a certain awe and wonder (I'm still a knobby-kneed little kid about it), and I am pleased. I feel as if I have shared or done something, so I trudge on willingly.

Cris—University

What is Metacognition?

What exactly is it that students are doing in these learning log entries? Among other things, they are asking themselves questions and making statements about their own thinking and writing processes, assessing the effectiveness of these processes, and consciously reflecting on the extent of their understanding. In short, they are performing acts of metacognition. Metacognition, in its simplest sense, can be defined as thinking about thinking. It is a conscious monitoring of one's own thinking process. It could be the ability to realize that you do not understand something another person just said. It could be paraphrasing aloud what someone has just told you to determine whether he will agree that that is, in fact, exactly what was meant. It could be the realization someone does not know enough about a particular subject to write effectively about it and needs to gather more information before beginning to write. It could be the discovery of the thinking and writing processes one goes through when composing a written text.

This kind of reflective, recursive thinking occurs naturally during the act of composing. In order to maintain or reassert their forward momentum while composing, all writers pause to review and reassess in some manner what they have already created. With more experienced writers this is often an ongoing, unconscious process or reappraisal and recurring analysis of such global composing considerations as content, purpose, audience, central focus, style, rhythm, etc. In some fashion or other, more experienced writers pose questions for themselves such as, "What do I want to say here?" "Why am I stuck and how can I get unstuck?" "What did I really mean to say in this section?" or "Who am I writing this for?" However effective their strategies may be, the exact means by which experienced writers regain their focus and reassert their progress in a developing work are frequently silent, solitary acts of which the writers themselves are not fully aware.

Less experienced writers also pause during the writing process, but they pause at different and sometimes premature points in the development of a piece, for different durations, and for different reasons than more experienced writers. Instead of asking themselves directional questions about content, purpose, or focus, they often get bogged down with issues of correctness related to grammar, mechanics, and usage which can interfere with the act of composing.[1]

For both more and less experienced writers, purposeful conscious monitoring of their own thinking and writing processes allows them to recognize the nature and effectiveness of their own problem-solving strategies. Conscious reflection enables students to discover how they are solving a problem as well as to explore how they feel about the product and the process of their problem solving. The insights students gain into their own problem solving processes as a result of engaging in metacognitive activities can become stepping-stones toward solving kindred problems posed by other writing tasks. The student who has become blocked in his thinking or writing and who consciously reflects on how he overcame his block, for example, may well be able to use that same insight, that same strategy in handling the problem when it arises again. Likewise, if a composition has gone particularly well, the student can benefit from reconsidering what worked in the piece and why.

Thinking and Writing About Thinking and Writing

Practicing this kind of purposeful reflection and self-monitoring enables students to incorporate effective metacognitive strategies as an ongoing part of their own thinking processes and problem-solving repertoire. Notice how Frank Ashby, a student in a Teacher Education course, is thinking and writing about thinking and writing in the following reflective paper. Through retracing his steps in composing this paper, he not only becomes better acquainted with his only thinking and writing processes, but he articulates a problem-solving strategy that he can use when writing future comparison/contrast essays:

My Experience In Writing My First Comparison/Contrast Essay

I subscribe to the Thomas Edison formula: ''Invention is 5% inspiration and 95% perspiration.'' Writing is 5% inspiration and 95% perspiration. Or to tell it another way, I ran across this piece written anonymously:

> Nothing in the world can take the place of persistence. Talent will not; nothing is more common than unsuccessful men with talent. Genius will not; unrewarded genius is almost a proverb. Education alone will not; the world is full of educated derelicts. Persistence and determination alone are omnipotent.

In writing the comparison/contrast assignment, I felt like I was an inexperienced Captain at sea in a ship without a rudder. Oh, I had my navigational charts and aids in the form of what we were told in class and the examples we were given to read. I knew that I was going to make mistakes and spend a lot of time writing and rewriting. So I took the attitude if this is what it takes to keep the ship safely afloat and arrive at the port of my destination—so be it.

The first thing that I did was read and interpret. After reading "Mariana" by Tennyson, I went back through it and retold the poem as a story deciphering the symbols and images as I went along. I did the same thing with the passage on "Miss Havisham" by Dickens. Now I felt that I was ready to write my introductory paragraph. I got out the prompt, studied it, and wrote what I was going to do. I looked in my book of quotations until I found one that could apply to both selections. The idea of Shakespeare's quote was how one sorrow could lead to another. In my introductory paragraph, I used the image of a snake. I resolved that I would refer to both the quote and image whenever it could help explain similarities and differences between the two women—as long as it wasn't too often or contrived. I wrote my paragraph. I rewrote my paragraph four times. After each rewrite, I would study what I had written. I discovered that the paragraph would sound better or could be improved by leaving something out or by adding something.

Before beginning the body of essay, I wrote about both women. I wrote about Mariana: all of the things that I found interesting enough to tell the story, and created a few images. I did the same thing for Miss Havisham. Soon, I realized that I had more information and ideas than I could develop in one essay. At this point, I felt that I had made a false start and had wasted my time. It was far from any form that I wanted. I began reading over what I had written about Mariana. I decided to cut out everything that didn't move the story from beginning to end. I ended up with four points: unrequited love, isolation, sorrow, and her impending death. And since they also fit Miss Havisham's story, I decided to compare and contrast those four points with both women. The four pages that I had already written were not wasted at all. I used parts of them as they fit. From this time on, I felt comfortable writing my essay. I had a watertight ship and my port was in sight. I had the focus I needed to do what I wanted to do. My only worry now was I hoped that I was delivering the right cargo.

After achieving the focus, I needed to write the body. It was still work. I went through four or five rewrites, each time shaping it. I would find a better way to say something; after reading the prompt again I would find something else to say; and sadly, some of my best phrases had to be left out because they didn't apply.

The summary was the easiest part to write. By then I knew the material well enough to write several explanatory paragraphs or sum up each story in a sentence. So I did both.

The paper about how one student wrote a paper is just one of a variety of techniques and strategies that can be used to enhance students' sense of themselves as thinkers and writers. Here are some additional ideas:

Metacognitive Strategies

- Foster students' understanding of their own process by having them think aloud into a tape recorder during the composing process.

- Have students share their process—what they had to think about in order to get started with a piece of writing—as well as to share their products.
- Use students' various approaches to thinking before and during writing (visualization of images, recollection of a personal experience, memory of a literary work they have read, creation of a narrative context for their writing, etc.) to demonstrate the many options students have available to them in the problem-solving process of writing.
- Have students explain how they got "unstuck" when they were "stuck" during the writing process.
- Have students make annotations in the margins of a piece of writing explaining the purpose for including particular paragraphs, details, quotes, uses of figurative language, etc.
- Have students write learning log entries about what they are thinking and writing about in your class. Entries can be completely open-ended or students can be asked to respond to a set of prompted questions. For example, here is a set of questions following the second writing assignment in a university-level composition class:
  - Did you find this assignment easier or more difficult than your first paper—the sensory/descriptive literary imitation? Explain why.
  - Please describe what you had to think about in order to write this paper.
  - What do you feel you did most successfully in this paper?
  - How do you feel about your performance in these first two papers overall?
  - What would you like to work on in the future papers?

The metacognitive strategies listed above are all aimed at helping to facilitate the students' own thinking and writing processes. As students engage in these metacognitive activities, our hope is that they will begin asking themselves reflective questions without any external prompting. Listed below are reflective questions that students can ask themselves at each stage of the composing process. Ultimately, these kinds of questions will become a natural part of the composing process as our students make the transition from inexperienced to experienced writers.

Some Metacognitive Questions for Stages of the Writing Process

Prewriting

- What do I want to write about?
- Have I brainstormed?
- What do I know about this topic?
- What do I assume about this topic?
- If I need more information, where can I find it?
- What do I want to say about this topic?
- Is there anything that I can draw from my last paper which will be helpful in this paper?
- Are there other ways of looking at this?

Prompt

- Is the prompt clear?
- What do I find confusing or unclear about this prompt?
- How can I go about getting clarification on this prompt?
- What are the key thinking and writing tasks that I need to engage in?
- Does the prompt break down into separate parts?
- How do I feel about the writing task?

Precomposing

- Who is my audience for this piece?
- Is there a ''supposed'' audience for this piece that is different from the ''real'' audience?
- What is my purpose in writing this piece?
- What is the main idea or central focus of this piece?
- Do my prewriting ideas seem to fit into any groups that will help me plan my composition?
- How will I organize what I have to say?
- Is this approach best suited to the kind of writing I'm doing?

Writing

- How would I respond to this as a reader?
- Do I like what I've written so far? Why or why not?
- Overall, am I responding to the requirements in the prompt?
- Do I want to continue working on this piece?
- Where do I go from here?
- While writing, have I made any discoveries that I didn't expect?
- Do these discoveries change my ideas about what my paper is about? If so, how?
- Have I justified what I have to say?
- Is the structure I decided on for my paper working out?
- If not, what other approach might be more successful?

Sharing

- What did I learn from responding to a peer's paper?
- What have I learned from listening to others talk about how they went about writing their drafts?
- What have I learned from the responses that have been made to my paper?
- Does my paper fulfill the requirements of the assignment?
- How do I feel about the responses that have been made to my paper?

Revision

- Does my paper say what I wanted it to say?
- How can I use what I learned during sharing to make my paper better?

- Where does my paper need work?
- In what specific ways will I change my piece to make it better? (Add, delete, substitute, rearrange)

Editing

- Which of the editing requirements for this paper do I feel the most unsure about?
- How can I get help with these editing concerns?
- Are there words that might be misspelled that I haven't looked up?
- Are there any words that I usually misspell that I should double-check?
- Are there places where capitalization and punctuation aren't clear or correct?
- Should I read my paper aloud to try to catch any punctuation or sentence errors?

Evaluation

- Which responses to my paper do I most strongly agree with?
- Which responses to my paper do I most strongly disagree with?
- How can I apply these comments to my next paper?
- What did I learn about my own composing process (which steps/which phase) from this assignment?
- What did I learn about the quality and quantity of my content in this paper? My use of form? My degree of correctness?
- To what other topics does this assignment lead me?

Modeling the Thinking/Writing Process

While collaborative talk in large groups or in smaller peer groups or individual self-questioning can be a rich source of metacognitive insights, one additional and often untapped resource in the classroom is the teacher. It has long been a tenet of the National Writing Project that teachers of writing must themselves write. As James Gray, founder and Director of the National Writing Project points out, "Teachers need to experience regularly what they are asking of students, and they need to discover and understand, through their own writing, the process [of writing] they are teaching."[2]

For those teachers who are already in the habit of modeling commitment to the writing process by writing along with their students, we suggest going one step further. Although it may sound risky, one of the best ways to demonstrate to inexperienced writers how a writer *thinks* through the writing process is for the teacher to compose out loud at the blackboard or on an overhead projector. Rarely, if ever, have students had the opportunity to listen to how a writer makes decisions and solves problems as he or she progresses through a writing task. Students often gain great insights into the composing process when they can hear their teacher struggling through the same assignment they themselves are writing.

After guiding students through prewriting and precomposing activities, when they are ready to compose their rough draft, begin your own piece on the board or on an overhead projector. As ideas, questions or phrases occur to you, articulate that inner speech aloud while simultaneously jotting down notes or phrases. Instruct students who have a clear direction for their own writing assignment to ignore you and continue with their own work. But those who are stumped as to how to begin or get stuck after the first few sentences can attend to your thinking/ writing process. Although it may feel humbling to you, it is quite illuminating for the students to see that the teacher can also get *stuck* in his or her writing. In fact, this may be the best pedagogical tool of all. For it is here that the students are able to see the difficulty of writing, even for the experienced teacher, and be exposed to the problem-solving process as you consider different ways to overcome the obstacle you have encountered.

The cardinal rule in the thinking/writing aloud demonstration is that students can listen in but cannot interrupt the teacher's process with questions or comments. As they sit back in their chairs, you can almost hear the students saying to themselves, *Let's see how he gets himself out of this one.* And, after observing you in this process, the students will come to see you not just as the teacher, but as a fellow writer—as someone who shares the same frustrations and triumphs as they do.

Sometimes, it is helpful to invite different students to take your place in the "writer's chair" and to think and write before their classmates. Exposure to a number of different writers will expand the students' repertoire of options.

We have found the metacognitive technique of modeling the thinking/writing process for students to be extremely valuable. It not only helps students to see how you compose, but helps them tune in to their own problem solving process and explore and refine their own thinking as they write.

A Cautionary Note

Much of what we do in the classroom helps students learn *what* to write. The use of metacognitive activities can allow students not only to see *how* to write but to discover *how they think* when they write. These activities should be used sparingly, however. Unrelenting imposition of metacognitive activities may actually backfire—making students over-conscious and inhibiting rather than facilitating their process. But when metacognitive activities are used judiciously, they enable students to review and appraise their thinking, writing, and problem solving, to consciously practice their effective strategies, to share them and to learn from the process of others, and to refine and incorporate them as elements of their processes as thinkers and writers.

Notes

1 Linda S. Flower and John R. Hayes, "The Pregnant Pause: An Inquiry into the Nature of Planning." *Research in the Teaching of English* 15 (October 1981): 229–343.
2 James Gray, "The California Writing Project." In *Practical Ideas for Teaching Writing as a Process.* Carol Booth Olson, ed. Sacramento: California State Department of Education, 1987: 1–3.

3 Operation Robot or How We Made Thinking/Writing Our Own

Picture students and teachers of any age busily working together, gluing scraps of foil, cardboard, or trash of the cleanest kind . . . and picture them talking to each other, maybe even to the *CARDBOARD*. They are experiencing the magic of tapping their own creativity. Through this process, the children are discovering that their ideas are so extraordinary that they can hardly wait to write about them! This is the picture of the robot lesson.

In the summer of 1986, we embarked on an adventure to make Thinking/Writing our own. We were team teaching a group of fourth through sixth graders, and our dream was to create a community of writers in our classroom. We chose to collaborate on a demonstration lesson on designing a Thinking/Writing Robot Friend and to use that initial lesson as a starting point on which to build a comprehensive writing unit. What follows is a brief description of our discovery process as we designed the lesson and the unit. By sharing our experience, we hope to provide you with ideas for and support you in making Thinking/Writing lessons your own.

In our initial design of the robot lesson, we envisioned a unit of activities that would involve each child in the application and synthesis level of Bloom's taxonomy and enable them to experience writing in each of the domains. We decided to link our lesson to the fun of creating a robot, the central focus and springboard for our writing unit. We wanted students to have an opportunity to develop not one, but four writing products, one in each of the four domains: sensory/descriptive; imaginative/narrative; practical/informative; and analytical/expository. Our goal was to motivate students not only to gain practice in thinking and writing skills, but to share the wonders of their imagination within a cooperative group setting. We collaborated to develop the lesson for our own classroom use, and although we did not see a need to write it according to the format of the Thinking/ Writing demonstration lessons presented in this book, we drew upon Thinking/ Writing concepts throughout the unit. We also did not formalize the prompts for each writing, other than the imaginative/narrative writing. In other words, we made Thinking/Writing our own by adapting and modifying it to suit our own audience and purpose. We encourage you to do the same.

We felt that it was important in the prewriting stage of our lesson to build a knowledge base before constructing robots. We decided to invite students to bring in magazine pictures, advertisements, or toy robots from home. We discussed robots as seen on television and in the movies and brainstormed possible things that a robot could do if it had certain specialty parts. Students verbally brainstormed possibilities for their robot's specialty parts and related functions. We charted their ideas on the board in the following format:

Brainstorming Format

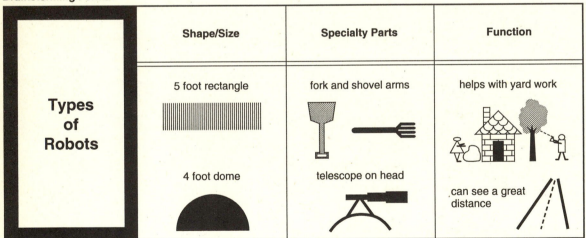

A few days before robots went into construction, students began collecting junk or odds and ends. We suggested they collect scraps of foil, milk cartons, cardboard, stray buttons, paper clips, orphaned mittens or gloves . . . anything that could become a part or an appendage of a robot. As can be expected, students are great scavengers, finding many novel uses for what may seem to be quite ordinary junk.

On the day of robot construction, students brought their junk to school. We found that they benefitted from building their robots together, rather than individually at home. The reciprocal sharing of ideas became a support system that encouraged students to experiment and discover unusual patterns of their creation. They worked in groups of four or five, gluing, discussing, sharing ideas, and assisting each other as needed. We allowed forty-five minutes to an hour for building, and any unfinished robots were completed at home and returned to school the following day. We considered all of these preliminary activities to be a part of the prewriting stage of the lesson.

Throughout the building stage, we were pleased to hear precise and descriptive language flowing spontaneously throughout our students' discussions. We felt that it was of utmost importance to get that wealth of language down on paper. We wanted to move quite naturally from the concrete to the abstract realm of language

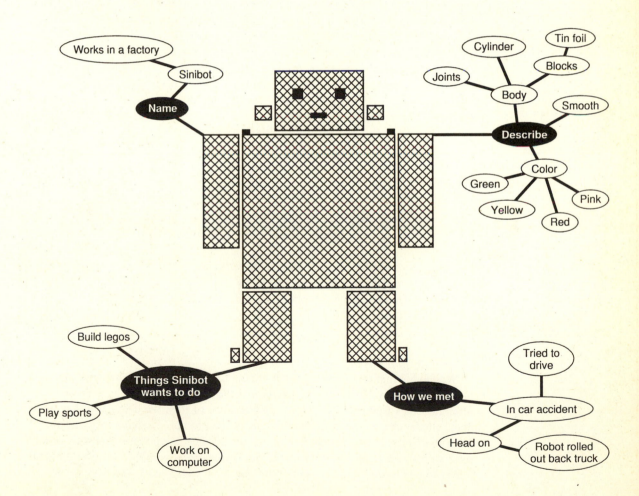

processing. That led us to the next step in our lesson—the shaping of that language in the precomposing stage of writing which took the form of a robot map. (See page 413.)

We wanted the students' robot maps to be vivid, detailed representations of their robots, so we provided them with colored pencils, markers, crayons, and felt pens. Focusing on the five senses, students drew their robot and brainstormed and recorded their descriptive words on and around their drawing. We stressed the importance of taking time on their drawings, looking closely and thinking carefully about their unique creations. We wanted the students to imagine their robot as real, and to observe and make note of every detail. They shared their maps with a partner, including fresh information that came to mind, so that they could tell each other *everything* they could think of about their robot.

Up to this point in the lesson, students had been *PREWRITING* and *PRECOMPOSING*, generating descriptive language based on the robot that they had created and observed. Students had been involved in a Thinking/Writing sequence that moved them from their concrete robot to the abstract area of sensory/descriptive language. This *SENSORY/DESCRIPTIVE* writing became an embedded part of the *IMAGINATIVE/NARRATIVE* writing assignment. We chose not to separate the sensory/descriptive piece from the larger piece of writing. We felt that for our purpose it made more sense to have students extend their ideas further into an imaginary realm by developing a story revolving around their robot and based on the following prompt:

Prompt:

Everyone has become quite curious about your robot friend. We would like you to tell us all about your robot. We are especially hoping that you will:

- Describe your robot and tell us your robot's name
- Tell us how you met and became friends
- Tell us what you and your robot like to do together

We have found that students often begin breezing through their writing only to discover that they have left out details that they especially want to include. This often becomes frustrating for them, and because of this, we decided to have students cluster around the three main points of the prompt. Students included words from their map in their cluster. The cluster became a guidepost that they could refer to throughout the writing stage. Sometimes they would think of additional things to add to their cluster. The following is an example of a student cluster:

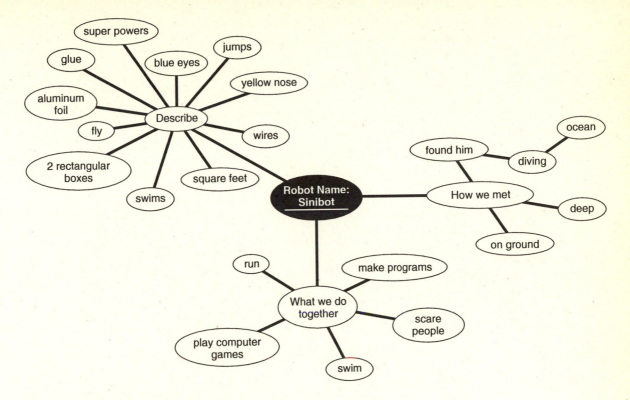

We encouraged the students to "think fun" when writing their stories, and to feel free to play with lots of ideas. We reminded them that this was only an initial writing, and that they would have an opportunity to make any changes desired.

You can see that as this particular lesson unfolds, the distinction between prewriting and writing becomes fluid, one stage of the process strengthening the other. Throughout the working of their papers, students moved back and forth between prewriting and writing in order to move their story forward.

The following day, students shared their writing with a partner. In our lesson, the *SHARING* stage was actually time with a response partner. We decided to use the response partner technique because we were trying to create a situation that invited students to support one another. We wanted the comfort level high enough so that students would not be afraid to seek advice from their peers. We had partners write down the things they liked best on a piece of paper. The partners also identified vivid word choices, so that those words could receive a "Golden Robot"—a rubber stamp robot.

Students then *REVISED* their writings, including the suggestions they received from their partner, provided they chose to integrate them into their paper.

Spending the time to explore each stage of the writing process in-depth gave us incredible pay-offs. Students sincerely cared about their writing and took time to make their writing special. Not only were students proud of their own writing, but they were also excited to hear the writing of other students in the room. A sample paper written by one of our students, George Kao, is included below:

My Robot

My robot is called Sinibot. He was made out of tape, aluminum foil, some wire, glue, two rectangular boxes, three paper towel rolls (the round cardboards), one long cylinder and two short cylinders, two cassette boxes, and four pieces of paper.

Its whole body is silver except the hands, eyes, nose, and mouth. The eyes are blue and white, the nose is yellow and the mouth is red. They are all taped down with tape. The hand is gray.

The shape of its head and body are all rectangular. The feet are kind of squared and rectangular. They're taped down with the legs. The shape of the hands are the shapes of mittens. The shape of its arm and legs are like a cylinder.

Sinibot has powers. It is super-strong, super-fast, and super-careful. It can walk or run very fast. It can jump (maximum height is 80 feet, if it jumps higher than it might lose pressure and break). It can swim (maximum depth is 80 feet or it might get too much pressure and leak, break). Also, it can fly (but if it flew one hour, it has to fly to the ground and rest for half an hour, and if it flew for two minutes, it would have to rest for one minute).

I found Sinibot when I was diving in the Pacific Ocean, and I was in a part that was not so deep. It's about $80\frac{1}{2}$ feet down there. It was very bright ground, but when I found Sinibot on the bright ground, it looked dead. I guess it was too deep for it.

Sinibot and I like to play on the computer a lot, and it can make a lot of cool programs because Sinibot is computerized. We also like to swim together. The funny part is when somebody sees Sinibot, they get up and run!

Since students were so intrigued with each other's robots, it seemed natural to follow the writing with a read-around. This gave everyone a chance to read each other's stories and have fun matching the stories to the robots around the room.

This is as far as we took this sensory/descriptive and imaginative/narrative lesson. We did not do a formal evaluation because we wanted to keep our lesson as nonjudgmental as possible. We felt this decision was imperative if our dream really was to build a community of writers.

Before we could move ahead to the *PRACTICAL/INFORMATIVE* domain, we needed to ask ourselves certain questions. What kinds of things would robots or kids with robots need to know how to do? How were we going to ensure that the students would be able to sustain their emotional attachment to their robots?

We had observed that the students were very fond of their robots as well as of the robot community within the room. We decided to create a scenario where students were going to be away from home on a weekend trip. We were banking on the fact that students would feel responsible for their robot's well-being. We discussed what happens when we leave pets behind, and they immediately responded that the animal had to be fed, walked, put in, put out, etc.

Keeping those ideas in mind, we took the next step and had students think about their own robots and their robot's special needs. We had students develop a practical/informative booklet, complete with illustrations, on the care and feeding of their robot. We did not spend a great deal of time prewriting and leading students into the writing. At this point, students were well-acquainted with their robots, since they had already created a kind of personal history for their robot when they wrote their first selection.

The second writing assignment seemed to flow naturally from the first assignment. We found that it kept the interest level high when we varied the format by having students make small booklets and draw to illustrate their points. We found that students enjoyed dealing with the hypothetical situation, and their writing became quite humorous.

In the final writing assignment, an *ANALYTICAL/EXPOSITORY* writing, each student explained why his robot was the best robot in the world. We felt that this topic stated a position that each student could readily and wholeheartedly defend. This writing topic also moved students into the evaluation level of the taxonomy. We followed the same writing process format—prewriting, precomposing, writing, sharing, responding, revising, editing, and evaluating throughout three of the four writing assignments. Evaluation of each separate assignment was done as a part of peer sharing.

At the end of the robot experience, students had participated in both affective and cognitive experiences and had completed writing tasks in the four domains while encountering the joy of cooperatively creating and discovering. They grew to respect themselves and each other as writers. We found that students were not struggling for something to say, that they were emotionally drawn to their writing, and that they felt a strong sense of commitment to their work. They left the writing experience feeling a sense of accomplishment and personal integrity and, hopefully, they were looking forward to writing again.

Our sense of accomplishment was tied to the pride we saw developing in our students. We saw the Thinking/Writing concepts developing naturally in sequence, one leading to another, even though the lesson was never formally written in Thinking/Writing style. The writing process made it possible for the students' writing, as well as our unit, to develop organically as ideas became seeded at each thinking level and stage of the process.

We were surprised to see that we could alternate the order of the writing process stages. Sometimes it was difficult to determine which was prewriting and which was precomposing. The exciting thing was that it really didn't matter. What did matter was that the writing process was supporting the students as they wrote, and it was leading to the outcome that we had in mind.

We have found that making Thinking/Writing our own was like designing our own robot. We had to give it our own shape and design useful appendages. It had to be comfortable to be with and easy to maneuver wherever we needed to go. It didn't require excessive maintenance, and there were plenty of accessible emergency parts. Piece by piece, it became our own creation. Please accept our invitation to make Thinking/Writing *YOUR* own!

4 The Lesson on How to Design a Lesson

Unless you decide to generate a Thinking/Writing lesson for staff development purposes or your school elects to develop a language arts curriculum based upon the Thinking/Writing model and involves you in the project, you may never have an occasion to write down a detailed description of the ladder of activities you construct to enhance the thinking and writing abilities of your students. But, if you are inclined to translate what you do into the stages of the Thinking/Writing process, you may find this annotated lesson design format useful. It is intended not as a set of absolute instructions, but as flexible guidelines to use as a point of departure when you make Thinking/Writing your own.

Writing Domain: _____

Decide if the writing falls primarily in the sensory/descriptive, imaginative/narrative, practical/informative or analytical/expository domains.

Thinking Level: _____

Determine the thinking level by analyzing what the key cognitive task of the writing prompt is.

Grade Level: _____

Although many lessons can be adapted for a range of grade levels, you may wish to gear the lesson for primary, elementary, intermediate, high school, or college.

Title

Select a title that indicates the focus and intent of the lesson

Lesson

_____

_____

Write an abstract that accurately describes the lesson and which will be easily understood by the reader.

Objectives

Thinking Skills

_____

_____

Writing Skills

_____

_____

- Clearly state the thinking skills and writing skills which the lesson focuses on.
- Make sure the objectives state the *WHAT, WHY* and *HOW* of the lesson.
- Use cue words from the taxonomy of thinking levels that accurately reflect the cognitive tasks to be fostered in the lesson and make sure that they are appropriate for the thinking level designated.
- Compare thinking and writing skills listed under the lesson objectives with the requirements of the prompt and with the criteria for evaluation to ensure that they are consistent.

The Process

- Write clear directions for each stage of the process throughout the lesson.
- Keep the audience for whom the lesson was intended (the classroom teacher) in mind throughout the process.
- Keep point of view (2nd person imperative) and tense (present) consistent.

- Provide adequate background information to orient the teacher to when this lesson might be introduced during a course of study, what prior thinking/writing experiences the students should have had, what the time frame for the lesson is, and what special resources, if any, are necessary.
- Define any unfamiliar terms.
- Describe the process in the lesson in such a way that it can be applied to other lessons.
- Consider whether the overall process of the lesson moves from concrete to abstract, oral to written, experiential to hypothetical, and from a writer base to a reader base.

Prewriting

_____

_____

_____

_____

- Design prewriting activities that generate ideas for writing.
- Use prewriting activities to create a knowledge base that will make the lesson accessible to a range of student learners.
- Actively involve the students in this phase of the lesson. Design activities that appeal to different learning styles.
- Make sure that the prewriting activities are adequate to prepare students for the introduction of the prompt and provide practice in the thinking skills required in the prompt.
- Consider if the prewriting activities stimulate the students' interest in performing the thinking and writing tasks designated in the prompt.
- Provide concrete examples of prewriting activities for the reader of the lesson, where applicable.

_____

Prompt:

_____

_____

_____

_____

- Make sure the prompt is clearly stated.
- Compare the prompt with the thinking and writing skills objectives to ensure that they are consistent.

- Use the same cue words in the prompt that are listed under the thinking skills objectives and require the same cognitive tasks.
- Consider whether the prompt is feasible. Does it have realistic expectations?
- Check to see that the prompt is geared appropriately given the grade level designated.

Precomposing

_____

_____

_____

_____

- The precomposing stage should be distinguishable from the prewriting stage. In addition to generating ideas for writing, design activities which help students to focus specifically on the prompt and to formulate a writing plan. The emphasis should be not only on the *WHAT* but on the *HOW* of writing in this stage of the process.
- Make sure that the precomposing activities are adequate to prepare students to think and write at the level required in the prompt.

Writing

_____

_____

_____

_____

- Give students an opportunity to generate more than one draft of their papers.
- Give students an adequate amount of time (either in or out of class) to write their papers.

Sharing

_____

_____

_____

_____

- Make provisions for students to give and receive feedback on their written work.
- Here and/or elsewhere in the lesson, introduce models (written either by the teacher or by the students) that show the students what a successful paper looks like.
- Give students specific criteria or guidelines on which to respond to each other's work.
- Here and/or elsewhere in the lesson, give students an opportunity to share (both orally and in writing) information about their process as thinkers and writers as well as their products. In other words, include a reflection or metacognitive component in the lesson.

Revising

_____

- Specifically build the revising stage into the lesson.
- Give students ample time to revise their work.
- Develop specific activities or guidelines geared for revision.
- Make sure that the lesson, overall, and the revising stage, in particular, has created the motivation for students to genuinely rethink and reshape their papers and not just recopy them.

Editing

_____

- Give students an opportunity to edit their finished drafts (individually or in groups) prior to submitting their work for evaluation.
- Give students specific criteria to look for when editing.
- Make some provision for the fact that the occurrence of error often increases as the cognitive task becomes more complex.

Evaluation

_____

_____

_____

_____

- Give students (or involve them in generating) a rubric, scoring guide or list of criteria on which their papers will be evaluated early on in the writing process.
- Encourage students to apply this rubric or scoring guide to their own writing during the writing, sharing, revising, and editing stages of the process.
- Make sure that the rubric or scoring guide clearly assesses the cognitive task required in the prompt.
- Check to see if the writing skills assessed are consistent with those delineated in the lesson objectives and in the prompt.
- Consider whether evaluation criteria include issues of fluency, form and correctness.
- Design a rubric or scoring guide which is flexible enough to allow for students to meet most but not all of the specified criteria and still do well on the paper.

Extension Activities

_____

_____

_____

_____

- Develop Extension Activities which are a logical extension of the demonstration lesson.
- Designate the thinking skills and writing skills objectives and ensure they are appropriate for the activity.
- Check to see that the Extension Activities clearly demonstrate how the conceptual skills fostered and the process described in the original demonstration lesson can transfer to new situations.
- Write instructions for the Extension Activities that are clear and complete enough to be useful to the reader.

Just as students need practice in a variety of thinking and writing tasks to tap the full range of their cognitive potential, so too their teachers need practice in thinking critically about critical thinking, in determining what it is they are asking their students to do when they ask them to write, and in carefully structuring activities to help get their students where they want them to go. Designing your own Thinking/Writing lesson—even if you intend it for no other audience than yourself—can be a rewarding learning experience which will provide you with this kind of practice. As one teacher put it, ''I learned that I sometimes ask students to leap tall buildings in a single bound. They would be more likely to make it with a ladder.''

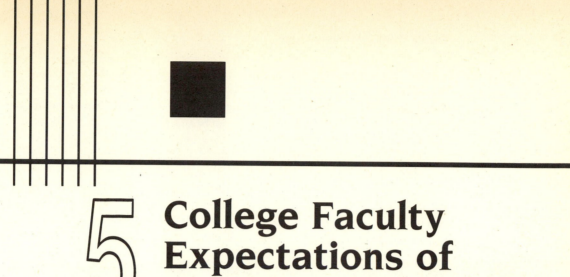

5 College Faculty Expectations of Students' Thinking and Writing Abilities

The *Statement on Competencies in English and Mathematics Expected of Entering Freshmen* stresses that a growing number of students who enter California colleges and universities are deficient in their basic academic skills and ill-prepared to meet the rigorous demands of higher education. Although the causes of underpreparation are various and complex, one of particular concern is the "lack of understanding among students, parents, and educators of the competencies expected of entering college students."[1] The *Statement on Competencies* addresses this issue by specifying a number of reading, thinking, writing, and mathematical abilities which must be introduced and practiced before students enter college in order to foster basic skills in communication and analysis, skills that are essential for academic progress across the curriculum.

It was reinforcing to turn to the English section of the *Statement on Competencies* and find this opening remark:

> Clarity in writing reflects clarity in thinking. College and university faculty expect students to be able to understand, organize, synthesize and communicate information, ideas, and opinions . . . Students will be required in their college courses to demonstrate these abilities by writing compositions, reports, term papers, and essay examinations.[2]

Not only did the authors of this report emphasize the interdependence of thinking and writing, but here, again, were the levels of thinking outlined in Bloom's taxonomy. Equally validating was the recognition that the "mastery" of the ability to generate ideas, formulate a thesis, logically develop and support an argument, and consciously manipulate language and sentence structure to inform and/or persuade a reader is a "cumulative process that begins in the lower grades and extends beyond college."[3]

We see our Thinking/Writing demonstration lessons as an attempt to provide continuity in the "cumulative process" of fostering basic academic competency. The writing skills delineated in the *Statement on Competencies* were a useful point of departure for the high school/college strand of our document. But in order to ensure that our continuum was truly articulated, we needed to get an accurate picture of the expectations of college faculty across the curriculum, as well as to see specific examples of the thinking and writing tasks students are called upon to perform. Thirteen faculty members at the University of California, Irvine from ten different disciplines agreed to participate in informal interviews. All were extremely receptive to what we were trying to do and provided valuable assistance. The opportunity for classroom teachers to exchange ideas and discuss mutual concerns with university professors was, in itself, a rewarding experience.

What we learned from these faculty members mirrors much of what we had already read, not only in the *Statement on Competencies,* but in the National Assessment of Educational Progress report, *Reading, Thinking and Writing.* Problems in student writing are often a reflection of problems in thinking. For instance, Amihai Glazer, Professor of Economics, noted lack of clarity in writing as one of his students' primary weaknesses and added, "If a student doesn't write well, he probably doesn't think clearly." Michael Butler, Dean of Undergraduate Studies, added that students seemed to have no notion of how to develop and support an argument in writing. Patrick Healy, Director of Instructional Development Services, felt that many students do not have "intellectual discipline" and seem unable to support generalizations with specifics. According to Richard Regosin, Chair of the Department of French and Italian, students do understand the concept of the thesis statement. However, they are weak at formulating their own theses and saying more than the obvious.

Most of the professors we interviewed felt it was not their job to teach thinking or writing in addition to their content; they expected students to have these skills well mastered prior to entering their courses. Michael Butler mentioned that these abilities should be fostered early on and emphasized the importance of providing students with practice in identifying main ideas, distinguishing between concepts, and analytically examining issues. Because analytical skills are often developed through reading, Mare Taagepera, Lecturer in Chemistry, stressed a need for critical reading as well as writing. On a recent reading comprehension test she gave to her Chemistry 10 students, 30% scored in the lowest percentile. In addition, she knows of high school teachers who have given up assigning a text in their chemistry classes because students either can't or won't read it. Naturally, when these students reach the university with their A's in chemistry, they're in trouble.

Both Gary Evans, Professor of Social Ecology, and Charles Lave, Chair of the Department of Economics, noted that very bright, verbal students often have difficulty translating ideas into writing. These same students, noted Rein Taagepera, Professor of Politics and Society, often talk around the topic at hand, fail to directly respond to the question, and often end abruptly without developing an adequate conclusion. Several professors suggested modeling as a way of communicating expectations of form and content to students. Evans also mentioned that the more explicit the test question or essay topic, the better the student response.

Although the majority of the people we interviewed were primarily concerned with content, mechanics and grammar are still a concern for some. Roland Schinzinger, Professor of Electrical and Computer Engineering, and Amihai Glazer were both disturbed about their students' deficiencies in spelling. In fact, Glazer fails papers with two or more spelling errors. Patrick Healy identified mechanical errors as one of the greatest problems he encounters, adding, ''If students can't use the language correctly, they can't communicate.'' Interestingly, Mare Taagepera said her foreign students who have been well disciplined in logical thinking, have no problem picking up the conventions of the language and presenting them in written form. She felt this reflected their strong background in working hard to achieve goals, unlike most native speakers.

In conjunction with this last thought is the one expressed by Charles Lave. Students do not like to rewrite or proofread their finished products. Unused to receiving constructive criticism, students rarely come in to conference about their writing or wish to rewrite for improvement. They simply never want to see what they've written again. Several professors added that it's as if students write a first draft and turn it in as a finished product. Time constraints on students and professors alike discourage requiring multiple drafts of assignments, but all felt a best effort on the student's part demanded time spent in editing *before* turning the assignments in.

On the bright side, students are good at creative writing. Michael Butler believes they display a more human voice in their writing than the students of twenty years ago. Professor Helen Weil, former Program Director for Russian, agreed that students displayed strengths in their personal style. Although voice is important, particularly in the humanities courses, Rein Taagepera is tired of creative people who don't observe closely. He said, ''An artist has to know what the brush and colors can do before he can be creative.'' It would seem that unorthodox writing with a flourish but without substantive and organized logic does not have a place in most disciplined courses. And if students have gotten away with it in high school, most professors agreed that they'll have trouble at UCI.

The professors we interviewed were kind enough to share with us examples of paper topics, essay exams and student writing. In order to determine what levels of thinking these assignments called for, we read and coded them according to the categories of Bloom's taxonomy. What follows is a sampler of the different types of questions we encountered.

As might be expected, science and math professors tend to give more tests that have short answers at the *knowledge* level. A student is asked to recall information, such as ''*List* three of the major discoveries of recent years which provide the principal evidence in support of the sea floor spreading hypothesis'' from Earth and Space Sciences 1 or, "*Identify* any four of the works, the basic plots of which are given below: a) 'A supernaturally strong but extremely simpleminded fellow works foolish and heroic deeds,' " and so on from Rein Taagepera's Soviet Society and Politics II class. The student has been given information, stores it, memorizes it, and *relates* it at a later date.

At UCI, more exam questions are geared to the next thinking level, *comprehension,* where students must translate information into their own terms. Again, the following questions are parts of exams, such as "*Discuss* (in no more than one page) one of the following topics, which must *not* be your own research topic during this quarter: a) Soviet space program" and so on from Soviet Society and Politics II or, "*Define* the Elastic Rebound Theory" from Earth and Space Sciences 1. The answers still rely on information that has already been given; however, the student must *understand* it in order to *explain* it.

With the third level, *application,* which involves applying learned material in new and concrete situations, the questions become longer and more complex. For example, John Hollowell, Director of Writing, selected an essay from the *LA Times* by Frank Trippett on "scofflaws," people who would never think of themselves as lawbreakers but who take increasing liberties with the law, as the point of departure for the following writing prompt for a Subject A Examination workshop for secondary English teachers and their students: "Examine several of Trippett's examples of scofflawry as well as discuss examples from your own experience to explain what you think motivates people to 'skirt the law.' Based on the examples that you discuss, do you agree with Trippett's conclusion that scofflawry is a sign of 'people's inability or unwillingness to govern their own behavior in the interest of others?' " The student must *choose* examples, *organize* them, *apply* them to the definition of scofflawry, and *decide* whether those examples support or refute Trippett's argument.

Yet most of the assignments given at UCI are at the fourth level, *analysis* (breaking down or analyzing). Most English professors definitely aim at this thinking level. From a humanities core course, HCC/A, comes the following assignment: "Write a well-organized, coherently *argued* essay of 2 1/2–3 typed pages in which you *analyze* the function of the description of the seasons in Part II (lines 491–535) of *Sir Gawain and the Green Knight* within the context of poem as a whole, keeping in mind that a major characteristic of the poem as a 'romance' is its way of limiting time to put it in a strict cyclic pattern." And from Astronomy 3 comes the following *compare/contrast* question: "Describe the differences in the assumptions made in a) the evolutionary models of the universe and b) the steady-state model of the universe."

Synthesis, the fifth level, deals with *creating* and *formulating* new products based on accumulated knowledge. Not as many questions were in this category. An example of this high level thinking comes from Education 102C: "At the conclusion of *Of Mice and Men,* Slim leads George away from the river and up towards the highway, reassuring him that he had to kill Lennie: there was no way out. Imagine that Slim and George head into town for a drink at Suzy's Bar. Please begin your paper at this point. In George's words, explain to Slim why you killed

Lennie. Remember that you must *become* George to write this paper. You are limited to his vocabulary, his perspective on life, and his level of sensitivity. In your dialogue, suggest either directly or indirectly: what Lennie meant to you, what significance the dream of the land and the farmhouse has or had for you, and your perception of what life will be like without Lennie.''

From our admittedly small sample, we determined that 70% of the thinking and writing tasks at UCI were at the analysis level or above. Typically, questions seemed to focus primarily at the *analysis* level and skip over *synthesis* to the last level, *evaluation.* From Philosophy 182 comes "Point at a place. Can you ever point to the same place again?" This evaluation question, like many posed across the disciplines, asks students to *assess* a situation and to *justify* their point of view based upon a careful *analysis* of the data.

By becoming more aware of the words we use to elicit student writing, such as *analyze, solve, value, interpret,* and so on, we can recognize the thinking skill that is called for in the writing task. Is it valid at that particular time? Have we gone too far and asked too difficult a question? Too easy? Have we given enough information so that students can tackle the problem? Rein Taagepera noted that apparently bright students often fail to answer the question. Perhaps this is due not so much to the fact that they do not have a command of the content as to the fact that they do not fully comprehend what it is they are being asked to do. Helen Rivera, Director of the Learning Skills Center at UCI, receives daily visits from bewildered students, assignments in hand, who want someone with authority to interpret questions for them and explain how one goes about analyzing, formulating, assessing, hypothesizing, and so on. If the same terms were used throughout their education and training in the process of thinking and writing at different levels, it would seem that the tasks we ask our students to perform would be more familiar and less formidable. Perhaps educators at all levels of the curriculum need to work together and communicate among themselves in order to help our students reach their highest potential. What are we asking? When are we asking it? How are we asking it? Why are we asking it? The interview sessions helped us focus on these questions and exchange ideas. This was a first step in sharing in the responsibility of fostering critical thinking and writing, K-University.

Notes

1 The Academic Senates of the California Community Colleges, The California State University, and the University of California, *Statement on Competencies in English and Mathematics Expected of Entering Freshman,* November, 1982: 2.
2 *Statement on Competencies:* 3.
3 *Statement on Competencies:* 4.

6 Evaluating the Thinking/Writing Demonstration Lessons and Overall Model

After we completed the first draft of our demonstration lessons, we started to pilot them in our classrooms. Almost immediately, we became aware of how enthusiastically our students were responding to the lessons and noticed that the quality of writing the students produced was improving. Several of us—Brenda Borron, Trudy Burrus, Shari Lockman, Carol Booth Olson, Laurie Opfell, Julie Simpson, and Glenn Patchell—met as a committee to design an evaluation tool that we hoped would statistically show the progress we had observed our students making in writing and thinking. Bolstered by previous successful studies of the benefits of using the writing process as a tool for teaching students to write conducted by our Writing Project site, we optimistically felt we could demonstrate our observations. We also looked at our Thinking/Writing evaluation as an opportunity to learn more about the effect of our educational model and demonstration lessons on student writers. In her essay, "Reflections on Classroom Research," Lucinda Ray cites one of the summarizing points made by James Britton in a class she attended at Bread Loaf School of English as being especially meaningful to her: "Research is not primarily a process of proving something; but primarily a process of discovery and learning."[1] Reflecting upon Britton's statement, she goes on to add, "This view of research is tremendously liberating for it allows classroom teachers to take seriously the ordinary business of their lives as teachers."[2] This is the view of research that we kept in mind as we embarked upon our initial Thinking/Writing study.

Two primary goals in our study were to test the effectiveness of individual demonstration lessons and to measure the impact of the overall model on student thinking and writing ability. A secondary concern of the study was to determine whether there was a change in students' attitudes toward writing before and after exposure to the Thinking/Writing lessons. We intuitively felt and hoped to demonstrate that students who participated in several lessons would write better and think better as well as feel better about writing. Since our whole model was based upon the premise that writing is a mode of thinking, we assumed that, given practice in writing and thinking, students would internalize these processes and do well on a writing assessment. Our problem was to provide an evaluation design that would test for each of our goals.

In designing our evaluation, we had the good fortune to work with George Hillocks, Professor of English and Education, University of Chicago, who took our work as teacher researchers very seriously and who gave generously of his time and expertise. His assistance in conceptualizing each of the components of our study was invaluable. Each of these components is described below:

Component #1: Evaluation of Thinking/Writing Demonstration Lessons

To test the effectiveness of the Thinking/Writing lessons, sixteen teachers (four seventh grade and four eleventh grade California teachers and four seventh and four eleventh grade Utah teachers) were selected to be their own experimental and control teacher by teaching two lessons in two of their classes. The first lesson was presented to one class, complete with all the steps in the writing process, and the final product was collected. In the other class, just the prompt for the same lesson was presented (without the steps of the writing process), and that product was collected. The process was reversed with the second lesson so that the class that wrote to the first lesson complete with all the steps in the writing process, then wrote to the second prompt cold and vice versa. Both sets of class papers (experimental and control) were collected and sent to the UCI Writing Project for scoring. In all, eight lessons were pilot-tested. Each lesson was paired with another lesson. The four lesson pairs were repeated twice with the lesson order reversed as in the diagram on the following page:

Thinking/Writing 7th Grade Evaluation

Teacher Code	Class	Week 1	Week 2
U7A	#1	E Cookie Lesson	C Thank You Ma'am
	#2	C Cookie Lesson	E Thank You Ma'am
U7B	#1	E Thank You Ma'am	C Cookie Lesson
	#2	C Thank You Ma'am	E Cookie Lesson

Thinking/Writing 7th Grade Evaluation

Teacher Code	Class	Week 1	Week 2
U7C	#1	E Persuasive Ltrs.	C Designing E.T.
	#2	C Persuasive Ltrs.	E Designing E.T.
U7D	#1	E Designing E.T.	C Persuasive Ltrs.
	#2	C Designing E.T.	E Persuasive Ltrs.

After taking a random sample of ten experimental and ten control papers per class per teacher, the papers were coded and scored using a discourse feature analysis including two 1–6 scales—for Content and for Form. The overall results are as follows:

Overall scores of all 640 essays. (Average of Content plus Form scores)	4.00
Treatment 1 Thinking/Writing	4.17
Treatment 2 Control (without Thinking/Writing steps)	3.82
Difference between: **Treatment 1 and 2**	$.35 \ (P < .0005; \ F = 22.8)$
State 1 (California)	4.07
State 2 (Utah)	3.92
State Difference	$.15 \ (P < .035; \ F = 4.4)$

As hoped, the groups receiving Thinking/Writing significantly exceeded the scores of the same groups on lessons without the Thinking/Writing steps. Somewhat surprisingly, the results also show a significant difference between the overall scores for California and Utah students favoring California. Since a comparison of reading scores indicates that there is no reason to believe that the California students were more able than their Utah counterparts, we speculate that differences may be the results of the training in the Thinking/Writing model which California teachers received and Utah teachers did not. (*Note:* These results were calculated by using a four way ANOVA-treatment by state by class by lesson—on the overall data. We are indebted to Bob Land, Lecturer, Department of English and Comparative Literature, University of California, Irvine, for computing these results and helping us to interpret them. We were pleased to see that the probability significance of $P < .000$ and $P < .0005$ are considerably below the .05 level normally used in educational research.)

Component #2: Evaluation of the Thinking/Writing Model

To test the effectiveness of the overall Thinking/Writing model, we conducted two separate evaluations—one evaluation of the impact of Thinking/Writing lessons implemented over a semester on the students of teachers who received inservice on the Thinking/Writing model, and one evaluation of the impact of Thinking/Writing lessons on the students of the UCI Writing Project Teacher/Consultants who actually developed the Thinking/Writing lessons.

Teachers Who Received Thinking/Writing Inservice

In the fall of 1985, six teachers of minority and underrepresented students—two from each of the three high schools in Santa Ana Unified School District—were trained in a six-day workshop on Thinking/Writing. During the course of the workshop, the teachers heard guest speakers, participated in our demonstration lessons and designed a Thinking/Writing lesson of their own based on the existing ninth-grade curriculum for Santa Ana students.

These teachers committed to teach Thinking/Writing lessons throughout the course of the 1985–1986 school year. The target number of lessons was 12. Each teacher also agreed to find a control teacher willing to devote one 45 minute class period to an in-class writing assignment. Since English classes are tracked in Santa Ana, an additional constraint was that the control teacher's class be tracked at the same level as that of the Thinking/Writing-trained teacher's class. In mid-May, a 45 minute, posttest only prompt was administered to the six control classes and the six experimental classes. The prompt was a descriptive assignment in which students were asked to describe a place which had made a strong impact on them. Papers for evaluation were selected on the basis of reading scores ranging from 8.5 to 10.9. Subsequently, random selection was used to create cells of ten papers per teacher.

Papers were scored holistically on a 1–6 point scale by four Writing Project teachers. Papers were read twice; papers with scores differing by two or more points were given a third reader. The overall results are as follows:

		Valley	Santa Ana	Saddleback	
School Group		**level 1**	**level 2**	**level 3**	**Totals:**
Exp	*level 1*	20 / 2.8	20 / 3.45	20 / 3.75	60 / 3.333
C-1	*level 2*	2.0 / 2.5	20 / 2.8	20 / 3.2	60 / 2.8
Totals:		40 / (2.65)	40 / 3.125	40 / (3.425)	120 / 3.067

diff - .3   diff - .65   diff - .65

Experimental Group .533/ higher

Lowest overall average ⟶

⟵ Highest overall avrage

Again, the students in the experimental treatment (Writing Project) outscored the control students. The difference was .533. The probability significance of P < .001 and P < .005 were again considerably below the .05 level normally used in educational research. Our guess is that the difference between the .35 in the California/Utah evaluation and the .53 scores in the Santa Ana evaluation is due to three things: 1.) the difference in the duration of the treatment (two weeks versus a semester); 2.) the difference in the training (anywhere from no exposure to limited exposure to Thinking/Writing in the California/Utah evaluation as compared with six full days with Santa Ana teachers); 3.) the fact that the Santa Ana teachers made Thinking/Writing their own by writing a demonstration lesson.

Thinking/Writing Teacher/Consultants

The tables for the evaluation of the students of our Thinking/Writing Teacher/Consultants versus the students of comparable control teachers are too complex to reproduce here. To summarize, five Thinking/Writing Teacher/Consultants and their control teachers gave their students a pre- and posttest at the beginning and end of a semester. They either analyzed two different poems by Stephen Crane or analyzed the poem "Mariana" by A.L. Tennyson and a passage on Miss Havisham in Charles Dickens' *Great Expectations*. Both matched sets were tested and verified by George Hillocks as being comparable in difficulty. Between the pre- and post-test, Thinking/Writing Teacher/Consultants and their control teachers taught approximately the same content, but the former group used the Thinking/Writing lesson format while the latter did not. These pre- and posttests were holistically scored on a 1–6 point scale. A fluency count was also conducted. While the control group actually lost .05 from pretest to posttest, the experimental (Writing Project) students gained .764. The difference between these two, .084, is statistically significant at the .008 level—meaning that a difference that large might be expected to occur by chance only eight times in 10,000 experiments.

Experimental students also outgained control students in fluency—averaging 35 more words on the post test as opposed to the control students gain of six more words. This difference was statistically significant at the .05 level.

Comparative Chart

1	California/Utah	+.35
2	Santa Ana	+.53
3	Thinking/Writing	+.84

As was noted previously, the results of our first evaluation of individual demonstration lessons involving teachers from California and Utah who had no exposure or limited exposure to the Thinking/Writing model yielded a .35 increase on the part of the experimental treatment (Writing Project) over the control treatment. These results were especially validating because they indicate that individual Thinking/Writing lessons have a definite impact on student writing whether or not the teachers of those lessons have received inservice training on the Thinking/Writing model. In the Santa Ana evaluation, the experimental (Writing Project) group outscored the control group by .53. Although it may be inappropriate to compare our evaluation of individual Thinking/Writing lessons which used the same students for the experimental and control treatments with a study of the overall Thinking/Writing model assessing different students (experimental and control) with the same prompt, we do think that the six days of inservice the Santa Ana teachers received in the Thinking/Writing model may account for the difference of .53 in that evaluation versus .35 in the California/Utah evaluation. More importantly, the teachers in the Santa Ana evaluation designed their own Thinking/Writing lesson. In making Thinking/Writing their own, we feel that these teachers internalized the process in a way that the teachers participating in the California/Utah evaluation did not. Finally, our guess is that the difference in the .53 increase we saw in the evaluation of the students of teachers who were inserviced in Thinking/Writing versus the .84 difference we see in the results for the students of our own Thinking/Writing Teacher/Consultants is due to the difference in six days of training versus six years of commitment to this model on the part of our Teacher/Consultants.

At this point, as teacher researchers, we were hooked. The results of these three studies empirically validated for us something we already knew by virtue of the quality of the papers we were receiving from our students: *The Thinking/Writing model does have a positive influence on student reading, thinking and writing ability.* But we only had educated guesses as to **why** this model has the potential to have such a significant impact on student writers and as to **what** factors contribute the most to this impact. Further, we realized that in our existing studies the number of students involved was relatively small. Our curiosity sparked, we were now ready to embark upon a large scale study that would enable us to test out some of those educated guesses and to explore student learners and learning in a way we hadn't had the opportunity to before.

The Presidential Grant for School Improvement Study

In the Spring of 1989, the UCI Writing Project received a Presidential Grant for School Improvement from the University of California Office of the President to address the following question: *What are the factors in curriculum design and staff development which can maximize teacher understanding and assimilation and thereby positively affect student reading, thinking and writing ability?* Our focus was on what impact a sequence of three literature-based Thinking/Writing lessons taught over a 17-week period would have on students of different ability levels in grades eight to twelve. Would they show growth in their reading, thinking and writing ability? Additionally, we wished to determine to what extent varying levels of exposure to staff development training on the Thinking/Writing model provided to their teachers would influence student performance. Does more staff development training on the part of the teacher mean better writing on the part of their students? As opposed to our earlier studies, we also planned to collect and score student writing at the final draft stage in addition to the timed writing they would do during pre-tests, and post-tests—a decision we felt was more in tune with the concept of writing as a process.

Evaluation Design: Experimental Treatment Groups

During August 1989, our large group of Thinking/Writing Teacher/Consultants wrote a set of new Thinking/Writing lessons that dealt with relatively short works of literature which involved specific cognitive tasks such as analyzing, interpreting, making inferences, persuading, etc., and which could be taught in a one to two-week period. A subcommittee of this group consisting of Brenda Borron, Pat Clark, Sue Ellen Gold, Jerry Judd, Carol Booth Olson, Glenn Patchell, and Julie Simpson edited these lessons and sent them on to George Hillocks for review. Hillocks again provided valuable assistance by selecting three of these lessons (all dealing with inferential reasoning and literary interpretation) to be taught in a sequence. We then identified and selected five experimental treatment groups involving eight to ten teachers per group:

Group 1—No UCI Writing Project Training

This group consisted of teachers who applied to and were accepted for an early admission program to the 1990 Summer Institute which required their participation in the research project. Group 1 was chosen from this population so that the teachers would be of equal caliber to and have similar motivation as Writing Project Fellows.

Group 2—Summer Institute Only

This group consisted of Writing Project Fellows from the 1989 Summer Institute only.

Group 3—Summer Institute Plus Follow-Up Course

This group consisted of Writing Project Fellows (1978–1988) who participated in a ten-week inservice course on *Fostering Critical Thinking Through Reading and Writing About Literature.* This group participated in all the in-class inservice activities but did not design their own Thinking/Writing literature-based lesson.

Group 4—Summer Institute, Follow-Up Course, Lesson Design

This group consisted of Writing Project Fellows (1978–1988) who attended the ten-week course on *Fostering Critical Thinking Through Reading and Writing About Literature* and who designed their own Thinking/Writing lesson based on a work of literature of their choice as a by-product of the inservice.

Group 5—Summer Institute, Follow-Up Course, Lesson Design, Peer Coaching

This group consisted of Writing Project Fellows (1978–1988) who either participated in the course on *Fostering Critical Thinking Skills Through Reading and Writing About Literature* or who are members of the UCI Writing Project's Thinking/Writing group, wrote a Thinking/Writing lesson based on a work of literature of their choice, and had three peer coaching visits from an experienced UCI Writing Project Teacher/Consultant.

The Evaluation Design

In February 1990, the fifty teachers implemented the following evaluation design:

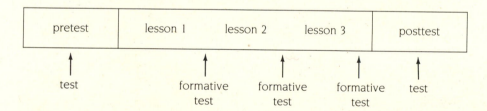

1. For the pretest, all fifty teachers administered a Thinking/Writing/Literature prompt to a randomly selected class. Students wrote to this prompt cold (without Thinking/Writing/Literature training). Students had the last 20 minutes of one class period in which the literature was read to them aloud while they read a copy silently and one 45 minute period the next day when they received and wrote to the prompt.

2. Teachers collected all papers.

Late February–Early May 1990

3. Teachers taught Thinking/Writing/Literature lesson #1. They took this lesson through all of the stages in the Thinking/Writing process. Teachers collected formative test #1 at both the rough draft and final draft stages.

4. All teachers taught Thinking/Writing/Literature lesson #2. They took this lesson through all of the stages in the Thinking/Writing process. Teachers collected formative test #2 at both the rough draft and final draft stages.

5. All teachers taught Thinking/Writing/Literature lesson #3. They took this lesson through all of the stages in the Thinking/Writing process. Teachers collected formative test #3 at both the rough draft and final draft stages.

May 1990

6. Teachers administered a posttest Thinking/Writing/Literature prompt which all the students wrote to cold. Students had the last 20 minutes of one class period in which the literature was read to them aloud while they read a copy silently and one 45 minute period the next day when they received and wrote to the prompt.

May/June 1990

7. The research committee matched formative tests #1, #2, and #3 and the pre- and post-test to ensure all student work was properly coded. They then randomly selected the papers of eight students per class for scoring. Papers were scored on June 23 by faculty and TAs from the UCI Department of English and Comparative Literature and UCIWP Teacher/Consultants not involved in the study. Papers were scored using a 1–6 scale. Papers received two scores from readers which were added for a total score on a 2–11 scale. All paper scores which diverged by two points were scored by a third reader.

8. The Research Committee reviewed and analyzed Metacognitive Logs from students in Group 5, as well as Teachers' Logs from all five Experimental Treatment Groups.

The Research Data

After completing the scoring of the pretests, posttests, and the three sets of student essays (an arduous task since our readers were scoring the work of eight randomly sampled students from the classes of 40 teachers for a total of 1,600 papers), we turned over the scoring sheets to Bob Land and anxiously awaited the results. Provided below is a summary of the major questions we addressed in the study and the results which pertain to each question.

What is the growth between pretest and posttest for the students across all experimental treatment groups?

Source:	df:	Sum of Squares:	Mean Square:	F-test:	P value:
TRAINING LEVEL (A)	4	19.285	4.821	1.565	.2068
subjects w. groups	33	101.691	3.082		
Repeated Measure (B)	1	15.195	15.195	15.081	5.0E−4
AB	4	2.196	.549	.545	.704
B × subjects w. groups	33	33.25	1.008		

The AB Incidence table

Repeated Mea...		PRESCORE	POSTSCO...	Totals:	GAIN
TRAINING LEVEL	ONE	7 5.589	7 6.571	14 6.08	.982
	TWO	8 5.359	8 5.75	16 5.555	.391
	THREE	7 5.321	7 6	14 5.661	.679
	FOUR	8 6.438	8 7.469	16 6.953	1.031
TR...	FIVE	8 5.259	8 6.632	16 5.945	1.373
	Totals:	38 5.601	38 6.495	76 6.048	.891

(Results were calculated using a two-way repeated measures ANOVA).

The growth of all groups from pretest to posttest was .891 on an 11 point scale. The probability of this gain occurring by chance alone is 1 in 5,000. We were pleased to see that all students grew significantly over the seventeen week period, regardless of the Experimental Treatment/Training Group they were in. We also conducted a fluency count of the gain in words between pretest and posttest of students across all groups.

Source:	df:	Sum of Squares:	Mean Square:	F-test:	P value:
TRAINING LEVEL (A)	4	63001.809	15750.452	1.618	.1931
subjects w. groups	33	321287.863	9735.996		
Repeated Measure (B)	1	204443.635	204443.635	61.985	1.0E−4
AB	4	14622.91	3655.728	1.108	.3691
B × subjects w. groups	33	108843.495	3298.288		

	Repeated Mea...	PREWORDS	POSTWOR...	Totals:	GAIN
TRAINING LEVEL	ONE	7 209.304	7 362.625	14 285.964	153.321
	TWO	8 212.359	8 285.984	16 249.172	73.625
	THREE	7 210.786	7 289.321	14 250.054	78.535
	FOUR	8 270.344	8 377.094	16 323.719	106.75
TR...	FIVE	8 204.354	8 313.828	16 259.091	109.474
	Totals:	38 222.029	38 325.76	76 273.894	103.731

The average gain in words across all five training groups was almost 104 words (103.7). For many students, the posttest gain represented 50% to 100% more words than they had written on the pretest. The probability of this gain occurring by chance alone is 1 in 10,000.

Given a constant number of Thinking/Writing/Literature lessons taught, what is the impact of the following degrees of teacher training upon student writing?

- No previous UCI Writing Project training;
- Writing Project Summer Institute training only;
- Writing Project plus ten-week Thinking/Literature course;
- Writing Project plus ten-week Thinking/Literature course (including one self-designed lesson);
- Writing Project, ten-week course, three follow-up meetings, peer coaching.

To our surprise, Training Group #1 outscored both Training Group #2 and Training Group #3. Because of this, the significance of the training effect across all five groups is not statistically relevant. We have some educated guesses as to why Group #1 fared so well which we drew from the teachers' metacognitive logs and interviews. Guess #1 is that this group applied for an early admission program to the 1990 Summer Institute that required that they participate in the study. They were honored to be selected and were on their "best behavior" because they wished to do especially well before joining the Writing Project Summer Institute. Guess #2 is that these teachers followed the lessons "religiously," were encountering many of the Writing Project strategies for the first time and were very enthusiastic about them, and, because of their lack of previous training, would (as one Group #1 teacher said) "try anything!"

Because this was somewhat of an anomaly, our research consultant, Bob Land, reran our data omitting Training Group #1 and also Training Group #5 (whose members he found to be usually experienced—including some Thinking/Writing Group members—and consequently, whose students showed the most growth). When only Training Groups #2, #3, and #4 were compared (T#2 = .391 Gain, T#3 = .677 Gain, T#4 = 1.03), the training effect was statistically significant. The probability is .0209 (or 2 chances in 100) that these differences would occur by chance alone.

Source:	df:	Sum of Squares:	Mean Square:	F-test:	P value:
TRAINING LEVEL (A)	2	57.413	28.706	4.722	.0209
subjects w. groups	20	121.593	6.08		
Repeated Measure (B)	4	27.885	6.971	7.332	1.0E−4
AB	8	3.68	.46	.484	.8643
B × subjects w. groups	80	76.068	.951		

Repeated Mea...		PRESCORE	MARIANA	GAME	LAST	POSTSCO...	PRE TO POST GAIN
TRAINING LEVEL	TWO	8 5.359	8 6.125	8 6.293	8 5.953	8 5.75	40 .391
	THREE	7 5.321	7 7.054	7 6.852	7 6.518	7 6	35 .678
	FOUR	8 6.438	8 7.969	8 7.797	8 8.031	8 7.469	40 1.031
	Totals:	23 5.723	23 7.049	23 6.986	23 6.848	23 6.424	

At the California Writing Project Directors' meeting held in Fall 1990, we discussed the fact that the 1989 Summer Institute Group (T#2) might have experienced that sense of what Piaget would call "disequilibrium" that many Writing Project Fellows go through in their first year after the Project. This led to an interesting discussion of whether we "overload" Fellows in the Summer Institute. With a ten session follow-up program where they participated fully but did not generate their own curriculum materials, Writing Project Fellows (T#3) had more impact on student progress. But the teachers who made the staff development training their own by creating their own curriculum materials based upon works of literature of their own choosing had the most impact of all (T#4).

What growth patterns, if any, emerge across all papers? What might account for these patterns?

Students in classes described by Writing Project teachers as heterogeneous, average or college prep, improved the most (1.18), followed by students described as ESL or remedial (.726), and then by those described as GATE or honors (.25), as noted on the table on page 443. (*Note: We could not separate the scores of ESL and remedial students, as we would have liked to do, because the reality is that many ESL students are unfortunately placed in remedial classes.*) This is also true of the word gain: heterogeneous, etc. (117.7), ESL/remedial (92.3), honors (74.5). It is important to note, however, that the GATE and honors students had the highest pre-test scores and fluency count, and, therefore, had less room for improvement.

Source:	df:	Sum of Squares:	Mean Square:	F-test:	P value:
TRAINING LEVEL (A)	4	2.419	.605	.349	.8419
ABILITY LEVEL (B)	2	11.335	5.667	3.272	.0562
AB	8	9.033	1.129	.652	.7269
Error	23	39.835	1.732		

The AB Incidence table on Y_1: GAIN

ABILITY LEVEL:		LOW	MEDIUM	HIGH	Totals:
TRAINING LEVEL	ONE	−1 .75	4 1.406	1 −.875	6 .917
	TWO	2 −.375	4 1.375	2 −.812	8 .391
	THREE	1 1.75	4 .406	2 .688	7 .679
	FOUR	0 •	5 .65	3 1.667	8 1.031
TR...	FIVE	2 1.304	5 2	1 −1.625	8 1.373
	Totals:	6 .726	22 1.182	9 .25	37 .891

Note: Low = ESL/Remedial; *Medium* = Heterogeneous/Average/College Prep; *High* = Gate/Honors.

The AB Incidence table

Repeated Mea...		PREWORDS	POSTWOR...	Totals:	GAIN
Class Ability	ESL/REME...	6 174.16	6 266.542	12 220.351	92.382
	MIXED/PR...	22 214.568	22 332.341	44 273.455	117.773
	HONORS	9 280.875	9 354.931	18 317.903	74.056
	Totals:	37 224.144	37 327.166	74 275.655	

By grade level, tenth graders improved the most (1.14), followed by eleventh graders (1.03) and eighth graders (1.0). (See the table on page 444.) Twelfth graders showed very little growth (.59) which we attribute to the boredom and "I'm out of here" syndrome. Ninth graders actually went down (−.334). There was some discussion at the California Writing Project Directors' meeting that perhaps ninth graders are in a "disequilibrium" that is not totally dissimilar from the one new Writing Project Fellows are in. That is, our Training Group #2 teachers expressed a certain sense of insecurity and a feeling of being "new kids on the block."

Source:	df:	Sum of Squares:	Mean Square:	F-test:	P value:
GRADE (A)	4	96.293	24.073	4.471	.0055
subjects w. groups	32	172.305	5.385		
Repeated Measure (B)	4	49.089	12.272	13.348	1.0E−4
AB	16	11.584	.724	.787	.6973
B × subjects w. groups	128	117.686	.919		

The AB Incidence table

Repeated Mea...		PRESCORE	MARIANA	GAME	LAST	POSTSCO...	Totals:	GAIN Pre to Post
GRADE	EIGHT	14 5.196	14 6.339	14 6.515	14 5.973	14 6.196	70 6.044	1.0
	NINE	3 4.792	3 6.042	3 4.917	3 5.333	3 4.458	15 5.108	−.334
	TEN	6 6.158	6 8.077	6 7.795	6 8.387	6 7.301	3 7.544	1.143
	ELEVEN	10 5.975	10 7.7	10 7.125	10 7.238	10 7.012	50 7.01	1.037
GR...	TWELVE	4 6.219	.4 7.969	4 7.438	4 7.344	4 6.812	20 7.156	.593
	Totals:	37 5.64	37 7.141	37 6.858	37 6.803	37 6.522	185 6.593	103.731

Does there seem to be a specific lesson (#1, #2, or #3) where student progress peaks?

In four of the five groups, the highest scores were on the first lesson—an analysis of setting as a mirror of character in A.L. Tennyson's poem, ''Mariana.'' This may be due to the fact that this lesson was the longest and most carefully structured. The succeeding lessons, an analysis of character through dialogue (specifically the closing line) of Richard Wilbur's short story, ''A Game of Catch'' and an interpretation of why the characters behave the way they do in Harold Pinter's play *Last to Go* built upon the ''Mariana'' activities but, by design, had fewer rungs in the instructional ladder.[3] We were interested to see if students would internalize certain strategies from their practice with ''Mariana'' and whether or not the teachers would feel free to add steps to the lessons if they determined there was a need. The *Last to Go* lesson was also particularly sophisticated. Eighth and ninth graders scores went down considerably on this lesson while tenth graders went up and eleventh and twelfth graders went down but only very little.

Some Preliminary Conclusions

The Thinking/Writing model appears to have a positive impact upon students across grade levels and in diverse ability groupings. We have no data regarding exactly how many lessons of this kind teachers might want to expose students to in order to derive maximum benefits. What we do know is that engaging in the guided practice of even one lesson seems to facilitate student growth. Judging by the post-test scores by grade level (cited on page 444), it also looks as if exposure to a series of lessons enables students to internalize problem solving strategies (in this case, related to inferential reasoning and literary analysis) that enabled these students to obtain a score on their post-test which is within range of the scores they obtained on full length lessons with prewriting and precomposing activities and multiple drafts.

As far as teachers are concerned, we cannot guarantee (nor would we want to) that teachers who have had no staff development training in the Thinking/Writing model will outscore some teachers with inservice training. What we can say is that teachers who do not have an opportunity for staff development can still expect to see student growth by experimenting with these lessons. If teachers do have an opportunity for some sustained staff development, that training will most likely positively influence the performance of their students. Further, if teachers are given time and encouragement to make what they learn their own by developing their own curriculum materials, they have an even greater influence on their students than those teachers who simply receive inservice training but do not translate that training into their own lesson ideas.

It's How You Feel that Counts

It's empirical! Thinking/Writing works. But far more important than pretest, post-test and word gain scores on data tables are the responses of teachers and their students.

The Teachers

"My students enjoyed the variety of prewriting and precomposing activities and they seemed to be stimulated—so that they had fun too! It was exciting and rewarding to pilot these lessons."

—Wendy Washington

"One of the most valuable things these lessons showed my students is that effective writing is difficult but rewarding work—that much thought and organization are necessary to generate something of clarity and value. I think my students came away with good feelings about themselves because they took a difficult piece of literature and made their own meaning from it. Suddenly, they began to understand and believe that they are not *boneheads* as they call themselves because they are tracked into *remedial* classes. This alone would be enough for me to call this a success.''

—Darlene Grierson

''My students' writing seemed to improve across the board. The careful stair-stepping of learning really made a difference.''

—Melody Allan

''The Thinking/Writing process has been valuable to the students and to me. I have learned as much as they and have many new ideas for making writing about literature more interactive. Many of my students who were hostile and resistant at first were very proud of their accomplishments.''

—Suzanne Durkee

''I had about three or four students who were identified as Special Ed. who had not written anything all year who started writing and wrote the most incredibly insightful essays about 'Mariana.' I think the sequential process really gave them confidence.''

—Bobbie Flora

The Students

''Writing was something that I dreaded, something that was just too hard. But this year, I've come to enjoy writing.''

—Chin-sop Yi

''I learned how to write this year. I found my process.''

—Sean Walters

''You ease us into the exercises—showing us the way for the first time, and then letting us do the exercises on our own . . . This internalization of technique is very critical in 'real' writing.''

—Doug Enright

''You gave me and other students time to do things that are complicated and difficult. You have found ways to make our work easier and simpler.''

—Liem Huynh

''I am a better student for having experienced these lessons. I now understand that if I take my time and think things through, I can write well.''

—Trisha Soni

An Invitation

Mary K. Healy, former Co-Director of the Bay Area Writing Project, noted in an article in *California English,* ''Teachers are already researchers because thoughtful teachers base so much of what they do on what they observe and on the reactions of their students.''[4] We invite you, as teacher researchers, to make Thinking/

Writing your own and to observe its impact on students' thinking, writing, and feeling for yourselves.

Notes

1 Quoted by Lucinda Ray, "Reflections on Classroom Research." *Reclaiming the Classroom: Teacher Research as an Agency for Change.* ed. Dixie Goswami and Peter R. Stillman. (Upper Montclair, N.J.: Boynton/Cook Publishers, Inc., 1987): 220.
2 Lucinda Ray, "Reflections on Classroom Research," 220.
3 If you wish to obtain copies of these lessons, write to Carol Booth Olson, University of California, UCI Writing Project, Department of Education, Irvine, CA 92717. We will send them to you at xeroxing and postage cost.
4 Mary K. Healy, "Teachers as Researchers: An Interview with Mary K. Healy," *California English* (January/February, 1987): 6.

Glossary
Virginia Bergquist, Susanna Tracy Clemans, Sue Ellen Gold, Mike O'Brien, Carol Booth Olson, and Dale Sprowl

Bibliography
Laurie Opfell and Sue Rader Willett

Glossary

Abstract   An abstract is a brief statement of the essential ideas of a book, article, essay, speech, etc. In the "Personalizing the Research Paper" lesson, for example, prior to conducting their search, students are asked to write an abstract in which they briefly explain what their topic is, why they have chosen it and how they intend to go about searching and writing. (*Thinking/Writing: Fostering Critical Thinking Through Writing,* 326).

Audience   An audience is the reader(s) of the writer's work. Students should write for a variety of audiences in addition to the teacher as evaluator or "giver-of-grades." A proposed hierarchical order of audiences is self, peers, trusted adult, teacher as collaborator, teacher as evaluator, and unknown audiences. It is important for writers to identify their audience so that they may choose the appropriate subject and a suitable way of communicating about it. (*Practical Ideas for Teaching Writing as a Process,* 73.)

Bloom's Taxonomy of the Cognitive Domain   Under the leadership of Benjamin Bloom, a committee of over 30 educators constructed a taxonomy (classification scheme) of educational objectives in the cognitive domain that delineates the intended behaviors that relate to mental acts or think-

*Note: Page references are made in many of the glossary entries to the California State Department of Education publication *Practical Ideas for Teaching Writing as a Process* (1987 Edition), compiled and edited by Dr. Carol Booth Olson, Director of the UCI Writing Project, a site of the California Writing Project. Information regarding this publication is available through the Bureau of Publications, California State Department of Education, to P.O. Box 271, Sacramento, CA 95802-0271. Page references are also made to lessons in this edition of *Thinking/Writing: Fostering Critical Thinking Through Writing.*

ing. The committee conceived of six major classes of educational objectives arranged in hierarchical order from simple to complex. The six major classes are:

Knowledge
Comprehension
Application
Analysis
Synthesis
Evaluation

The KNOWLEDGE level requires such skills as remembering specifics: facts, terminology, events, and relationships. COMPREHENSION encompasses the ability to understand the meaning of the material or ideas contained in it. This stage also involves translation of knowledge from ideas and thought into print. APPLICATION includes the ability to apply what has been learned to new situations and to make appropriate generalizations or to derive principles. ANALYSIS is the breaking down of material into its component parts and the discovery of the relationships and organization of those parts. SYNTHESIS involves composing the parts of the material into something original—a creative act in which elements or parts are put together to form a new whole predicting on the basis of a new formulation. EVALUATION refers to making judgments according to a set of criteria. Evaluation includes rating, ranking and persuading. [See *Taxonomy of Educational Objectives—Handbook I: Cognitive Domain*, ed. Benjamin Bloom (New York: David McKay Company, Inc., 1956.)]

Brainstorming   Brainstorming is a generic term given to a wide variety of strategies used for generating ideas. These include listing, clustering, charting, mapping, etc. For example, in the "Operation Robot" lesson, students are asked to verbally brainstorm possible things a robot could do it if had specialty parts like forks for arms. After this discussion, students chart their ideas on the board in the following format:

Brainstorming Format

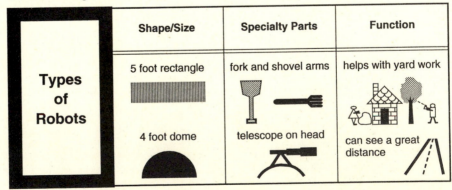

(**Thinking/Writing: Fostering Critical Thinking Through Writing,** 346.)

Charting   Charting involves organizing words or ideas in columns, list or chart form to help students categorize information and see relationships. For example, in the "Darwin Redone" lesson, students brainstorm a list of four legged animals such as the one below:

dog	sheep	zebra	wolf
cat	goat	giraffe	rhinocerous
elk	hamster	bear	antelope
deer	rat	koala	wildebeast
skunk	mouse	opossum	horse
chipmunk	rabbit	raccoon	elephant
cow	lion	aardvark	coyote

Then, they chart these animals—grouping them according to common elements related to appearance, habitat, behavior, etc:

milk-givers	hibernating	carnivorous	house pets	etc.
cow goat	bear	lion bear coyote	dog cat	

(*Thinking/Writing: Fostering Critical Thinking Through Writing*, 232.)

Checklist   A checklist is a list of things, names, criteria, etc., to be checked off or referred to for verifying, ordering, comparing, etc. In the Thinking/Writing lessons, checklists are often used in the revising stage of the composing process as in the "Bobby B. Bored" lesson:

Revising Checklist

- ☐ Did I show the behavior of a bored student using factual information based on my observation?
- ☐ Is my writing so vivid that someone else can visualize what I am describing?
- ☐ Did I describe clear sights and sounds?
- ☐ Did I use precise nouns, descriptive adjectives, active verbs, and at least one simile or metaphor?
- ☐ Does my writing have an interesting beginning, middle and end which are logically connected and flow smoothly?

(*Thinking/Writing: Fostering Critical Thinking Through Writing*, 52.)

Clustering   Clustering is a nonlinear, brainstorming activity that generates ideas, images and feelings around a stimulus word until a pattern becomes discernible. As students cluster around a stimulus word, the encircled words rapidly radiate outward until a sudden shift takes place, a sort of "Aha!" that signals an awareness of that tentative whole which allows students to begin writing. It can be done as a class (on the board or on paper) or individually. Example:

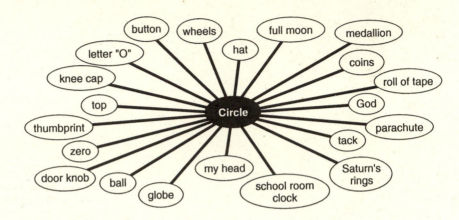

(*Practical Ideas for Teaching Writing as a Process,* 17–19 and 23.)

Correctness   Correctness as a goal of writing is the ability to use the conventions of written English—capitalization, punctuation, word choice, grammar, usage, spelling, and penmanship—in order to communicate effectively.

Dialogue   Dialogue is the passages of conversation within a written work. For example, in the "Persuasive Letters" lesson, student partners practice argumentation through a silent, written dialogue in which they role-play the persuader and the audience whom that person is trying to persuade. The directions for this dialogue are as follows:

- On a lined sheet of paper, the *PERSUADER* should ask the *AUDIENCE* to do what he/ she is trying to persuade him/her to do.

    Example: "Mom, will you let me take three friends to Farrell's for my birthday?"

- The *AUDIENCE* should read the question silently, then write a response according to his/her first possible reaction and return it to the *PERSUADER*.

    Example: "No, Farrell's is too expensive."

- The paper is to be passed back and forth in this manner until the audience is convinced or the *PERSUADER* gives up.
- The *PERSUADER* should then read over the dialogue and enter new *POSSIBLE RE-ACTIONS* and *POSSIBLE ARGUMENTS* on the chart.
- Now, have the students switch roles and do the exercise again so that both students' charts are complete.

Enter more *POSSIBLE REACTIONS* and *POSSIBLE ARGUMENTS* on the chart.

Who	What	Possible Objections of Audience	Possible Arguments of Persuader
Mom	Let me take 3 friends to Farrell's for my birthday.	1. "It's too expensive." 2. "I don't know where Farrell's is." 3. "I don't have time."	1. "I'll help pay with my allowance." 2. "There is a Farrell's only 2 blocks from school." 3. "You don't have to come."

(*Thinking/Writing: Fostering Critical Thinking Through Writing,* 296)

Dialectal Journal   The dialectal journal is a double-entry note-taking process which the student can keep while reading literature. It provides the student with two columns which are in dialogue with one another, not only developing a method of critical reading but also encouraging habits of reflective questioning. In the "Thank You Ma'am" lesson, students use a form of the dialectical journal to analyze the characters in Langston Hughes' short story. For each character—Roger and Mrs. Jones—students write three sets of double-entries to look at what the characters say, what they do, and what others say about them. The example below shows how information taken directly from the text in column one gets analyzed and interpreted in the following column:

What Roger Says	What Roger's Comments Tell the Reader	What Roger Does	What Roger's Actions Tell the Reader	What Others Say About Roger	What These Statements Tell the Reader About Roger
Example: "I didn't aim to."	Roger did aim to steal her pocketbook. He is either really ashamed of what he did or he is trying to talk his way out of what he did. Maybe both things are true.	**Example:** Struggles to get away from Mrs. Jones.	Roger is nervous about what Mrs. Jones is going to do with him. His impulse is to escape from her clutches.	**Example:** "Ain't you got nobody at home to wash your face?"	Roger's face is dirty and he's also very thin. There's probably no one at home to take care of him.

(*Thinking/Writing: Fostering Critical Thinking Through Writing,* 246)

Domains of Writing   Domains are categories which delineate the purposes of writing and which have a distinctive place in writing and thinking development. The four domains include sensory/descriptive, imaginative/narrative, practical/informative and analytical/expository. *Sensory/descriptive* writing involves presenting a picture in words, one so vivid that the reader or listener can recapture many of the same perceptions and feelings that the writer has had. The main intent of *imaginative/narrative* writing is to tell a story—sometimes real, sometimes imaginary. The forms may range widely, but the main idea is to tell what happens. In the *practical/informative* domain, students are required to provide clear information. Finally, the goal of *analytical/expository* writing is to analyze, explain, persuade, and influence. (*Practical Ideas for Teaching Writing as a Process*, 81–87)

Editing   When editing, a writer concerns himself with correctness. Like revision, editing occurs continuously throughout the writing process and is for some writers automatic. Revision is actually the reshaping of thought while editing is the polishing of that thought. For most student writers, formal editing takes place immediately before the final evaluation step in the writing process. The goal is for the paper to stand alone without needing interpretation or explanation by the writer because of distractions caused by errors in the conventions of written English. (*Practical Ideas for Teaching Writing as a Process*, 158)

Evaluation   Evaluation is final feedback given to a writer when a paper is completed—usually in the form of a score or letter grade. It is important that the criteria on which papers will be evaluated be communicated to students early on in the writing process. (*Practical Ideas for Teaching Writing as a Process*, 8)

Fast Writing or Quick Writing   Fast writing (also called quick writing) is a method of freewriting that helps a writer achieve fluency. The student is asked to write as much as possible without stopping in a limited amount of time. The instructor also emphasizes that the student should not be concerned with correctness. For example, in the ''Thank You Ma'am'' lesson, students are asked to quick write their own ending to Langston Hughes' short story after a portion of the text is read to them. (*Thinking/Writing: Fostering Critical Thinking Through Writing*, 241)

Fluency   Fluency is the ability to express ideas comfortably and easily in writing. Prewriting strategies promote fluency.

Form   In determining the form of a piece of writing, the writer must respond to the requirements of the writing task, work through and choose a shape or format for the piece, execute a plan which fulfills that format, and select the domain and style of writing based upon the audience. The form of any work should be appropriate to its purpose, its content and its audience.

Framing   Framing is a way of showing students how to write an assignment by providing a teacher-generated structure. For instance, students who have clustered their ideas about ''My Terrible Day'' may not know how to sequence their thoughts. Framing can provide the class with a model that allows the students to see the process. Example:

It had been a terrible, horrible, no good, very bad day.

I woke at _____.

By noon, _____.

In the evening, _____.

Freewriting   Freewriting is nongraded, nonstructured writing. From this "stream of consciousness" writing a student can sometimes find a topic. Freewriting is also used as an exercise to eliminate self-consciousness and ease the constraints of correctness. In the "Justifying a Decision" lesson, for example, as preparation for reading Arthur Miller's *The Crucible,* students are asked to freewrite about a time when their decision to do something they were strictly forbidden to do resulted in their getting caught.
(*Thinking/Writing: Fostering Critical Thinking Through Writing,* 312)

Guided Imagery   Guided imagery uses visualization to stimulate writing ideas; the students watch the "movie screens" in their minds. The teacher slowly narrates a setting or story using sensory detail to elicit impressions or images, pausing often to give students time to develop their own mental pictures of the words they are learning. This method is especially helpful as a prewriting activity for sensory/descriptive and imaginative/narrative writing. (*Practical Ideas for Teaching Writing as a Process,* 93–94.) The following is a guided imagery from the "On The Nose" lesson:

Begin to direct the students' focus inward upon their personal experiences by dimming the lights and using the following questions to guide the students' imagery. Say to them:

- Close your eyes and relax. You may put your head on your desk or sit with your back straight and your eyes closed. The important thing is that you are as comfortable and relaxed as you can be.
- Imagine that all the tension in your body is running down from your head and right out through your toes. Picture it evaporating into the air and floating away as lightly as a fluffy white cloud. Your whole body is relaxed and you feel calm and peaceful.
- Breathe slowly and deeply, enjoying this calm and peaceful feeling.
- Turn your attention to the smells that make you think of school. Smell and imagine:
  - a row of lunches lined up at the back of the room;
  - the smell of a hot meal as you stand in the lunch line;
  - the smell of a pencil being sharpened;
  - the smell of wet coats drying near the furnace on a rainy day;
  - the smell of grass being cut on a warm spring day.
- All those special smells bring back vivid memories for us. Now think of a smell that is special to you.
  - What is that smell like?
  - Where are you when you smell it? Are you at home? Away? Are you inside? Outside?
  - Is this place familiar to you? Unfamiliar?
  - What do you see as you look around this place?
  - Are you moving or are you still?
  - What are you touching? What is touching you? What do you feel?
  - What kind of sounds surround you?
  - What do you taste?
  - How does this place make you feel?

Slowly, turn up the lights and have the students draw a picture (on art paper) of the place that they visualized, incorporating as many details as they can into the drawing. This will help them visualize and, later, generate language. Many students will choose to finish their pictures at home.
(*Thinking/Writing: Fostering Critical Thinking Through Writing,* 87–88)

Holistic Scoring   When scoring holistically, an evaluator judges a piece of writing based on an overall impression of how well the piece fulfilled the objectives of the assignment. Thus, holistic scoring helps objective evaluation because the scorers follow a rubric of specific traits that should appear in the writing. Examples of these traits might be: (1) complete coverage of the topic, (2) excellent fluency, (3) effective structure, and (4) freedom from mechanical errors. The better the student achieves these traits in his piece of writing, the higher the numerical score he receives.
(Practical Ideas for Teaching Writing as a Process, 185–187)

Learning Log   A learning log is a student's informal written response to class information, unlike the journal, which usually deals with personal experience. Cognitively, the log is a place for students to think "out loud" on paper—to question, sort through, clarify or challenge what they are learning and may be shared with the teacher to enable him or her to ascertain the students' comprehension. Affectively, the log is a place where students can express how they are feeling about the learning experiences taking place in class and share with the teacher as a partner in dialogue rather than as an assessor. The teacher can respond either by addressing the student individually (orally or in writing) or by opening up issues to class discussion. Provided below are three sample learning log entries from the same student:

> 9/10/85: Well, today I'm in English again! No—I don't want to be but have to be! Well, today we're supposed to be doing a talk about the stupid paper I wrote about yesterday, but the teacher sent me and Michelle out of class because we didn't have the paper, and it was in our locker and she wouldn't let us go get it. This is boring!

> 9/11/85: Today we got together in groups and discussed things about ourselves. I met some people today that are in our group. I guess it's gonna be cool. Three more minutes until the bell. I have to go home! I'm dying of starvation. I'm getting pretty proud of myself because today I made a friend that was my worst enemy for two years. Bye Bye.

> 9/12/85: Well, I've got three minutes to tell you everything I have to. I feel fine about my writing. My writing makes me feel good because I write down what I feel, think, and believe, so if people don't like it, that's ok, because it's me and they don't have to be me.
> *(Practical Ideas for Teaching Writing as a Process,* 79–80)

Mapping   Mapping is a composing method that can best be described as graphic outlining. Rather than organizing primary, secondary and tertiary ideas in outline form, students choose a geometric shape or simple picture to depict the ideas. This is a more organized form of clustering. Samples:

Oreo

From the "How Does Your Cookie Crumble?" lesson.
(Thinking/Writing: Fostering Critical Thinking Through Writing, 289)

Kick the Can	Pac Man
• Similar to Hide & Seek except you have to find all the other players.	• Electronic game in which you move a lever to manipulate a visual image of "Pac Man."
• Materials are a tin can and a base.	• Pac Man eats dots to get points.

Similarities of Games

- Both involve strategy.
- Both involve some sort of movement.
- Both have obstacles that must be overcome.
- Both are fun and challenging.

Differences of Games

running around	vs staying in one place.
physical	vs visual
simple materials	vs complex machine
played with a group	vs played alone or with a partner
outdoors	vs indoors

Conclusions About Growing Up During The Depression And Now

- Electronic games are now available, whereas they were not then.
- Technology has made life easier today but also more complex.
- Life is lived at a much faster pace now.
- Activities were more oriented around the home and family then, whereas now we go outside our neighborhoods for entertainment.

From the "Pac Man or Kick the Can?" lesson. (*Thinking/Writing: Fostering Critical Thinking Through Writing,* 197) [See also Owen Boyle and Marilyn Hanf Buckley, *Mapping the Writing Journey* (Berkeley: Bay Area Writing Project Publications, No. 15, 1981)].

Metacognition   Metacognition, in its simplest sense, can be defined as thinking about thinking. It is a conscious monitoring of one's own thinking process. It could be the ability to realize that you do not understand something another person has said. It could be paraphrasing aloud what someone has just told you to determine whether he will agree that that is, in fact, exactly what was meant. It could be the realization that someone does not know enough about a particular subject to write effectively and needs to gather more information before beginning to write. (*Practical Ideas for Teaching Writing as a Process,* 16)

Microtheme   A microtheme is a minicomposition which allows students to formulate a writing plan. On a 3 × 5 card or piece of 8½″ × 11″ paper, students can select headings related to both the form and content of their papers and to begin to think about where they will be heading in their writing. For example, here are the microtheme instructions in the "Birth Order Essay" lesson:

	Birth Order Essay
○	
	Introduction
	Main Body
○	
	Conclusion
○	

Under **Introduction,** sketch out an idea for how you will open your paper in a way that will engage your reader and explain how you will integrate the information on birth order theory. For example, will you begin with a quote from a secondary source, an anecdote, some dialogue, description, etc.?

Under **Main Body,** outline the main points you intend to make, noting the specific examples you intend to use for support.

Under **Conclusion,** summarize your finding about the relevance or irrelevance of birth order theory.

(*Thinking/Writing: Fostering Critical Thinking Through Writing,* 169)

Modeling   Through modeling, the teacher provides examples or models for students, either by other students or by professional writers, to emulate so that they may better understand what it is that they are being asked to produce. For example, in the "Your Romantic Childhood" lesson, students are given Walt Whitman's poem ":There Was a Child Went Forth" to use as a model for developing a free verse poem about their own childhood. (*Thinking/Writing: Fostering Critical Thinking Through Writing,* 147) One way a teacher might model his or her own thinking and writing process would be to create a draft of the same assignment the students are working on on the board and think aloud and write while students observe. (*Practical Ideas for Teaching Writing as a Process,* 16)

Note Taking/Note Making   Note taking/note making is a strategy to encourage students to think critically about what they are learning—to question, sort through, puzzle over, clarify, or comment on information. In one column of a piece of paper, students simply record what they are learning—(i.e., take lecture notes, record the results of experiments, work through the steps of a problem, copy down a passage of text, etc.) In the right-hand column, students make notes about the notes they took. The note making column may be cognitive or affective or a mixture of the two. Reprinted below is a note-taking/note-making exercise from ''The Laws of Probability'' lesson.

Note Taking	Note Making
1. What is the ratio of heads to the total number of flips after the first 25 flips? H/F: 14/25 What is the ratio of tails to flips after 25 flips? T/F: 11/25	1. What observation can you make about this? *Heads seem to fall more often than tails.*
2. What is the ratio of heads to the total number of flips after the first 50 flips? H/F: 22/50 What is the ratio of tails to the total number of flips after the first 50 flips? T/F: 28/50	2. What observation can you make about this? *Now, tails are occurring more often than heads.*
3. What is the ratio of heads to the total number of flips after the second 50 flips? H/F: 27/50 What is the ratio of tails to the total number of flips after the second 50 flips? T/F: 23/50	3. What observation can you make about this? *The ratio is even closer, although heads came up more often than tails.*
4. What is the overall ratio of heads to the total number of flips after 100 flips? H/F: 49/100 What is the overall ratio of tails to the total number of flips after 100 flips?	4. What observation can you make about this? *The more often we flipped the coin, the more even the ratio got.*

Note Taking	Note Making
T/F: 51/100 5. What can you predict about future flips?	5. *Maybe if we did it again, heads would win. If we continued, though, it would eventually come out 1:2.*

(Thinking/Writing: Fostering Critical Thinking Through Writing, 302)

Peer Editing   Instead of the teacher marking errors, peers or classmates assume the role of editors. By editing one another's writing, students often become more proficient in editing their own writing. In the "Bobby B. Bored" lesson *(Thinking/Writing: Fostering Critical Thinking Through Writing,* 43), students conduct a read-around to search for misspelled words, sentence fragments or run-ons, and errors in punctuation.

Peer Partners   A teacher uses peer partnerships so that students may help one another through any of the stages of the writing process. Peer partners are particularly useful for giving feedback and differing viewpoints during the sharing and revising stages of the writing process. Students often "hear" better when the critique comes from a peer. (See the definition of Dialogue for a description of how peer partners help each other anticipate objections to a request they are making and think of logical reasons to overcome those objections.)

Point of View   Point of view is the viewpoint from which a story is narrated. Point of view includes: *who* (first person, third person, omniscient, and stream of conscious narration); *when* (past, present, future, and flashback); and *where* (from a distant perspective, in the midst of the action, from beyond the grave, and so forth.) *(Practical Ideas for Teaching Writing as a Process,* 114–117.) One effective way to help students internalize the concept of point of view is to ask them to become a character in a work of literature they have been reading and to speak in that character's voice as in "A Letter From the Heart of Darkness" lesson. *(Thinking/Writing: Fostering Critical Thinking Through Writing,* 269)

Precomposing   Helping students generate ideas for writing is often not enough to enable them to organize and articulate their thoughts. Precomposing activities help students to focus on the specific requirements of the writing assignment as well as to formulate a writing plan. For instance, once students were given *The Grapes of Wrath* writing assignment (see Prewriting definition below), a teacher might draw Highway 66 on the board and have the class reconstruct the Joad's journey from Oklahoma to California. Students could then select one or more scenes that had a significant impact on them and write a paragraph explaining why the cruelties and kindnesses exemplify Steinbeck's quote. Finally, they might list three other events in the novel which their scene mirrors.

Prewriting   Prewriting generates ideas for writing. Taking a wide range of forms—class discussion, brainstorming, visualizing, freewriting, etc.—prewriting aims to stimulate the free flow of thought. In the writing process, prewriting usually precedes the introduction of the writing assignment (prompt) and may set the stage for thinking and writing about a given topic without specifically addressing it. For example, the following is an application level question on *The Grapes of Wrath:*

Steinbeck says, ''The people in flight from the terror behind—strange things happen to them, some bitterly cruel and some so beautiful that the faith is refired forever.'' Please illustrate his statement by giving one example of a cruelty and one example of a kindness that are representative of the events of the novel as a whole.

In order to prepare students to consider the significance of Steinbeck's remark in the context of the novel, one might begin having students freewrite about what the terms *cruelty* and *kindness* mean to them and then to think about a time when their own faith in humanity was restored when they saw, heard about, or personally benefitted from an act of kindness performed by another human being. This latter activity will provide practice in the skill of application called for in *The Grapes of Wrath* assignment.

Primary Traits   In evaluation, the primary traits are those considered to be the most important in a student's writing. Generally, no more than five traits are identified for one assignment. A point system is used to denote a student's grade on each of those traits in his writing assignment. For instance, if organization is an important concern for the assignment, on a scale of 5 to 1, a score of 5 would indicate excellent organization, and a score of 1 would indicate the writer's failure to organize the paper in a coherent manner.
(*Practical Ideas for Teaching Writing as a Process,* 197–198)

Prompt   The prompt is the writing task or assignment. Effective prompts provide specific directions for the writing task. They not only explain what is required in terms of the content of the final piece of writing, but describe what is required in terms of fluency, form, and correctness. Prompts can be open-ended, allowing for student choice, or closed-ended. The more specific the prompt, the clearer the criteria for evaluation, the better able the student is to respond effectively.

Read-around Groups   Read-around groups give students the opportunity to share their own writing, as well as to read and respond to each other's writing anonymously at several stages in the process of any assignment. Students write for a specified amount of time and then place code numbers rather than their names on their papers. Then, they form groups (preferably of four) to read all the papers of the other groups of four in the class. At the teacher's signal, the group leader passes the set of papers to another group who reads them very quickly (usually 30 seconds to one-minute per paper.) At the end of the 30-second to one-minute interval, the teacher signals the readers to pass the paper they have just read to the right. As soon as all of the papers have been read, the group must come to consensus on the paper they liked best. In addition to reader appeal, papers can be read-around for beginnings, middle and/ or endings, for language use, for organization, for correctness, or for any other feature specified by the teacher or the class.
(*Practical Ideas for Teaching Writing as a Process,* 148–151)

Recursive   The composing process—prewriting, precomposing, writing, sharing, revising, editing, and evaluation—involves all levels of critical thinking and is a recursive process. It is termed ''recursive'' because the process is not strictly linear. Writers often ''go back to go forward.''
(*Practical Ideas for Teaching Writing as a Process,* 8)

Response Forms or Sharing Sheets   Response forms or sharing sheets are forms of written feedback used primarily during the sharing stage of the writing process to provide the writer with reactions to his or her work in progress. The example on the next page is a sharing sheet from the ''Watermarks'' lesson

```
┌─────┬──────────────────────────────────────────────────────────┐┐┐
│     │                    Sharing Sheet                         ││││
│     ├──────────────────────────────────────────────────────────┤
│     │ 1. Your paper does/does not "hook" me to read it because... │
│  ◯──┤                                                          │
│     │ 2. I like the following "showing" details in your paper... │
│     ├──────────────────────────────────────────────────────────┤
│     │ 3. I would like to read more "showing" about...          │
│     ├──────────────────────────────────────────────────────────┤
│     │ 4. I can/cannot tell what came first, second, etc., because... │
│     ├──────────────────────────────────────────────────────────┤
│     │ 5. The parts I have trouble understanding are...         │
│     ├──────────────────────────────────────────────────────────┤
│     │ 6. After reading this paper, what your watermark means to me is... │
│  ◯──┤                                                          │
│     │ 7. What I think this watermark means to you today is...  │
└─────┴──────────────────────────────────────────────────────────┘
```

(*Thinking/Writing: Fostering Critical Thinking Through Writing*, 111)

Revising   Revision involves a commitment to fully engage in the challenges of the writing task—to make the effort to discover and articulate our ideas for ourselves, and the detachment to get enough distance from the writing in order to take the perspective of a reader. Revising requires a writer both to appraise his writing and then to make the necessary changes. The writer examines his ideas and then the words chosen to express his ideas and how these words work together in phrases, sentences, and paragraphs to communicate his ideas and then adds, deletes, substitutes, and rearranges to enhance his communication. Revision can occur after a single word is written, a total composition, or at any place in between. A teacher can facilitate revision by asking questions which address surface level changes as well as meaning changes. A writer then rereads his paper with specific objectives in mind.
(*Practical Ideas for Teaching Writing as a Process*, 155–160)

Rubric   A rubric is a scale or set of criteria which delineates the key features of a writing task. It often has a numerical scale attached to it that is used as a basis for evaluating the final written product. (*Practical Ideas for Teaching Writing as a Process*, 185–187) Provided below are the criteria for a 6 paper for the ''Justifying a Decision'' lesson:

Sample Rubric

6 This a paper that is clearly superior, well-written, carefully organized, insightful, and technically correct. It does all or most of the following well:

- Maintains the character's attitude, point of view and language traits throughout the whole paper
- Shows in detail and with depth of perception the moment of decision and the character's psychological and emotional responses to that moment
- Justifies the character's decision as the best possible one he could make—doesn't apologize for or excuse the decision

- Moves through time easily and with appropriate verb tenses
- Varies sentence structure and length
- Demonstrates mastery of the conventions of written English (punctuation, capitalization, pronoun reference, agreement, spelling)

Scoring Guide   A scoring guide is another term for a rubric.

Secondary Traits   In evaluation, the secondary traits are those considered to be of secondary importance in a writing assignment. They are often areas such as format and mechanics. A point system is used to denote a student's grade or success in addressing those requirements (*Practical Ideas for Teaching Writing as a Process,* 197–198). For example, in the ''Handy News'' lesson, the primary traits involve accurately describing how a person who works at the school uses his or her hands to do a job, while the secondary traits involve neatness and the number of errors in correctness.
(*Thinking/Writing: Fostering Critical Thinking Through Writing,* 206)

Sentence Combining   Sentence combining is a teaching technique devised to help students write fewer choppy sentences and attempt sentences with more complex syntactical structures. It is a means of increasing a writer's options in terms of fluency, form, and correctness, enabling the writer to enhance his or her own style. Instruction in sentence combining usually involves presenting students with specific exercises. For example:

- I ate the hambugers.
- *Henry* also ate the hamburgers.
- They were *soggy.*   } *Henry and I ate the soggy, stale hamburgers quickly.*
- They were *stale.*
- We ate them *quickly*

(*Practical Ideas for Teaching Writing as a Process,* 163–164 and 168–170)

Sharing Groups (Writing-Response Groups)   Sharing groups are composed of students who are willing to share their own writing as well as respond to the writing of their peers. The goal of sharing groups is to provide the writer with *movies* of peoples's minds while they hear his or her words. Sharing group members can play the roles of supportive listener, constructive critic, and editor.
(*Practical Ideas for Teaching Writing as a Process,* 139–143)

Showing, Not Telling   The assumption behind the showing, not telling technique is that most students have not been trained to show what they mean. Showing, not telling encourages students to dramatize their writing by ''showing'' with specific details that paint pictures in the reader's mind. It involves giving students a *telling sentence* such as *The room was vacant* or *The lunch period was too short* and asking them to expand the thought in that sentence into an entire paragraph. Students are challenged not to use the original statement in the paragraph at all. Rather, they must *show* that *The room was vacant* without making that claim directly. Reproduced below is a showing paragraph for the telling sentence, *The roller coaster was the scariest ride at the fair.*

As I stood in line, I gazed up at the gigantic steel tracks that looped around three times. The thunderous roar of the roller coaster sounded like a thunder cloud that had sunk into my ears and suddenly exploded. The wild screams of terror shot through me like a bolt of lightning and made my fingers tingle with fear. Soon I heard the roar of the roller coaster cease. As the line started to move forward, I heard the clicking of the turnstile move closer and closer. Finally, I got onto the loading deck and with a shaking hand gave the attendant my ticket.

It seemed like I barely got seated when I felt a jolt which signified the beginning of the ride. While the roller coaster edged up the large track, I kept pulling my seatbelt tighter and tighter until it felt like I was cutting off all circulation from the waist down. At the crest of the hill, I caught a glimpse of the quiet town which lay before me and gave me a feeling of peace and serenity. Suddenly my eyes felt like they were pushed all the way back into my head, and the town had become a blur. All I could see was a mass of steel curving this way and that as the roller coaster turned upside down. I was squeezing the safety bar so tight that my fingers seemed to be embedded in the metal. I could see the landing deck, and I let out a deep breath that had been held inside ever since the first drop. As the roller coaster came to a halt, I felt weak and emotionally drained. When I stepped off onto the deck, I teetered a bit to the left, but caught my balance quickly when I saw my friends waiting for me at the exit gate. I tried to look ''normal,'' while trying to convince them in a weak voice that, ''Oh, it was nothing.''
(*Practical Ideas for Teaching Writing as a Process,* 51–56)

Stylistic Imitation   Stylistic imitation involves emulating an author's word choice, uses of figurative language (similes, metaphors, symbols, imagery, analogies, etc.), syntax, rhetorical devices (such as foreshadowing, irony, hyperbole, etc.), tone, and point of view. For example, in the ''A Letter From the Heart of Darkness'' lesson, students are asked to *become* Marlow, the protagonist of Conrad's novel, and to write a letter describing Marlow's experiences in the Congo. In order to *become* Marlow—to see through his eyes and speak through his voice—students must carefully analyze Conrad's distinctive style and imitate it.
(*Thinking/Writing: Fostering Critical Thinking Through Writing,* 269)

Thinking Skills Objectives   The thinking skills objectives are the key cognitive tasks which students practice in a Thinking/Writing lesson. For example, in the ''Thank You Ma'am'' lesson, students are asked to write their own ending to Langston Hughes' short story. The writing prompt requires that students function at the synthesis level of Bloom's taxonomy. The specific thinking skills objectives call for students to *speculate* about the ending of the story based upon facts from the portion of the story they have read, to *formulate* their own ending, and to *compose* that ending.
(*Thinking/Writing: Fostering Critical Thinking Through Writing,* 241).

Time-line   A time-line is a graphic representation of a sequence of events or activities. In the study of literature, developing time-lines often helps students to reconstruct what happened in the text. In the ''After the Storm'' lesson, for example, students are asked to fill in the following timeline—retracing Santiago's actions from the time he lands on shore to the end of the book:

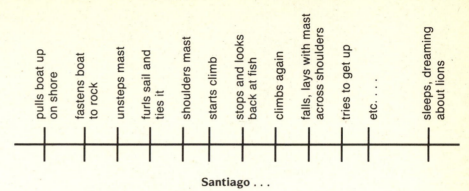

Santiago . . .

(Thinking/Writing: Fostering Critical Thinking Through Writing, 258)

Tone Tone is an author's attitude toward his or her subject and is communicated in writing through word choice and phrasing. In the ''Laws of Probability'' lesson, students are asked to review these two opening statements in a persuasive letter to determine which tone is more likely to convince their audience that a claim they have made is invalid:

Dear Sarah,

Your claim that heads will come up more than tails is completely invalid. How can you say it's common knowledge? According to the laws of probability, you are dead wrong. My experiments prove that you can't possibly be right.

Dear Rick,

You know, up until last week, if you had flipped a coin and asked me to pick heads or tails, I would have picked heads too. I guess, like you, I just had a hunch that heads would come up more often than tails. But in my class we've been conducting experiments and learning about the laws of probability. Let me tell you about what we did so that I can explain why what you believe in is mathematically unfounded.

What they learn in the ensuing discussion is that *what* a writer says will affect the reader differently depending on *how* it is communicated. The writer's tone plays a major role in how information is communicated.

(Thinking/Writing: Fostering Critical Thinking Through Writing, 308)

Transition Transition is the word, phrase, sentence, or group of sentences that relates a preceding topic to a succeeding one or that smoothly connects a piece of writing. Words commonly used to mark transitions are noted in the chart below:

Transitional Words

To mark an addition:
   and, furthermore, next, moreover, in addition, again, also, likewise, similarly, finally, second, in the same respect, just as . . . so, concomitant with, interestingly

To emphasize a contrast or alternative:
   but, or, nor, neither, still, however, nevertheless, on the contrary, on the other hand, conversely, despite, aside from, although, even though

To mark a conclusion:
   therefore, thus, in conclusion, consequently, in consequence, as a result, in other words, accordingly, hence, subsequently, in summary, in the final analysis, finally, ultimately, in retrospect

To introduce an illustration or example:
   for example, for instance, thus, hence, significantly, that is, again

(*Thinking/Writing: Fostering Critical Thinking Through Writing*, 307)

Venn Diagram   Venn Diagrams are overlapping circles often used in mathematics to show relationships between sets. In language arts instruction, Venn Diagrams are useful for examining similarities and differences as in the character study of Marlow and Kurtz in the ''A Letter From the Heart of Darkness'' lesson:

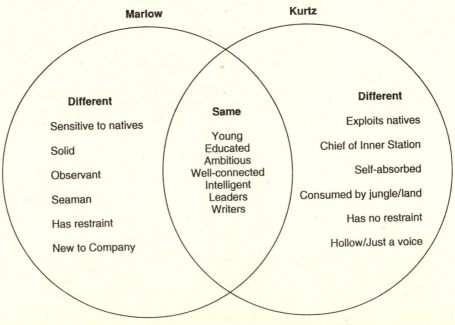

(*Thinking/Writing: Fostering Critical Thinking Through Writing*, 277)

WIRMI   WIRMI is an acronym for "What I Really Mean Is . . . ." A planning strategy developed by Linda Flower and John R. Hayes, WIRMI's can be used to select or focus on a train of thought, to prepare for writing or to sum up one's thinking. [See Linda Flower and John R. Hayes, "Plans That Guide the Composing Process," in *Writing: The Nature, Development and Teaching of Written Composition,* Volume 2, ed. Carl H. Frederiksen and Joseph F. Dominic (Hillsdale, N.J.: Lawrence Erlbaum Associates, 1981), 44.] For example, in the "Birth Order Essay," students bring a piece of expressive writing starting with the lines "What I really meant to say was" with them to a conference with the teacher on the first draft of their essay. The teacher can then verify if the student's intended message came across clearly. Here are two sample WIRMI's:

> *What I really meant to say was . . .*
> Even though people should not be categorized quickly like inanimate objects, the assumption that we all see things differently may be based on the way we've been raised—possibly birth order expectations. This awareness may help us understand ourselves and others more easily.

> or

> *What I really meant to say was . . .*
> More than anything I've read in the field of psychology, the study of birth order has given me some creditable insight into the interactions of siblings within the family and later on into their adult lives.

(*Thinking/Writing: Fostering Critical Thinking Through Writing,* 173)

Writing   During the writing stage of the composing process, students allow their ideas to take shape by putting words to paper. Because writers may lack a conscious awareness of what they specifically want to communicate, writing becomes a process of discovering on the conscious level what they are thinking about a given topic. This movement of an idea to the conscious level allows for spontaneity and creativity and should not be impeded in the first draft by concerns with correctness.
(*Practical Ideas for Teaching Writing as a Process,* 7)

Writing Skills Objective   The Writing Skills objectives are the key writing strategies which students practice in a Thinking/Writing lesson. The "Thank You M'am" lesson (described under Thinking Skills Objectives) calls for students to write in the imaginative/narrative domain. While composing their own ending to Langston Hughes' short story, students will employ the writing skills of *narration, showing, not telling,* and *dialogue.*
(*Thinking/Writing: Fostering Critical Thinking Through Writing,* 241)

Bibliography

Applebee, Arthur. *Writing in the Secondary School: English and the Content Areas.* Urbana, Ill.: National Council of Teachers of English, 1981.

Applebee, Arthur, et al. *Reading, Thinking and Writing.* National Assessment of Educational Progress, Report No. 11–L–01, 1981: 31.

Applebee, Arthur; Anne Auten and Fran Lehr. *Writing in the Secondary School.* National Council of Teachers of English. Research Report No. 21, 1981: 93.

Applebee, Arthur N. and Judith A. Langer. "Instructional Scaffolding." *Language Arts* 60 (February 1983): 168–175.

Ault, Ruth. *Children's Cognitive Development: Piaget's Theory and the Process Approach.* New York: Oxford University Press, 1977.

Bamburg, Betty. "Composition Instruction Does Make a Difference." *Research in the Teaching of English* 12 (February 1978): 47–59.

Bereiter, Carl. "Development in Writing." In *Cognitive Processes in Writing:* 73–96. Lee W. Gregg and Erwin R. Steinberg, eds. Hillsdale, NJ: Lawrence Erlbaum Associates, 1980.

_____. *Must We Educate?* Englewood Cliffs, NJ: Prentice-Hall, 1973.

_____. "Development in Writing." In *Testing, Teaching and Learning.* R.W. Tyler and S.H. White, eds. Washington, D.C.: National Institute of Education, 1979.

Berthoff, Ann E. "Tolstoy, Vygotsky, and the Making of Meaning." *College Composition and Communication* 29 (October 1978): 249–255.

_____. *Forming, Thinking and Writing.* Portsmouth, NH: Boynton/Cook, 1982.

Bigler, Mary. "Creative Writing Ideas." *English Journal* 69 (December 1980): 91–92.

Birnbaum, June C. "The Reading and Composing Behavior of Selected Fourth- and Seventh-Grade Students." *Research in the Teaching of English* 16 (October 1982): 241–260.

Blau, Sheridan. "Competence for Performance in Revision. In *Practical Ideas for Teaching*

Writing as a Process: 139–144. Carol Booth Olson, ed. Sacramento: California State Department of Education, 1987.

Blau, Sheridan, et al. "The Crisis in Literacy." *The Center Magazine* (November/December 1980): 54–61.

Bloom, Benjamin. *All Our Children Are Learning: A Primer for Parents, Teachers, and Other Educators.* New York: McGraw-Hill, 1981.

_____. *Every Kid Can; Learning for Mastery.* Washington, DC: College/University Press, 1973.

Bloom, Benjamin, et al. *Taxonomy of Education Objectives, Handbook I: Cognitive Domain.* New York: Longmans, 1956.

Bloom, Benjamin, et al. *Taxonomy of Educational Objectives: The Classification of Educational Objectives: The Classification of Educational Goals. Handbook II: Affective Domain.* New York: David McKay, 1956.

Bracewell, Robert J. "Writing as a Cognitive Activity." *Visible Language* 14 (1980): 400–422.

Brand, Alice G. "The Way of Cognition: Emotion and the Writing Process." *College Composition and Communication* 38 (December 1987): 443.

Bridwell, L.S. "Revising Strategies in Twelfth Grade Students' Transactional Writing." *Research in the Teaching of English* 14 (1980): 197–222.

Britton, James, et al. *The Development of Writing Abilities* (11 – 18). Urbana, IL: NCTE, 1975.

Bronson, David B. "Education, Writing, and the Brain." *Educational Forum* 46 (Spring 1983): 327–335.

Bruner, Jerome. *Social Foundations of Language and Thought.* New York: Norton, 1980.

Buckley, Marilyn H., and Owen Boyle. *Mapping the Writing Journey.* Berkeley, CA: Bay Area Writing Project, 1981.

Camp, Gerald. *A Success Curriculum for The Remedial Writer.* Berkeley, CA: Bay Area Writing Project, 1982.

_____. *Teaching Writing: Essays from the Bay Area Writing Project.* Portsmouth, NH: Boynton/Cook Publishers, 1982.

Caplan, Rebekah. *Writers in Training: A Guide to Developing a Composition Program for Language Arts Teachers, Grades 7–12.* Palo Alto, CA: Dale Seymour Publications, 1984.

Caplan, Rebekah, and Catherine Keech. *Showing Writing: A Training Program to Help Students to Be Specific.* Berkeley, CA: Bay Area Writing Project, 1980.

Cooper, Charles et al. "Tonawanda Middle School's New Writing Program." *English Journal* 65 (November 1976): 56–61.

Cooper, Charles, and Lee Odell, eds. *Evaluating Writing.* Urbana, IL: NCTE, 1978.

_____. *Research in Composing: Points of Departure.* Urbana, IL: NCTE, 1978.

Costa, Arthur L. *Enabling Behaviors.* General Learning Press: Foundations of Education Series, 1976.

_____. *Developing Minds: A Resource Book for Teaching Thinking.* ASCD Publications: 611–85362, 1985.

Covino, William A. "Making Differences in the Composition Class: A Philosophy of Invention." *Freshman English News* 10 (Spring 1981): 1–4.

Daiute, Collette A. "Psycholinguistic Foundations of the Writing Process." *Research in the Teaching of English* 15 (February 1981): 5–22.

D'Angelo, Frank. *A Conceptual Theory of Rhetoric.* Cambridge, MA: Winthrop Publishers, 1975.

_____. ''An Ontological Basis for A Modern Theory of the Composing Process.'' *Quarterly Journal of Speech* 64 (1978): 79–85.

_____. *Process and Thought in Composition*. Cambridge, MA: Winthrop Publishers, Inc., 1977.

_____. ''In Search for Intelligible Structure in the Teaching of Composition.'' *College Composition and Communication* 27 (May 1976): 142–147.

D'Arcy, Pat, and Mary K. Healy. *What's Going On: Language Learning Episodes in British and American Classrooms, Grades 4–13*. Portsmouth, NH: Boynton/Cook Publishers, 1982.

Diederick, Paul. *Measuring Growth in English*. Urbana, IL: NCTE, 1974.

Elbow, Peter. *Writing Without Teachers*. New York: Oxford University Press, 1973.

_____. *Writing With Power: Techniques for Mastering the Writing Process*. New York: Oxford University Press, 1981.

Elkind, David. *Children and Adolescents*. New York: Oxford University Press, 1974.

Emig, Janet. *The Composing Processes of Twelfth Graders*. Urbana, IL: NCTE, Research Report, No. 13, 1971.

_____. ''Nonmagical Thinking: Presenting Writing Developmentally in Schools.'' In *Writing: Process, Development and Communication*, 21–30. Carl F. Frederiksen and Joseph F. Dominic, eds. Hillsdale, NJ: Lawrence Erlbaum, 1981.

_____. *The Web of Meaning*. Dixie Goswami and Maureen Butter, eds. Portsmouth, NH.: Boynton/Cook Publishers, 1983.

_____. ''Writing as a Mode of Learning.'' *College Composition and Communication* 28 (May 1977): 122–127.

Falk, Julia. ''Language Acquisition and the Teaching and Learning of Writing.'' *College English* 41 (December 1979): 436–447.

Fenstermaker, John J. ''Freshman Composition: An Overlooked Perspective on Accountability.'' *Teaching English in the Two Year College* 6 (Spring 1980): 213–215.

Flanigan, Michael and Diane S. Mendez. ''Perception and Change: Teaching Revision.'' *College English* 42 (November 1980): 256–266.

Flavell, John. ''Metacognition and Cognitive Monitoring: A New Area of Cognitive-Developmental Inquiry.'' *American Psychologist* 34 (October 1979): 906–910.

_____. ''On Cognitive Development.'' Presidential Address, Society for Research in Child Development, 1982.

Flower, Linda. ''A Cognitive Process Theory of Writing.'' *College Composition and Communication* 32 (December 1981): 365–387.

_____. *Problem Solving Strategies for Writing*. New York: Harcourt Brace Jovanovich, Inc., 1981.

_____. ''Writer-Based Prose: A Cognitive Basis for Problems in Writing.'' *College English* (September 1979): 19–37.

Flower, Linda, and John R. Hayes. ''The Cognition of Discovery: Defining a Rhetorical Problem.'' *College Composition and Communication* 31 (February 1980): 21–32.

_____. ''Identifying the Organization of Writing Processes.'' In *Cognitive Processes in Writing*: 3–30. Lee W. Gregg and E.R. Steinberg, eds. Hillsdale, NJ: Lawrence Erlbaum Associates, 1980.

_____. ''Plans that Guide the Composing Process.: In *Writing: Process, Development and Communication*: 41–58. Carl H. Frederiksen and Joseph F. Dominic, eds. Hillsdale, NJ: Lawrence Erlbaum Associates, 1981.

_____. ''The Pregnant Pause: An Inquiry into the Nature of Planning.'' *Research in the Teaching of English* 15 (October 1981): 229–243.

_____. "Problem Solving Strategies and the Writing Process." *College English* 39 (1977): 449–461.

_____. *Protocol Analysis of Writing Processes.* Toronto, Canada: American Educational Research Assn., 1978 (ERIC ED 155 697).

_____. *Uncovering Cognitive Processes in Writing: An Introduction to Protocol Analysis.* Los Angeles: American Educational Research Assn., 1981 (ERIC ED 202 035).

Fraigley, Lester, and Stephen Witte. "Analyzing Revision." *College Composition and Communication* 32 (December 1981): 400–414.

Francoz, M.J. "The Logic of Question and Answer: Writing as Inquiry." *College English* 41 (November 1979): 336–339.

Frederiksen, Carl H., and Joseph F. Dominic, eds. *Writing: The Nature, Development, and Teaching of Written Communication: Volume 2: Process, Development and Communication.* Hillsdale, NJ: Lawrence Erlbaum Associates, 1981.

Furth, Hans. *Piaget for Teachers.* Englewood Cliffs, NJ: Prentice-Hall, 1970.

Gagné, Robert M. *The Conditions of Learning.* New York: Holt, Rinehart & Winston, 1965.

Gallagher, James G. *Productive Thinking of Gifted Children in Classroom Interaction.* CEC Research Monograph, Series B, No. B-5, 1967.

Gardner, Howard. *Frames of Mind: The Theory of Multiple Intelligences.* New York: Basic Books Inc., 1983.

Ginsburg, Herbert, and Sylvie Opper. *Piaget's Theory of Intellectual Development: An Introduction.* Englewood Cliffs, NJ: Prentice-Hall, 1969.

Giroux, Henry A. "Teaching Content and Thinking Through Writing." *Social Education* 43 (March 1979): 190–193.

Graves, Donald. "An Examination of the Writing Processes of Seven-Year Old Children." *Research in the Teaching of English* 9 (Winter 1975): 227–241.

_____. "How Do Writers Develop?" *Language Arts* 59 (February 1982), 173–179.

_____. "Patterns of Child Control in the W.P." In *English in the Eighties.* Robert D. Eagleson, ed. Australia: AATE (Australian Association for the Teaching of English), 1982.

_____. "A Six-Year-Old's Writing Process: The First Half of First Grade." *Language Arts* 56 (October 1979): 829–835.

_____. *Writing: Teachers and Children at Work.* Portsmouth, N.H.: Heinemann Educational Books, 1983.

Gray, James. "The California Writing Project." In *Practical Ideas for Teaching Writing as a Process.* Carol Booth Olson, ed. Sacramento: California State Department of Education, 1987: 1–3.

Gregg, Lee W., and Ervin R. Steinberg, eds. *Cognitive Processes in Writing.* Hillsdale, N.J.: Lawrence Erlbaum Associates, 1980.

Grindal, Gracia. "Freshman English: A Rhetoric for Teachers." *College English* 39 (December 1977): 442–448.

Guilford, J.P. *The Analysis of Human Intelligence.* New York: McGraw-Hill Book Company, 1971.

_____. *The Nature of Human Intelligence.* New York: McGraw-Hill Book Company, 1967.

Guthrie, John T. "Research: Documentation and Memory." *Journal of Reading* 26 (October, 1982): 94–95.

Haley-James, Shirley, ed. *Perspectives on Writing in Grades 1–8.* Urbana, IL: NCTE, 1981.

Hays, Janice, ed. *The Writer's Mind: Writing as a Mode of Thinking*. Urbana, IL: NCTE, 1983.

Hays, Janice, et al. "Facilitating Reading, Writing, and Thinking with Collaborative Learning." Paper presented at the Pacific Northwest Writing Consortium Conference: Writing, Learning and Belonging. Seattle, Washington, 1984.

Healy, Mary K. *Using Student Writing Response Groups in the Classroom*. Berkeley, CA: Bay Area Writing Project, 1980.

_____. "Teacher as Researcher: An Interview with Mary K. Healy." *California English* (January, 1987): 6.

Hillocks, George. *Research on Written Composition: New Directions for Teaching*. Urbana, IL: NCRE/ERIC, 1986.

_____. "What Works in the Teaching of Composition: A Meta-analysis of Experimental Treatment Studies, *American Journal of Education* (November 1984): 133–170.

Holland, Robert M. "Piagetian Theory and the Design of Composing Assignments." *Arizona English Bulletin* 19 (October 1976): 17–22.

Hunter, Madeline. "Madeline Hunter in the English Classroom." *English Journal* 78 (September 1989): 17–18.

Irmscher, William F. "Writing as a Way of Learning and Developing." *College Composition and Communication* 28 (December 1977): 333–337.

Jordan, Michael P. "Short Texts to Explain Problem-Solution Structures—and Vice Versa: An Analytical Study of English Prose to Show the Relationship Between Clear Writing and Clear Thinking." *Instructional Science* 9 (October 1980): 221–252.

Kantor, Ken, and Jack Perron. "Thinking and Writing: Creativity in the Modes of Discourse." *Language Arts* 54 (October 1977): 742–749.

Kirby, Dan, and Tom Liner. *Inside Out: Developmental Strategies for Teaching Writing*. Portsmouth, NH: Boynton/Cook, 1981.

Krathwohl, David, et al. *Taxonomy of Educational Objectives: The Classification of Educational Goals Handbook II: The Affective Domain*. New York: David McKay, Co., 1956.

Kurfiss, Joanne. "Developmental Perspectives on Writing and Intellectual Growth in College." In *To Improve the Academy: Resources for Student, Faculty and Institutional Development,* 136–47. Vol. III. L. Wilson and L. Buhl, eds. Pittsburgh, PA: Professional and Organizational Development Network in Higher Education, 1984.

_____. "Intellectual, Psychosocial and Moral Development in College: Four Major Theories." Washington D.C.: Manual for Project QUE (Quality Undergraduate Education), Council for Independent Colleges, 1983.

Langer, Judith A., and Applebee, Arthur N. *How Writing Shapes Thinking: A Study of Teaching and Learning*. Urbana, IL: National Council of Teachers of English, 1987.

Larson, Richard, ed. *Children and Writing in the Elementary Schools*. New York: Oxford University Press, 1975.

Lauer, Janice. "Writing as Inquiry: Some Questions for Teachers." *College Composition and Communication* 33 (February 1982): 89–93.

Leathard, D.A. "Writing and the 'Subject'—A Scientist's View." *Use of English* 25 (Winter 1973): 129–133.

Lehr, Fran. "Developing Critical Reading and Thinking Skills." *Journal of Reading* 25 (May 1982): 804–807.

Lundsford, Andrea. "Cognitive Studies and Teaching Writing." In *Perspectives on Research and Scholarship in Composition*. Ben W. McClelland and Timothy R. Donovan, eds. New York: The Modern Language Association of America, 1985.

Lundsteen, Sara W., ed. *Help for the Teacher of Written Composition, K–9.* Urbana, IL: NCTE/ERIC, 1976.

Macrorie, Ken. *The I-Search Paper: Revised Edition of Searching Writing.* (Portsmouth, NH: Boynton/Cook Publishers, Heinemann), 1988.

Madaus, G.F., E.N. Woods, R.L. Nuttal. ''A Causal Model Analysis of Bloom's Taxonomy.'' *American Educational Research Journal.* Vol. 10: 253–262.

Mandel, Barrett J. ''Losing One's Mind: Learning to Write and Edit.'' *College Composition and Communication* 29 (December 1978): 362–368.

Matsuhashi, Ann. ''Pausing and Planning: The Tempo of Written Discourse Production.'' *Research in the Teaching of English* 15 (1981): 113–134.

Meeker, Mary N. *The Structure of the Intellect: Its Interpretation and Uses.* Columbus, OH: Merrill, 1969.

Medway, Peter. *Finding a Language: Autonomy and Learning in School.* London: Chameleon, 1980.

Miles, Curtis. ''The 4th R: Reasoning Microthemes: Writing and Thinking Intertwined.'' *Journal of Developmental and Remedial Education* 6 (Fall 1982): 9–32.

Moffett, James. *Active Voice: A Writing Program Across the Curriculum.* Portsmouth, NH: Boynton/Cook, 1981.

_____. *Coming on Center: English Education in Evolution.* Portsmouth, NH: Boynton/Cook, 1981.

_____. *Teaching the Universe of Discourse.* Boston: Houghton Mifflin, 1968.

_____. ''Writing, Inner Speech, and Meditation.'' *College English* 44 (May 1982): 231–246.

Moffett, James and Betty Jane Wagner. *Student-Centered Language Arts and Reading, K–13: A Handbook for Teachers.* Boston, MA: Houghton Mifflin, 1976.

Mohr, Marian. *Revision, the Rhythm of Meaning.* Portsmouth, NH: Boynton/Cook, 1984.

Murray, Donald. ''First Silence, Then Paper.'' In *Forum: Essays on Theory and Practice in the Teaching of Writing,* Patricia L. Stock, ed. Portsmouth, NH: Boynton/Cook, 1983.

_____. *Learning by Teaching: Selected Articles on Writing and Teaching.* Portsmouth, NH: Boynton/Cook, 1982.

_____. ''Teaching the Motivating Force of Revision.'' *English Journal* 65 (January 1976): 106–111.

_____. ''Teaching the Other Self.'' *College Composition and Communication* 33 (May 1982): 140–147.

_____. ''Writing Before Writing.'' *College Composition and Communication* 29 (December 1978): 375–381.

_____. *A Writer Teaches Writing: A Practical Method of Teaching Writing.* Boston, MA: Houghton Mifflin, 1968.

Myers, Miles. ''Five Approaches to the Teaching of Writing.'' *Learning* (April 1976): 38–41.

Nyberg, David. ''Skill School v. Education School: An Essay on Carl Bereiter's Pedagogics.'' *Educational Theory* 26 (Spring 1976): 214–222.

Odell, Lee. ''The Classroom Teacher as Researcher.'' *English Journal* 65 (January 1976): 106–111.

_____. ''Piaget, Problem Solving and Freshmen Composition.'' *College Composition and Communication* 24 (February 1973): 36–42.

_____. ''The Process of Writing as a Process of Learning.'' *College Composition and Communication* 31 (February 1980): 42–50.

_____. "Responding to Student Writing." *College Composition and Communication* 24 (December 1973): 394–400.

Olson, Carol Booth. "Fostering Critical Thinking Though Writing." *Educational Leadership* 42 (November 1984): 28–39.

_____. "Personalizing Research in the I Search Paper." *Arizona English Bulletin* 25 (November 1983): 147–163.

_____. "The Thinking/Writing Connection." In *Developing Minds: A Resource Book for Teaching Thinking:* 102–107. Arthur L. Costa, ed. ASCD Publications: 611-85362, 1985.

_____, ed. *Practical Ideas for Teaching Writing as a Process.* Sacramento: California State Department of Education, 1987.

Paul, Richard W. "Bloom's Taxonomy and Critical Thinking Instruction." *Educational Leadership* (May 1985): 36–39.

Perl, Sondra. "The Composing Processes of Unskilled College Writers." *Research in the Teaching of English* 13 (December 1979): 317–336.

_____. "Understanding Composing." *College Composition and Communication* 31 (December 1980): 363–369.

_____. "Unskilled Writers as Composers." *New York University Education Quarterly* 10 (Spring 1979): 17–22.

Perry, William G. *Forms of Intellectual and Ethical Development in the College Years.* New York: Holt, Rinehart & Winston, Inc., 1968.

Piaget, Jean. *The Psychology of Intelligence.* London: Routledge & Kegan Paul LTD, 1950.

Pianko, Sharon. "A Description of the Composing Processes of College Freshman." *Research in the Teaching of English* 13 (1979): 5–22.

_____. "Reflection: A Critical Component of the Composing Process." *College Composition and Communication* 30 (October 1979): 275–278.

Ponsot, Marie and Rosemary Dean. *Beat Not the Poor Desk: Writing: What to Teach, How to Teach It and Why.* Portsmouth, NH: Boynton/Cook, 1982.

Powers, William. "Notes Toward a Theory to Underlie the Teaching of Writing." *Freshman English News* 6 (Fall 1977): 19–23.

The Random House Dictionary of the English Language. New York: Random House, 1983: 531.

Ray, Lucinda. "Reflections on Classroom Research." *Reclaiming the Classroom: Teacher Research as an Agency for Change.* eds. Dixie Goswami and Peter R. Stillman. Upper Montclair, N.J.: Boynton/Cook Publishers, Inc.: 1987, 220.

Raymond, Michael W. "Reading, Thinking and Writing in the Literature Class." *Exercise Exchange* 26 (Fall 1981): 34–37.

Rose, Mike. "Teaching University Discourse." In *Teaching/Writing/Learning:* 117–128. Ian Pringle and Aviva Freedman, eds. Ottawa: Canadian Council of Teachers of English, 45 (February 1983).

_____. "When Faculty Talk About Writing." *College English* 41 (November 1979): 272–279.

Rivers, William E. "Developing a Critical Habit of Mind: An Approach to Teaching Applied Writing." *ABCA Bulletin* (December 1979): 29–32.

Sagar, Carol. "Improving the Quality of Written Composition." *Language Arts* 54 (October 1977): 760–762.

Scardamalia, Marlene. "How Children Cope With the Cognitive Demands of Writing." In *Writing: Process, Development and Communication:* 81–104. Carl H. Frederiksen and Joseph F. Dominic, eds. Hillsdale, N.J.: Lawrence Erlbaum Associates, 1981.

Schwab, David. "Writing as Thinking: Solving the Mystery of Deduction." *Exercise Exchange* 25 (Spring 1981): 18–21.

Shaughnessy, Mina. *Errors and Expectations.* New York: Oxford University Press. 1977.

Sheerer, Martin. *Handbook of Social Psychology: Vol 1.* Cambridge, MA: Addison Wesley, 1954.

Shuman, R. Baird. "What About Revision?" *English Journal* 65 (December 1975): 41–43.

Shuy, Robert W. "Toward a Developmental Theory of Writing." In *Writing: Process, Development and Communication:* 119–132. Carl H. Frederiksen and Joseph F. Dominic, eds. Hillsdale, N.J.: Lawrence Erlbaum Associates, 1981.

Smith, Frank. *Writing and the Writer.* New York: Holt, Rinehart & Winston, 1982.

Smith, Myrna J. "Bruner on Writing." *College Composition and Communication* 28 (May 1977): 129–33.

Sommers, Nancy. "Need for Theory in Composition Research." *College Composition and Communication* 30 (February 1979): 148–156.

_____. "Responding to Student Writing." *College Composition and Communication* 33 (May 1982).

_____. "Revision Strategies of Student Writers and Experienced Adult Writers." *College Composition and Communication* 31 (1980): 378–388.

Stallard, Charles K. "An Analysis of the Writing Behavior of Good Student Writers." *Research in the Teaching of English* 8 (Fall 1974): 206–218.

Stock, Patricia L., ed. *FFORUM: Essays on Theory and Practice in the Teaching of Writing.* Portsmouth, NH: Boynton/Cook, 1983.

Strong, William. *Sentence Combining and Paragraph Building.* New York: Random House, 1981.

Taba, Hilda. *Thinking in Elementary School Children.* U.S. Department of Health, Education and Welfare. Cooperative Research Project No. 1571, 1964, 25.

Tate, Gary and Edward P.J. Corbett, eds. *The Writing Teacher's Sourcebook.* New York: Oxford University Press, 1981.

Taylor, Karl K. "Doors English—The Cognitive Basis of Rhetorical Models." *Journal of Basic Writing.* (Spring/Summer, 1979): 52–66.

Tiedt, Iris. *Individualizing Writing in the Classroom.* Urbana, IL: NCTE/ERIC, 1975.

Van Nostrand, A.D. "The Inference Construct: A Model of the Writing Process." *ADE Bulletin* 57 (May 1978): 13–20.

Voyat, Gilbert. "Open Education and the Embodiment of Thinking, Reading, and Writing." *ADE Bulletin* 6 (September 1975): 8–10.

Vygotsky, Lev S. *Mind in Society: The Development of Higher Psychological Processes.* Cambridge, Mass.: Harvard University Press, 1978.

_____. *Thought and Language.* Cambridge, MA.: M.I.T. Press, 1962.

Wason, P.C. "Specific Thoughts on the Writing Process." In *Cognitive Processes in Writing:* 129–138. Lee W. Gregg and Erwin R. Steinberg, eds. Hillsdale, NJ: Lawrence Erlbaum Associates, 1980.

Text Credits

pp. 14–16: Bloom, B. S., Englehart, M. D., First, E. J., Hill, W. H., & Krathwohl, D. R. (1956). *Taxonomy of Educational Objectives. The Classification of Educational Goals: Handbook I: Cognitive Domain.* New York: David McKay.

p. 36: From ''Colors'' by M. Mackles in *Wishes, Lies, and Dreams: Teaching Children to Write Poetry* by Kenneth Koch. Reprinted by permission of Chelsea House Publishers.

p. 72: ''My Papa's Waltz,'' copyright 1942 by Hearst Magazines, Inc. from *The Collected Poems of Theodore Roethke* by Theodore Roethke. Used by permission of Doubleday, a division of Bantam Doubleday Dell Publishing Group, Inc.

p. 77: Adapted from ''My Senior Prom'' in *English Skills*, John Langan, ed. Copyright © 1977 McGraw-Hill Book Co. Reproduced by permission of the Glencoe Division of Macmillan/McGraw-Hill School Publishing Company.

pp. 285–287: From ''Thank You, Ma'am'' by Langston Hughes in *The Langston Hughes Reader.* Copyright © 1958 by Langston Hughes. Copyright renewed 1986 by George Houston Bass. Reprinted by permission of Harold Ober Associates Incorporated.

Name Index

The names of contributing authors to this book appear in **boldface** type.

Subject Index